Sartre, Imagination, and Dialectical Reason

Reframing the Boundaries: Thinking the Political

Series Editors: Alison Assiter and Evert van der Zweerde

This series aims to mine the rich resources of philosophers in the "continental" tradition for their contributions to thinking the political. It fills a gap in the literature by suggesting that the work of a wider range of philosophers than those normally associated with this sphere of work can be of relevance to the political.

Titles in the Series

Kierkegaard and the Matter of Philosophy, Michael O'Neill Burns
Arendt, Levinas and a Politics of Relationality, Anya Topolski
The Risk of Freedom: Ethics, Phenomenology and Politics in Jan Patocka, Francesco Tava, translated by Jane Ledlie
Nietzsche's Death of God and Italian Philosophy, Emilio Carlo Corriero, translated by Vanessa Di Stefano
Lotman's Cultural Semiotics and the Political, Andrey Makarychev and Alexandra Yatsyk
Axel Honneth: Reconceiving Social Philosophy, Dagmar Wilhelm
Sartre, Imagination, and Dialectical Reason: Creating Society as a Work of Art, Austin Hayden Smidt
Erotic Experience and Sexual Difference in Contemporary Continental Philosophy, Zeynep Direk (forthcoming)

Sartre, Imagination, and Dialectical Reason

Creating Society as a Work of Art

Austin Hayden Smidt

**ROWMAN &
LITTLEFIELD**
───────INTERNATIONAL
London • New York

Published by Rowman & Littlefield International, Ltd.
6 Tinworth Street, London SE11 5AL
www.rowmaninternational.com

Rowman & Littlefield International, Ltd. is an affiliate of
Rowman & Littlefield
4501 Forbes Boulevard, Suite 200, Lanham, Maryland 20706, USA
With additional offices in Boulder, New York, Toronto (Canada), and London (UK)
www.rowman.com

Copyright © 2019 by Austin Hayden Smidt

All rights reserved. No part of this book may be reproduced in any form or by any electronic or mechanical means, including information storage and retrieval systems, without written permission from the publisher, except by a reviewer who may quote passages in a review.

British Library Cataloguing in Publication Information
A catalogue record for this book is available from the British Library

ISBN: HB 978-1-78661-167-3

Library of Congress Cataloging-in-Publication Data Available

ISBN: 978-1-78661-167-3 (cloth)
ISBN: 978-1-5381-5307-9 (pbk)
ISBN: 978-1-78661-168-0 (electronic)

Contents

Acknowledgements	vii
Abbreviations	ix
Glossary of Terms	xi
Introduction: Rediscovering Sartre in a Completely Natural Way	1

Part I: The Living Logic of Action in *Critique of Dialectical Reason* — 13

1. Dialectical Reason and the Paradoxico-Critical Orientation of Thought — 15
2. Dialectical Logic and the Pervasion of Seriality: Toward a Fresh Reading of Sartre's *Critique of Dialectical Reason* — 51
3. The Field of Possibles: The Practico-Inert and the Exigency of Objective Conditions — 73
4. Pluridimensional Seriality — 89
5. Freedom and the Logic of the Group — 117

Part II: Toward an Imaginative Logic of Action — 157

6. The Logic of Poetic Imagination — 159
7. A Tale of Two Logics — 175
8. Creating Society as a Work of Art — 189
9. Prolegomena to Any Future Critique of Political Economy — 231

Conclusion	267
Bibliography	271

Index 279
About the Author 287

Acknowledgements

"With hope in our hearts, and bricks in our hands, we sing for change" (Rise Against). The present effort is both my hope and metaphorical brick. This project is the outcome of years of scattered concerns, from the philosophical, to the political, to the artistic. It was encountering the work of Latin American Liberation Theologians, particularly José Miranda, that sparked the fire in my heart for wedding together theoretical abstraction with material praxis. After this, the wish of Marx to realize religious concerns through political means seemed the perfect transfiguration of the Social Gospel and Liberation Christianity that constituted my early formative intellectual journey. While I no longer have the same attachments to the confessional church, this work signals a trajectory for the continuing elaboration of similar concerns for global justice that have consumed my heart and mind for years.

This work's germination began during my time at the University of Nottingham, where I was introduced to the *Critique of Dialectical Reason* and to Philip Goodchild's inventive critique of political economy. It reached flower among the philosophy department at the University of Dundee. In particular, James Williams, Michael O'Neill Burns, Brian Smith, Scott Gallacher, and Ashley Woodward helped form many of these thoughts through stimulating conversation and consistent support. As a research assistant for Matthew Ally's *Ecology and Existence: Bringing Sartre to the Water's Edge*, I was encouraged and challenged by a reading of Sartre that eschewed the typical received Sartrean scholasticism. Matthew's persistent friendship and insight has had tremendous impact on this project. The North American Sartre Society and the UK Sartre Society have both provided bountiful environments for the steady flow of creative Sartre scholarship from which I have gleaned much. And of course, I would be remiss if I did not thank the team at Rowman & Littlefield International. In particular, Reframing the Boundaries:

Thinking the Political series editors Alison Assiter and Evert van der Zweerde provided enthusiasm and guiding hands to bring this book to completion. Their insight and suggestions have only changed my work for the better. Any shortcomings rest squarely on my shoulders. Beyond this, the unquantifiable hours of conversation with Troy Polidori over the years has been the single greatest contributor to my growth as a thinker. For all of these amazing gifts in my life, I am forever grateful.

Of course, none of the above would have been possible if not for the unwavering support system of my family and friends. Mom, Aunt Debbie, Pop, Fran, and Elly—we are small and non-traditional, but you have been the safety net that has allowed me to vagabond around the world and experiment with ideas and cultures in the pursuit of something-not-yet-realized. I hope you see this book as a beacon toward that something. I love you. And to the friends I've made around the world—whether in the theater, the classroom, the pub, the gym, on set, digital space, or elsewhere—thank you.

"Als Ik Kan"

Abbreviations

BN—Being and Nothingness
CDR—Critique of Dialectical Reason (Volume One, unless otherwise specified)
EH—Existentialism Is a Humanism
FI—The Family Idiot
MR—Materialism and Revolution
PI—The Imaginary: A Phenomenological Psychology of the Imagination
SM—Search for a Method
TE—Transcendence of the Ego: An Existentialist Theory of Consciousness

Glossary of Terms

Affect

Affect refers to pre-personal, pre-subjective experience. It does not refer to emotion or feelings. Rather, affect refers to interaction and encounters that stimulate bodily responses. It most corresponds to Spinoza's *affectus* as interpreted by Deleuze.[1]

Analytical Reason

Analytical Reason investigates the world by separating the observer from the observed. The observed is analyzed as a sequence of externally related, discrete units, much like mathematical variables. Sartre attributes analytical reason to Positivist Rationalists and Positivist Marxists. It is a relativism insofar as analytical reason can only observe relative parts of an externally autonomous Reason. It corresponds with the Constructivist orientation of thought and the philosophy of external relations.

Apocalypse

This term is derived from Malraux's *Days of Hope* (sometimes translated as *Man's Hope*). In the novel, it refers to the fraternity of unwavering hope among soldiers in hopeless circumstances who cannot but fight their way out of hopelessness. In *Critique of Dialectical Reason*, apocalypse is the term that describes the awakening of humanity out of the inhuman conditions of serial existence.

Dialectic of Nature

The dialectic of nature is a theory of the dialectic as an Eternal Reason. It is a law that determines all human interaction and physico-chemical processes. Sartre argues that the dialectic of nature is a "metaphysical hypothesis." It corresponds with the Constructivist orientation of thought.

Dialectical Reason

Dialectical Reason is defined in contradistinction to analytical reason. It is both method and movement. As method, Sartre refers to it as the "law of intelligibility." This means that dialectical reason is the rational structure of Being, the logic of totalization. It is derived squarely from the relation between "men and matter." As movement, as (in)humans overcome conditions of scarcity toward the next moment of objectification, such is dialectical reason. It is not reducible to abstract thinking (although thought is a moment of praxis, a moment of dialectical movement). Rather, for Sartre, dialectical reason is lived (*le vécu*). This is why he refers to it as the "living logic of action." It accords with the Paradoxico-Critical orientation of thought and the philosophy of internal relations.

Empathy

Empathy is not to be understood with regard to compassion or feeling in any sense. It refers to a contagious, affective (i.e., unconscious and automatic) vicarious experience of a common goal. Empathy is what characterizes the fusion of the group.

Formal

Formal refers to the many grouped as one. A formal construct is one in which a multiplicity is united into a singular category. *Critique of Dialectical Reason* is a formal investigation in that it seeks to encompass the manifold of lived experienced under particular conditions into simple, abstract logical (i.e., the living logic) concepts. These concepts are considered formal in that they contain the many in the one; the many are not reduced to the one. In this way, the one opens up to the infinite constellation of meanings contained within it. These formal concepts are historicized *a priori*. They are processes and sets. They are both the result and condition of dialectical totalization.

Infinite Seriality

Infinite Seriality is Sartre's term for the confluence of horizontal and vertical serial alienation. It is the purely descriptive component of the formal concept, Kaironic Seriality.

Kaironic Seriality

Kaironic Seriality has a dual meaning. It describes the social fact of existence by calling the age of capitalist hegemony Impossible and simultaneously declares that it is never not the opportune moment to act in antagonism to serial power structures. Whereas Infinite Seriality is purely descriptive, Kaironic Seriality is descriptive insofar as it identifies the stakes of inhuman serial existence as the Impossible, and it is prescriptive insofar as it is the formal fact that this impossibility is no longer possible. It is not Sartre's term, but the author's. It is a useful construct insofar as it serves the ends of this project by clearly nominating a foe that must be perpetually negated through vigilant action.

Logic

Logic in *Critique of Dialectical Reason* means "intelligibility." It is the *sense* of the elemental formal structures of dialectical reason. While not identical to dialectical reason, logic cannot ever be understood apart from dialectical reason. It is not akin to formal logics in the tradition of propositional logic, first-order logic, model-theoretic logic, or any other analytical system. It is best understood in relation to the philosophy of internal relations, whereby interpenetrating abstractions co-constitute one another through dialectical tension.

Mediation

There is always mediation between persons and the conditions into which they are thrown. (In)humans are not self-sufficient, but must look outside themselves in order to survive. Breathing air, walking on various terrain, using tools, speaking words: all of these demonstrate that the human predicament is necessarily a mediatory condition. There is no such thing as immediacy in real material terms.

Orientations of Thought

Transcendent/Onto-Theological: Any position that views the totality of what can be known within a set limit that is dependent upon a transcendent beyond which itself is ineffable, superlative, and groundless. Ex. Aristotle, Augustine, Aquinas.

Constructivist: Delimits all that is sayable or sensical while remaining outside of that totality. Ex. Kant, Russell, Carnap, Ayer, Foucault, analytical reason, dialectic of nature.

Generic: Alain Badiou's self-designation. Any self-referential position that recognizes the paradoxes of totality and thus denies the being of totality as such in favor of infinite worlds. When given the choice between completeness and consistency, this orientation chooses consistency. Ex. Badiou, Gabriel.

Paradoxico-Critical: Paul Livingston's addition to the three orientations that Badiou articulates. Any position that recognizes the paradoxes of self-reflexivity but does not reject totality as such. When given the choice between completeness and consistency, this orientation chooses completeness. Ex. Deleuze, Derrida, Agamben, Ollman.

Praxis

Praxis is the logic of human activity. Sartre refers to praxis and totalization in interchangeable terms, with nuances differentiating them based on the context of the discussion. Similarly, praxis is dialectical reason, the *lived* of the living logic of action. It describes (in)human activity in its perpetual interiorization and exteriorization of the situation into which it is thrown at any and every given moment. Praxis is not generic action. It is the re-organization of the material environment through totalization.

Subjectivity

Subjectivity has two senses:

1) It is part of the process of totalization. It is described, in mereological terms, as a system of interiority.

2) It is the gap between interiorization and exteriorization, the differential. It is the spark of life initiated by the apocalypse.

These two senses are not contradictory but envelop one another. The first sense is the abstract logic of totalization. The second is the particular motive force of the former. Under inhuman conditions, the second sense is dormant and must be awakened by the apocalypse. But this language is merely an abstraction. In real material terms, subjectivity is never entirely dormant. Sartre's point is to describe how and why subjectivity emerges under conditions of serial alienation.

Telepathy

This does not refer to extra-sensory perception. Telepathy, in our usage, is the real, material, contagious spread of affect in the group-in-fusion.

Totality

Totality is a correlative of the imagination. Sartre refers to totality as being practico-inert. He argues that reason conditioned by closed totalities (à la Lukács) leads to dogmatic insensitivity to the multiplicity.

Totalization

In contradistinction to totality, totalization is an open-ended process. This is the unceasing movement of dialectical reason. If totality is a correlative of the imagination, totalization is a correlative of praxis.

NOTE

1. Gilles Deleuze, "Lectures on Spinoza," http://deleuzelectures.blogspot.ie/2007/02/on-spinoza.html.

Introduction

Rediscovering Sartre in a Completely Natural Way

Interviewer: Are you sorry that young intellectuals don't read you any more, that they know you only through false ideas of you and your works?

Sartre: I would say it's too bad for me.

Interviewer: For you, or for them?

Sartre: To tell the truth, for them too. But I think it is just a passing stage.

Interviewer: Basically you would agree with the prediction Roland Barthes made recently when he said that you will soon be rediscovered and that this will take place in a completely natural way?

Sartre: I hope so.[1]

Making the conditions for liberatory socio-political practice intelligible has been a central preoccupation among theorists and activists alike since Marx made this a primary concern in the mid-nineteenth century: from his indictment of religious mystification, to Lenin's concerns about the transformation of human nature in *State and Revolution*; from Audre Lorde's "The Master's Tools," to Butlerian performativity; and more recently from Žižek's transcendental materialism and Malabou's plastic brains, to Badiou's set-theoretical subtractive subject. The common thread connecting these disparate persuasions is an interest in fundamental questions pertaining to exploitation, oppression, self-awareness, and human motivation. Generally speaking, it is understood that by comprehending who we are in the worlds that we inhabit can instigate the proper action to combat injustice. Jean-Paul Sartre's *Critique of Dialectical Reason* (hereafter *CDR*) must be understood within this tradition of critique.

There is a type of 1940s Sartrean Scholasticism that overdetermines *CDR* reception. By focusing on the classic and paradigmatic Sartrean motifs, a hermeneutical rigidity sets the limits and issues the demands for how the rest of Sartre's ideas are interpreted. The present book is an effort to combat this tendency and to re-introduce *CDR* with this dogmatism. More than this, the present book is also an exploration of broader political philosophical concerns. Sartre's political works have been tragically lost among the sea of more fashionable theorists and orientations of late. The present effort is, in part, an attempt to situate Sartre among these concerns in order to demonstrate the lasting validity of particular Sartrean insights that have been largely swept away in the tumult of post-phenomenological concerns. There will be both re-introductions and novel conceptual creations throughout. Thus, both Sartre scholars and those less familiar with the internal debates surrounding Sartre's mature philosophical writings will find value in the present work. The author encourages readers of all stripes to take a proactive and experimental imaginative approach when reading. Make connections beyond the limits of these pages. Allow the beckoning of the universal to inflect the particulars. And maintain an awakened spirit for sites of potential expansion in future projects. In this way, we can take the steps toward rediscovering Sartre in a completely natural way.

Sartre's oft-neglected tome investigates the formal conditions of structural and historical anthropology.[2] Divided into two volumes, *CDR* undertakes a formal[3] and logical[4] investigation into the historicized *a priori* conditions of social life.[5] Abstractly analyzed as heuristic devices, these "elementary formal structures" are 1) the result of dialectical totalization, 2) the condition(s) of any and all praxis, and 3) the intelligibility of what Sartre refers to as "practical ensembles."[6] Simply stated, in *CDR*, Sartre is seeking to develop a logic for the analysis and creation of new humanisms, analyzing what the human *is* under particular historical and structural conditions and then seeking to provide the necessary tools to envision alternatives. For him, dialectical reason is the way to do this. Logic, for Sartre, is not a reformulation of thinking "from a higher standpoint" à la Hegel. Rather, it is the development of an orientation to the world, one that is defined by dialectical reason.

Dialectical reason is a form of thinking and acting. It is a particular disposition and comportment of thought and action toward material realities. It is "praxis" understood as totalization, which is the human creating from within conditions that are not of his/her choosing. It is the intelligibility of history. Thus, *CDR* is at once a criticism of analytical reason and also a criticism of particular rationalities within Marxism that are either positivist, totalized, and/or idealist. In *CDR*, Sartre advocates a form of rationality that is both structural and historical, but that is purely lived (*le vécu*). Thus, dialectical reason is a *living logic of action*. In his words, "[It] appears in the course of praxis as a necessary moment of it; in other words, it is created anew in each action (though actions arise only on the basis of a world entirely constituted by the dialectical praxis of the past) and becomes a theoretical and practical method when action in the course of development begins to give an explanation of itself."[7] The meaning of this will become clearer as this project unfolds.

Through his analysis, Sartre develops a series of abstract concepts that serve as points of departure in which complex and concrete analyses can subsequently take place. The most notable of these terms for the present project are 1) praxis (as totalization), 2) seriality, and 3) the group.

Praxis is how Sartre characterizes the entirety of material human existence in a Marxian fashion—identifying the human with labor: "[The] truth of a man is the nature of his work. . . . But, this truth defines him just insofar as he constantly goes beyond it in his practical activity."[8] This experience of one working, being defined by her work, and surpassing her situation is what Sartre would call one's "praxis-project." It is the essential identity marker of human existence. That said, we must distinguish Sartre's use of "work" here from wage-labor. Sure, this is part of one's praxis-project, but by speaking about the human "constantly [going] beyond [this truth] in his practical activity," he is expanding on his earlier notion about the transcending nature of consciousness (i.e., consciousness transcending one's situation in aiming toward the possible beyond it). To reduce praxis to wage-labor is to miss the robustness of Sartre's reconceptualization of subjectivity as a system of interiority. The latter encompasses the entirety of embodied and embedded human activity—"practical activity"—into his redefined understanding of humanity in *CDR*. Part of the reason seriality is alienating is because it reduces the human to an inhuman actor mediated and determined by market relations. This is precisely one reason the Sartrean notion of "apocalypse" has a transformative effect on subjectivity—it reconstitutes the human, in praxis, as something other than a node in the swirling mediacy of market sociality. Thus, to speak of the human merely in terms of wage-labor would be to reduce praxis to a serial logic. And while praxis can be understood as antipraxis (i.e., serial praxis), this mode of praxis is only made intelligible by understanding the serial conditions that constitute it as such.[9]

Praxis is also how Sartre would redefine his notion of freedom in *CDR*. Eschewing voluntarist ideas of freedom being related to one's capacity to choose within a given context, praxis defines the human in her persistent overcoming of the scarce material reality in which one finds herself thrown at each moment. Freedom is thus understood as interiorizing the milieu of scarcity (i.e., negating it) while at the same time re-exteriorizing a new condition, from objectification to objectification, that itself can be taken up in a new interiorization. The result is a concrete notion of dialectical movement that is firmly rooted in the activity of human beings in material conditions. In other words, the dialectic, for Sartre, is just that movement of human beings as they overcome their present situation in seeking to satisfy a need.

As humans engage in this dialectical process, praxis is meant to be revealed through comprehension. In his words, this comprehension through dialectical reason is the "translucidity of praxis to itself."[10] For Sartre, praxis's comprehension is the human function of Marxist anthropology. This is the source of class consciousness that will awaken the proletariat to the truth of their situation and motivate them toward just ends. This means that the function of Marxist anthropology is precisely to enable humanity to comprehend existence. Not a detached metaphysical notion of existence—but concrete historical existence. And this only happens through praxis comprehending itself in creating history, which itself is already a product of itself. As you can see, this framing is quite a self-referential and idealist philosophical doctrine. Despite Marx's efforts to ground Hegel, Cornelius Castoriadis's assessment seems apt when he remarked that Marx "preserved [the] true philosophical content" of Hegel's dialectic—"rationalism . . . [and that] every rationalist dialectic is necessarily a closed dialectic."[11] What defines Hegel's dialectic as closed is that the real is rational and that "logos precedes nature." As such, "This essence [of logos preceding nature] cannot be destroyed by setting the dialectic 'on its feet.' . . . A revolutionary surpassing of the Hegelian dialectic demands not that it be set on its feet but that, to begin with, its head be cut off."[12] This latter idea of cutting the head off the closed dialectic is what Sartre endeavors to do by grounding dialectical reason in the materiality of concrete praxis, despite the paradoxical self-referential and idealist slick that floats on the surface of the Marxist project *per se*.

However, a problem arises: since material conditions under the logic of capital are characterized by scarcity, the dialectic is marred by *seriality*. Seriality is the result of scarce material conditions mediating human relations, causing conflict, competition, violence, and radical alterity. As persons within collectives are united externally by shared objects in the milieu of scarcity, they are deemed *inessential* in the service of the goal of the collective or institution, which is given *essential* status. Sociality, under the conditions of seriality, is therefore perpetually embattled in a field of subjective and objective conflict. For Sartre, even political parties themselves exhibit the force of seriality over their members by instituting a serial logic by which the individual members of the party would take it up as their "own" and subsequently live it. This adoption of the institutional logic and then expression of it as one's own is understood as the self-domestication of the human. It is not truly a free act, as the adopted logic was pre-destined by the pre-existent institution. Therefore, the persons adopting such a logic are trapped within the serial conditions of the institution.

What this leads to is false comprehension. That is, Sartre does not believe that under serial conditions praxis has the tools available to be able to comprehend itself. The tools themselves, so to speak, are conditioned by a serial logic. As such, they reproduce illusory self-comprehension. This is why *Search for a Method* (*SM*) and *CDR* are methodological projects through and through. And this is why Volume One of *CDR* (more so than Volume Two) must be read as a formal investigation into the logical abstractions that might reveal the grounds of this comprehension. As Sartre would say, the project of *CDR* concerns "comprehending the comprehension" of praxis.[13] This means that a Marxist comprehension of anthropological history is not possible until this comprehension itself can be comprehended.[14]

All is not lost though. When the pressures of this serial entrapment are felt deeply, an irruption of freedom bursts forth. This is the apocalyptic moment for Sartre, and out of this event a group-in-fusion emerges, uniting people in a common action in their shared antagonism to the impossibility of living under serial conditions any longer. This notion of the apocalypse and the constitution of the group-in-fusion is where Alain Badiou derives his notion of the Event.[15] Like Badiou's later formulation, a space is opened in Being that allows for the recreation of subjectivity itself. Whereas under serial conditions, people are "inhuman" and marked by alterity, conflict, competition, and ultimately incomprehension, once the freedom of the fused group irrupts, new humanisms are created. Unfortunately, the affective power of the Event is understood as an upsurging flash, irrupting from and through the conditions of seriality. And while it has a genuine effect on the constituent process of praxis and the material conditions, the ubiquity of seriality ensures that such moments are insufficient to transform the situation entirely in freedom. However, post-Eventual situations are not mere cascades back into a previous serial condition, for the people have been changed. They have experienced freedom and their subjectivities have been re-constituted. They are now a new people.

It is generally assumed that Sartre was unconcerned with complexes of mediation and relationality, and that ultimately Sartre was a theorist of the Cartesian individualist tradition unable to provide viable ideas for social or political life. Thinkers like Raymond Aron, Lévi-Strauss, Wilfrid Desan, and even Thomas Flynn all place Sartre in this camp.[16] They claim, to differing extents, that Sartre's later work is still trapped within the individualist paradigm that he established in his early existentialist writings. This has been the dominant mode of reception of *CDR*. They see it as a work of individualism seeking to vindicate itself in the social realm, or, in Flynn's case, as a social ontology that gives primacy to individual praxis and which lacks "an ontology of relations."[17] According to Edouard Morot-Sir, *CDR*'s effort to provide a novel social theory fails catastrophically, for as he states, *"la mariée est trop belle."*[18] In other words, Sartre's attempt to wed together "methodological individualism" with any meaningful social theory is nothing but a fanciful endeavor.

As a brief aside, it must be acknowledged that the history of Sartre reception is far more complex than merely drawing a line between individualism and social theory. In *Being and Nothingness* (*BN*), Sartre does explore inter-subjective relations. In fact, the mode "being-for-others" is a term that necessarily denotes the relationality of lived experience. It also must be noted that the three modes of being (in-itself, for-itself, and for-others) are abstractions that in lived experience co-inhere within embodied existence. This means that there are no pure "for-itselfs" walking around. Rather, Sartre's investigation was to unveil the truth of phenomenological ontology as it is expressed in its various modes. And he did this by investigating what he formulates as the three basic modes of phenomenological ontology.

The problem in *BN* is that his investigation ends up diminishing the possibility for any lasting or valuable inter-subjective relations. He does discuss the "us-object" and "we-subject" as modes of social being-together. However, both of these terms end up deficient. The we-subject is the term given the most positive treatment of the intersubjective modes. However, the we-subject is merely a temporary state where individuals suspend their individual freedom for a single purpose. And even while this might seem a useful way of being-together, there is always suspicion that the Other will betray your confidence and depart from the task. And, of course, inevitably it is only a short-lived positive relation because once the task is complete, there is no longer any union of interests.

CDR signals a shift in that Sartre develops a genuine understanding of the conditions of free social ensembles. It might be argued that *CDR* takes the concept of the "we-subject" and expands it, seeking to make the conditions under which this mode of being-together might be made intelligible (as it does have a lot of resonance with his group logic in *CDR*). However, this is a claim that is outside the scope of the present project. The point here is merely to note that although Sartre's ontology in his earlier writings is far more complex than a crude Cartesian accusation would suppose, it is also the case that he is often lumped into this category, and I would argue that there is often a residue of this interpretation in even the most sympathetic of *CDR* readers.

Therefore, against the dominant mode of *CDR* reception, the tack of the present project presents Sartre as a theorist who bridges the gap between many modernist and postmodernist concerns. Following the works of Christina Howells, Nik Farrell Fox, and Elizabeth Butterfield, this project views *CDR* as providing a transition from simplistic, modernist political readings that tout the centrality of the pre-constituted subject, to postmodern concerns with the dispersal of power relations that condition subjective constitution, structural institutional potency, and the relations between the two. This is not to claim that a division between the modern and postmodern is neatly drawn. Rather, the point is to note that Sartre's investigation in *CDR* eschews the categorization that has often peppered its reception. Rather than read the endeavor as an effort to wed together existentialism and Marxism into a modernist project, our hope is to illuminate a prescience in the conceptual abstractions he develops, one that straddles a Marxian context that cannot be shucked and that also incorporates the anxieties that echo from the post-war European landscape.

In a sense, the true potency of *CDR* has yet to be mined. Rather than establishing a social ontology or set of normative models that can aid in the construction of social life, *CDR* is a work of *logic*. That is, *CDR* investigates the formal, logical conditions of social life in its various forms (collectives, groups, organizations, institutions, classes, political parties, etc.) in order to make their emergence and functionality intelligible. As he makes explicit, the dialectic is "the living logic of action."[19] The result is not to suggest which groupings are superior. Instead, Sartre wants to equip future theorists with a foundational logical disposition that will aid further investigation into the mechanisms that drive anthropological history. In his words, "If our critical investigation actually yields positive results, we shall have established *a priori*—and not, as the Marxists *think* they have done, *a posteriori*—the heuristic value of the dialectical method when applied to the human sciences, and the necessity . . . of reinserting it within the developing totalisation and understanding it on this basis."[20] This is why he refers to *CDR* as a "prolegomena to any future anthropology."[21] What *CDR* investigates are the conditions under which dialectical reason can come to comprehend itself.

Once this fresh reading of *CDR* has been articulated in part I, we turn to creation and reconstruction in part II. After establishing the above reading, we will pick up precisely where Sartre stopped in his investigation in Volume One. This will be pursued in two ways: 1) by further explicating the logic of the dynamic power relations that make up social life, and 2) by theorizing ways in which such a logic can be deployed in the perpetual transformation of life. In light of this, the two most pressing political concerns of this project will be 1) micro-political and 2) macro-political. The micro-political concerns will regard the logic of subjective constitution and horizontal political action. The macro-political concerns will focus on the logic of transforming structural and systemic power relations.

There have been many theorists in recent years who have sought to think "the people" (such as Enrique Dussel and Alain Badiou) or against a notion of the people (ex. Hardt and Negri) in order to empower global political liberatory praxis. Micro-political theorists (ex. William Connolly and Todd May) are less concerned with large-scale political endeavors, favoring instead horizontal and local political disruptions/transformations. What I endeavor to demonstrate are the ways in which both micro- and macro-political concerns are crucial in the development of an imaginative disposition that seeks the transformation of the human in the creation of new social and political ensembles.

Therefore, the first half of the book is a creative but thoroughly exegetical reading of the formal constructions that Sartre develops in *CDR*, paying particular attention to praxis, seriality, and the group. The second half of the book explores the deployment of these notions in conjunction with Sartre's early work on the imagination. Guiding this section is the claim that Sartre unwittingly develops a theory of praxis in *CDR* that presupposes his earlier work on the imagination, and that this earlier work in fact supplements how praxis ought to be understood in *CDR*. The result is that a renewed understanding of the "living logic of action" in *CDR* emerges as an *imaginative logic of action*. With the latter, imagination becomes a latent, embedded moment of praxis itself in the latter's perpetual recreative, active antagonism to serial conditions in seeking to ground comprehension.

By incorporating the imagination into Sartre's living logic of action, two results follow: 1) by further explicating the logic of the dynamic power relations that make up social life, a more robust set of analytical tools emerge with which novel social and political theory can develop, and 2) by theorizing ways in which such a logic can be deployed in the perpetual transformation of life, a creative, forward-looking, utopic thought is developed. This will be done primarily through a creative exegesis of *Critique of Dialectical Reason*: Volume One, as well as key secondary texts that have engaged with Sartre's mature political thought. There will be appeals to Sartre's other works as well, insofar as these resources either clarify the terms contained in *CDR* or develop related notions that contribute to the overarching development of the logical project of *CDR*.

At the outset, it is imperative to note that this present project will primarily focus on Volume One of *CDR*. Volume Two is a valuable text for fleshing out the project that was begun in Volume One. However, it is of secondary importance for two reasons. First, Sartre himself abandoned the project. The reasons for this are subject to speculation. For example, Robert Bernasconi insightfully argues that Sartre left the project of Volume Two to those who were better equipped to address the meaning of history at that stage of historical development, namely the colonized.[22] The implication is that Fanon's *The Wretched of the Earth* serves as a sequel in that in order for philosophical practice to seek comprehension, it must not remain a European exercise, but must dialectically incorporate a more holistic notion of the complex character of the proletariat if dialectical reason is truly to make praxis translucid to itself. Alternatively, Fredric Jameson suggests that existentialism's passing popularity in light of the rise of structuralism, its transdisciplinary generality, and its "notorious stylistic difficulty" have made *CDR* the critical target of all manner of philosophers, social scientists, historians, and political theorists.[23] Sartre himself would later state that he believed *CDR* was "too idealistic" and wanted to engage in projects that were squarely concrete. Hence his move toward the massive biographical-historical work on Flaubert. Whatever the reasons, what matters for the aims of this project is that Volume Two is an incomplete bundle of writings that were not intended to be published, and as such, they will be treated with a sense of caution so as to not risk overvaluing ideas that Sartre himself did not take public.

The second reason Volume Two is of secondary importance for the present project, and more importantly, is that Volume One sets the logical framework for future investigation into history. Sartre first needed to explore the historical and structural conditions of social ensembles by establishing a living logic of action through his analysis of the logic of dialectical reason before he could proceed to investigate the single meaning of history. If the tools of comprehension remained ever illusive, then seeking a progressive elaboration of the meaning of dialectical unfolding would be a vacuous endeavor. Without getting too ahead of ourselves, on the penultimate page of Volume One, reflecting on the investigation up to that point, Sartre remarks,

> If History really is to be the totalisation of all practical multiplicities and of all their struggles, the complex products of the conflicts and collaborations of these very diverse multiplicities must themselves be intelligible in their synthetic reality, that is to say, they must be comprehensible as the synthetic products of a totalitarian praxis.[24]

Making the logic of these "synthetic products" intelligible through a fresh reading of Volume One is thus our primary concern, so that we can press their use as far as possible in establishing an orientation that is both perspicuously critical of material conditions and unwaveringly creative. There will be references to Volume Two, but only insofar as they serve this end. As such, the theoretical paradigm Sartre establishes in Volume One is the stage on which this present investigation plays out. That means that Volume One will not only serve as the primary exegetical source, but it will also frame the form of the investigation proper. And despite the difficulties of the verbose language, as Jameson states, "with a little practice its rhythms fall into place."[25]

By the end, through this analysis, we will have developed new tools with which future theorists can undertake abstract analyses of social ensembles and their historical and material effects, and activists will be equipped with a logical disposition that will aid them in constructing local action and large-scale policy. This will require both the analysis of real, concrete material conditions and an indomitable creative imaginative spirit. Without the former, politics is nothing but idealistic utopianism. Without a creative imaginative spirit, politics rests in a conservative self-perpetuation. By bringing them both together, we develop the necessary tools to resist stasis, develop sensitivities to the ever-emerging concerns of social and political communities, and remain optimistic in our abilities to perpetually recreate our worlds.

Sartre stated that if his investigation in *CDR* accomplished nothing more than enabling him "to define the problem, by means of provisional remarks which are there to be challenged and modified, and if they give rise to a discussion and if, as would be best, this discussion is carried on collectively in working groups, then I shall be satisfied."[26] Following the path laid by Sartre, the present project seeks to take this mantle, expand it further, and lay it at the feet of future groups, with the hope that further development of this investigation will lead to 1) a reintroduction and expansion of *CDR* scholarship and 2) a set of fluid practical devices that can be employed in future socio-political activities.

NOTES

1. Jean-Paul Sartre and Michel Contat, "Sartre at Seventy: An Interview," *The New York Review of Books*, originally published August 7, 1975, accessed June 12, 2016, http://www.nybooks.com/articles/1975/08/07/sartre-at-seventy-an-interview/.
2. Jean-Paul Sartre, *Critique of Dialectical Reason*: Volume One, ed. Jonathan Ree, trans. Alan Sheridan-Smith (London: Verso, 2004), 69.
3. "Formal" refers to the many grouped as one. A formal construct is one in which a multiplicity is united into a singular category. *Critique of Dialectical Reason* is a formal investigation in that it seeks to encompass the manifold of lived experience under particular conditions into simple, abstract logical notions. These notions are considered formal in that they contain the many in the one; the many are not reduced to the one. In this way, the one opens up to the infinite constellation of meanings contained within it. These formal notions are historicized *a priori*. They are both the result and condition of dialectical totalization.
4. "Logic" in the language of *CDR* means "dialectical intelligibility." While it is related to dialectical reason, the terms are not interchangeable. Chapter 1 will elaborate further on Sartre's deployment of dialectical reason in its self-referential founding and movement and will clarify in what sense "logic" is to be understood in this project.
5. Sartre, *CDR*, 11.
6. Ibid., 818.
7. Sartre, *CDR*, 38.
8. Jean-Paul Sartre, *Search for a Method*, trans. Hazel Barnes (New York: Alfred A. Knopf, 1963), 93.
9. This will be elaborated in chapters 4, 5, 7, and 9.
10. Ibid., 91.
11. Cornelius Castoriadis, *The Imaginary Institution of Society*, trans. Kathleen Blamey (Cambridge: Polity Press, 2005), 54 and 55.
12. Ibid., 55.
13. Sartre, *CDR*, 696.
14. Keen observers might note how such a project could lead to an infinite regress wherein the comprehension of comprehension itself must be subject to its own process of comprehension. And this criticism would not be invalid were it not for the approach that Sartre assumes in *CDR* (what we will identify in chapter 1 as the "Paradoxico-Critical" orientation of thought).

15. Alain Badiou, interview with Emmanuel Barot, "Entretien avec Alain Badiou, par Emmanuel Barot," in *Sartre et le Marxisme*, ed. Emmanuel Barot (Paris: La Dispute, 2011): "I must say that in effect [my] notion of event finds its genesis . . . in the descriptions of the group-in-fusion, and particularly all the episodes of the French Revolution interpreted by Sartre in this way."

16. Although Flynn is one of the most astute early readers of *CDR*, his emphasis on individual praxis in *CDR* ultimately places his reading into the Cartesian camp with the majority of readers. He does, however, contribute valuably to the text as a whole, and he will be mostly referred to favorably throughout this project.

17. Thomas Flynn, *Sartre and Marxist Existentialism* (Chicago: University of Chicago Press, 1984), 206. Against this view, it could be argued that *CDR* is only concerned with an ontology of relations, insofar as an ontology can be derived from the formal, logical investigation. That is, the shift in *CDR* from his earlier work takes place precisely under a rubric of social mediation. This social mediation can only be understood as relational. In other words, what Sartre assumes, not so much develops, is an ecology of material relations between (in)humans and the material field in which they live and create. For this reading, see Matthew Ally, *Ecology and Existence: Bringing Sartre to the Water's Edge* (Lanham, MD: Lexington Books, 2017).

18. Edouard Morot-Sir, "Sartre's Critique of Dialectical Reason," *Journal of the History of Ideas*, 22, no. 4 (1961): 575.

19. Sartre, *CDR*, 38.

20. Sartre, *CDR*, 66.

21. Ibid., 66.

22. Robert Bernasconi, "Fanon's *The Wretched of the Earth* as the Fulfillment of Sartre's *Critique of Dialectical Reason*," *Sartre Studies International*, 16, no. 2 (2010).

23. Fredric Jameson, "Foreword," in Sartre, *CDR*, xiii–xvi.

24. Sartre, *CDR*, 817.

25. Jameson, "Foreword," in Sartre *CDR*, xvi.

26. Ibid., 41.

Part I

The Living Logic of Action in *Critique of Dialectical Reason*

Part I is the analytical and exegetical component of the present project. We begin in chapter 1 by setting the trajectory. This is done through an analysis of Sartre's stated effort to validate his own approach in *CDR*. In a word, this chapter will establish the methodology of our own practice in reorienting ourselves to *CDR*. Chapter 2 serves as a preface to the exegetical work in the subsequent chapters by establishing the orthodox readings of *CDR* in order to problematize them. These readings will be categorized as the "ontological and normative" readings. We will come to see how they were formulated and why and in what ways do they fail to adequately convey crucial elements in Sartre's investigation into dialectical rationality.

Chapter 3 begins the exegetical investigation of *CDR* by beginning with an examination of familiar Sartrean concepts: scarcity, worked matter, and the practico-inert. Some of this will be familiar (both for those familiar with Sartre and the uninitiated), but much of it is a nuanced reading of these terms that provides novel angles by which we can examine terms under the scrutiny of the particular methodology that we previously established in chapter 1. This chapter will not discard previous scholarship on these or related terms but provide suggestions for how we might better understand the logic of the exigency of material conditions through our fresh take. This chapter ends by heightening the human predicament. Chapter 4 then further explores the depths of this condition through a complete analysis of a term that is often given only cursory treatment: seriality. This chapter serves as the most crucial for understanding how and why praxis is not translucid to itself (insofar as it is not under serial conditions). The reason this chapter is so important for the foregoing investigation is that it establishes the stakes of praxis's self-awareness by intensifying the forces that suppress it.

The final chapter of part I is the foil to chapter 4. If chapter 4 establishes the depths of the human predicament, chapter 5 articulates under what conditions the grip of seriality is loosened. This chapter will investigate the logic of the group. We work through all the formulations of the group that Sartre develops in order not to identify which stage of group formation is the most desirable as a practical ensemble, but to understand the various living logics that constitute each of these group modes. Once our exegetical investigation reaches this point, we will have covered the central terms of *CDR* that inform our project. The next step is to turn to the more speculative portion of the book. By establishing our fresh reading of *CDR*, we will be better positioned to investigate how the imagination is a central component to the living logic of action that Sartre develops in *CDR*, and what implications this has for creating new humanisms and perpetually creating society as a work of art so that praxis will be better equipped to confront the dominance of serial alienation.

Chapter One

Dialectical Reason and the Paradoxico-Critical Orientation of Thought

Prior to developing a fresh reading of *CDR*, it will be crucial to orient our practice so we can decode some of the "rhythms" of the text. Sartre's use of particular terms may, at times, seem novel or even obscurantist.[1] However, although he does not always signal to whom, his arguments arise out of contextual concerns within the Marxist tradition. Viewing himself as a Marxian ideologist rather than a philosopher proper,[2] Sartre's gesture is to work within the Marxian historical paradigm and to clarify and/or correct certain tendencies that gained ascendency.

Most forcefully, Sartre argues that if Marxism is to have sustained value it must *found* itself. This is because Sartre was unconvinced that Marxism had properly articulated a foundation for dialectical reason. In the opening pages of *CDR*, he states, "The totalising thought of historical materialism has established everything except its own existence. . . . [We] do not know what it means for a Marxist historian to *speak the truth*."[3] This bold assertion is due to Marxism's self-containment as a serial discourse. Sartre supposes that Marxism had been enclosed in its own self-reinforcing, serial circularity whereby Marxism itself was a reified totality (what Sartre might call a practico-inert image) that mediated and determined all potential praxis. The result is that Marxism, as reified totality, became a static object immune from the processual flow of becoming, which in turn stifled the dialectic. The very orientation meant to illumine the dialectic instead became its foreclosure.

Therefore, the dialectic establishing itself in dialectical intelligibility becomes the task for Sartre. That is, in what way is the dialectic both method and movement? And how is this to be understood if we are to claim that there is a single meaning to history?

The task in Volume One thus becomes less about understanding that truth *per se* than about *discovering* and *grounding* how to speak that truth in the first instance. This, at least, is where he begins. Not seeing himself as a Marxist historian, Sartre intends to investigate the philosophical foundations of anthropological history that will reveal the intelligibility of the dialectic itself. He refers to this as the "unveiling of being" and the establishment of the "validity of this unveiling."[4]

This chapter will proceed by exploring both this unveiling and its validity. Section 1.1 will construct a conceptual narrative pertaining to the separation of *logos* from *mythos*. The reason for this is to position Sartre's project in *CDR* within a set of concerns that have loomed over debates about rationality. Other conceptual narratives could be drawn. Which is to say that this is only one charted path among others in a network of shared concerns. But its validity is useful for the present project in that it covers the broad concerns in a short amount of space without sacrificing accuracy.[5]

Section 1.2 expands on this conceptual narrative by addressing Sartre's criticism of Georg Lukács's totality. Particularly, we pay attention to how the logic of totality operates by pre-figuring praxis through the fabrication of a rigid and fixed *telos*. Inverting the existentialist maxim—"existence precedes essence"—the logic of totality imposes essence onto the manifold of praxis and stifles its becoming. Then we introduce Sartre's speculative proposal of totalization as an alternative logic for the unveiling of being.

Sections 1.3 and 1.4 explore the validity of the unveiling of Being that Sartre proposes. Criticisms from Claude Lévi-Strauss frame this portion of the discussion. We will briefly address his accusation that *CDR* is an ethnocentric fetishization of the French Revolution. But what most concerns us is the charge that *CDR* is contradictory. We answer this charge by reading *CDR* through the lens of the Paradoxico-Critical orientation toward thought and Being as elaborated by Paul Livingston (this orientation will be explained below). The reason we frame the argument in this way is that Livingston's four orientations of thought present useful templates that allow us to place Sartre's project. Where Lévi-Strauss sees simple contradiction, we will offer that Sartre productively employs a paradoxical poetic.

The conclusion of the chapter will lead us into our exegetical examination of *CDR*. We will come to see Sartre's project as endeavoring to articulate that in order to properly unveil Being we must possess the proper tools of comprehension. While Sartre speculatively proposes to unveil Being, his primary concern is to elucidate the path to that end. However, for Sartre, the road is fraught with diversions and obstacles. Recognizing this and charting a strategy to clear the way is what grounds the validity of his investigation into dialectical reason.

1.1 THE UNVEILING OF BEING: THE SEPARATION OF *LOGOS* FROM *MYTHOS*

How are we to understand what Sartre means by the "unveiling of being"? For this, it would be useful to turn briefly to the history of a debate surrounding rationality in order to situate the Sartrean project. This will not be an exhaustive investigation. Our intent is to situate the concerns of *CDR* within a conceptual context moreso than the historical. Therefore, we ask for a little leeway in crafting a particular conceptual narrative. Its value will become increasingly clear as this project unfolds, right through to the final chapter.

Historian Martin Jay has charted the developing notion of reason from ancient Greece through to the Frankfurt School criticisms of formal and instrumental reason. What is sometimes termed "the Greek Miracle," Jay explains how the unfolding elaboration of reason must be understood within the context of the separation of *logos* from *mythos*.[6] This is not to suggest that there was a clean rupture between the two concepts, for there are traces of each embedded within the other. Rather, what is meant by "separation" is that a trajectory was initiated that charted paths for two dispositions to the world that would feign at the idea of a clean rupture. What this means is that, at the very least, a performative forcing tendentially began to view the world according to a single template, one that would actively seek to neglect the value of the other.

The mythological disposition is characterized by narrative, allegory, and metaphor, whereas *logos* depends "on impersonal discursive argumentation and inferential deduction to generate not only meanings but also knowledge."[7] There is a privileged *sense* in the autonomous development of *logos* that bore a special relation to the world, one that was able to access deeper truths, or even truth in itself. Sometimes reducible to language as such,[8] *logos* as separate from *mythos* implies a shift in metaphysical evaluation; away from holistic syntheses of cultural life, toward technological evaluations of the relationship between word and reality. Jay refers to the increasing autonomous relation between *logos* and reality as developing a metaphysical sense of Reason. That is, *logos* develops a perfect metalanguage that "seeks the singular meaning of 'the word' and claims it can be entirely adequate to whatever it references in the world (or beyond it)."[9] This adequacy is due to the fact that Reason itself, as *logos*, expresses itself through particular instantiations or articulations. We will call this tendency the Greco-Christian orientation.

Plato uses the word *methexis*, or participation, to explain the relation between the Forms and the many. Accordingly, this participatory relation implies a deep ontological connection. The Forms and the many are not externally related, autonomous modes of Being. Although Plato does afford metaphysical primacy to the Forms, the many are best understood as expressions or instantiations (even if only in a corrupted sense) of the Forms. Aristotle seems to have misunderstood this participatory relation. He would charge that Plato was merely a Pythagorean who unsubstantively changed the idea of *mimesis* to *methexis*. Usually rendered "imitation," philosopher Hans-Georg Gadamer suggests that *mimesis* is better read as "re-presentation."[10] The significance in the shift, then, from *mimesis* to *methexis* in Plato, is that *methexis* implies a taking part or a sharing. Not merely re-presenting the thing (as in Aristotle), but taking part in the thing. With regard to the Forms, there is thus a sense in which the many take part—ontologically—in the universal. They share its Being.

The metaphor of the theater is useful here. In the same sense that the audience shares in the performance of the play, so too do the many share in the Forms. There is a distinction between the two. But this distinction is one of mutual participation. For as the audience need the actors, director, stage hands, and writer, so too do the many require prompting by the Forms. By extension, the Forms are expressed in the many as the performance is expressed through its reception in the imagination of an audience. Of course, the play can exist on its own (whereas an audience is not an audience without the performance). Which means, by analogy, so too can the Forms exist on their own. However, for present purposes, the potential independence of the Forms is secondary. What to keep in mind is the participatory relation—as a sharing or taking part—that Plato elaborates through his use of the term *methexis*. For him, the emphasis on *methexis* as opposed to *mimesis* is on *how* the many could take part when taking part.

Although Aristotle was right to point out the shift from *mimesis* to *methexis*, this alteration is not merely rhetorical. Rather, as Gadamer notes, the emphasis on *methexis* initiates the "Socratic-Platonic ground which Plato entered with the flight into the *logoi* and which he introduced to the world with the name 'dialectic.'"[11] When *mimesis* is employed, it is understood that there is an ontological distance maintained between the thing and its re-presentation. However, *methexis* is a relationship of participatory mutuality. It "implies that one thing is there together with something else."[12] And this ontological participatory mutuality opens up the space for *logos* and dialectic (in the Platonic sense) to reason both *toward and in participation with* the Forms.

The Christian tradition elevated the significance of *logos* even further.[13] In the Gospel of John, we read that, "In the beginning was the *logos*, and the *logos* was with God, and the *logos* was God." The opening words, ἐν ἀρχῇ ἦν ὁ λόγος, view the *logos* not only as being a discourse but as being the very foundation, the *arche*, of the world. This *logos* is that through which everything in the world came to be. And as we know from Genesis 1, of which John 1 is an intentional retread, God spoke the world into existence. Thus, there is a sense in which *logos* carries connotations of 1) discourse and language, 2) invocation or the call, and 3) the grounds by which points 1 and 2 are expressed. For Christianity, this expression is the self-revelation of God in the person of Jesus, the Messiah. In verse 14 of John we read that this *logos* "became flesh and dwelt among us." This irruption of the transcendent into the immanent is the unveiling of the very Being which is the ground of reality itself—*logos* showing itself through *logos*. This is not to claim that the Christian use of *logos* is devoid of *mythos*. On the contrary, the intimate relation between the two can hardly be separated at this point. However, what this does indicate is that there was a decisive intent to imbue *logos* with a special relation to Truth: it is both the ground of truth and that which makes truth known.

If *logos* and dialectic, for Plato, are enabled by the shift to *methexis*, the shift in the early Christian tradition can be said to be one in which the very thing about which *logos* reasons is the *logos* in which it participates. What this ultimately means is that there is a sense in which the world is rational. It can be known. And in a way, it is meant to be known. For Plato, knowing that which is rational comes through dialogue, philosophy, and tending toward the Forms in life as one who most closely approaches death. For Christianity, it mostly comes through right *doxa*, believing in the *logos* who mediates our relation to the *logos*. However, because of the indwelling of the Holy Spirit, the capacity for right *doxa* is universally enabled by *logos* itself. The primary point for both is that ultimately Reality is rational *in se*. Later thinkers as historically separated as Ibn Sina (Avicenna), Aquinas, and Leibniz would echo this Greco-Christian sentiment, albeit in their own ways, by maintaining that reality itself is always already rational and perfect.[14] What is more, this metaphysical understanding of Reason carries certain demands with it. As the Roman poet Seneca declared, "Virtue is nothing other than right reason."[15] Thus, there is also an ethical dimension that is embedded within the metaphysical idea of Reason. Not only is Reality rational, but it can and ought to be known.

However, as Max Weber would come to show, the formalization of *logos* as distinct from *mythos* and unique in its capacity to speak Reality led to the expansion of a particular type of Western rationalization that he examined in its categorial variations. Distinguishing between many subvariants of rationality, Weber was mostly concerned that instrumental reason "was becoming disembedded, that ongoing rationalization had produced a cold instrumentality largely devoid of spirit."[16] The disenchantment of the world through the expansion of technical capitalism in Weber's eyes is the fulcrum point at which *mythos* and *logos* became entirely distinct. While the precise definitions of Weber's terminology have been subject to considerable confusion and debate, it is sufficient to assert that the increasing efficiency-minded approach of instrumental reason to the neglect of value and emotion were distressing. Which is to say, regardless of where the borders between instrumental and value-based rationalities are ultimately drawn, Weber was concerned with any form of reason that would reduce the meaning of social action to *techné*. Such is a world reduced to the "that" and "what" to the neglect of the "why" and "how."

The triumph of instrumental reason, therefore, maintains the metaphysics of the Greco-Christian notion of Reason but completely discards the ethical dimension that is implicit in the participatory ontology of Plato or the logocentrism of Christianity. Commenting on the negative implications of instrumental reason for Weber, Jay notes that the "momentum of technological rationalization, the imperative to develop new technical tools whose ends were uncertain [was] an expansion whose inexorable power to shape our lives seemed to recognize no limits."[17]

This endless expansion of instrumental reason would lead the first generation of the Frankfurt School theorists to wage an all-out war against the very division between *logos* and *mythos* that led to this cold rationalization of Reason. Although not the primary point of the present project, situating Sartre's *CDR* within this trajectory demonstrates its validity as a proto-text of critical theory. To a large extent, *CDR* can be read as a forerunner to many of the concerns that the Frankfurt School would take up. When understood in this light, we will be able to reframe the value of this overlooked text as a practical device for social analysis. While the Frankfurt School theorists engaged in more detail, and more explicitly, with instrumental reason, they are nevertheless part of the same family of concern as Sartre.

This family of concern revolves around the status of Reason as such. Though the first generation of the Frankfurt School theorists can hardly be characterized as dogmatic rationalists, they do share a sense with Greco-Christian notions of Reason that Reason is objective. That is, that Reason somehow exists in the world and is knowable, or at least that it could be.[18] While Sartre would not be comfortable with the axiom, "Reason is objective," his investigation in *CDR* endeavors to make the "rational structure of Being intelligible."[19] And by this "rational structure of Being" he means *the dialectic*.

This approach problematizes the trajectory of the Greco-Christian orientation. For Sartre, a critique of dialectical reason must ground rationality as both existential (subjective/singular) and historical materialist (objective/universal). Thus, when Sartre remarks that comprehension (*Verstehen*) is the "translucidity of praxis to itself" what he means is that dialectical comprehension is something fundamentally other than a participatory relation between praxis and its material conditions. The real is rational for Sartre. However, to understand his divergence with the metaphysical conceptions of Rationality addressed in this subsection and to signal the differences between his own ideas from the Frankfurt School, one has to understand his debate with Lukács pertaining to totality.[20] While the connection between Lukács and the Frankfurt School is tangential, the reason for bringing them together is to give an indication as to how Sartre's project differed from the latter's attempt to circumvent the problems associated with the Greco-Christian orientation. And this difference is due to Sartre's elaboration of seriality which cannot be understood without appealing to the mediatory conditions that induce serial thoughts and feelings which stifle praxis's ability to comprehend itself.

1.2 THE UNVEILING OF BEING: TOTALITY AND TOTALIZATION

In *Search for a Method* (*SM*), Sartre sets out to develop the grounds of a "philosophical anthropology." According to Hazel Barnes, Sartre believed that the "existing tools and methods of the natural sciences, of traditional sociology and anthropology, are not adequate. What is needed is a new kind of Reason."[21] What is meant by "Reason" is the totalizing historical relation between Being and comprehension: the dialectic. This new kind of Reason would eschew the problems that he identifies within the Marxist tradition and its efforts to ground its thinking of the world in totality. In *CDR*, Sartre focuses his criticism on positivist/analytical reason and the dialectic of nature. In *SM*, his concern was with what he saw as the enclosed totalized thought represented in the ideas of Lukács and articulated by the dogmatism of the U.S.S.R..[22] Understanding how Sartre's criticism of analytical reason in *CDR* maps onto his engagement with Lukács will allow us to see how his thought remained consistent even if the target's location shifted. This will also help us to begin to understand a central concern for the present work pertaining to Sartre's elaboration of seriality as not only a condition of alienated existence, but also as a mode of thinking and acting as anti-dialectical—i.e., counter-revolutionary.

1.2.1 Sartre Contra Lukács and Totality

According to Sartre, Lukács and the U.S.S.R. were dispositionally blind to the individual and variant concerns of the proletariat. In effect, for Sartre, "Marxism stopped."[23] It had run into a limit that required a re-examination and correction. In his mind, this stop could be most clearly seen in the encircling totality of the U.S.S.R., as the party leaders "reserved for themselves the right to define the line and to interpret the event."[24] It is worth noting that the historical event that sparked Sartre's ire toward the Soviet Union and that raised his suspicion toward the orthodox Marxism of the mid-1950s was the U.S.S.R.'s invasion of Hungary in 1956. Writing for *L'Express* in November after the invasion of Budapest, Sartre wrote:

> I completely and unreservedly condemn Soviet aggression. Without blaming the Russian people, I repeat that their present government committed a crime. [. . . All] the crimes of history are forgotten, we have forgotten ours, and the other nations will forget them little by little. There may come a time when one will forget that of the USSR if its government changes and if newcomers try to apply truly the principle of equality in relations between socialist nations or not. For now, there is nothing else to do but condemn. I reluctantly, but entirely, break my relations with my friends, the Soviet writers, who do not denounce (or deny) the massacre in Hungary. We can no longer have friendship for the ruling faction of the Soviet bureaucracy: horror dominates.[25]

This "horror" led to his break with the PCF, as they would not waver in their support of Stalin: "It is and will be impossible to reestablish any sort of contact with the men who are currently at the head of the French Communist Party. Each sentence they utter, each action they take is the culmination of 30 years of lies and sclerosis."[26] This sclerosis seemed to indicate that there was a dogmatic rigidity that characterized a particular disposition of Marxism, one that he believed needed to be overcome if historical materialism were to remain unscathed from the (rightful) criticisms directed toward the Soviet Union in light of their unethical invasion of Hungary. We might say that the U.S.S.R. was operating according to a deficient horizon of meaning. The hermeneutical grid by which they took up the world predisposed them to an insensitivity toward anything that did not conform with party dogmatism. This tendency inscribed a limiting and limited paradigm that determined all political, social, economic, and cultural interactions between the U.S.S.R. and any other entity (not to mention within the borders of the U.S.S.R. itself). Not maintaining any sensitivity to potential truths that would disrupt party dogmatism, Marxism was trapped in a narcissistic reproduction of mediated and self-legitimized totality.[27]

Lukács was Sartre's target as the source of this dispositional totality because, as Jay notes, "Lukács's faith [was] in a wholeness yet to be achieved."[28] As Sartre read him, Lukács articulated a fixed *telos* in which class consciousness would merge with Being. Therefore, the future, fixed end of history was already charted. It was merely humanity's job—or the party's job—to realize it at whatever cost. This immunized the party from any form of criticism, internal or otherwise. For, as the possessors of truth, the dogma of the party, the dogma conditioned by totality, ensured their legitimacy. The individual components or any potential dissonance must therefore submit to the overall "Hegelian idea . . . which creates for itself its own instruments."[29] This teleological thought inverts Sartre's existential commitment to existence preceding essence by prioritizing essence (the future-to-come of totalized Being). The totality is given ultimate status which then subsumes the particularities of the manifold of concrete existence underneath it. It would not be a stretch to note the Greco-Christian logic embedded within this frame of thought. For Lukács, the rationality of class-consciousness was not transparent to praxis, but separate from praxis as a pre-constituted totality to be realized. Whereas for Sartre, ironically, this only leads to a false comprehension, where praxis is determined by an autonomous Other rather than constructing itself in dialectical freedom.

Instead of this form of subsumption to a transcendent totality-to-come, Sartre proposed to discover a type of reason that would entail a comprehensive study of the complex and variegating manifold of historical forces. For him, this meant the irreducibility of concrete subjectivity and objectivity. Or as Pietro Chiodi remarks, "Sartre's philosophy became not that of the individual but of the *whole*, in the sense of being the problem of a totality in which the individual finds himself placed within the perspective of the totalized, while yet preserving his own particularity as *totalizing* existent."[30] If Lukács is guilty of erecting a static and suppressive formal *a priori telos*, Sartre's endeavor is to construct a dynamic and stimulative historicized *a priori logic* (what he will come to term "the living logic of action" in *CDR*).

A fuller investigation into the distinction between totality and totalization would receive treatment in *CDR*. But at the time of *SM*, Sartre was primarily concerned with the Stalinist writings of Lukács from the 1930s and 1940s that he believed valorized closed totality over open-ended totalizations. (Side note: So as to not be accused of conflating, it is admitted that Sartre's reading of Lukács is restricted to a particular set of writings. Had Sartre spent time engaging the earlier *History and Class Consiousness*, for example, he may have discovered in Lukács's own writings a position tending closer to his own. This is not to suggest he would not still be critical, but to mention that there was a shift in Lukács's own intellectual trajectory. Whether or not he was familiar with this shift is of secondary importance for the time being. However, it ought to be noted that considering *History and Class Consciousness*'s formative influence on Merleau-Ponty's *Adventures of the Dialectic* which was published two years prior to *SM*, and considering that *CDR* is most assuredly a response to many of the criticisms contained therein, he must have at least been aware of it at a cursory level.)

Back to the critique. The reason Sartre directed his attention to Lukács is because he believed that the concept of totality elaborated by Lukács was also the paradigmatic orientation of a Marxism in need of transfiguration. Further to this, it could be argued that what Sartre identified in Lukács was precisely a theory of seriality. Termed "objective possibility," Lukács related consciousness to the whole of society which in turn "makes it possible to infer the thoughts and feelings which men would have in a particular situation if they were able to assess both it and the interests arising from it in their impact on immediate action and on the whole structure of society. That is to say, it would be possible to infer the thoughts and feelings appropriate to their objective situation."[31] G. A. Cohen refers to this type of scientific socialism as the "obstetric conception of political practice."[32] According to this approach, the solution to capitalism is contained within the problem itself. It is, therefore, only up to the socialist theorist to better elaborate the problem in order to make the solution known. In a word: history is pregnant with socialism's inevitable birth. Understanding this inevitable solution in relation to its conditioning problem allows the socialist theorist to work backwards from the solution to interpret the various complexities of the problem as the birth pangs of what is sure to come. However, for Sartre, this is an imaginative act of inscription and forcing that imposes an interpretation on the problem by a rigid and fixed image of a solution.

This imputation of class consciousness is a forcing of serialized class interests onto the manifold. By giving the proletariat a means for apprehending society from within, Lukács believed that his articulation of class consciousness reconciled the division between theory and praxis. For praxis and theory are ever-intertwined, as the solution to the problem of historical exploitation is embedded within the problem itself insofar as the problem is accurately articulated—or even more forcefully, as the problem has reached its consummation. Merleau-Ponty subsequently praised Lukács for defending a "Marxism that incorporates subjectivity into history without making it its epiphenomenon."[33] The point being that, according to Merleau-Ponty, praxis had been placed into the hands of the active agents of history—the proletariat. But Sartre would only see this incorporation of subjectivity as an embrace that smothers. Even though his thought developed to an orientation that could be more intensely classified as totalized totality, the early writings of Lukács would not have escaped Sartre's criticism precisely because, for Sartre, "there could be no original meta-subject who created history, forgot its original creative act through the mystifying effects of reification, and then would regain it in the revolutionary act of becoming both subject and object of the whole."[34] In other words, the future totality-to-come, for Lukács, would always be a transcendent *analogon*, a practico-inert correlative of the imagination that limits and demands how life is to be lived by mediating social relations, even among the proletariat, through the contagion of mediated inertia.

The result of this framework of rationality is that class consciousness is a reified horizon that ultimately alienates those who it is supposed to motivate toward liberation. Totality is the possibility to be realized; hence Sartre's reference to Lukács's argument as an "idealist dialectics."[35] What he means is that the Lukács's logic of the dialectic is not found in the materiality of subjectivity and its mediated relation with the conditions into which it is thrown, but in the future image that is posited as the possibility of proletarian realization. An Aristotelean schema of potential and act can be detected here; one that requires a notion of a formal cause that Sartre would reject. For Aristotle, an essence is assumed by the formal cause. As Kant explains,

"Essence is the first inner principle of all that belongs to the possibility of a thing."[36] Thus, the essence of the realized is already contained in the possible, which means that the real is given only mediatory status insofar as it is already prefigured by its essence contained in the possible. Therefore, Lukács's totality mediates any present practical ensemble by pulling them toward that fixed, prefigured future possible. Regardless of its makeup, regardless of its complexity or variation, any proletarian practical ensemble would therefore be, in Sartre's terms, anti-dialectical insofar as they are conditioned by seriality. To invert Sartre's great existentialist maxim: essence precedes existence. However, beyond merely the ontological implications of this inversion, there are drastic epistemological implications for praxis's ability to comprehend itself and its material environment.

This is not to suppose that Sartre necessarily rejects a Hegelian or Marxian rationality. While he may not project a future Rationality that mediates the present and pulls it toward its realized essence, he would aver that the world both is and is not rational, and that through dialectical reason it could be in the process of becoming more rational. However, the unveiling of being does not refer to either a past notion that needs to be remembered (á la Heidegger) nor to a future totality that is to be realized (á la Lukács). Instead, Sartre offers his idea of totalization as a system of interiority as an alternative notion to reveal the rationality of Being.

1.2.2 Totalization and the Arche of the Unveiling of Being

In a series of lectures given in Rome shortly after the publication of *CDR*, Sartre explains this system of interiority in mereological terms (i.e., pertaining to the relation between parts and wholes). Again targeting Lukács, someone potentially "damaging for the development of Marxist studies," Sartre explains that his concern is primarily that of "subjectivity, or subjectivation, and objectivity or objectivation."[37] What he means by this will become clear. But he makes it a point at the outset to note that he is not referring to "subject and object." He continues by saying, "The subject is a different, far more complex problem."[38] This is a problem that the present project will work through in chapter 5 as we investigate the logic of the group, and then in part II as we develop the imaginative logic of action in the construction of new humanisms. For now, understanding what subjectivity means, for Sartre, requires that we understand what totalization is in contradistinction to totality.

Sartre states that subjectivity is a "certain type of internal action, an interior system—*systéme en intériorité*—rather than the simple, immediate relationship of the subject to itself."[39] This immediate relationship of a subject to itself ought to be considered within the entire gamut of philosophical ideas broadly construed within the so-called "turn to the self." This would include Descartes's *cogito*, Kant's transcendental unity of apperception, Husserl's transcendental ego, or even later ideas such as Michel Henry's auto-affectivity. Having already written a treatise criticizing Husserl's transcendental ego and expelling any notion of the self to second-order reflective construction,[40] Sartre is not concerned with rehashing his argument against this type of subjectivity. Instead, he elaborates on conceptions he articulated in *CDR* pertaining to totalization.

Referring to the "Introduction" of the 1857 draft of the *Grundrisse*, he notes that Marx understood the dialectic as being a synthetic connection between humankind and the material environment. What he means is that there is always mediation between people and the conditions into which they are thrown. Humans are not self-sufficient, but must look beyond themselves in order to survive. Breathing air, walking on various terrain, using tools, speaking words: all of these demonstrate that the human condition is necessarily a mediatory condition. There is no such thing as immediacy in real material terms. Therefore, the "psychosomatic unit" (his new term for subjectivity in these lectures), is perpetually engaged in a synthetic process of interiorizing and exteriorizing the field of mediations that surround him/her at all times. He defines this as a system of interiority in this way:

> A material system is defined as having an *interior* or, if you prefer, as marking off a domain within the real world, when the relationship between its parts involves the relation of each to the whole. Reciprocally, the whole is no more than the sum of its parts insofar as it is involved as a whole in the relations that the parts have with each other.[41]

Now, let's compare the above quote with the following definition of totality:

> A totality is defined as a being which, while radically distinct from the sum of its parts, is present in its entirety, in one form or another, in each of these parts, and which relates to itself either through its relation to one or more of its parts or through its relation to the relations between all or some of them.[42]

These two definitions are extremely similar. Both are mereological descriptions. In the first, Sartre presents a material system. In the second, a being. Both the material system and the being are described in relations of parts to whole, where the parts involve the relation of each to the whole and the whole is involved in the relations of each part. But the crucial distinction is in the following clause when speaking about totality: "while radically distinct from the sum of its parts." This clause marks the enclosure of totality as a correlative of the imagination. We might say, without too much infused conceptual baggage, that a totality is a practico-inert set. It is a set that encompasses the totality of objects contained within it. It mediates the relations of the objects contained therein, but the totality itself is other than those objects. What is more, in the totality, as opposed to the material system, the whole is present in its entirety in each of these parts. This is not the singular-universal as dialectical totalization. It is the inert, enclosed totality as such. Which means that in the totality, the whole is only present in each of its parts as an abstraction. The implication being that even the parts of the whole are inflected with the inertia of the whole as they reinforce one another by layering and infusing inertia within inertia.

The material system, by contrast, is defined by this clause: "the whole is no more than the sum of its parts." This implies that there is no enclosure of the whole as in totality. Something else is going on with the material system that ensures it is not a totality. This something else is precisely that the material system is a *totalization*. Sartre remarks on the similarity of the definitions between totality and totalization in *CDR*. However, he draws a clear distinction by emphasizing that, "[totalization] is a developing activity, which cannot cease without the multiplicity reverting to its original statute."[43] What he means is that totalization as an act of subjectivity—a system of interiority—cannot cease without the parts becoming a totality (inertia). Therefore, if totality is a correlative of the imagination as a practico-inert object, then totalization is the "undifferentiated correlative of praxis."[44] And it is at this point where Sartre wants to found his investigation by remarking that, "dialectical Reason is the very movement of totalisation."[45] Said otherwise, subjectivity, as the *system of interiority*, is the *arche* of dialectical reason.

The stakes of this, for Sartre, are thoroughly ethical. If the world is a closed totality, then the consequences for our actions are diminished. We are parts in the larger whole, but our individual participation in the coming-to-be of that totality are secondary. However, retaining the open-endedness of totalization necessitates an ethical responsibility for our action as we are co-creators with history as it also creates us. This is why he was so critical of the dogmatism of the U.S.S.R.'s self-legitimized invasion of Hungary. There was ultimately no way for them to be held accountable for their actions. Similarly, any orientation that is characterized by totality will carry similar implications. The micro-actions of the present and subsequent unfolding of history are granted secondary importance to the totality (which is itself only an inert *analogon* to begin with). Thus, we can catch a glimpse of how Sartre is seeking to unveil the rationality of Being. While his notion of totalization remains speculative at this point, it does suggest a way beyond the stifling obstetric model of political practice. We begin with a criticism of what Sartre identifies as the problem, but without advancing a solution just yet. This is because, as we will come to see, Sartre does not believe that we have the tools of comprehension at our disposal. This is what would motivate his writing of *CDR*. Praxis is not yet translucid to itself. In order for totalization to provide the ground for dialectical reason, comprehension itself must be comprehended. Thus, we now turn to the second task of this chapter: to investigate the validity of the unveiling of Being to see how we might understand how comprehension might come to be comprehended.

1.3 THE VALIDITY OF THE UNVEILING: DIALECTICAL REASON AND THE PARADOXICO-CRITICAL ORIENTATION

Right up to the point where we can distinguish between totality and totalization in the unveiling of Being, we run into a limit, a paradox. And this limit is best articulated in the staunch criticisms leveled by Claude Lévi-Strauss. Ironically, it is his indictment of the paradoxical unveiling of Being in *CDR* that reveals to us the validity of this unveiling.

Lévi-Strauss's criticisms of *CDR* can be boiled down to two categories: 1) ethnocentrism and 2) contradiction/paradox. The former concern of ethnocentrism will not be our primary focus. The bulk of the argument will rest on our engagement with the second category. However, as to not neglect the charge of ethnocentrism, it will briefly be addressed.

1.3.1 Lévi-Strauss's Charge of Ethnocentrism

We grant that *CDR* is a thoroughly Western text. Most of the examples from which Sartre draws are Western examples. However, when discussing counter-finality, he does spend time referring to deforestation in China. That said, this too could be construed as an ethnocentric reading of a regional particularity in order to justify his own presuppositions. Regardless, what Lévi-Strauss really has in mind when he charges Sartre with ethnocentrism is 1) a fetishization of the French Revolution and 2) a perceived disdain for "native" communities.

Sartre's fetishization of the French Revolution has more recently been pointed out by Alain Badiou as well. Badiou is heavily indebted to Sartre as a thinker of rupture. However, their divergences will form a current that guides the rest of this book. Badiou's claim is that Sartre is less a thinker of political revolution than of historical revolution.[46] Sartre's focus on the formation of the group in the apocalyptic irruption at the Bastille seems to indicate that his only hope for genuine intersubjective solidarity could arise under similar circumstances rather than in any organized proletarian effort. This is something we will address in chapter 5 and again throughout part II.

For Lévi-Strauss, the problem of *CDR* "is reducible to the question: under what conditions is the myth of the French Revolution possible?"[47] Snide humor aside, there is something substantive in this criticism. Namely, does *CDR* merely seek to understand the conditions of a particular historical moment (or even moments), or do its ambitions have greater scope and applicability? In a sense, this is precisely the question that *CDR* puts to itself.

Volume One is not concerned with making intelligible particular domains of anthropological history in scientific terms. Rather, Sartre is investigating particular expressions of practical ensembles, those that are immediately familiar to French Marxists, in order to provide a corrective to the rational foundation upon which Marxism might proceed. Like a parable teaching greater truths, Sartre is fabulating in order to reveal the underlying logics that make the unveiling of Being intelligible. In his final interview with Simone de Beauvoir before his death, he claimed: "I invented mythical societies: good societies in which one ought to live. It was the irreal that became the meaning of my politics; it is [for] something like that that I entered into the political."[48] This does not mean that his concerns were purely fanciful. As we will continue to develop through to the end of this book, the irreal is a central component in the formal approach that aids praxis in comprehending comprehension.

What to take from this, for now, is that Sartre's project is not investigating the conditions of the French Revolution as an end, but merely as a formal exercise for the extraction and distillation of abstractions that aid in revealing the logic of freedom. Of course, this does not excuse one for being limited in his analysis. If Sartre is unfairly neglecting alternative forms of practical ensembles to the detriment of identifying the source of the intelligibility of history, then such sources ought to be announced so the investigation can be strengthened. It is therefore not trite to point out that Sartre himself creates space within pages of *CDR* for correction and further elaboration.[49] This is also perhaps why Volume Two was never completed. Perhaps Sartre himself realized the over-reach of trying to articulate the single meaning of history by analyzing a particular region of world history. Unfortunately, we must leave that question to pages yet to be written.

To the present task, we must also understand that there is a sense in which Sartre's *CDR* is a text for *this* history. He is not engaging in ethnography or anthropology as such. He is seeking to understand the historical moment of life lived under capitalist hegemony. This is what he means when he identifies himself as an ideologist, thinking and living in the wake of Marx. One cannot exceed the Marxian moment, which implies the critique of political economy. Thus, *CDR* is an intentional project working within the larger endeavor of the critique of political economy. In this way, it could be argued that *CDR* is not merely a prolegomena to any future anthropology, but that it is a prolegomena to any future political economy, insofar as political economy must be understood from within a revised understanding of subjectivity and the dialectic. This is because he is not developing a theory of human or social evolution. He is seeking to regressively analyze the conditions of precisely *this* history, as it has been conditioned by capitalist hegemony, as interpreted through Marx's critique.

The second point about Sartre's denigration of "native" peoples is one that ought to be considered, because if Sartre is seeking to identify the law of intelligibility of history rooted in the relation between the psychosomatic unit that is concrete subjectivity and the material world, it would be unfortunate to exclude potential sources of information and integral components that highlight varying processes of totalization. In a section referencing Sartre's brief remarks on Deacon's work with Ambrym natives and their drawing of diagrams in the sand to communicate marriage rules and kinship systems, Lévi-Strauss censures Sartre by saying, "It seems even less tolerable to [Sartre] than to Levy-Bruhl that the savage should possess 'complex understanding' and should be capable of analysis and demonstration."[50] Initially, it bears noting that the quotation of "complex understanding" is not attributable to Sartre. These words are Levy-Bruhl's.[51] Further, the accusation against Sartre seems spurious. In fact, Sartre expressly articulates that he is not concerned with whether or not abstract thought is an intrinsic human capacity that is expressed to varying degrees of complexity. Rather, what he is seeking to demonstrate by mentioning the Ambrym native is that abstract thought is not a capacity possessed *per se* but is intrinsic within the practico-inert mediations of the organization. It is important to note that at this section of Sartre's investigation he has already explored the logic of the group and the logic of the pledge; the latter which mediates through fear and pledged-praxis.[52] These totalities are part of the analysis of the Ambrym native in that the pledge is always present in the articulation of any social schematic; in this instance, the matrimonial schematic.

The point that Sartre is making is that when the native draws out the diagram explaining the matrimonial relations of the tribe, he is not merely articulating abstract knowledge in a vacuum. Rather, as Sartre says, he is "guided by the synthetic understanding which defines his membership in the group."[53] But this synthetic understanding itself is not communicated because the transmission of the information takes place through the creation of an inert object. Thus, Sartre's point is not to slight the native's capacity for thought, but rather to illuminate how synthetic knowledge is exteriorized in practico-inertia to one that is exterior to that organization (in this case, Deacon) and how this conditions understanding. This dovetails with the second category of Lévi-Strauss's criticisms of *CDR*.

1.3.2 Lévi-Strauss's Charge of Contradiction and the Four Orientations

Related to this last point, Lévi-Strauss accuses Sartre of inconsistency and contradiction when speaking about the relations between analytical and dialectical reason. First, he claims that Sartre employs analytical reason himself while decrying its status as inferior to dialectical reason.[54] Second, he asserts that his own understanding of dialectical reason is better found in the savage mind, as one that entirely encloses everything within its classificatory categories of schematization.[55] And third, he accuses Sartre of developing a paradoxical system that, "offers not a concrete image of history but an abstract schema of men making history of such a kind that it can manifest itself in the trend of their lives as a synchronic totality."[56]

In order to understand the crux of this threefold argument about the perceived contradictions and paradox of *CDR*, it will be useful to frame our response through the lens of what Paul Livingston, following Alain Badiou, refers to as "orientations of thought."[57] In his book, *The Politics of Logic*, Livingston outlines three orientations of thought developed by Badiou that establish various relations between thought and Being:

1. Transcendent (what Livingston terms the Onto-Theological)
2. Constructivist (what Livingston terms the Criteriological)
3. Generic (same)

1. The Transcendent/Onto-Theological orientation

> sets up the totality of being by reference to a privileged being, a "super-existence" that assures the place of everything else, while at the same time obscuring its own moment of institution or the grounds of its own authority. Thus, the totality is conceived as the determined order of an exact placement of beings, while it is covertly regulated by an exemplary Being, conceived as superlative, transcendent to the order of things, and ineffable in its terms.[58]

Livingston calls this orientation Onto-Theological following Heidegger. And in reference to the present chapter, we might say that the Greco-Christian orientation to Reason would fit in this category. The privileged being to which the Greco-Christian model refers would be Reason or *logos* as the ineffable limit of Reality.

2. The Constructivist/Criteriological orientation is seen in the critical tradition inspired by Kant and finds its zenith in the twentieth-century linguistic turn.

> This is the orientation that relates to the totality of what is sayable about Being by means of an explicit tracing of the structure and boundaries of language. [. . . The] totality of existence is regulated by the discernible protocols of a meaningful language, comprehensible in themselves and capable of distinguishing between the sayable and the non-sayable . . . drawing [a] regulative line between sense and nonsense. [. . . Here], the totality of the sayable is itself understood as comprehended by the determinate syntactical rules for the use of the language in question, and thus as not only a bounded but a finite whole,

outside of which it is possible for the theorist or the inventor of languages unproblematically to stand.[59]

This orientation of thought will come to be seen below in both Positivistic Science/Marxism (i.e., Analytical Reason) and the Dialectic of Nature that Sartre criticizes in *CDR*. Although prior to the linguistic turn, Positivistic Science/Marxism and the Dialectic of Nature fit within the Kantian transcendental schematic in that they draw a line around totality and then formally stand above or outside by asserting their own regulative law of articulation. Connecting this with the previous two sections, this orientation operates according to technical or instrumental rationality. It is concerned with the "that" and "what." But incapable of truly addressing the "how" and "why." Lukács's logic of totality would also fit.

3. The third orientation is Badiou's own position, the Generic:

> Thus, applying no norm *other than formal consistency*, the generic orientation relentlessly pursues, along the diagonal, the existence of all that which escapes constructivism's limitative doctrine of thought. [. . .] Badiou thereby shows how the apparatus of set theory leaves open the possibility, beyond anything constructivism can allow, of the "generic set" which, though real, is completely indiscernible within ontology, and hence also the possibility of the extension of any determinate situation by means of a generic "forcing" of the indiscernible which realizes, at its infinite limit, a new truth.[60]

The Generic shows the limit of any Constructivist orientation's ability to introduce genuine novelty beyond what any existing language can articulate. It is only through set theory that the radically new can be introduced outside the transcendental schematics of Constructivism or the enclosed totality of the Onto-Theological orientation.[61]

However, Livingston introduces one more orientation of thought that he believes Badiou has neglected. He terms this the Paradoxico-Critical orientation. It operates

> by tracing the destabilizing implications of the paradoxes of self-reference at the boundaries of the thinkable, or sayable. [. . . Given] the paradoxes that force a choice, whereas Badiou's generic orientation decides for consistency and against completeness, the paradoxico-critical orientation is based on the decision for completeness and against consistency.

This is the orientation that most aligns with Sartre's dialectical reason in *CDR*. It might not be apparent *prima facie*, but once we take a closer look into Sartre's conception of totalization vis-à-vis totality, then aligning Sartre with the Paradoxico-Critical orientation of thought will make sense. As well, it will help us work through Lévi-Strauss's threefold criticism of the contradictory/paradoxical nature of *CDR* and suggest that perhaps the dialectical reason of the savage mind might be closer to Sartre's orientation than Lévi-Strauss allows.

If we depict this visually, we can say that the Onto-Theological orientation views the totality of what can be known as contained within limits established by an ineffable beyond that itself has no ground, or no need of *founding* (Figure 1.1). Thus, all thought is contained within these established limits.

The Constructivist orientation draws a line around all that is sayable and demarcates between sense and nonsense. However, the theorist stands outside looking in, observing, analyzing, and redrawing the boundaries while remaining unscathed from any self-referential criticism (Figure 1.2). Where the Onto-Theological orientation finds its source in the ineffable, the Constructivist is essentially an-archic. There is no (knowable) beyond that shores up what is sayable or unsayable other than the endless re-inscription and enclosure by Constructivist theorists. This is the culmination of the Greco-Christian logic (i.e., the separation of *logos* from *mythos*).

Badiou's Generic orientation proceeds quite differently. In this disposition, totality itself is rejected. There is no world of all worlds but infinite worlds that overlap and interpenetrate (Figure 1.3). These worlds (or intra-worldly phenomenological orders) are transcendentally indexed, but only contingently so. The universality of the generic ensures that worlds are not reducible to conditions of thought or language (as in the Constructivist orientation). Rather, there is an excess that is forever beyond, but not ineffable (as

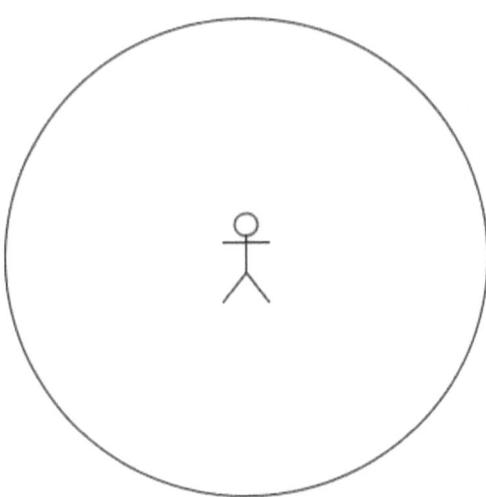

Figure 1.1. The Onto-Theological Orientation.

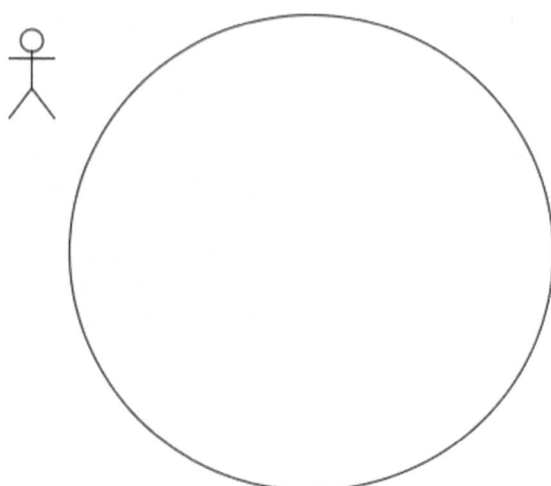

Figure 1.2. The Constructivist Orientation.

in the Onto-Theological). This is because, for Badiou, the Generic orientation is grounded on the universality of the void that produces the effects of the intra-worldly phenomenological orders.

And finally, the Paradoxico-Critical orientation can be thought in terms of the limits of totality itself being stretched and twisted which then perpetually transforms the scope, the sense, the relations, and the variations of intensity of the very totality (Figure 1.4). If Badiou appeals to the paradoxes of self-reference (think Russell's Paradox) in order to eschew the One, this orientation affirms the paradoxes of self-reference in favor of the One. It rejects any world beyond language and its structure *per se*. It does not necessarily seek to resolve the aporia elicited by the boundaries of self-reference. But rather, perpetually creates within a whole that itself is being recast and reshaped by its own inward expressiveness.

This is, of course, quite abstruse and difficult to comprehend. However, there is a poetics involved in understanding the Paradoxico-Critical orientation. And this is part of the very disposition itself. To seek to determinately define an orientation that is processual and paradoxical is to betray its very lifeblood.

Perhaps providing a brief litany of thinkers classified within the orientation that best describes their thought will help situate the notion a bit better:

1. Onto-Theological thinkers: Aquinas, Aristotle, and more recently theologian John Milbank. This orientation is loosely affiliated with a

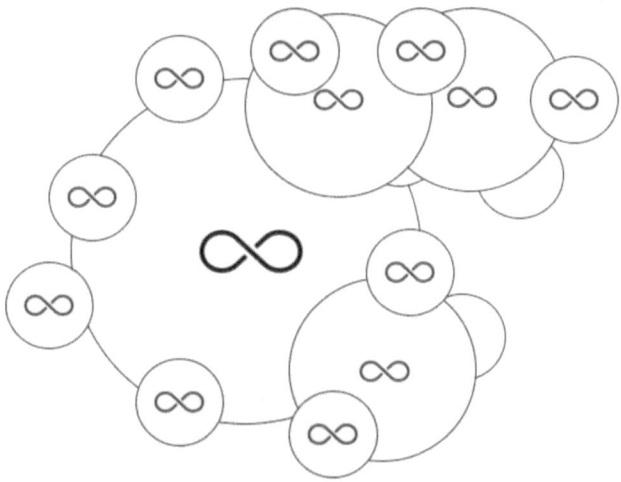

Figure 1.3. The Generic Orientation.

religious worldview, although religious mysticism could be Paradoxico-Critical.
2. Constructivist thinkers: Kant, Russell, Carnap, Ayer, and Foucault are emblematic figures of this orientation.
3. Generic: Badiou.
4. Paradoxico-Critical thinkers: Deleuze, Derrida, Lacan, Irigaray, Kristeva, and Borges.

While all the figures classified within the Paradoxico-Critical orientation have been identified as "postmodern" thinkers (whether rightly or wrongly), the Paradoxico-Critical orientation is not to be understood strictly as a postmodern concept. Rather, it is an orientation that seeks to navigate between the polarities of the Generic and Constructivist. It refuses the sufficiency of instrumental reason and thus would not be satisfied with the conceptual narrative that culminates in the separation of *logos* from *mythos* (and all the attendant results that issue therefrom), but also rejects the transcendence of the generic outside. Accordingly, neither would it retreat into a form of religious esotericism, even if it would avow a holism. The great difference between the Onto-Theological thinkers and the Paradoxico-Critical ones is that the former feign at an articulation of the One, when in point of fact, they end up espousing a metaphysical dualism.

Now let's tie this to the discussion pertaining to Sartre and the validity of the unveiling of Being. To start, Sartre's criticism in the opening pages of *CDR* is directed toward two broad camps[62]: the first is the Positivist Ration-

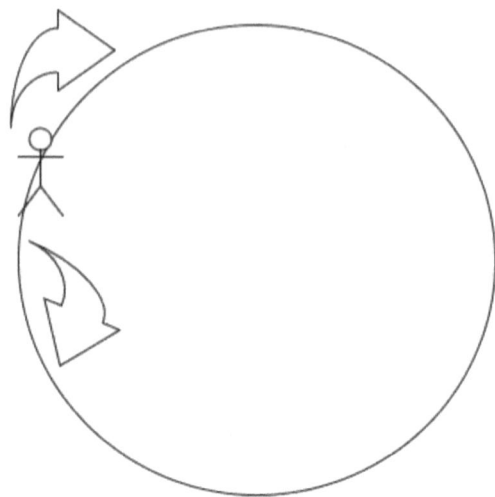

Figure 1.4. The Paradoxico-Critical Orientation.

alists and Marxists of scientific socialism, and the second is the dialectic of nature. The Positivist Rationalists assert that the real is rational, however can only ever give relative expressions that correspond to this reality. Thus, facts become simple correlations between observable nature and the measurement of that observation. This is the pure saturation of *techne* and instrumental reason. For Sartre, it is relativism. Facts are truth insofar as they relatively describe portions of the Rational which is only ever re-presented. But nevertheless, the assumption by Positivist Rationalists is that the Rational is knowable as an external metaphysical reality to be discovered. However, analytical reason is unaware of its own ground. The mind "prejudges nothing . . . [and] sees Reason as independent of any particular rational system."[63] Therefore, positivist rationalism is to be understood as an-archic. Unlike dialectical reason, that is squarely concerned with grounding itself by unveiling the rational structure of Being through self-referentially investigating the validity of this unveiling, Positivist Rationalists are "unconcerned with the ground of their inductions."[64] This is because they do not have a thorough conception of totalization.

But physicists or chemists are not the only ones who draw Sartre's criticism for being Positivists. Marxists too have "played the Positivist game."[65] By incorporating the tools of instrumental reason, Positivist Marxists engage in the game of interpretation much like scientists, seeking to predict future events squarely based on the sequential causal relations between entities in external relation. The problem here is that the dialectic ensures that the future is absolutely new and irreducible to observation. Sartre admits that Marx did make predictions, but claims that he actually disqualified himself from doing so because positivist rationalism asserts that the future is a repetition of the past insofar as the present order of succession reenacts a previous one. Thus, for Sartre, "Marxism as dialectic must reject the relativism of the positivists" insofar as only dialectical reason asserts the truth.[66] It is not merely a perspective on the truth, but truth insofar as the component parts of knowledge are instantiations of the totalizing whole, which in turn mediates the parts in a system of interiority.

Sartre's other target in the opening of *CDR* is the dialectic of nature, which similarly asserts a metaphysical form of Rationality. Taking Engels as an example, the latter is unable to think novelty because the Rational is enclosed with a totality of which there is no outside. However, unlike the relative rationality of the Positivists, the dialectic of nature, similar to Kant, asserts transcendental laws that themselves have no foundation. As Sartre states, the dialectic of nature "has a curious similarity to those Ideas of Reason which, according to Kant, were regulative and incapable of being corroborated by any particular experience."[67] Thus, there is an "Eternal Reason" for Engels that establishes a pre-constituted law.[68] In a sense, the dialectic of nature becomes a reified projection of historical dialectics, for Sartre. It becomes a transcendental category that governs all particulars. This is why he states unequivocally that the dialectic of nature is nothing more than "a metaphysical hypothesis."[69] He would elaborate further on the irrationality of this anarchic dogmatism:

> The procedure of discovering dialectical rationality in praxis, and then projecting it, as an unconditional law, on to the inorganic world, and then returning to the study of societies and claiming that this opaquely irrational law of nature conditions them, seems to us to be a complete aberration.[70]

The dialectic of nature is thus a type of dogmatic metaphysical rationality that sees the world as itself being Rational as a derivative of an observable dialectic in praxis. Accordingly, the dialectic in the world is the rationality of the rational world that is its own principle of sufficient reason. Thus, the dialectic of nature ends up subsuming "man" or "dissolving man" into a singular and regulative totality. Contra this position, in actual fact, for Sartre, the dialectic must be understood both in its universality and its particularity. In Sartre's words, the intelligibility of the dialectic is as a totalizing system of interiority, not a universal law of nature or a totality. This does not mean that he precludes the possibility of science one day discovering a dialectic of nature in physical processes themselves. However, his concern is that if such a day comes, it will require that the dialectic be found "where it is there to be seen,"[71] as opposed to, as in the case of the Engelsian dialectic of nature, being discovered in human societies and then projected into the inorganic.

Simply stated, positivist rationalism/Marxism and the dialectic of nature are subject to the same criticism as Lukács: they are closed systems of totality. They all operate according to a formal limiting of the space where reason must reason. They set strict parameters and then condition in what ways thought can proceed. They are thus beholden to the practico-inert correlative of the imagination that externally mediates its relations. In the case of positivism, this leads to relativism and a reproduction of the past; for the dialectic of nature, metaphysical speculation and dogmatic idealism, rather than synthetic analysis and concrete dialectics. It is the latter two that must characterize dialectical reason.

But this doesn't validate the unveiling of the rational structure of Being in dialectical reason. That is, there still needs to be a way to ground the investigation into the rational structure of Being. And this is where Livingston's taxonomy provides assistance.

1.3.3 CDR and the Paradoxico-Critical Orientation

It seems quite obvious to assert that analytical reason (as associated with positivist rationalism and positivist Marxism) ought to be understood within the Constructivist orientation. Livingston includes Russell, Carnap, and Ayer into this schema as prime examples of Constructivists.[72] Russell's fight against the doctrine of internal relations and Carnap's and Ayer's logical positivism draw a line around that which is sayable (or rational) but exclude themselves and their praxis from this bounded, finite totality. That is, there is a stark demarcation between autonomous thought and Being. However, Foucault also fits into this camp. Any intuition that asserts that what exists is controlled and determined by that which is sayable is Constructivist. For Foucault, this takes the form of unmasking the actual historical foundations (i.e., power relations) that constitute institutional power structures. The lines, for Foucault, are merely redrawn. This is precisely how Sartre defines analytical reason and it's inability to reason synthetically. Recall Sartre's criticism of the U.S.S.R.'s invasion of Hungary. In their totalized thinking, they were immune from any criticism because they drew the lines around the event, defining it from their external position, and justifying their action based on the rules of the game that they themselves were not subject to (in fact, which had no meaning to them whatsoever).

But so too ought the dialectic of nature be understood as Constructivist. While not concerned *per se* with language, the dialectic of nature establishes a totality outside of which the regulative Idea of the dialectic, so construed, stands in determining sense and nonsense. This regulative Idea itself is unable to be criticized by the manifold of existential concerns over which it determines the sayable contra the non-sayable. Thus, the dialectic of nature becomes a "determinate syntactical [rule] . . . outside of which it is possible for the theorist [or party] . . . to stand,"⁷³ again, precisely because the theorist or party draws the lines in the first place.

Compared to the Constructivist orientation, Sartre's consideration of dialectical reason must be thought of within a different schematic for three reasons: 1) it rejects closed totality, 2) it proceeds from a self-referential recognition of its own paradoxes, and 3) it discovers and grounds the paradoxical nature of the rational structure of Being—i.e., the dialectic itself. The only question that remains is, "In which of the two remaining orientations are we to situate dialectical reason?"

Remember that the Generic orientation is Badiou's description of his own system of thought. Relying on the discoveries of set theory, Badiou argues that the Generic orientation is different from the Onto-Theological and the Constructivist in that the Generic insists upon the relevance of actual and multiple infinities to reasoning about Being. This schema allows for a realist conception of thinking about beings as such and Being as a whole. But the whole of Being must not be understood as a closed totality. Rather it is "whole" *as a formal discursive consistency*. We could say that Badiou, like Sartre, wants to reject any notion of a closed totality in favor of an open system (although what this means is different for each). He would go so far as to say that, in fact, there is no such thing as *the* World, but infinite worlds. That is, this orientation "lends privilege to indefinite zones, multiples subtracted from any predicative gathering of thoughts, points of excess and subtractive donations. Say all existence is caught in a wandering that works diagonally against the diverse assemblages expected to surprise it."⁷⁴

However, for Badiou, this orientation differs from Sartre in that although Sartre wants to reject any notion of a closed totality he is not actually averse to the idea of a different type of totality. That is, his entire argument unfolds within the rubric of a project investigating the potential to articulate a single meaning of History. This is a type of whole that is not defined by the types of indefinite zones and multiples that Badiou articulates in his infinite worlds orientation. Precisely because Sartre is not concerned with the ontological findings of set theory that Badiou articulates, it cannot be claimed that dialectical reason is therefore a formal discursive consistency. Instead, the dialectic is a paradoxical self-referential emergent that does not position itself, as does the Generic orientation, beyond or before its own embeddedness within *logos*; or what amounts to the same, within the dialectic itself. So whereas existence for Badiou wanders "diagonally against the diverse assemblages expected to surprise it," for Sartre it is *co-constitutive* with the diverse assemblages that surprise it.

This difference can be summarized by what Livingston claims is a difference in how the final two orientations "consider the status of totality."⁷⁵ When given a choice between consistency and completeness, the Generic orientation chooses consistency. However, the final option that Livingston presents chooses completeness instead. This is the Paradoxico-Critical orientation. By affirming an inconsistent totality, this orientation documents the inconsistencies that arise when language attempts to speak the whole as One.[76] This One is not a pre-constituted totality, but rather is itself an emergent multiplicity-as-One insofar as it is synthesized in its articulation. There is a self-referentiality that is not a paradoxical aporia, but that is productive—i.e., autopoetic. In Sartrean terms, we can say that this orientation pertaining to the relation between thought and Being accords with dialectical reason as the latter attempts to make intelligible the whole of history through its own inconsistencies. Although it is not concerned primarily with language, dialectical reason can be seen as Paradoxico-Critical because it is an orientation concerned with the relation between thought and Being insofar as this relation itself is perpetually seeking its own ground in its articulation of the very relation. As Sartre explains in *SM*:

> The motivation of the enterprise is one with the enterprise itself; the specification and the project are one and the same reality. Finally, the project never has any *content*, since its objectives are at once united with it and yet transcendent. But its *coloration*—i.e., subjectively, its taste; objectively, its *style*—is nothing but the surpassing of our original deviations. This surpassing is not an instantaneous movement, it is a long work; each moment of this work is at once the surpassing and, to the extent that it is posited for itself, the pure and simple subsistence of these deviations at a given level of integration. *For this reason a life develops in spirals; it passes again and again by the same points but at different levels of integration and complexity.* [Last emphasis added][77]

This is Sartre again explaining his system of interiority, subjectivity, totalization. This is the logic of dialectical reason, the validity of its unveiling the structure of Being. That is, the validity of the unveiling is precisely that which is constructed in the very process of unveiling. The law of the dialectic is not a universal *a priori*. First it is a resultant, and then it becomes a redoubled *de facto*, not *de jure*, law of intelligibility insofar as totalization synthesizes the movement of the dialectic in subjectivity as the latter interiorizes situations of objectivity. As Sartre plainly states, "[If] dialectical Reason is to be rationality, it must provide Reason with its own reasons."[78] And just a couple pages later, he continues: "[If] there is such a thing as a dialectical reason, it is revealed and established in and through human *praxis*."[79] This is because dialectical reason establishes its own limits and scope, its own reason and foundation. It is both lived and known, with neither knowing or living taking precedence, for they are both moments of the same movement of totalization. This is why Sartre would say that humankind both creates and submits to the dialectic, and that this contradiction must itself be lived dialectically.[80]

This paradox of both creating and being created by the dialectic, of working with and beyond and thereby stretching the very limits of rationality, is why dialectical reason accords with the Paradoxico-Critical orientation of thought rather than the Generic. There is no outside of the system of interiority. Thus, while Sartre adamantly criticized closed systems of totality, there is a sense in which his own method was itself a disjunctive totality, a paradoxical totality—*totalization*. Thus, we can agree with Livingston's simple barometer to help delineate between the Generic and Paradoxico-Critical; that given a choice between completeness and consistency, Sartre chooses, albeit with qualification, completeness. Understanding Sartre's orientation of thought as Paradoxico-Critical, we can now better address Lévi-Strauss's threefold criticism that *CDR* is contradictory/paradoxical.

1.4 THE VALIDITY OF THE UNVEILING: LÉVI-STRAUSS AND DIALECTICAL REASON

1.4.1 Addressing Lévi-Strauss's Charge of Contradiction/Paradox

The first criticism about the contradictory nature of *CDR* is that Sartre employs analytical reason while decrying its inferiority to dialectical reason. He states that it is a "curious paradox; for the work entitled *Critique de la raison dialectique* is the result of the author's exercise of his own analytical reason: he defines, distinguishes, classifies and opposes."[81] While he uses the word "paradox," it seems most accurate to assume that Lévi-Strauss is not employing the term productively as in the Paradoxico-Critical orientation, but rather as a critical remark about perceived contradictions in the text. He continues on the next page by saying, "[If] dialectical and analytical reason ultimately arrive at the same results, and if their respective truths merge into a single truth, then, one may ask in what way they are opposed and, in particular, on what grounds the former should be pronounced superior to the latter."[82] While it is certainly true that Sartre utilizes analysis in his regressive investigation into the conditions under which history might be made intelligible, it is not necessarily the case that such analysis is akin to analytical reason. When we frame the issue in terms of the orientations of thought, then it becomes clear that what Lévi-Strauss is failing to capture is that analytical reason and dialectical reason don't, in fact, "arrive at the same results." Analytical reason is that expression of rationality that is anti-dialectical in that it is shot-through with serial thoughts and affect. Dialectical reason, on the contrary, is that expression of rationality whereby praxis is translucid to itself. The former makes comprehension incomprehensible, whereas dialectical reason is comprehension comprehended. Thus, Sartre's project in *CDR* is an investigation into *how* and *why* these two tendencies are, in fact, distinct, and then further, a speculative proposal for how we can develop the necessary tools to allow dialectical reason to—perhaps for the first time—comprehend in full. Thus, the validity of Sartre's project is still at stake. Which requires that we understand 1) what dialectical reason is, 2) whether or not it has been properly expressed, and 3) if not, why? and what can be done?

If a given analysis is seeking the relative truths in a metaphysical Reason to be discovered, or if it is attempting to stand outside the given field of observation, then the analysis tends toward a positivistic/analytical rationality. This is not what Sartre is doing. He may begin by using certain tools of analysis that resemble the *techne* of analytical reason, but the goal is to start *in media res* in order to regressively discover the foundations of dialectical reason and its intelligibility from within already existing practical ensembles. Therefore, analytical and dialectical reason won't reach the "same results" because analytical reason is a relativistic endeavor commenting on the correlation between externally-related entities and the observational measurement of these autonomous objects of analysis. Whereas dialectical reason is a system of interiority—what Sartre will call the "living logic of action" in *CDR*—that integrates all models of rationality. It constitutes itself while dissolving all other constituted reasons (analytic included) in order to constitute new reasons which it then in turn transcends and dissolves. This is why when Lévi-Strauss claims that Sartre abandons a solid starting point from which to begin his investigation, Jacob Rump writes: "What [Lévi-Strauss] calls the 'secondary incidentals' of society—the series, groups and collectives differentiated and examined in Sartre's text—are insufficient for establishing the anthropological foundations of society *only if* we assume that the foundations sought are purely analytic and static."[83] But as we have explained, in light of the Paradoxico-Critical orientation of thought, dialectical reason is not purely analytic and static but is a perpetual process of autopoetic construction as it founds itself in its creation of itself.

1.4.2 Addressing Lévi-Strauss's Claim That the Savage Mind Is Properly Dialectical

Lévi-Strauss's second criticism is that his own understanding of dialectical reason is better found in the savage mind, as one that entirely encloses everything within its classificatory categories of schematization. He bolsters his argument by claiming that the savage mind seeks to timelessly "grasp the world as both a synchronic and diachronic totality."[84] The savage mind, according to Lévi-Strauss, creates images of the world "which facilitate an understanding of the world in as much as they resemble it."[85] We interpret this to mean that Lévi-Strauss supposes that the savage mind creates images that serve as regulative principles, inasmuch as these principles are representations of the world (i.e., totalities). As such, Lévi-Strauss's reading of the savage mind from within his own Constructivist orientation does not seem *prima facie* dialectical in the Sartrean sense. This explanation of the savage mind has much more resonance with Charles Taylor's conception of Social Imaginaries, in that the totalities that mediate social relations are static, practico-inert objects rather than systems of interiority. We will engage with Taylor further in chapter 6. For now, the point is that we must argue that the logic of the savage mind, as Lévi-Strauss describes it, does not have a sufficient notion of praxis that would break the serial mediatory control mechanisms introduced through inertia that entrap it within the Constructivist orientation.

However, how much of Lévi-Strauss's language describing the savage mind is an accurate description of the savage mind as a Constructivist orientation and how much is attributable to his own project from within his understanding of the analytical-dialectical divide? Although there is a distinction between Lévi-Strauss's own orientation and that of the savage mind that he is seeking to defend, in the closing words of the book he remarks that

> The entire process of human knowledge thus assumes the character of a closed system. And we therefore remain faithful to the inspiration of the savage mind when we recognize that the scientific spirit in its modern form will . . . have contributed to legitimize the principles of savage thought and to re-establish it in its rightful place.[86]

This valorization of the savage mind can only be read as a statement of Lévi-Strauss's own self-congratulatory posturing of his position as similarly constructed as a "closed system." His appeal is directed to the rest of the scientific community as a charge to similarly adopt the "principles of savage thought and to re-establish it in its rightful place." In a sense, he is suggesting that the split that was initiated between *mythos* and *logos* be reversed, and that the totalized thought of the savage mind, which is a genuine expression of human knowledge of the world, serve as an example of how to overcome the effects of that gap. However, it must be asked: is classifying human knowledge as essentially a "closed system" the best way to overcome this gap? And further, is it the case that the savage mind or that Lévi-Strauss's own positions are in fact closed systems?

As Livingston notes, the seeds of the Paradoxico-Critical orientation lie in the Structuralism of Lévi-Strauss and those of his ilk. He notices that there is a "fundamental reflexive consideration of the One of language as such . . . that essentially yields the paradoxico-critical orientation."[87] This is because the One of which Lévi-Strauss speaks is not a fixed or closed totality. Rather, it draws limits but not from an external position. Instead, the limits of Structuralism and the savage mind that enclose everything are both within and without the totality it thinks; as it is creating its own limits, as it transcends them, in its construction of them.

Later identified as a certain "exercise of structure" by Roland Barthes, implicit within the Constructivism of Structuralism is an activity of ongoing movement.[88] The timeless schematization that Lévi-Strauss identifies in the savage mind and the two-stage system whereby he claims anthropologists observe and analyze data in order to grasp the historical antecedents so they can bring the facts to the present in a meaningful totality, only to then repeat this on "a different plane and at a different level,"[89] is thus better understood by what Barthes refers to as "the functional." He explains: "Subsequently and especially, [the functional] highlights the strictly human process by which men give meaning to things."[90] This is what characterizes the totalizing schematization and classification that Lévi-Strauss notices in the savage mind. He claims that this true "dialectical reason" of the savage mind is very different from Sartre's, but perhaps if we understand the functionality and activity of the "fundamental reflexive consideration" of the savage mind's structural system, we can begin to see that Lévi-Strauss's own orientation was not so far removed from Sartre's. This does not mean that they were identical. Nor does it mean that in *The Savage Mind* Lévi-Strauss was deploying the Paradoxico-Critical orientation. But it does suggest that there is greater nuance than either may have been willing to concede. Even later in Lévi-Strauss's life, he concedes the need for a stronger role of activity in understanding structural analysis that moves him explicitly closer to Sartre and the Paradoxico-Critical orientation. He claims, "[The] linguists have taught us this. Every system—linguistic or otherwise—is in *constant disequilibrium with itself*, this is the motor of its internal dynamism. . . . But, in addition to this, there are other things, which we can never reduce. History is there in front of us, as something absolute in front of which we must bow down [emphasis added]."[91] This "constant disequilibrium" ensures that given the same choice between completeness and consistency, just like Sartre, perhaps with some qualification, he would choose completeness.

1.4.3 Addressing Lévi-Strauss's Assertion That CDR Is an Abstract Schema

All of this brings us to the third and final criticism that Lévi-Strauss levels against Sartre's perceived contradictory labor in *CDR*. The claim is that Sartre does not offer "a concrete image of history but an abstract schema of men making history of such a kind that it can manifest itself in the trend of their lives as a synchronic totality."[92] In a sense, this goes to the heart of the rest of the present project. To say that Sartre does not offer a "concrete image of history" is not a criticism. In fact, as we will elaborate in the coming chapters, this is almost a tautology. Volume One of *CDR* is an intentional regressive analysis of the conditions of history in order to make them intelligible. His project is not intended to offer a concrete image of history *per se*, but to illumine the reasons why history is unintelligible in the first instance, and then to offer a solution toward intelligibility. This is a different project. Thus, this criticism lands as a red herring. And it is a common scent that leads many readers of *CDR* off the trail. Therefore, by being aware of this tendency, it is our hope that we will not be enticed by the overwhelming presence of byways that might deter our focus.

By resolving our focus, we can see that Sartre's foray into such a regressive analysis is to unveil the rational structure of Being and to validate this unveiling. Or perhaps it would be more accurate to say: to unveil the rational structure of Being *by* validating its unveiling. As we have been arguing throughout this chapter, Sartre employs a Paradoxico-Critical orientation of thought toward the relation between thought and Being. When we situate him thusly, the ends of our project come into scope. That is, in the construction of what we will call a "hypo-logical" reading of *CDR*, examining Sartre's regressive analysis of practical ensembles through the lens of the Paradoxico-Critical orientation will enable us to see the text in its pluridimensional complexity as a synthetic analysis. We will endeavor to do this by examining the various practical ensembles to reveal the various logics that make these ensembles intelligible in totalization (not totality). "Logic" here means *intelligibility*. It is the intelligibility revealed by dialectical reason as the latter seeks to discover itself and found itself through the investigation into the practical ensembles which are both the results and creators of this dialectical reason.

Logic, for Sartre, is not an action of *ratio*. Rather, logic is lived. This is why he refers to a "living logic of action." As praxis seeks to comprehend itself in its articulation of itself in a field of mediated material conditions, this logic of action becomes inaction under serial conditions. This is why he says "if" when he writes, "[If] there is such a thing as a dialectical reason, it is revealed and established in and through human *praxis*." The point of the "if" is that dialectical reason as the unveiling of being is not guaranteed. Under conditions of Kaironic Seriality, comprehension is, in fact, not comprehended. There needs to be a development of an orientation that will allow dialectical reason to be properly dialectical. There must be a *critique* of dialectical reason in order for there to *be* dialectical reason. This is why we refer to our reading of *CDR* as "hypo-logical." We cannot assume the presence of a pure logical frame. We must also employ a Paradoxico-Critical orientation to, at once, reveal the speculative proposal and to simultaneously construct a productive method of revelation. And this method must not follow the trajectory mapped by the Greco-Christian separation of *logos* from *mythos* but will work through this separation in seeking to articulate a grounding of dialectical reason.

What does it mean to "work through this separation"? Only that, in *CDR*, Sartre is working toward rejecting the binary between thought and Being that characterized his early phenomenological investigations. No longer are *noema* and *noesis* or for-itself and in-itself distinct modes of being. Instead, praxis and the material environment are co-constitutive in a paradoxical dance of cross-pollination, with neither term to be viewed as primary. Whether or not his project is successful will be up to the determination of the reader. However, adjusting our expectations so that we do not impose an overdetermined hermeneutical prism onto the text is required. *CDR* is not seeking to develop a system in full. Rather, its scope is much more humble (while its depths extremely ambitious): *CDR* is laying down the groundwork to chart new territories of praxis. It is asking "how?" and "why?" while leaving judgements of "what" and "that" to future fellow travelers.

Having determined dialectical reason's significance as a system of interiority and validated its *arche* as Paradoxico-Critical, we will follow Sartre by setting out "from lived experience (*le vécu*) in order gradually to discover all the structures of *praxis*."[93] These structures are what we are calling here the formal, logical constructions of *CDR*'s hypo-logic. These formal constructions, therefore, become the dialectical intelligibility of particular moments of totalization. This is why we will speak of the "logic of the group" or "the logic of seriality." What this is referring to is the dialectical intelligibility of the various regressive syntheses under investigation at each stage of the project. To do so is to abstract from their unfolding material existence for heuristic purposes; that is, again, to reveal the truth of their intelligibility. What this will allow us to do is then rebuild a dialectical logical disposition (i.e., an orientation of dialectical reason) that can then become a "motive force."

Sartre himself said that he would reconstruct a "progressive definition of 'the rationality of action.'" This was his intention with Volume Two. However, the project at hand is different from setting out to construct a progressive definition. Rather, the goal of the present project is to extract those foundational elements of dialectical intelligibility so as to flesh out how this dialectical intelligibility can develop a dialectical disposition that is thoroughly regressive/analytical and creative/productive—what we will call the *imaginative logic of action*—so that future work can be done in the service of constructing a progressive definition of the rationality of action. Therefore, in order to understand the conditions of praxis seeking to comprehend itself, we turn to an exposition of Sartre's most ambitious work, *Critique of Dialectical Reason*: Volume One, *Theory of Practical Ensembles*.

NOTES

1. Please refer to the glossary for clear definitions of some of the more complex terms.
2. Sartre, *SM*, 8
3. Sartre, *CDR*, 19.

4. Ibid., 19.
5. For an excellent overview of this network of concerns, see Thomas Flynn, *Sartre: A Philosophical Biography* (Cambridge: Cambridge University Press, 2014).
6. Martin Jay, *Reason After Its Eclipse* (Madison: University of Wisconsin Press, 2016), 3–18.
7. Ibid., 4.
8. Giorgio Agamben, "Vocation and Voice," *Qui Parle*, 10, no. 2 (1997): 95.
9. Jay, *Reason*, 5.
10. Hans-Georg Gadamer, "Plato as Portraitist," in *The Gadamer Reader: A Bouquet of the Later Writings*, ed. Richard E. Palmer (Evanston, IL: Northwestern University Press, 2007), 310.
11. Ibid., 311.
12. Ibid., 311.
13. The elaboration of Christian metaphysics here is of course shorthand for a much larger set of concerns within the field of theology. For example, there is considerable internal debate pertaining to the metaphysical underpinning of the relation between thought/existence and Being. One of the most strident contemporary nodes of the debate concerns the school of Radical Orthodoxy's defense of participatory metaphysics pitted against the covenantal ontology of Bruce McCormack et al. For a brief overview of the debate and the implications drawn therefrom, see Jared Michelson, "Covenantal History and Participatory Metaphysics: Formulating a Reformed Response to the Charge of Legal Fiction," *Scottish Journal of Theology*, 71, no. 4 (2018): 391–410.
14. Jay, *Reason*, 21, and Thomas Aquinas, *The Summa contra Gentiles*, first and second books (Dominican Studio, 2000), 46.
15. Lucius Annaeus Seneca, *Letters on Ethics: To Lucilius*, trans. Margaret Graver and A. A. Long (Chicago: University of Chicago Press, 2015), 196.
16. Martijn Konings, *The Emotional Logic of Capitalism* (Stanford, CA: Stanford University Press, 2015), 50.
17. Jay, *Reason*, 25.
18. The Frankfurt School theorists have not all been united in their views on what this means, but there is a tendency from Horkheimer, to Marcuse, to the second generational ideas of Habermas that the gap between subjective and objective Reason needed to be understood and overcome. See, for example, Max Horkheimer, *Eclipse of Reason* (New York: 1947); Herbert Marcuse, *Reason and Revolution: Hegel and the Rise of Social Theory* (Boston: 1960); and Jürgen Habermas, *The Philosophical Discourse of Modernity: Twelve Lectures*, trans. Frederick Lawrence (Cambridge, MA: 1987).
19. Sartre, *CDR*, 33.
20. This project is not an investigation into the relation between Sartre and the Frankfurt School. While such would be a fruitful further endeavor, the present comparison is intended to conceptually situate Sartre's investigation of dialectical reason. The assumption is that the reader has at least a cursory familiarity with the Frankfurt School. As such, keeping their diverse views in mind will be an added benefit.
21. Hazel Barnes, "Introduction," in *SM*, xi.
22. Sartre, *SM*, 21–22.
23. Ibid., 21.
24. Ibid., 22.
25. Jean-Paul Sartre, "Après Budapest Sartre Parle," *L'Express*, November 9, 1956, http://www.lexpress.fr/informations/apres-budapest-sartre-parle_590852.html.
26. Ibid.
27. It is worthwhile to note that Sartre's criticism of this self-legitimized totality is a type of precursor to the criticisms of legitimacy that emerged in the next decade. See Jürgen Habermas, *Legitimation Crisis* (London: Heinemann, 1976) and Jean-François Lyotard, Geoffrey Bennington, Brian Massumi, and Fredric Jameson, *The Postmodern Condition: A Report on Knowledge* (Manchester: Manchester University Press, 1984).
28. Martin Jay, *Marxism and Totality: The Adventures of a Concept from Lukács to Habermas* (Berkeley: University of California Press, 1984), 332.

29. Sartre, *SM*, 53.
30. Pietro Chiodi, *Sartre and Marxism*, trans. Kate Soper (Sussex: The Harvester Press, 1976), 112–13.
31. Georg Lukács, *History and Class Consciousness* (Cambridge, MA: MIT Press, 1971), 51.
32. G. A. Cohen, *If You're an Egalitarian, How Come You're So Rich?* (Cambridge, MA: Harvard University Press, 2001), chapters 3 and 4.
33. Maurice Merleau-Ponty, "Sartre et l'ulta bolchevisme," in *Les Aventures de la Dialectique* (Paris: Gillimard, 1955), 57.
34. Jay, *Marxism and Totality*, 352.
35. Jean-Paul Sartre, *What Is Subjectivity?*, trans. David Broder and Trista Selous, Kindle ed. (London: Verso, 2016).
36. Immanuel Kant, *Metaphysical Foundations of Natural Science*, ed. Michael Friedman (Cambridge: Cambridge University Press, 2004), 3.
37. Sartre, *What Is Subjectivity?*
38. Ibid.
39. Ibid.
40. Jean-Paul Sartre, *The Transcendence of the Ego: An Existentialist Theory of Consciousness*, trans. Forrest Williams and Robert Kirkpatrick (New York: Hill and Wang, 1991).
41. Sartre, *What Is Subjectivity?*
42. Sartre, *CDR*, 45.
43. Ibid., 46.
44. Ibid., 46.
45. Ibid., 46.
46. Alain Badiou, *Pocket Pantheon: Figures of Postwar Philosophy*, trans. David Macey (London: Verso, 2009), 25.
47. Claude Lévi-Strauss, *The Savage Mind* (London: Weidenfeld and Nicolson, 1966), 254.
48. Simone de Beauvoir, La Cérémonie des adieux, suivi de entretiens avec Jean-Paul Sartre, Août-Septembre 1974 (Paris: Gallimard, 1981), 479.
49. "If these initial investigations have done no more than enable me to define the problem, by means of provisional remarks, which are there to be challenged and modified, and if they give rise to a discussion and if, as would be best, this discussion is carried on collectively in working groups, then I shall be satisfied." Sartre, *CDR*, 41.
50. Lévi-Strauss, *The Savage Mind*, 251.
51. See Bradley W. Patterson, *Redefining Reason: The Story of the Twentieth Century "Primitive" Mentality Debate* (Bradley Williams Patterson, 2011), 243–44.
52. This will be explored fully in chapter 5.
53. Sartre, *CDR*, 503.
54. Lévi-Strauss, *The Savage Mind*, 245.
55. Ibid., 245.
56. Ibid., 254.
57. Paul Livingston, *The Politics of Logic: Badiou, Wittgenstein, and the Consequences of Formalism* (New York: Routledge, 2012), 51–62.
58. Ibid., 54.
59. Ibid., 54.
60. Ibid., 55.
61. This could be understood as a type of dialectical reason. It is not the one found in *CDR*, but it does seem clear that Badiou, in many ways, is seeking to correct certain ontological problems that he finds in the orientation of *CDR*. It is not the place here to develop this idea further, but such an investigation into the relation between the Generic orientation of thought as a type of dialectical reason and Sartre's Paradoxico-Critical dialectical reason would be a very fruitful path of exploration.
62. Sartre, *CDR*, 18–32.
63. Ibid., 20.
64. Ibid., 19.
65. Ibid., 23.

66. Ibid., 23.
67. Ibid., 29.
68. Ibid., 29 note 14.
69. Ibid., 33.
70. Ibid., 33.
71. Ibid., 34.
72. Livingston, *The Politics of Logic*, 54.
73. Ibid., 54.
74. Alain Badiou, *Briefings on Existence: A Short Treatise on Transitory Ontology*, trans. Norman Madarasz (Albany: SUNY Press, 1998), 55.
75. Livingston, *The Politics of Logic*, 58.
76. Ibid., 59.
77. Sartre, *SM*, 105–106.
78. Sartre, *CDR*, 31.
79. Ibid., 33.
80. Ibid., 36.
81. Lévi-Strauss, *The Savage Mind*, 245.
82. Ibid., 246.
83. Jacob Rump, "Lévi-Strauss, Barthes, and the 'Structuralist Activity' of Sartre's Dialectical Reason," *Sartre Studies International*, 17, no. 2 (2011): 5.
84. Lévi-Strauss, *The Savage Mind*, 263.
85. Ibid., 263
86. Ibid., 269.
87. Livingston, *The Politics of Logic*, 94.
88. Roland Barthes, "The Structuralist Activity," *Partisan Review*, 15, no. 3 (1967): 83.
89. Lévi-Strauss, *The Savage Mind*, 253.
90. Barthes, "The Structuralist Activity," 86.
91. Claude Lévi-Strauss, Marc Augé, and Maurice Godelier, "Anthropologie, Histoire, Idéologie," in *L'Homme*, 15, nos. 3–4 (1975): 183.
92. Lévi-Strauss, *The Savage Mind*, 254.
93. Sartre, *CDR*, 39.

Chapter Two

Dialectical Logic and the Pervasion of Seriality

Toward a Fresh Reading of Sartre's
Critique of Dialectical Reason

"Tell [Sartre] that each time I sit down at my desk, I think of him. He writes such important things for our future, but he has not found readers at home who yet know how to read and among us he has not found any readers at all."
—Frantz Fanon[1]

CDR is generally read as a work of ontology and/or normative social theory. Thomas Flynn refers to it as a work of social ontology; Kristian Klockars and Gavin Rae suggest that Sartre prescribes that certain practical ensembles ought to be pursued over others; and Nina Power, Alain Badiou, Peter Hallward, and Brian Smith present Sartre as primarily a thinker of historical rupture. These three interpretive tendencies influence the majority of contemporary *CDR* scholarship. While there is merit in each of these tendencies, and while the theorists mentioned have influenced this author in immeasurable ways, they all employ (in his or her own way) a rushed hermeneutic: what we shall classify as the ontological and normative readings of *CDR*. This hermeneutic is rushed in that it hurries over the hypo-logical to reach the ontological and normative. Rather than reading *CDR*, first, as Sartre's effort to make comprehension comprehensible, these theorists all seek to elaborate dialectical reason in its presumably revealed intelligibility. While not wrong to extract normative or ontological value from the text, this misstep ensures that the novelty of *CDR* as a prolegomena remains obscured. What this section will elaborate, then, is how this dominant tendency has come to be, where it goes awry, and, following Fanon's prompt in the epigraph above, how we can move toward a fresh and productive reading.

By presenting a survey of the orthodox interpretation first, we better situate the debate. This will allow us to then problematize the ontological and normative readings so we can reconstruct the textual resonance prior to investigating the abstract, formal structures themselves. We begin in section 2.1 by presenting the standard circular reading of *CDR*. This is the *prima facie* reading that tends to dominate textual reception. This interpretation is not wrong so much as it is limited. Section 2.2 then begins our deconstruction of this superficial reading as we aim toward our goal of elaborating a hypo-logical hermeneutic. We address Sartre's hope against hope displayed throughout his life, before more substantively criticizing positional misunderstandings within *CDR* interpretation. Our hope with this section is that we can source some of the reasons why *CDR* has been read the way it has. Of course, the intent is not to censure, but to understand how we have perhaps misarticulated certain textual resonances, and how these interpretations have then dominated *CDR* reception on the whole. The goal throughout this chapter is that we can move toward an interpretation free from fogged lenses.

Section 2.3 closes the chapter by highlighting the aporia that Sartre identifies in history. This problematization of the concept of history is crucial for further understanding of Sartre's unique approach in *CDR*. We address Raymond Aron's criticism that Sartre was wedding together methodological individualism with dialectical materialism and Lévi-Strauss's critique that Sartre gives history a mystical status. We show how both of these accusations miss the mark, and then turn toward an elaboration of Sartre's notion of history as an aporetic concept. This culminates in a discussion of why *this* history is inherently incomprehensible: Kaironic Seriality. The introduction of this concept at this point signals to chapters 3 and 4 which will further clarify the problems facing dialectical reason and how they might be addressed.

2.1 CIRCULARITY IN THE *CRITIQUE*

A common criticism of Sartre's philosophy is that he is unable to escape pessimism regarding social relations. In *Being and Nothingness* (hereafter *BN*), this is undoubtedly the case as he describes the human "project" as consciousness surpassing its present "situation" toward the unbounded possibles that might be realized through the radical freedom of the for-itself, as the latter seeks to create itself, create meaning, and overcome the viscous nature of the present, which continually threatens the for-itself with the Impossible—annihilation, death, collapse into the in-itself. Because other free for-itselfs all have the same project (structurally),[2] there necessarily arises conflict in the social sphere as one consciousness seeks its own ends over and against the desired ends of any and every other for-itself. Therefore, the for-itself, in the mode "being-for-others," is haunted by an unceasing competition with others, as individual consciousnesses transcend/negate one another in a field of subjective competition. Unlike Taylorist readings of the dialectic, there is no dyadic struggle that results in a "higher synthesis."[3] There is no hope for resolution. Sartre seems to suggest that the conflictual nature of intersubjectivity is irreconcilable—an absolute result of the ontological freedom of the for-itself. It is this conflictual phenomenology that has led many readers to focus exclusively on various pessimistic soundbites taken from Sartre's massive corpus: "hell is other people"; "man is a useless passion"; or existence is "absurd." Taken as definitive characterizations of Sartre's philosophy, such maxims often neglect Sartre's most ambitious work, *Critique of Dialectical Reason*, in which he investigates, through a regressive analysis, the formal conditions of reciprocal relations between individuals and the material conditions in which the former are always-already situated.

In *CDR*, Sartre retains much of the language/structure of his earlier works (the project, the situation, facticity, freedom, the field of possibles, intending toward the beyond, etc). However, he modifies their content significantly by turning from consciousness toward human labor to define human existence. The conceptual shift from defining human existence as *consciousness* to *praxis* is profound, primarily because it incorporates the human being completely in its embedded material facticity. In his later work, Sartre characterized facticity as the entirety of material human existence in a Marxian fashion—identifying the human with labour: "[The] truth of a man is the nature of his work. . . . But, this truth defines him just insofar as he constantly goes beyond it in his practical activity."[4] This latter experience of one working, being defined by her work, and surpassing her situation is what Sartre would call one's praxis-project. It is the essential identity marker of human existence. Like the intending, surpassing, negating consciousness of BN, the human-as-praxis is characterized by arising within a given situation of exigence, which requires that it be surpassed. This necessity is not an *a priori* mandate derived from analytic reason but arises from the contingent relation between humans and their material conditions. Comprehending this relation (as do historical materialist theorists) is not done from an external position, but is part of the dialectical process itself—an internal moment of praxis, which by its very existence marks the "being-past of Being, or the movement by which Being becomes what it has been."[5] Rejecting economistic and structuralist readings of Marx alike, Sartre re-articulates the paradox of Marx's dictum that "Man makes his own history, but he does not make it out of the whole cloth; he does not make it out of conditions chosen by himself, but out of such as he finds close at hand."[6] In Sartre's words, "[Men] make history to precisely the same extent that it makes them."[7] The dialectical relationship between humans and their material conditions is thus the *source of dialecticity*. Eschewing any notion of a dialectic of nature, he locates the dialectic purely in the contingent historical relation between human praxis and the situation in which the latter finds itself.[8]

Although a *de facto*, relational necessity, the dialectic is also comprehended as contingent. Arising because of the relationship between humans and scarce material conditions, history is always understood in relation to scarcity, "which explains fundamental structures (techniques and institutions)—not in the sense that it is a real force and that it has produced them, but because they were produced in the *milieu of scarcity* by men whose *praxis* interiorises this scarcity even when they try to transcend it."[9] For this reason, Sartre remarks that the original contingency (i.e., scarcity) "shows us . . . both the necessity of our contingency and the contingency of our necessity."[10] Defined not as temporally, historically, or ontologically prior (at least in the first instance), but as formally and logically prior to praxis, scarcity is the original situation into which every human being is thrown at each given moment. In other words, human beings are always immersed in a situation characterized by an original negation in relation to need. Therefore, persons are perpetually embattled by transcending their present situation toward a beyond of possibles.

This process parallels the for-itself's tendential targeting of its own absolute realization as the in-itself-for-itself in *Being and Nothingness*, a project which necessarily leads to existential angst. Although he implies that perhaps beauty might be that which releases humanity from "total frustration," beauty must not be conceived as real. Rather, it "is no more a potentiality of things than the in-itself-for-itself is a peculiar possibility of the for-itself. It haunts the world as an unrealizable. To the extent that man realizes the beautiful in the world, he realizes it *in the imaginary mode* [emphasis added]."[11] Taken as hopelessness by Ronald Aronson,[12] Sartre's tending toward the "imaginary mode" is actually rather positive. Although not recognizable as such until *Critique of Dialectical Reason*, one's praxis-project interiorizes imagined futures, which means that one's praxis-project continually recreates imagined futures through the negation of negation in seeking de-alienation. *CDR* ought to be perceived as a step in Sartre's journey out of the pessimistic trap of total frustration that he caught himself in due to his earlier phenomenological commitments. By infusing beauty into praxis's desire to comprehend itself and history, Sartre develops a heuristic that will enable us to envision an aesthetic ethical orientation of political praxis. To this we will return. Chapter 6 will be a brief exposition of Sartre's investigation into the image and the imagination in his early works, and then chapter 7 will synthesize the formal analysis of *CDR* with the findings of chapter 6 as we seek to ground an imaginative logic of action.

For now, it must be emphasized that the dialectic is a process from "objectification to objectification." As praxis works in a pre-constituted situation, its subjectivity is inscribed on the objective world. Matter is therefore understood as "worked-matter." By storing labor, the material world becomes a field of preserved, inert striving. Likewise, in the same movement, the individual interiorizes the pre-existent material conditions in her praxis as she totalizes herself and the field of objective possibilities with which she is faced (recall the discussion in chapter 1 about totalization and the material system contra totality and the closed set). This activity of interiorization, exteriorization, re-interiorization, re-exteriorization describes the flow of totalization. It is the accumulating, spiral movement of praxis that creates new situations of exigence and freedom in the unfolding of historical praxis at both the individual and group levels. In other words, totalization can well be described as the particular Sartrean notion that redefines the dialectic in the formal terms he establishes in *CDR*.

At this point, it is crucial to note that—in itself, as a formal notion—worked-matter is not a threat to praxis. However, once worked-matter takes on the alienating characteristics that condition it in the milieu of scarcity, it becomes "practico-inert." For Sartre, the practico-inert is a field of dehumanizing mediations that act as the source of "negative reciprocity." According to Pietro Chiodi, the practico-inert is the field produced by the praxis-project as the latter imprints itself upon

> the inertia of [matter] . . . which, in escaping the finality of the constituting dialectic, becomes available for insertion into heterogeneous dialectical totalizations whose orientation is counter-final relative to the finality of the constitutive process. The effect of this is to render material external to the project and opposed to it as necessity to freedom.[13]

What he means is that praxis's self-inscription on matter is the necessary condition that both opposes praxis and creates the conditions for its freedom. Because of praxis's inscribed significations into the material field, praxis returns as counter-finality, opposed to the heterogenous projects of dialectical totalization. This occurs as a result of the milieu of scarcity that is internalized and which conditions totalization's tendency toward inscribing counter-final ends. The result is that a *serial collective* is formed. Externally objectified by its own product (i.e., the practico-inert), the series is a collective of *inhumans* insofar as they are robbed of freedom over their product and its finality, as the product is utilizable by others in a field of objective competition. That is, a serial collective is characterized by inhuman-actors, whose projects are stifled by the stasis arising from confronting projects in a given horizon, which in turn marks each person in *competition* and *alterity* in relation to one another.

Since, therefore, the practico-inert negates the humanity of the praxis-project, it must itself be negated. There must be a "reaffirmation of man."[14] Such occurs through the irruption of the "group-in-fusion." The group-in-fusion is established by its common praxis in seeking a particular objective. Not united in external relations (as is the serial collective by the necessity of the practico-inert), the group-in-fusion humanizes its constituents through an "apocalypse."[15] Sartre characterizes the group-in-fusion as freely snatching from the practico-inert field its inhumanizing power of "mediation between men in order to confer power on each and everyone in the community, and thus establish itself . . . as the means whereby the materiality of the practical field is placed again in the hands of free communized praxis."[16] When such occurs, alterity is curbed and the members of the fused group are viewed as Same insofar as they are each products of the group and the common activity of the free individual *praxes* that constitute the *praxis* of this particular formal mode of group formation.

Through the apocalyptic upsurge of group activity in the face of an imminent threat (i.e., the Impossible), Sartre espouses a theory of social relationality that is able to skirt a destiny that is bound for the mere repetition of alienation. Achieved through "mediated reciprocity," de-alienation occurs through the communized, free praxis of the group-in-fusion. Their primary task being "to snatch from worked-upon material its inhuman power of mediation between men in order to confer it on each and everyone in the community," the group-in-fusion exhibits a novel social arrangement in which the dehumanizing powers of seriality are dissolved in the irruption of humanity, perhaps even for the first time.

However, a pressing question arises: how is such a group able to sustain itself in its de-alienation despite its perpetual totalization within the practico-inert field? And this is where interpreters claim that we again encounter Sartre's social pessimism. After the initial, free, instantaneous upsurge (i.e., the apocalypse), the group is then threatened with dissolution into seriality. As Fredric Jameson notes, there are at least three ways the group can dissolve: 1) "it can . . . disperse back into seriality," or, by institutionalization, it can develop 2) bureaucracy, and/or 3) dictatorship.[17] Not wishing such a fate, an oath (or "pledge") is sworn: "when freedom makes itself the communal praxis of establishing the permanence of the group by way of producing itself its own inertia in mediated reciprocity, this new *statut* is called *the oath*."[18]

Although there is a momentary experience of de-alienated sociality in the group-in-fusion, this *instant* is fated to dissipate after the oath is made (if not prior). In the face of the event, the pre-constituted group was faced with the Impossible, which instigated a united front against a violent foe. By negating this violence with violence and revolutionary resistance, the moment of apocalypse offered a glimpse of absolute de-alienated communized praxis (mediated reciprocity). However, after the initial upsurge, the group is faced with simple and sudden ossification into a serial collective or an institution because of the absolute presence of the practico-inert in the milieu of scarcity. Therefore, an oath is made to preserve the group. However, the very effect of the sworn oath produces a "permanence" which fails to maintain the pure freedom of the apocalypse. In other words, the oath is a "reflective act," instituted by the group to retain the affective impetus that was initially experienced during the apocalyptic moment. Unfortunately, the reflective act is insufficient in three ways:

1. It is a forced reproduction (re-presentation) of a previous spontaneous, affective experience.
2. It establishes a *being* of the group, which negates the free *becoming* of the apocalypse.
3. It creates an *image* whose object is both absent and present; one that is inert and completely produced by the collective imaginative consciousness of the group; that has no creative capacity in itself (it teaches nothing); and that is devoid of the infinite depth of the real (spatio-temporality).[19]

As such, the "pledged group" begins to mineralize. Roles, and eventually functions, are rigidly delineated. This self-imposition of inertia—*in itself*—is not to be viewed as opposed to freedom, for each individual "freely" swears the oath in order to preserve her freedom and the commonality of the group. However, its insufficiency comes precisely as an unintended consequence (i.e., counter-finality) of the introduction of inertia into the life of the group. As the group settles into its permanence (whether merely perceived or actual is of no consequence at this point), it becomes more and more organized, and each member becomes identified by her function in fulfilling the role that pre-destines her action in the objective of the organized group. Still though, the organization is not viewed itself as an alienated ensemble. It isn't until institutionalization becomes formalized that inertia and alterity inhere as the constitutive and affective mediators of the institution. In the institution, each member becomes a cog in the larger wheel. Like the experience of the collective in basic seriality writ large, the *members* of the institution are *inessential*. By contrast, the *institution* is *essential*.

2.2 REJECTING THE PESSIMISTIC READING OF *CDR*

Such is the basic formula that we find in *CDR*. Groups emerge in antagonism to serial conditions that constitute basic human existence. However, basic human existence is really understood as *inhuman* existence, as each individual's life is pre-destined by the milieu of scarcity that ensures competitive relations of alterity in its social expression. Freedom is possible through the irruption of the group-in-fusion, but that soon collapses once permanence creeps back into the group, and institutionalization is the ultimate outcome of the life of the group. Thus, there is a path from series, to group, to institution. At least this is how *CDR* is generally read. Even the most sympathetic readers of Sartre's revolutionary work read it through this pessimistic lens. As Nina Power notes:

> In the end, for Sartre, revolts will always crystallise. The fusion of the group will always reach a certain point and coalesce. Things fall apart, or rather, things slip back into seriality, often on a grander scale. . . . Whilst this appears to be a wholly pessimistic conclusion, creeping inertia destroying all possibility of active change, nevertheless it is inescapable.[20]

While it is true that this is the dominant reading of *CDR*, there is something missing in such a pessimistic interpretation: hope and a proper understanding of the pluridimensional logic of dialectical rationality that is espoused in *CDR*; or, referring back to chapter 1, we might say that there ought to be greater attention paid to the system of interiority that we articulated according to the Paradoxico-Critical orientation.

2.2.1 Sartre's Hopefulness

It is not a trivial point to note that Sartre himself never veered from his hope for the revolution. In his final interview with Benny Lévy, although unable to firmly ground his reasons for being hopeful, Sartre remarked that, "The world seems ugly, bad, and without hope. That is the tranquil despair of an old man who will die within it. But that is precisely what I resist, and I know that I will die in hope; but it is necessary to create a foundation for this hope."[21] Although this final interview has been the subject of much critical scrutiny, and instigated controversy upon its original publication, the elements under examination pertain to claims that Benny Lévy manipulated the older Sartre through loaded questions and that through his sheer will and youthful vivacity, overran Sartre, who had always been known to be accommodating to the views of his interviewers anyway.[22] Of particular concern are indications that Sartre may have adopted a form of Jewish Messianism, which was curiously close to Lévy's own views.

Not under scrutiny are the instances of Sartre's future-oriented disposition. Considering a great motive force of his intellectual and political career was driven by empowering human beings with the freedom of choice in the midst of a constraining world, it hardly seems out of character that Sartre would retain a hopeful outlook. Beyond this, the articulated desire to create a "foundation for this hope" fits precisely within the paradoxical self-referential productivity of dialectical reason that characterizes *CDR*. His hope was not in some pre-figured future as in mystical Messianism, but rather in *founding* the hope that was always-already hoping. This Paradoxico-Critical hopeful tendency in the Lévy–Sartre interviews is an echo of Sartre's invocation of Malraux's conception of apocalypse that he employs to describe the irruption of the human out of the domination of inhuman seriality.[23] In a sense, there is nothing one can do but hope. This is what the apocalypse indicates. Under situations of great pressure, when threatened by the Impossible, the very impulse of life facing death is hope against hope. This will be clarified and elaborated more fully below. For now, what matters is that this search for a "foundation" for hope is precisely what the pessimistic readings of *CDR* overlook (or at least de-emphasize). For although "revolts will always crystallise" in concrete historical circumstances, the persistence of freedom-as-praxis ensures that this crystallization itself is only one component of the logic of totalization.

2.2.2 Eschewing Orthogonal Reciprocity

More substantively, the pessimistic readings of *CDR* are due to a positional misreading of the text itself. That is, these readings underestimate the *formality* of the text. The result is that they tend to read *CDR* as though it were an analysis of history itself, or as a linear logic, rather than a synthetic logic. The terms deployed (group, praxis, series, collective, institution, etc.) are best understood in their enfolded and enfolding synthesis (with both diachronic and synchronic moments contained therein). As such, what we have in *CDR* is *theory construction*. Sartre is developing abstract, formal constructions to help us think through concrete material historical actualities. There are of course going to be historical, ontological, and normative implications that can be drawn from this construction. But first and foremost, Volume One of *CDR* must be considered in its *heuristic* purposes: exploring the formal conditions of *anthropological history*.[24] In the end, what Volume One of *CDR* develops is not so much a definite system (à la Hegel or Badiou) but a set of theoretical constructions that allow future theorists and activists to apply them (in so far as they are deemed useful) to social and historical realities. In Sartre's words:

> Volume One of the *Critique of Dialectical Reason* stops as soon as we reach the "locus of history"; *it is solely concerned with finding the intelligible foundations* for a structural anthropology—to the extent, of course, that these synthetic structures are the condition of a directed, developing totalization. [Emphasis added][25]

That is, Volume One stops at the point when we can articulate the formal abstractions that will open up history for further analysis. And this further analysis is done through dialectical reason as praxis seeks comprehension.

If a locus is the site where something occurs, then we must take Sartre to mean that Volume One brings us to an understanding of *how* and *why* history occurs. In other words, Volume One examines the mechanisms that drive anthropological historical movement (i.e., the mechanisms of totalization). These mechanisms are the "intelligible foundations" for a structural anthropology. They are "synthetic structures." And these synthetic structures condition a directed and developing totalization. In other words, totalization is conditioned by the synthetic structures (praxis, practico-inert, worked matter, collective, group, organization, institution, etc.), which means that totalization, as the movement of history-as-dialectical, can only be made intelligible through analyzing these synthetic structures in the first instance. For, they reveal how and in what ways totalization is either dialectical or anti-dialectical; comprehensible or incomprehensible; free or serial. Further, as this project will defend, the synthetic structures of Sartre's "structural anthropology" are composites of 1) *diachronic history and praxis* and 2) *synchronic structure and situatedness*. Another way of phrasing this is that Sartre's structural and historical anthropology is grounded by a logic that refuses to reduce either the absolute of concrete praxis or the absolute of objective material conditions into the other. Both praxis and objectivity must be maintained as co-constituting absolutes in dialectical relationality.

However, this must be done without resorting to any sort of orthogonal privileging. Orthogonal literally means "right-angled." In statistics, it is used to describe variates that are treated independently. For Peter Caws, orthogonal privileging is the independent relation between the variates thought and Being, existence and structure, for-itself and in-itself, and praxis and the situation. As an analogy, we can imagine a right-angled relation between any *x* and any *y* where the two vectors diverge in equal proportion. It is this inverse proportionality that Caws is drawing upon.

How the concept of "orthogonal privileging" relates to Sartre's thought needs to be unpacked a bit in order to understand a common tendency among readers of *CDR*. Caws claims that there is an orthogonal reciprocity between existence and structure. In *Being and Nothingness*, he claims there was a swing toward the side of existence, whereas *CDR* moves the pendulum back toward the middle.[26] However, the notion of orthogonal reciprocity only has abstract conceptual explanatory value when considering terms that are externally related.[27] This is the very approach that *CDR* rejects. In Sartre's dialectical project, the two notions don't shift in inverse proportion to one another, but rather infuse one another in totalization. This is not to say that they can be reduced to one another. Rather, it is to say that the two terms themselves are never separated (except abstractly), and as such there is no law whereby one's increase necessarily implies the other's decrease. In fact, *CDR* could be said to give *primacy to both*. It is not a perfectly balanced theory, where existence and structure are given equal priority as terms in relation *to* one another. Rather, Caws's setup (and those that follow a similar logic) must be rejected in favor of thinking of the two terms as enveloping and infusing one another in a co-constituting synthetic relation. Instead of there being an external relationship, there is an internal *chassé-croisé* of intensive variation. Again, we must bear in mind Sartre's rigorous criticism of analytical reason, which is defined precisely by external relations. Orthogonal reciprocity must therefore be thought of in terms of the Constructivist orientation of thought; whereas our goal must be to maintain the Paradoxico-Critical orientation, in order to resist the tendencies of analytical reason.

Once orthogonal reciprocity is eschewed, a space is opened wherein non-pessimistic readings of *CDR* can emerge. First of all, Sartre's negativity regarding human freedom in situations of scarcity is not necessarily inversely proportional to the possibility for de-alienation. Rather, the two have a relationship of cross-contamination, like two intensities that co-constitute one another within the same field of possibilities. Sure, there are methods of analysis that will focus on the depths of alienation and the ubiquity of scarcity. And at the same time, such analyses will produce a seemingly dire sense toward overcoming such alienation.[28] But Sartre must also be read as an emancipatory thinker who never wavered from his commitment to the idea of freedom (even if its definition shifts throughout his writings). For every serial condition necessarily contains the latent potency of transformation and re-creation. Freedom (praxis/existence) and seriality (objectivity/structure) are not two concepts in external, inverse, proportional relation to one another. They are interpenetrating, synthetic, material realities that imbue one another with the efficacy of the other. They are internal to one another, and one's strength doesn't mean the necessary depletion of the other. In fact, there is no *a priori* law of necessity regarding their proportional relation.

2.2.3 CDR Is Not a Theory of History

This leads to a second and more basic point regarding the positional misreadings of the text: *CDR* isn't a pessimistic reading of history, or practical ensembles, or inter-subjective relations—precisely because it is *not* a theory of history *in se*. That is, *CDR* develops a pulsating, spiraling, dialectical *logic*—not a linear or progressive view of the way things unfold, or even could unfold. To suppose that *CDR* is pessimistic is to suppose that Sartre's theory moves from group, to series, to group, to series, always ending up in seriality. And while seriality is pervasive and inescapable in many ways, serial relations are just as exposed to dissolution through the emergence of the group logic as groups are threatened by the serial logic. That is, the relation between alienation and de-alienation is one where neither has primacy in terms of its possible realization. They are both possible, *logically*. The group is always threatening irruption within serial conditions. And likewise, seriality is always there to threaten the ossification of the group. But this stasis is never final, because the logic of the apocalypse ensures that the irruption of humanity can and will break forth.

Sartre's point, therefore, is to *make intelligible the conditions under which group freedom can emerge, with the hope of equipping humanity with a set of formal, logical constructions that can aid it in overcoming serial conditions* (whether finally or at least to as great a degree as possible). But this desire (so far as we can surmise that such is his desire, and in so far as it is not fully realized in his logical investigation) does not mean that the relation between alienation and de-alienation is somehow circular and pessimistic. It is sporadic and rather hopeful. *CDR* is an investigation and development of a logic. As such, the only pessimism is in the eyes of those readers who have no hope in using the "living logic of action" that he places at the feet of future theorists for them to further develop.[29] Andrew Dobson exhibits this pessimism clearly when he claims, "To the extent that philosophers have only interpreted the world and never changed it, the *Critique* is no guide to social revolution."[30] This is precisely the interpretation that we must reject in order to develop a productive Paradoxico-Critical reading of *CDR*. For, the pessimism is merely in the interpretation and application of the text because of hermeneutical misgivings. In itself, *CDR* is an open and logically neutral formal investigation.[31] As Sartre says, groups have a "serial destiny" but also that it is always the case that "seriality may . . . be transformed into a community."[32] Therefore, a rejection of pessimism in the establishment of a proper dialectical logic is the first guiding principle of this chapter and will serve as a crucial foundation for the elaboration of the imaginative logic of action in part II.

2.3 *IN MEDIA RES*:
PROBLEMATIZING HISTORY AND KAIRONIC SERIALITY

Once the negative baggage of pessimism is cleared, *CDR* is able to speak forth afresh. With that, the second guiding principle of part I: the depths of seriality are so pervasive that it is not a rhetorical flourish to claim that our history, the *this history* that Sartre analyzes in *CDR*, is aptly characterized as the *age of seriality*.

2.3.1 La mariée est trop belle:
Contra Aron and Methodological Individualism

To be clear, Sartre's notion of history is somewhat ambiguous and has been the subject of much scrutiny. Aron and Lévi-Strauss are perhaps the two most notable critics of Sartre's understanding of history. For Aron, the *Critique* tends toward the following objective: to establish ontologically the foundations of methodological individualism. . . . Sartre also intends to reduce all human, socio-historical reality to individual *praxis*, which, according to him, is the sole ontological reality or, at the very least, is the ontological origin of practice-oriented ensembles or of the anti-dialectic wherein individual *praxis* is alienated and seems to disappear.[33]

The first thing of note is a point that was discussed in the previous section. Aron is operating under the orthogonal logic of interpretation. As such, his reading is both reductive and pessimistic.

The second point to note is that Aron's reading of *CDR* is really just a reading of *BN* superimposed *into* the text of *CDR*. As he states, "The reconciliation of ontological individualism and dialectical totalization . . . lends itself to a pessimistic reading; it presents us a new version of the myth of Sisyphus."[34] Obviously for Aron, this means that Sartre's effort to wed together Existentialism and Marxism is a piece of wishful thinking. Or, as Edouard Morot-Sir put it, "*la mariée est trop belle*."[35] But the idea that "ontological individualism" is primary in *CDR* misses the complexity with which Sartre investigates the terms of the text. More egregiously, it ignores the persistent statements by Sartre that the terms in the early development of his argument are merely "simple" and "abstract," with the dialectical complexity accumulating toward a crescendo in the middle and later parts of the text. Therefore, it takes patience to not judge the early, simple, abstract terms as encompassing the entirety of Sartre's elaboration of concepts in *CDR*. Instead, a more complete reading will transform the simple and abstract notions once they have been folded into the more complex and concrete notions that are developed in the later portions of the volume. More on this later.

For now, it needs to be emphasized that *CDR* is not a work of Cartesian individualism. In fact, for Sartre, the individual is itself an abstract notion. As he would come to say in the Volume Two of *CDR*, "[There] is no atomic solitude. There are only ways of being together. Solitude appears within ways of being together."[36] As Nina Power quips, it is "capitalism that creates the 'erroneous' impression that there are only individuals."[37] Therefore, what we can derive from this is that individualism is a particular contingent phenomenon that arises within this particular history—the capitalist history. And this thread of thought is crucial to keep in mind throughout Sartre's investigation in *CDR* as a whole. He is not trifling with universals or metaphysical absolutes. Rather, he is developing a transcendental historical materialist account of anthropology. As such, the facts of history are contingent in their necessity, and likewise necessary in their contingency. This harkens back to his maxim from "Existentialism is a Humanism" that "existence precedes essence," but without the Cartesian phenomenological ontological baggage. Again quoting Power:

> What Sartre was obliged to do, therefore, in the *Critique*, was use existentialism to unblock the "stopped" really existing socialism, and the abuses of Marxism, without letting the Cartesianism of the earlier project seep back in and reify the dialectical comprehension he was trying to pursue. He thus introduces a hierarchy of mediations which make up the *Critique* and allows it to grasp the process which produces the person within a given society at a given moment.[38]

Thus, while *BN* was undoubtedly a work that fits within the Cartesian individualist legacy, *CDR* proceeds from a different foundation—one that develops a logic of totalization that asserts both the complex system of interiority of subjectivity and the concrete situatedness of objectivity in mediatory co-constitution and integration. It assumes that "the concept of Man is an abstraction,"[39] claims that individual actions are "acts without an author,"[40] and ends by re-emphasizing that individual and group actions are "constructions without a constructor."[41] It is these notions that have led some readers of *CDR* to claim that it is a text that "occupies a transitional space between modernist and postmodernist categories, integrating elements of each into a constellated and synthetic whole."[42]

While it isn't the primary concern of the present project, one thing must be emphasized: *Critique of Dialectical Reason* is not a work of Cartesian individual *ontology*. In fact, it is not a work of ontology at all (in the first instance). As was mentioned in the previous section, Sartre is engaging in theory construction first and foremost. This means that the primary purpose of *CDR* is to investigate the formal conditions under which an historical and structural anthropology might be made intelligible. And even though Sartre does place a measure of emphasis on individual praxis, this is better understood as an entry point into the broader investigation, which would get progressively more complex, thereby problematizing the simple and abstract notions from the earlier portions of the investigation in order to establish a living logic of action in a pluridimensional reality. Not that individual praxis would become obsolete at the deeper stages of complexity, but that it must be understood in its proper place in the material system of totalization.

Therefore, Aron's interpretive mistake (as well as Flynn's, Desan's, and even the postmodern reading of Nik Farrell Fox) is that he fails to grasp the extent of the formal and theoretical nature of *CDR*. Thomas Flynn comes close by claiming that *CDR* is "hypothetical."[43] However, it does a disservice to the applicability of Sartre's investigation to say that *CDR* is hypothetical. While there is certainly fabulation throughout, *CDR* is not investigating a world that *could be*. Nor is it offering suppositions. No, he is regressively investigating the formal conditions of the world that *is*, and then providing the reader with imaginative tools to create therefrom. As we will explore further, what is crucial for Sartre is both rigorous analysis of real material conditions and an imaginative logic that can create new worlds—with neither receiving primacy. Therefore, it would be better to speak of *CDR* as *hypological*. This neologism has value in that the logic of dialectical reason in *CDR* is not the *logos* of the Greco-Christian orientation. Nor is it akin to the *ratio* of analytical reason. It is thus an under-logic, one rooted in the material flow of the dialectic itself. Never divorced from its thrownness in existence or from its own disruption and re-articulation through totalization. To speak of *CDR* as "hypo-logical" is, therefore, to incorporate embodied labor as a moment of praxis seeking to comprehend comprehension.

2.3.2 The Aporia of History: Contra Lévi-Strauss

Lévi-Strauss's criticism comes from a different direction. For Lévi-Strauss, Sartre is an historicist who valued "history above the other human sciences and formed an almost mystical conception of it."[44] Perhaps because he did not have access to Volume Two, but this mystical conception that he perceives misses Sartre's designation of history as being essentially aporetic. As the result and creator of integrated systems of interiority—that is totalizations within totalizations—history is aporetic, for Sartre, because every practical ensemble is riven with splits and contradictions. "Society, from afar, seems to stand unaided; from close to, it is riddled with holes."[45] Scarcity of time, scarcity of means, and scarcity of knowledge—plus the structural milieu of scarcity that conditions these subvariants—ensure that every praxis must struggle in a milieu of antagonism that is itself unintelligible from the perspective of analytical reason. This is because analytical reason reduces history to a mathematical formula. When discussing military academies studying past battles, Sartre writes: "A certain schematization . . . is enough to transform the comprehensive study of the battle into a formal theory, into a quasi-mathematical calculus of possibles. The reality of the conflict fades—ultimately we find a calculus of probabilities."[46]

We discussed this approach in chapter 1 with reference to the Constructivist orientation of thought that totalizes a given field but that reserves a privileged outside position for the theorist to analyze the given totality. When history is examined in this way, it becomes a mathematical formula and loses the unique elements of totalization, particularization, and paradox, which Sartre refers to as the three features of dialectical intelligibility in Volume Two.[47] The once-lived totalization with all its nuance and particularities of passion and circumstance, strategy and maneuver, stakes and intentions, is totalized into a sequence of externally-related variables. This will not give us access to the dialectical intelligibility of totalization. This is why the investigation in Volume One into the formal elements of dialectical intelligibility is so crucial to found before examining the meaning of history. It illuminates the complexity of totalization and reorients the investigation from a Constructivist to a Paradoxico-Critical disposition. The former can only ever give an analytical intelligibility of totalized parts mediated by totality (ex. the singular historical event as closed set). The Paradoxico-Critical orientation, on the other hand, is what enables processes-in-becoming to be made intelligible in their pluridimensional complexity.

But a Paradoxico-Critical orientation, in this case the particular Sartrean expression of it as a critique of dialectical reason, also provides a way of investigating concrete historical realities without imputing a teleological idealism into the field of study (remember our discussion of Lukács in chapter 1). By starting with an examination of a given situation and then regressively investigating the synthetic conditions of that situation, elemental structures are revealed as the intelligibility of that particular situation. These elemental structures are strictly derived from the situation itself as resultants. They were discovered, if you will. Only after, only once the logic of that given situation is discovered and when dialectical reason is comprehensible, does the investigation proceed toward history writ large. Thus, the aporia of history is precisely in its complexity as a totalization composed of totalities and totalizations in concrete material situations that yield productive contradictions and paradox.

Thus, for Sartre, history isn't mystical at all. He is not placing history in the realm of *Geist* à la Hegel. Rather history is the result of concrete human relations between humans and between the material conditions in which they find themselves thrown at all times. In other words, "history" is the abstract term we ascribe, at singular moments of analysis, to the totalizing process of concrete relations between (in)human actors and the situations into which they are perpetually thrown. History then is the result of the dialectical movement between (in)humans and their overcoming of their situation as they tend toward future possibles. This is where Sartre's investigation begins and ultimately ends. He is seeking to make the conditions of history intelligible so that he might be able to understand if there is a single meaning of history. Simply divided, Volume One is concerned with the former and Volume Two with the latter. However, the conditions of historical intelligibility and the single meaning of history are not something known *a priori*. Nor can they be described as having any sort of mystical characteristics, as they are exclusively the result of concrete (in)human reality that is not yet known. And they can only be known through a dialectical reason because history is a material result of the dialectical movement itself.

Lévi-Strauss seems to further confuse this fact by drawing a strict line between history (diachrony) and anthropology (synchrony).[48] He then proceeds to criticize Sartre for supposedly camping in the historical/diachronic theoretical realm while ignoring the anthropological/synchronic. The problem with this argument is that, for Sartre, neither diachrony nor synchrony has priority. They are both held in dialectical tension. That is why Sartre claims to be investigating the formal conditions for a *structural and historical* anthropology. Diachrony *and* synchrony characterize his investigation. As Jacob Rump states,

> The *Critique of Dialectical Reason* is thus able to recognize the important role that structure plays in our world and in our history, without subsuming the possibility of free human praxis to an outright determinist and structuralist account that would reduce history to the playing out of a deterministic rationality, a history that would be, in effect, not really ours.[49]

In other words, what Rump is saying is that Sartre skirts both Lévi-Strauss's and Aron's criticism in the same move: he is able to preserve the *freedom of praxis* and the *objectivity of material conditions* without reducing history to either voluntarism or determinism. And this is done not by hypothetical theorizing or by grand system creation, but through a formal investigation of the history that we live—this is what Sartre calls his regressive analysis of the formal conditions of history.

2.3.3 The Pervasion of Seriality

This leads us to what is perhaps the most unique aspect of our investigation so far. Outside of few exceptions, readers of *CDR* get trapped in the simple abstract moments of the investigation.[50] They are too wedded to an orthogonal logic. That is, they read *CDR* through the Constructivist orientation. The results are that readers either emphasize praxis or objectivity (with the overwhelming majority of readers emphasizing praxis). In order to avoid this pitfall, this project will endeavor to maintain an equal footing between praxis and objectivity. However, since the majority of literature expositing or engaging with *CDR* spends the majority of time on the freedom of praxis, the irruption of the group out of serial conditions, and the pessimism of group life as it falls back into seriality, the rest of this chapter will take a different approach. These will be the final preparatory remarks before we begin the formal exegesis of *CDR* that will reveal the underlying logical structure of the formal abstractions of Volume One.

Thomas Flynn claims that, "The two most significant conceptual innovations in the *Critique* are the practico-inert and the mediating third."[51] By contrast, the present claim is that the single most significant conceptual innovation is "seriality." In order to give this notion its due exposition, by the end of this chapter, it may seem that the pendulum has swung from the "primacy of praxis" to the "primacy of seriality." However, this is not the case. The purpose in focusing on seriality is to problematize the historical situation to its utmost so that the stakes of political action can be properly understood in their urgency. And the notion of seriality is a very keen notion in revealing the depth of alienation that inheres in bodies and that impinges upon social, political, and economic life. This is where the term *Kaironic Seriality* becomes useful.

As will be explained further in the chapters 3 and 4, Sartre's notion of seriality has both diachronic and synchronic characteristics. "Inhumans" find themselves conditioned by varying degrees and intensities of seriality based on temporal activities and structural realities. Moving from one series to the next is not a simple, linear activity whereby the serial ties are cut off from one *statut* to the next. Rather, the intensive variations of horizontal and vertical serial complexity are so replete that seriality is not a minor fact that threatens human freedom in flashes or instants. It is the very truth of our existence—this is what is meant by Kaironic Seriality. We live in an age of serial alienation under capitalist hegemony. Like total depravity in Calvinist theology, seriality pierces each person and threatens each group to their constitutive cores. However, this is where the similarity with Calvinism ends. For in the latter, God is required to have chosen the elect from eternity past in order to redeem them from the sure fate of eternal separation from Godself. Sartre requires no appeal to transcendence. Instead, it is the exigency, terror, and rage that arises from the impossibility of living under serial conditions that sparks the apocalypse. Life lived in Kaironic Seriality therefore also means that it is always the opportune time to act. And this apocalypse is what opens up space for "a new and positive humanism,"[52] one that will foreclose how praxis can resist the pressures of anti-dialectical rationality in the establishment of an authentic dialectical reason.

Since therefore Volume One of *CDR* is a prolegomena to any future anthropology, and further, since Sartre was seeking to ground an historical and structural anthropology, the most productive way to read *CDR* is as a *formal, logical investigation into the grounds by which we might be able to develop new humanisms*. That is, it is a hypo-logical investigation into the social and historical, in order to ground the development of ways by which humans *might come to exist*. Since, for the Sartre of the *Critique*, humanity does not exist, Volume One provides reasons *why* humanity does not exist (Kaironic Seriality) and provides tools for thinking through *how* humanity could come to exist under conditions of scarcity. In short: dialectical reason is made intelligible through the articulation of the prospects for the emergence of humanity.

Therefore, the rest of part I will proceed from where Sartre ended *CDR*: *in media res*. Because the first volume of *CDR* is the regressive analysis of the regressive-progressive method, it is appropriate to read it somewhat out of order, backwards even at times. As discussed above, many commentators misinterpret the extent of the logic of group formation because they are stuck within an orthogonal logic. Also, they often approach the text as though

Sartre were developing an historical or linear theory of the emergence of institutions. This was clearly not his intent, nor does it provide the most fruitful orientation for mining the depths of the theoretical content provided. Instead, Sartre was looking at alienation and institutional oppression all around him. He then regressively worked backwards to unpack the complex pluridimensionality of social relations so as to break them up into intelligible components. Thus, what Sartre develops in *CDR* is what he calls a "living logic of action," with the purpose being that political action (as dialectical rationality) could be understood, grounded in real material conditions, and wielded appropriately against the suppressive forces of alienation and the violent instruments of oppression. Now, it is crucial to turn to the key components of this living logic of action so that we can understand precisely what Sartre saw as the formal conditions of an historical and structural anthropology.

NOTES

1. Frantz Fanon, quoted in Robert Bernasconi, "Fanon's *The Wretched of the Earth* as the Fulfillment of Sartre's *Critique of Dialectical Reason*," Sartre Studies International, 16, no. 2 (2010): 37.
2. This is not to imply that the projects are the same in their individual content, but that each for-itself is stuck within the in-itself/for-itself relation, with all the resultant phenomenological effects this implies.
3. Charles Taylor, *Hegel* (Cambridge: Cambridge University Press, 1975), parts II and V.
4. Jean-Paul Sartre, *Search for a Method*, trans. Hazel Barnes (New York: Alfred A. Knopf, 1963), 93.
5. Juliette Simont, "*The Critique of Dialectical Reason*: From Need to Need, Circularly," *Yale French Studies*, no. 68 (1985): 113.
6. Karl Marx, *The Eighteenth Brumaire of Louis Bonaparte*, trans. D. D. L. [1897] (New York: Mondial, 2005), 10.
7. Sartre, *CDR*, 97.
8. Ibid., 27–29. Later he clarifies that he isn't in a position to absolutely deny or affirm whether nature might be itself dialectical, but that this isn't his concern for understanding dialectical reason: "if there is such a thing as a dialectical reason, it is revealed and established in and through human *praxis*, to men in a given society at a particular moment of its development." Ibid., 33.
9. Ibid., 127.
10. Ibid., 124.
11. Jean-Paul Sartre, *Being and Nothingness*, trans. and ed. Hazel Barnes (New York: Washington Square Press, 1993), 195.
12. Ronald Aronson, *Jean-Paul Sartre: Philosophy in the World* (London: Verso, 1980).
13. Pietro Chiodi, *Sartre and Marxism*, trans. Kate Soper (Sussex: The Harvester Press, 1976), 49.
14. Ibid., 56.
15. Sartre's use of "apocalypse" is derived from Malraux and has very little to do with eschatological notions that are found in monotheistic theological formulations. Instead, it is better understood in the literal sense of the term as being a "revealing" or "appearing" (*CDR*, 357). See also Badiou, *PP*, 19.
16. Chiodi, *Sartre and Marxism*, 68.
17. Fredric Jameson, "Foreword," in Sartre *CDR*, xxxii.

18. Sartre, *CDR*, 439.

19. The first two of these points will be addressed in part I, with the third addressed in part II.

20. Nina Power, "The Terror of Collectivity: Sartre's Theory of Political Groups," *Prelom*, 8 (2006): 102.

21. Benny Lévy, "Today's Hope: Conversations with Sartre," *Telos*, 44 (1980).

22. For a detailed and nuanced account of the controversy, see Ronald Aronson, "Sartre's Last Words," *Hope Now: The 1980 Interviews* (Chicago: University of Chicago Press, 1996). Aronson is critical of what he calls the "asymmetrical" relation between the aged Sartre and Lévy. For a more sympathetic account, see Ronald E. Santoni, "In Defense of Lévy and 'Hope Now': A Minority View," *Sartre Studies International* 4, no. 2 (1998): 61–68. And also see Jean-Pierre Boulé, "Revisiting the Sartre/Lévy Relationship," *Sartre Studies International*, 4, no. 2 (1998): 54–60.

23. This is discussed fully in chapter 5.

24. This phrasing is important because it highlights that neither history nor anthropology are supplemental to the other term. To speak of history is to speak of anthropology, and vice versa.

25. Sartre, *CDR*, 69.

26. Peter Caws, "Sartrean Structuralism?," in *Cambridge Companion to Sartre*, ed. Christina Howells (Cambridge: Cambridge University Press, 1992), 294.

27. In this notion of "orthogonal reciprocity," I am also including Thomas Flynn's extremely influential reading of *CDR* that claims that it must be read through the lens of a "primacy of praxis." See Thomas Flynn, *Sartre and Marxist Existentialism* (Chicago: University of Chicago Press, 1984). This reading has influenced a great many commentators, including Elizabeth Butterfield, *Sartre and Posthumanist Humanism* (Frankfurt: Peter Lang, 2012) and Kristian Klockars, *Sartre's Anthropology as a Hermeneutics of Praxis* (Aldershot, UK: Ashgate, 1998)—among many others. As we will elaborate further in this chapter, there is no primacy of praxis in *CDR*. Granted, praxis is one absolute that is irreducible. However, the other absolute of objectivity is also "primary." Therefore, it is better to avoid using any language of primacy that would give prominence to either praxis or the situation, as each term of the dialectic is dependent upon the other and co-constituting of the other in their internal relationality.

28. See for example, István Mészáros, *The Work of Sartre: Search for Freedom and the Challenge of History* (New York: Monthly Review Press, 2012). For Mészáros, Sartre's notion of scarcity precludes the possibility for any liberatory political action. We will engage with this criticism (and others in a similar vein) throughout this chapter and in chapter 5.

29. It is quite unnecessary to examine the supposed motivations behind these misreadings, at least for our present purposes. What matters then is identifying what readings are less than maximal in presenting us with the necessary tools for developing an imaginative logic of action within a faithful reading of *CDR* in relation to Sartre's oeuvre and then making the appropriate corrections to establish a more fruitful reading that will enable broad applicability.

30. Andrew Dobson, *Jean-Paul Sartre and the Politics of Reason* (Cambridge: Cambridge University Press, 1993), 83.

31. This might be a rhetorical overstatement. I'm not sure there is such a thing as neutrality. But my point is to wrest *CDR* from the clutches of pessimistic over-determination by demonstrating the fluidity of the powers of seriality and the subsequent reasons for the perpetual potential for the dissolution of seriality, which then curbs the pessimistic reading in favor of one that sees *CDR* as a tool with greater applicability.

32. Sartre, *CDR*, 679.

33. Raymond Aron, *History and the Dialectic of Violence: An Analysis of Sartre's Critique de la Raison Dialectique*, trans. Barry Cooper (Oxford: Basil Blackwell, 1975), 200.

34. Ibid., 202 and 210.

35. Edouard Sir-Morot, "Sartre's *Critique of Dialectical Reason*," *Journal of the History of Ideas*, 22, no. 4 (1961): 575.

36. Jean-Paul Sartre, *Critique of Dialectical Reason*: Volume Two, ed. Arlette Elkaim-Sartre, trans. Quintin Hoare (London: Verso, 2006), 431.

37. Nina Power, "From Theoretical Antihumanism to Practical Humanism: The Political Subject in Sartre, Althusser and Badiou" (PhD thesis, University of Warwick, 2007), 84.

38. Ibid., 199, note 509.
39. Sartre, *CDR*, 183.
40. Ibid., 152.
41. Ibid., 754.
42. Nik Farrell Fox, *The New Sartre: Explorations in Postmodernism* (London: Continuum, 2003), 4. Also see Christina Howells, *Sartre: The Necessity of Freedom* (Cambridge: Cambridge University Press, 1988).
43. Thomas Flynn, *Sartre, Foucault, and Historical Reason*, Volume One: *Toward an Existentialist Theory of History* (Chicago: The University of Chicago Press, 1997), 119.
44. Lévi-Strauss, *The Savage Mind*, 256.
45. Sartre, *CDR*, Vol. 2, 13.
46. Ibid., 8.
47. Ibid., 11.
48. Lévi-Strauss, *The Savage Mind*, 256.
49. Rump, "Lévi-Strauss, Barthes, and the 'Structuralist Activity' of Sartre's Dialectical Reason," 6.
50. Two notable recent exceptions are Elizabeth Butterfield, *Sartre and Posthumanist Humanism*, and Matthew Ally, *Ecology and Existence*.
51. Flynn, *Sartre, Foucault and Historical Reason*, Vol. 1, 125.
52. Sartre, *CDR*, Vol. 2.

Chapter Three

The Field of Possibles

The Practico-Inert and the Exigency of Objective Conditions

"A materialist dialectic will be meaningless if it cannot establish, within human history, the primacy of material conditions as they are discovered by the praxis of particular men and as they impose themselves on it."
—Jean-Paul Sartre[1]

This chapter inaugurates our hypo-logical, Paradoxico-Critical reading of *CDR*. We investigate terms that are familiar to the scholarship on the text, but do so by concentrating on central, overlooked components of the overall dialectical flow of Sartre's investigation. For readers less familiar with the internal debates on *CDR* reception, the hope is that this will also serve as an introduction to a productive reading that will cover familiar concerns in the larger political philosophical landscape.

Section 3.1 examines the logic of scarcity as a human fact. We explore how Sartre conceptualizes scarcity as both necessary and created. And then we close the section by examining how the human fact of scarcity re-conceptualizes the human in *CDR* as *inhuman*. Section 3.2 then works through the often overlooked distinction between worked matter and the practico-inert. We start by revealing the logic of worked matter as the passive motor of history, before explaining that, through the limits and demands introduced through signification, the practico-inert is the basic mediatory force of totalization. Section 3.3 introduces the two ways the practico-inert functions as mediator: 1) exigency and 2) seriality. The purpose of this section is to present the logic of exigency that impinges upon praxis through the introduction of alienation (i.e., seriality). We advance the idea that it is the return of stolen praxis that sets the limits and demands of exigency that underpin the logic of seriality. As the lead-in quote to this chapter indicates, this helps us understand the qualities of the material conditions that are encountered by praxis. This will help set the terms for the further elaboration of the dialectical relation between praxis and material conditions in chapter 4, where we fully investigate the logic of pluridimensional seriality.

3.1 SCARCITY AS A HUMAN FACT

Scarcity is *not* an ontological fact. This is crucial to understand. It is not the original sin of the world that presents a natural lack as an indomitable force of Nature. Rather, scarcity, for Sartre, is a *contingent* fact of history. Granted, it is a *fact* of our history. But nevertheless, scarcity must not be treated with metaphysical or essential ontological significance that makes it a monstrous power that cannot be defeated. As Sartre makes clear, scarcity is a human fact rather than the "malignity of a cruel Nature."[2] What does this mean, that "scarcity is a human fact"? Elizabeth Butterfield explains this nicely for us:

> As long as we are free, we are changing, and we are never satisfied, whole, or complete. Scarcity therefore arises from the fact that in our freedom, humans always demand more. In this way, we *create* a field of scarcity around us. Sartre is not implying that scarcity does not arise from actual objective lacks in the environment; some lacks really do exist. But it is our human projects which interpret these lacks in terms of our needs and desires, defining the field around us as "scarce" in some way. For this reason, Sartre understands scarcity to be a contingent human fact, and not the evil of a cruel Nature.[3]

In this quote, we encounter two crucial points for understanding Sartre's notion of scarcity: 1) scarcity is *created* and 2) scarcity is *necessary*.

3.1.1 Scarcity Is Necessary

The extent to which scarcity is necessary is understood, first, through the relation of the biological organism to basic material needs: hunger and thirst. Second, scarcity is necessary in that our particular history is one that is only understood as a history driven by the conflicts arising within the milieu of scarcity. As Butterfield was quoted above, "[Some] lacks really do exist. But it is our human projects which interpret these lacks in terms of our needs and desires." That is, as basic biological organisms, there are needs that arise based on lack. But this lack itself is something that developed in two ways: 1) in terms of our embeddedness and connectivity with the material environment in which we find ourselves; and 2) because of the ways in which human beings have totalized the material environment at each point of the dialectical flow of history (and ultimately because of the accumulating results of this movement over long periods of time).

This can't be reduced to mere psychological longing based on unsatisfied desires (although psychological longing is a result of the milieu of scarcity). Nor is scarcity a fact of subjective constitution (at least in the first instance). Sartre rejects any notions of human nature that might make scarcity an essential identity-marker of the human condition. Scarcity does get interiorized and human beings become "scarce men" and "men of scarcity." But this interiorization is not a fundamental lack of the human being, but rather the result of living life mediating materiality. Thus, it is best to understand the logic of scarcity as being a *relational fact* that exists as a mediatory result developed over time, in *this* history. In Sartre's words, scarcity is what has made us *"these* particular individuals producing *this* particular History."[4] Again, Sartre emphasizes both the necessity and the contingency of scarcity.

This history is the *de facto* result of scarcity, insofar as (in)humans in scarce material conditions have produced it as such. This is the typical dialectical language that tends to spin readers of *CDR* in circles. But it ought not do so. What Sartre is developing is not so much foundational universals, but rather seeking to give explanatory power to the concrete, material conditions of this historical experience. And in relation to scarcity, what Sartre wants to focus on is the ways in which scarcity conditions our relations with others and with nature. Therefore, Sartre is making a similar move as his parry in *BN* when he refused to do metaphysics in favor of phenomenological ontology; except in *CDR* he hesitates to develop a social ontology in favor of a formal investigation into the logic of would-be social ontologies. The result is that he defines scarcity's necessity, not as being a fundamental fact of the state of Nature or Being, but rather scarcity becomes a *necessary formal construct* that can aid social theorists in understanding the conflictual nature of social reality. And he is content to let it lie there.

3.1.2 Scarcity Is Created

Scarcity is also *created*. This is a unique point that Butterfield rightly emphasizes. This is not merely to say that scarcity is contingent. To say that scarcity is created is to say that scarcity is a social construction. That is, scarcity, as a logical, formal condition of human relations, is a condition that is created by the perpetual totalizing flow of the dialectic. It is formal in that it serves as a window by which the landscape of the material field is viewed. It directs our view through a particular lens, inscribing and sorting the *hyle* of the field of significations. And it is logical in the Sartrean sense of being a constitutive component of the living logic of action—i.e., as an expression of the intensive variation of totalization. Sartre says it is "a certain moment of human relations, which is constantly being transcended and partially destroyed, but which is always being reborn."[5] This is crucial, because what Sartre is effectively saying is that scarcity *as such* is not an ontological precondition so much as it is constantly being reproduced through totalization. It is praxis that reconstitutes scarcity in its efforts to transcend the present situation of scarcity, only to then reconstitute scarcity anew in the next moment of objectification. Thus, from objectification to objectification, scarcity is being transformed and reproduced based on the multiplicities that are being transformed and reproduced in praxis's aiming toward the possible in its creative project.

Sartre does muse about the possibilities of alien species or other practical organisms living in conditions outside of scarcity: "relations of immediate abundance between other practical organisms and other milieux are not inconceivable *a priori*."[6] However, such ideas are merely speculative and theoretical, and therefore they do not really concern him in understanding the formal conditions of *this* history. Thomas Flynn suggests that Sartre leaves room for theorizing about a possible "socialism of abundance."[7] For Flynn, sustained freedom is only possible under such conditions.[8] However, for Sartre, in a world without scarcity "our quality as men [would disappear] and since this quality is historical, the actual specificity of our History would disappear too."[9] Thus, scarcity is what has defined us as "men" (or as "humanity"—as these terms are interchangeable "according to taste" for Sartre). Thus, a post-scarcity world would be a world in which "humanity" itself would be re-created/re-cast as something other than what it is and has been in *this* history. Likewise, history itself would be other, for *this* history is and has been characterized in relation to scarcity. Therefore, a post-scarcity world would be a new "history," with a new "humanity."

3.1.3 The Man of Scarcity: The Inhuman

Considering we are in *this* history, the whole of (in)human development must be understood in relation to scarcity. Scarcity explains fundamental structures, institutions, and techniques, "not in the sense that it is real and that it has produced them, but because they were produced in the *milieu of scarcity* by men whose *praxis* interiorises this scarcity even when they try to transcend it."[10] The result is that the history of humanity—in the milieu of scarcity—is the history of "non-human man."[11] "Man" is non-human, not merely in a theoretical sense, or in a relation of exterior social relations (although such do hold). But more emphatically, "man" is non-human because of one's interiorization of the conditions of scarcity through totalization, which then come to mark each *inhuman body* as beings defined by scarcity in themselves. One can almost be excused for thinking that ontologically non-humans are imbued with scarcity. Sartre makes it clear, however, that this non-humanity is not a depletion of some pre-existent human nature to which humans must return. Rather, non-humanity is only understood through a negative differential relation to the concept of "humanity," as not in fact being that which is called "human."

It is, therefore, a negative designation based on the negation of the image(s) of the human that are proffered in philosophical, anthropological, and scientific discourses. It is curious to note, however, that most of these designations are themselves negative definitions, separating the human from what they are not (ex. humans are not animals). Concerning these discourses, Adam Kotsko has remarked that, "the procedure is to place humanity in a general category and then single out the distinctive trait that marks us off from other members of that category. One popular definition along these lines is that humanity is an animal (the general category) that possesses reason (the distinctive trait)."[12] Therefore, according to this model, the human is that animal that is superior precisely in its negative differential relation to the field of all other animals who do not possess this essential trait (as has been inscribed by humans drawing the lines in the first place—think: Constructivist orientation). Essentially, the human's identity *as human* is therefore an essentialization of a negative trait that is constructed according to analytical reason.

Kotsko continues, however, by offering an alternative framing for understanding the concept of the human:

> this brings me to another classic definition of the human from Aristotle, namely that the human being is a political animal. This definition, like the ones drawn from Agamben, has nothing to do with the "content" of our lives, which does not necessarily differ from that of animals, but instead concerns its "form"—our relationship to our own activities, capacities, and fellow human beings. We are human because we form human communities, in which we give ourselves a variety of tasks and responsibilities, by means of human languages that we pass on and teach to other human beings. The human being is the animal that engages with humans, as a human. This definition is admittedly tautological, but it is tautological in a way that fits with the human form of existence. *Humanity is not a property we possess or a substance that we are made out of, but an ongoing project undertaken in collaboration with other human beings.* [Emphasis added][13]

It is that final sentence that best summarizes how we are to understand Sartre's re-conception of the logic of the (in)human in *CDR*. It is the ongoing project of totalization in a milieu of scarcity that is paradoxically both form and matter, structure and history that characterizes the logic of the (in)human. Therefore, if the concept of the human, as constructed by analytical reason, is actually an essentialization of an original negation, then there must be a negation of this negative designation of the human.

To summarize, once more, we turn to Kotsko: "Humanity does define humanity wrongly, and the only solution is for more human beings to become involved in the fight for the full recognition of their fellow human beings' humanity. What basis do we have to dispute the reigning definition of humanity? Our own ability to recognize ourselves and others as human."[14] In other words, in order to be able to understand humanity (i.e., for praxis to be translucid to itself), we must acquire the tools necessary for comprehension. Until then, comprehension is marred by the serial rationality of "men of scarcity." Therefore, rather than view the inhuman as an ontological category, it is more proper to understand it in its heuristic capacity as a Paradoxico-Critical formal designator that indicates how and why scarcity marks humans as inhuman. To fully understand this, we need to understand how inhumans reproduce serial thoughts and feelings in anti-dialectical rationality. This will be the subject of chapter 4. For now, let us make a note to remember that Sartre's problematization and novel re-conception of the human in *CDR* is as man of scarcity—the inhuman.

3.2 WORKED MATTER, THE PRACTICO-INERT, AND THE EMERGENCE OF EXIGENCY

There is an oft missed distinction betwees worked matter and the practico-inert. The practico-inert is that intractable inertia that arises from others' praxis on worked matter. Although the distinction is slight, it is important to note that worked matter, as such, is not an alienating mode of being. If it were, then all praxis would lead to alienation (à la Hegel's notion of objectification). But this isn't the case for Sartre. Objectification in itself is not alienating. It is only when confronted by the mass of stored labor from others, culture, past history, etc., that "matter" becomes alienating—that is, as practico-inert.

3.2.1 The Logic of Worked Matter

In itself, worked matter "functions as an inert universal memory [that] records and conserves the forms impressed on it by earlier labour."[15] It is the material fingerprint of (in)human activity upon the material world. Worked matter, therefore, is an abstract notion that designates the ways in which matter stores praxis, preserving it in itself as the new objective mediation that (in)humans encounter at each moment of totalizing praxis. Sartre does not have a term for matter that is non-worked. All matter for him is worked matter. This makes obvious sense in cultural environments, where material objects are tools of past labor that persons employ in their perpetual activities to create new tools or work upon material environments. The hammer, for instance, is an obvious worked tool. In itself, it bears the past praxis of the craftsman or the machines that built it. When a person uses this hammer, she is using an already-worked material device. She can either use this tool to create other tools (for example, hammer the metal basin of a wheelbarrow back into proper shape), or she can perform a more streamlined task of hammering a nail into a board. Of course, the uses are far more extensive than just these two examples. However, these examples serve to show two categories of use for worked tools: 1) to work on worked matter in a simple unilateral relation or 2) to worked on a tool that itself will become a tool for future use.

However, understanding natural environments is where Sartre's idea becomes a bit more complex. For Sartre, all matter has already been "worked." In what is an indication of an idealism that remains in his project, Sartre claims, "If it is true that matter effects an initial union between men, this can only be *to the extent that* man has already made a practical attempt to unify it, and that it has passively received the seal of that unity."[16] In other words, there is no conception of "nature" in the typically modernist sense whereby there is a split between the world of humans and the pure world of nature, for nature itself has already been worked. One way of thinking about this is with regard to rainfall. Rain can be seen as a natural phenomenon. However, within the Sartrean paradigm, rainfall is already worked matter. From the chemicals in the air that affect its acidity, to the regional gathering techniques in locations around the globe, rainfall can only be understood as being a product of past praxis. Likewise, the oceans on the face of the Earth are polluted with oil and agricultural farming runoff; they are charted on maps to signal paths between continents; they are named and divided up into national territories and international waters respectively; they have been the sites of military conflict; they have been plundered for resources—and all of this *modifies* (i.e., works) the material space.

What is more, in this perpetual modifying and unifying moment of totalization, the limits and demands of how matter can be modified are established by material exigency calling forth to praxis. As was quoted in the previous paragraph, this is what Sartre means when he claims that matter effects an initial union between humans "*to the extent that* man has already made a practical attempt to unify it." It is the "to the extent" that causes pause. This is because the *extent* by which matter unifies humans in totalization is established by the limits and demands that have been infused into matter as the counter-final conditions set by past praxis. And this setting is the "seal of that unity"—i.e., the practico-inert. Therefore, the *logic of worked matter* reveals it to be a "passive synthesis whose unity conceals a molecular dispersal [which] conditions the totalisation of organisms whose deep bonds of interiority cannot be masked by their dispersal. This synthesis, therefore, represents the material condition of historicity. At the same time, it is what might be called the passive motor of History."[17] It is this "molecular dispersal" (and the limits and demands it issues) that Sartre calls the practico-inert. It is only by first understanding the basic logic of worked matter as the *passive motor* that the practico-inert becomes intelligible as the *active motor* that (metaphorically) conditions lived experience in accordance with the logic of worked matter.

3.2.2 The Logic of the Practico-Inert

There is a real sense in which matter, as objectified praxis, takes from individuals their "temperature" (*la chaud*).[18] This temperature could also be called their impetus, their vitality. And as such, it pacifies bodies by making them inert in relation to the external inertia, as the former exteriorizes itself as an inert object to comport itself with the instrument. In this sense, there is a "transubstantiation" between matter and praxis, a *chassé-croisé* where praxis takes on the inhuman inertia of matter at the same time that matter takes on the vitality of praxis. This cross-contamination results in the construction of the practico-inert field when other transubstantiated praxis-inertias are synthesized into a static totality. Therefore, the practico-inert field is replete with indefinite amounts, intensities, and variations of *la chaud*. As Elizabeth Butterfield states, "[Unlike] being-in-itself, the practico-inert is not separate from free human praxis—just the opposite: the practico-inert bears the marks of praxis through and through, as it is invested with human meanings."[19]

Returning to the example of the hammer for a moment, once we understand the practico-inert as the "seal of unity" replete with its own limits and demands stored from past praxis that return in counter-finality to present praxis, then we begin to understand how the logic of the practico-inert differs than the logic of worked matter. It is through considering the constellation of significations that inhere within the hammer that articulate how the tool uniquely exerts its powers of mediation. The hammer is not presented as an already-worked *Gestalt* device bearing the past praxis of craftsmanship and/or machinic labor. More than this, the entire history of hammer craftsmanship is contained therein, along with all the meanings, values, potential uses, past uses, and expected future uses; plus all the forbidden activities (ex. don't use a hammer on screws), non-standard uses (ex. in an art piece or a shabby-chic photo spread), nefarious uses (ex. as a weapon), etc. It is this field of significations that forms the logic of counter-finality that haunts praxis's engagement with the practico-inert field.

It is paramount, therefore, that we understand *that* and *how* the practico-inert field becomes the fundamental realm of sociality for Sartre.[20] Inhuman actors, in the milieu of scarcity, are "united" through mediatory relations conditioned by the practico-inert field. At the same time, matter is mediated by the praxical relations of inhuman actors as they seek to overtake (*dépasse-

ment) their present *statut* in aiming toward future possibilities. In this future-oriented activity, praxis interiorizes the practico-inert situation, appropriates it, makes it one's own ("freely"), and then re-exteriorizes it through objectification. This new objectification becomes the new practico-inert *statut* that will in turn be re-interiorized by praxis and subsequently re-exteriorized. This division between interiorization and exteriorization must be understood as an abstract delineation, for in practice, the activity takes place simultaneously at varying velocities of appropriation and flight. As such, to speak of it as though it were a temporal, sequential process is a metaphorical device to establish the internal logic of totalization.

There is another element, however, that we need to grasp at this point: the *resuscitating power* of the interiorization of totalization. That is, not only does worked matter have the power to mineralize the vitality of praxis and then synthesize it into the practico-inert field, but praxis, in the same totalizing movement, breathes *life* into the stored praxis in the practico-inert field. The reason we can speak of it as coming to life is because the reader of a book, for example, appropriates the mineralized praxis of the author as a moment of her praxis (which itself is life), thus resuscitating the inert praxis in a new mode, a mode that now belongs to the praxis (i.e., life) of the reader—this is why Sartre refers to it as *practico*-inert. When this is done, counter-finality has been introduced, for even if the author's intended goal was to have the piece written and read, one's specific interiorization of the written piece as a moment of totalization is unique to her project, and as such, is counter-final to the ends of the original praxis-project. Thus, there is both life and death, both human and inhuman in totalization at every step. It is only in the abstract that we can separate these "moments" of the dialectic and speak of them as moments of totalization; in reality, they occur simultaneously as shifting variations of intensity. Underlying this process is a theory of time and space that is beyond the scope of the present project. Suffice it to say, for now, that Sartre is attempting to develop spatio-temporal concepts that are themselves calcified derivations of the process of becoming. Even in his later work, he never wavered from his commitment to *becoming* over and against *being* as a primary ontological characteristic. Thus, the simultaneity of the moments of the dialectic must be held in tension: they are both unique in their role within totalization and also indistinguishable except through theoretical abstraction. The goal, as ever, for Sartre is to avoid what we might call "violent abstraction" in the pursuit of developing productive, lived, formal abstractions.

Thus, once the practico-inert is understood as both *practico* and *inert*, its logic as the basic mediator of social relations becomes useful. Next, we explore the two ways practico-inert functions as a mediator: 1) in exigency and 2) in seriality. The former creates the conditions of the latter; the practico-inert is the logic that grounds both and reveals their intelligibility; and the entire logical chain is what threatens social existence with perpetual alienation.

3.3 EXIGENCY AND THE DEMANDS OF RETURNED PRAXIS

> "Is it still necessary to state that not technology, not technique, not the machine are the engines of repression, but the presence, in them, of the masters who determine their number, their life span, their power, their place in life, and the need for them?"
>
> —Herbert Marcuse[21]

3.3.1 Need and Organic Subjectivity

Early in *CDR*, Sartre claims that, "Everything is to be explained through need."[22] For him, need is the basic motivation of action.

> [Need] is the first totalising relation between the material being, man, and the material ensemble of which he is part. This relation is *univocal* and *of interiority*. . . . Need is a negation of the negation in so far as it expresses itself as a *lack* within the organism; and need is a positivity in so far as the organic totality tends to preserve itself *as such* through it.[23]

In relation to the need of the organism, the material environment presents itself as an infinite field of possibilities of satisfaction. In this sense, Sartre seems to preserve at least some semblance of his earlier notions of freedom from *Transcendence of the Ego*, *Being and Nothingness*, and *Existentialism Is a Humanism*. However, it must be kept in mind that at this stage in his investigation he is using simple abstract concepts so that he can build his accumulating dialectical investigation toward the more complex and lived abstractions of dialectical reason. What is important about his understanding of need at this stage of his argument is the logical framework that it establishes between a basic understanding of individual praxis and the material conditions within which praxis totalizes. This basic understanding is what Kenneth Anderson refers to as "organic subjectivity."[24]

However, "organic subjectivity" is only Sartre's foray into his investigation of the relation between praxis and the objective material conditions in which praxis acts. Another way of saying this is that, at the outset of his investigation, Sartre uses the notion of need in this simple manner so that he can start his discussion and then complicate it further, leading to its eventual transformation in a more concrete and complex phase of the dialectical investigation. This occurs through the introduction of signification in the concept of the practico-inert. Like a folded extension ladder that gets one to the second floor and is then brought up to help climb to the next level once the second floor is reached, so too is the basic formulation of the term "need" preserved at the next stage of investigation. However, if the gap between the second and third floors is greater than that between the first and second, this requires that the extension ladder unfold and extend in proportion to the limits and demands of the task. Similarly, this requires that the conceptual tools used to reach the next stage of analysis transform in the unfolding moments of the dialectical investigation. This does not mean that a notion of organic subjectivity is itself discarded. Rather, praxis must be understood in every level of abstraction and complexity as the various levels inhere within one another in a given body. Therefore, an individual is at the same time organic, serial, and common to varying degrees of intensity, at various times.

3.3.2 Ethical Motivation and the Role of Exigency in the Practico-Inert

Sartre acknowledges the layers of complexity that circle around his unfolding investigation when he notes in these early pages that this basic notion of need is "ignoring for the moment the collective constraints" that define concrete need in its historical, material reality.[25] The reason he finds this approach valid is that it first establishes the basic logic that governs his understanding of need. And this logic is that of *ethical motivation*. That is, need is the basic cry of an organic subject that acts and moves in the milieu of scarcity, overcoming its present situation in seeking to satisfy a perceived lack. This is the basic (organic) motivation of praxis: to transcend the present *statut*, in aiming toward a future-not-yet-realized, in order to satisfy a need. It is this organic tendency that transfigures his earlier phenomenological understanding of intentionality. Quoting Butterfield, "[The] experience of needs leads us to constitute the world as a place in which something *must* be done—or, morally speaking, in which something *ought* to be done . . . 'true morality' arises from the most fundamental human needs, and makes progress toward an ideal future of 'integral humanity.'"[26] Therefore, what is most useful in Sartre's formal investigation into organic subjectivity is that there is an indomitable ethical spirit at the core of the (in)human condition.

That said, this so-called "ethical spirit" is rendered effectively impotent. It is buried under layers of alienation. The reason this ethical spirit is impotent is because of the mediatory particularities of the practico-inert field. If history weren't lived under conditions of scarcity, and if relations between humans weren't mediated by the practico-inert field, it would be possible to speak more fruitfully about a free ethical spirit in which human actors could seek ethical ends. However, because of the *de facto* state of affairs, there are demands that are placed upon (in)humanity that determine the conditions of their actions. This is what is meant by *exigency*.

As was mentioned at the end of the section 3.2, there are two ways the practico-inert functions as a mediator. The first of these ways is exigency.

For Sartre, in order to understand need in the abstract, we must first understand how praxis is subordinated to the field of exigencies. This field presents the demands placed upon praxis that predestine the possibilities for the (in)human in any given situation. As he states,

> [In] so far as [one] is dominated by matter, his activity is no longer directly derived from need, although this remains its fundamental basis: it is *occasioned in him*, from the outside, by worked matter, the practical exigency of the inanimate object. In other words, the object designates its man as one who is *expected to behave* in a certain way. [Emphasis added][27]

Let us especially reflect on the clauses "occasioned in him" and "expected to behave." In a very simple sense, these can be understood in terms of pure functionality. An object has a limited array of options for its use. These options are imposed on a potential user and ultimately dictate the way(s) in which the user can operate with the object. Of course, the user can always create new ways of using the object—this is the freedom of praxis. However, there is an inscribed set of parameters that impinge upon the freedom of the user. Objects, of course, impose varying strengths of varying demands. These options are the result of manifold possibilities: size, quantity, legal parameters, cultural expectations, personal pleasure, etc. But the important point, for Sartre, is that these exigencies exist 1) as a limit, 2) as a demand, and that 3) these limits and demands are themselves interiorized by praxis in totalization. This is how scarcity is interiorized through the mediatory role of the practico-inert. The human fact of scarcity, introduced through the limits and demands of counter-final significatory exigencies, is taken up as part of one's praxis-project in totalization. With every act of interiorization-exteriorization, new exigencies are inscribed into the object as the limits and demands it enforces are perpetually modifed. In Sartre's words, individuals "interiorise the exigency of matter and re-exteriorise it as the exigency of man."[28]

This must not be taken as dire hopelessness. According to Thomas Flynn, although it is true that exigency "restricts the effective choices which lie open to . . . praxis," it is also the case that exigencies "generate solidarity as they convey responsibility"[29]—again, an appeal to the ethical spirit. With this, Flynn introduces both a foreclosure and a disclosure of freedom within the logic of exigency. It has a bivalent nature. It both limits freedom by placing demands upon praxis, and also calls forth to praxis, beckoning it to come—to transcend one's present *statut* in solidarity with those who are experiencing the common demands of the practico-inert field. Thus, without jumping too far ahead, but also hinting at the future of this unfolding investigation, it might be accurate to say that there are *serial exigencies* and *free exigencies*. However, in order to firmly ground these two modes of exigency, it will be crucial to develop respective logics based on a solid understanding of the depths of seriality and the power of freedom in the irruption of the apocalypse. To that end, it is first necessary to investigate the formal nature of exigency itself. That is, *why* is it that exigency demands?

3.3.3 The Logic of Exigency: The Return of Stolen Praxis

In an insightful article, Christopher Turner expounds on this very problem. Illuminating a fact that is rarely discussed in the literature, Turner states that it is the return of stolen praxis itself that confronts praxis in a new situation of exigence. He poignantly notes,

> [If] the matter that acts against the praxis of the human being is matter that has been acted upon by the human being and transformed, and if in this praxis matter has been invested with its efficaciousness by being stamped by human aims, then what really opposes human praxis is not so much matter itself, not even "processed matter," but rather human praxis itself *through* matter.[30]

Although a simple enough observation, the implications are vast and foundational for understanding the logic of exigency (and subsequently seriality) which is summed up by Sartre in this pithy quote: "Man is mediated by things to the extent that things are mediated by man."[31] For Sartre, as for Turner as well, inscribed in the matter that mediates "man" is the multiplicity of humanity. This is not an eisegetical imposition. Rather, as we have made clear throughout the project thus far, Sartre rejects the notion of the individual subject in *CDR*. In his efforts to construct a dialectical theory of "practical ensembles," we must understand *l'homme* here as referring to humanity. This does not mean that there is no room for any discussion of individual praxis. Rather, what it implies is that all individual praxis is simultaneously singular and multiple. Singular in its concrete particularity as a contracted moment of totalization, and multiple in its interiorization-exteriorization of the molecular dispersal through the practico-inert field. Therefore, worked matter becomes an alienating mediatory concept (i.e., the practico-inert) because of the presence-absence of the multiplicity of others embedded in it. In this sense, we can speak of the practico-inert as a Sartrean "image." It is a present-absence of the multiplicity of others. And like the image, it is impoverished as a totality. It is only when awakened by praxis that it becomes excessive, as free praxis appropriates the totality, brings to life the inert-praxis, and tends toward future possibles. This will be explored further in part II.

Seeking to shore up our explanation of the logic of exigency as the return of stolen praxis, let us remark that as the past praxis of others is turned against new praxes in the process of totalization through the limits and demands imposed by the practico-inert field, the exigent demands become, at once, more clearly intelligible, and simultaneously shadowed. The demands become clear in that their source has been identified: humanity. But this clarity is muddied by sheer complexity. For, this is more than a simple understanding of counter-finality. Yes, in one sense, the return of stolen praxis is understood as being counter-final. However, this haunting by past praxis means that the multiplicity that confronts praxis in the practico-inert field that conditions and mediates social life is an infinite molecular dispersal of the praxis of others. Therefore, what confronts praxis in each moment of totalization is the indefinite scope of past praxis itself. As Christina Howells succinctly states, "Human alienation and lack of individual control over history arise not because man is *not* making history but because he is not making it alone."[32]

Therefore, the logic of the practico-inert as conditioned by exigency has been made intelligible: it is precisely the return of stolen praxis that confronts praxis as a multiplicity, setting infinite limits and making infinite demands as praxis both interiorizes and overcomes the molecular dispersal of mineralized praxis saturated in a milieu of scarcity. But, the now-intelligible logic of the practico-inert only highlights the penultimate step in our articulation of the broader synthetic logic of alienation. The final step is to excavate a concept that has not received its due treatment in *CDR* scholarship—seriality. Seriality is the formal, synthetic notion that encapsulates scarcity, need, worked-matter, the practico-inert, and exigency in one. However, in Trinitarian fashion, seriality itself has a tripartite nature: diachronic, synchronic, and Kaironic. The next chapter will investigate the logic of seriality in its synthetic pluridimensionality, with the hope being that the predicament of humanity will be made intelligible, and that the germinations of its overcoming will begin to bud.

NOTES

1. Sartre, *CDR*, 33.
2. Ibid., 140, note 21.
3. Butterfield, *Sartre and Posthumanist Humanism*, 31.
4. Sartre, *CDR*, 123.
5. Ibid., 134.
6. Ibid., 735.
7. Flynn, *Sartre, Foucault and Historical Reason*, Vol. 1, 124.
8. We address fully the notion of a "socialism of abundance" and the various interlocutors that have mused about the pessimism surrounding Sartre's seemingly over-focus on scarcity in the final pages of this chapter. Here, we are content to lay down the basic understandings of the formal logic of scarcity.
9. Sartre, *CDR*, 124.
10. Ibid., 127.
11. Ibid., 130.
12. Adam Kotsko, "Insan Nedir," in Sabah Ülkesi (October 8, 2018), http://www.sabahulkesi.com/2018/10/08/insan-nedir/ (last accessed December 7, 2018). Translation

provided on author's blog: https://itself.blog/2018/10/10/what-is-human/ (last accessed December 7, 2018).
    13. Ibid.
    14. Ibid.
    15. Sartre, *CDR*, 122.
    16. Ibid., 122.
    17. Ibid., 122.
    18. Ibid., 169
    19. Butterfield, *Sartre and Posthumanist Humanism*, 28.
    20. Sartre, *CDR*, 318.
    21. Herbert Marcuse, *An Essay on Liberation* (Boston: Beacon Press, 1969), 12.
    22. Sartre, *CDR*, 80.
    23. Ibid., 80.
    24. Kenneth L. Anderson, "Transformations of Subjectivity in Sartre's *Critique of Dialectical Reason*," *Journal of Philosophical Research*, 27 (2002).
    25. Sartre, *CDR*, 80.
    26. Butterfield, *Sartre and Posthumanist Humanism*, 34.
    27. Sartre, *CDR*, 186.
    28. Ibid., 190–91.
    29. Flynn, *Sartre and Marxist Existentialism*, 82 and 83.
    30. Christopher Turner, "The Return of Stolen Praxis: Counter-Finality in Sartre's *Critique of Dialectical Reason*," *Sartre Studies International*, 20, no. 1 (2014): 39.
    31. Sartre, *CDR*, 88.
    32. Howells, *The Necessity of Freedom*, 102.

Chapter Four

Pluridimensional Seriality

"*Reality*, at the level of serial impotence, is the impossibility of living."
—Jean-Paul Sartre [1]

This chapter presents an analysis of Sartre's development of the broad term *seriality*. Although Sartre's use of the term is complex and often unclear, this chapter develops a tripartite division of conceptual terms that clarify the logic of seriality in its pluridimensionality. These terms are not Sartre's but are derived from a close reading of the variant intensities in his deployment of "seriality." *Diachronic* and *synchronic* seriality describe the variations within the alienating social force that Sartre singularly refers to as "seriality." *Kaironic Seriality* refers to Sartre's analysis of *this* history as an age of seriality and declares the impossibility of living under serial conditions any further. It both describes the Impossible and heralds the opportune moment to overcome this predicament.

At times, he does use modifiers to tinge his use of the term, but he is inconsistent in his deployment of these modifiers and doesn't spend any time developing how they function in their particular iterations. That said, the terms diachronic and synchronic do appear throughout *CDR*, mostly referring to the movement of totalization which is "both synchronic (in the ensemble of the present) and diachronic (in its human depth)."[2] However, twice Sartre does seem to attach the terms diachronic and synchronic to seriality. In the chapter "The Place of History," he remarks that, "group action is always doomed to synchronic alienation except when the practical community is identical to all the individuals in the common field; then it is doomed without qualification to diachronic alienation."[3] Here, he clearly separates the two terms intending to highlight the distinct experiences between diachronic and synchronic alienation. Teasing out the specifics of these distinct terms in their relation to seriality will be the task of sections 4.2 and 4.3.

The only other time he aligns the terms "diachronic" and "synchronic" with "seriality" is on the page prior to the previous quote where he avers that "objectified praxis must necessarily allow itself to be modified by a double alienation (both synchronic and diachronic)."[4] It is this experience of "double alienation" that is developed below as Kaironic Seriality. This term is useful in that it brings together the temporal and spatial, the singular and structural, and the horizontal and vertical dimensions that are contained within the terms diachronic and synchronic. However, whereas the latter two terms are useful only insofar as they make intelligible the distinct experiences of seriality under either lateral or vertical conditions, Kaironic Seriality fuses the two dimensions together to help us better understand the compressed nature of the Impossible, and the virtual potency articulated by the logic of the apocalypse that dissolves the alienating force of seriality. As such, Kaironic Seriality will come to be seen as the complex, polyvalent experience of alienated existence that Sartre develops through an exploration of the logic of seriality in the milieu of scarcity, and it will also indicate how it is always the opportune moment for the apocalypse to irrupt.

Section 4.1 develops the tripartite, Trinitarian logic of seriality. Understanding the plurality of dimensions to the logic of seriality is paramount if we are to grasp the extent to which the exigencies of the practico-inert field produce serial thoughts, feelings, and actions. By deepening the stakes in this way, we also unveil how and why pluridimensional seriality must be overcome.

Section 4.2 examines the logic of diachronic seriality and establishes the basic inhuman experience of competition, alterity, and inessentiality. We look at Sartre's most notable examples that articulate this foundational logic: the bus queue and the radio broadcast. This sections ends by establishing that seriality is marked by destiny, not freedom. Inhumans enter in and out of serial contexts that are prefabricated and that impose serial exigencies onto their praxis, making it an anti-praxis. This is the beginning of understanding the logic of the anti-dialectic which reveals why it is that Sartre did not believe that dialectical reason yet had at its disposal the necessary tools of comprehension.

The intensity of the logic of seriality and the tendency toward incomprehension is magnified in section 4.3, where we explore the variegating structural power of synchronic seriality. Understanding objective spirit as the "medium for the circulation of significations" will allow us to understand how synchronic seriality imposes the demands of the entirety of culture upon any and every moment of totalization. What this means is that language, thought, and the very structures of the unconscious are predestined by culture writ large. If section 4.2 elucidates human destiny as characteristic of basic serial life, then section 4.3 indicates how inhumans are structurally predestined to reproduce this inhuman existence.

The chapter ends with section 4.4, where we defend the construction of the concept Kaironic Seriality. First, we chart a conceptual narrative that defines *kairos* as both a descriptive and prescriptive concept. As descriptive, *kairos* articulates a dual sense of now and not-yet, while declaring how to identify the opportune moment to act. Betwixt between the world that is and the world that could be, *kairos* straddles concerns for both material analysis and hopeful creation. Thus, by first establishing the logic of *kairos*, we then apply it to Sartre's analysis of seriality in *CDR*. We end the chapter by asserting that it is never not the opportune time to act and signal the way forward in elucidating the conditions for embodying an art of opportune action.

4.1 THE TRIPARTITE NATURE OF SERIALITY

There is a Trinitarian logic at work in Sartre's notion of seriality. The perichoretic relationship between the diachronic, synchronic, and Kaironic ensures that violent abstraction does not deter the investigation into the formal conditions of concrete, material existence. Of course, Sartre is still wont to utilize simple abstraction for the purpose of building his dialectical argument. However, it bears to be repeated until it becomes a mainstay in Sartre studies: *CDR*'s concern with abstraction is insofar as it brings the reader from the simple to the complex, with the concepts themselves becoming more complex as the investigation unfolds. Therefore, this section will proceed in like fashion. Seriality will be examined in each of its levels of conceptual abstraction, enfolding them into one another, as each stage of the investigation progresses. In the end, the logic of seriality will reveal a robust theory of alienated social existence that will give insight into the depths of the human predicament.

The use of "human predicament" follows William Connolly's prompting in *A World of Becoming*. As he states, "A predicament is a situation lived and felt from the inside. It is also something you seek strategies to ameliorate or rise above."[5] Our use of this term is deliberate in that it provides a clear definition of the experience of living life in Kaironic Seriality and also connects us with William Connolly's work, which will be explored in part II, as we work toward building strategies to ameliorate this predicament.

Before that, however, we must begin our investigation into the logic of seriality. We start with a declarative: seriality is the social fact of alienation. It describes the unity of individuals within a social field that is conditioned by scarcity and the practico-inert. Sartre calls this "unity" a "unity of flight."[6] It describes the gathering of inhumans who are in relations of alterity in the social field. Thus, this "unity" is hardly solidarity. Returning to a point suggested by Thomas Flynn that was addressed in chapter 3, there is a sense in which exigency unites individuals. However, this unity is non-directional. That is, it is characterized as being not directed toward a unified task or goal. It does not issue forth from common, mediated praxis but emerges from *without* and is imposed *upon* praxis.

Only under particular conditions does the logic of seriality and its effects become intelligible to praxis. As we addressed in chapter 3, for Sartre, history is understood in relation to scarcity. As such, under serial conditions, in the milieu of scarcity, the logic of serial unity establishes the "human predicament." This predicament is characterized by negative reciprocal relations between inhumans. However, simultaneously, it hints at ways this predicament can be overcome.

Seriality conditions all life lived within a given social context. The extent to which persons are so conditioned—the scope of the demands that impinge on their freedom—is the subject of this section. For now, it is sufficient to note that the products of (in)human striving are all structured by a serial logic. Sartre puts it thusly, "There are serial feelings and serial thoughts; in other words a series is a mode of being for individuals both in relation to one another and in relation to their common being, and this mode of being transforms all their structures."[7] That is why it is appropriate to speak of the human predicament—the inhumanity of life on Earth—as being conditioned thoroughly by a serial logic. For, this serial logic is the very orientation that frames the relation between serial inhumans and their projects, as their projects are products of serial thoughts, feelings, and actions.

Kristian Klockars prefers to view seriality as a "typology" that makes any "concrete social field, real constellation of social formations or any society intelligible." Thus far, we are in agreement. However, he further claims that seriality only "describes society as a static field, and not on the level of practices and history in process."[8] This is precisely where Klockars fails to comprehend the perichoretic nature of the abstract variations of seriality. For Sartre, totalization is intelligible as both diachronic and synchronic. It is diachronic insofar as totalization is temporalization, and synchronic insofar as the conditions of praxis in the practico-inert field are structural. Another way of stating this is that the *diachronic* accords with micrototalization, whereas the *synchronic* accords with macrototalization. As Thomas Flynn writes,

> Sartre distinguishes *micro-* and *macrototalizations*. . . . [The] former refers to the concrete totalizing praxis of the organic individual whereas the latter denotes the social, cultural world as a network of significations occupying the space between the individual agent and physical nature, that conditions individual praxis and connects it with a web of meanings it may not have chosen.[9]

Therefore, totalization has both micro and macro components. What this means with regard to seriality is that totalization takes place under both micro and macro serial conditions. At the same time, the perichoretic nature of seriality conditions micro- and macrototalizations.

In lived, concrete praxis, however, these layers or modes are concretized into a *concrete universal*. Flynn explains that, "the concrete universal is the 'incarnation' of this web of meanings in both its temporal (diachronic) and its structural (synchronic) dimensions."[10] Incarnation is therefore the most contracted or compressed point of pluridimensional seriality. In this sense, if we might indulge a metaphor, the diachronic is the Holy Spirit, the synchronic is the Father, and the concrete universal (what we will name "Kaironic") is the Son (i.e., the incarnation, which includes both the revelation of the Truth and points toward liberation). As with the Holy Spirit, the diachronic flows through the immanent life of history. The Father is the transcendent structure that bears the laws and codes. And the Son is the *dépassement*. Comprehending this perichoretic Trinitarian logic prepares the investigation for the problematization to come. That is, in what follows, the basic components of serial logic will be unpacked and examined for their intelligibility and efficacy. The result will be that each component will be grasped in its own alienating capacities. However, in the end, once they are enfolded back into one another, a monstrosity will emerge. And the impossibility of continuing to live *inhuman* life under monstrous serial conditions will pave the way for the only hope of resurrecting *human* life.

4.2 DIACHRONIC SERIALITY

Diachronic seriality is the most basic form of the logic of seriality. It is understood as temporal and horizontal. And it produces the model of the inhuman gathering that Sartre calls the *collective*. According to Nik Farrell Fox, "[Collectives] are not substances but a set of ongoing practical relations between individuals."[11] They are understood as fleeting unities that emerge through temporal succession depending on the collective object around which a particular group of persons is united. So collectives form and reform based on the external object that unites them as a *series*. However, this object is understood as an "index of separation."[12] In other words, it imposes serial exigency upon the members of the collective. In this way, Sartre insists that the collective is "anti-dialectical."[13] As anti-dialectical, the collective is a site of isolation with others. What this means is that, for Sartre, the collective shares a common *being*; but one that alienates by uniting individuals under the forced exigence of an external Other (i.e., practico-inert object) that limits the free praxis of the individuals by making them inessential (i.e., interchangeable), conflictual, and other (i.e., every Other is other than himself and other than the Others).

4.2.1 The Bus Queue: The Logic of Basic Seriality

The most notable example that Sartre uses to describe the collective is the bus queue. In the bus queue, individuals are united by the collective object, the bus. Each has a place in the queue, a particular number that defines this person by a quantity in relation to every Other. Each person, therefore, is an Other to every other Other. Because there are a limited number of seats (scarcity), there is a conflictual relation between the members of the collective. And because each person is a mere quantity, each is replaceable by another number. Therefore, in relation to the collective object, as united in flight under these particular temporal conditions, the individuals are impotent. Their actions are constrained by the demands established by the logic of the series.

According to Flynn, collective objects "keep serial individuals apart under the pretext of unifying them [in a horizontal inhuman relationship called] 'recurrence.'"[14] This recurrence infects the individuals across the collective and creates a false sense of solidarity. They feel as though they are "in this together." This false unity is what Sartre calls their "unit-being" or their "identity."[15] Identity, therefore, is ultimately an alienating self-imposition whereby members of a collective are united in alterity by an external object that limits their freedom by imposing exigency upon them. They, in turn, interiorize this exigency and become cogs in the diachronic serial wheel of recurrence. What is more, it bears noting that the logic of the series is produced in advance of any particular individuals arriving to enter into it in a given moment (as the aggregate of past praxis turned practico-inert). One then "freely" enters into the series by "queueing" (in the bus example) and as such self-serializes oneself as one "actualises his being-outside-himself as a reality shared by several people and which already exists, and awaits him, by means of an inert practice, denoted by instrumentality, whose meaning is that it integrates him into an ordered multiplicity by assigning him a place in a prefabricated reality."[16]

4.2.2 The Radio Broadcast: Indirect Gatherings and Public Opinion

That said, the bus queue, for Sartre, is a limited and superficial example.[17] It serves its purpose in establishing the logic of basic seriality. But he moves to add complexity by discussing what he calls "indirect gatherings." His example of an indirect gathering is a radio broadcast. With the radio broadcast there is a genuine "lack of two-way communication [which inhibits] group formation and engenders feelings of extreme impotence and passivity."[18]

The result of these feelings of impotence and passivity is that a collective—as united by *public opinion*—becomes defined by contagion. And as Sartre states, public opinion as a common material object in its practico-inert development "creates the unity of the discontent."[19] This is a social reality that produces various serial effects: fear, anger, riot, stagnation, resentment, complacency, etc. The point being that this complex variation of the "formula of the series" does not create an identity of commonality, but rather an identity of alterity.

This argument prefigures the potential rejoinder that one might contest by suggesting that common public opinion about a political candidate, for example, is uniting in a commonality. For Sartre, such a "unity" is merely another example of a fleeting unity, as such public opinion remains conditioned by the exigencies of the practico-inert field within that particular set of electoral significations. The truth of the opinion is something prefabricated by Others in the collective, and then imposed on the members in the series as the collective object that mediates the relations between the members of the series who express only the opinion of the series.

However, individuals are not constrained by a *unilateral* relation with the collective object. One is alienated first by the interiorization of the situation (or one's complicity with the serial condition) that is imposing itself from without, thus creating an alienation from oneself, a destruction of one's own potential claim to humanity. One is also alienated from the Other, as one is made an Other to oneself. As an Other, as an interiorized alienated non-human, one is marked in alterity as the Other non-human (who has undergone the same process of alienation) is Other in relation to the external system. This is what Sartre refers to as "the self-domestication of man" through interiorization (and subsequent exteriorization) that is crucial to the understanding of hostile social relations under conditions of seriality.

4.2.3 The Logic of Diachronic Seriality: Destiny

The logic of diachronic seriality should now be intelligible. Individuals are united externally by practico-inert objects. A collective is formed. The members of the collective are marked by competition, alterity, and inessentiality. Individuals enter in and out of various prefabricated series in temporal succession; some of which are more basic (the collective/bus queue) than others (the indirect gathering/radio broadcast). These serial conditions are interiorized and exteriorized in a process of micrototalization. And the result of all this is that the passive activity of the series (both the individual members of the series and the series in its fleeting unity) is driven, not by need, but by *destiny*. That is, the basic logic of diachronic seriality reveals the foundational fact that life under serial conditions is not free—but *predestined*. In Sartre's words, "[Destiny] is an irresistible movement [that] draws or impels the ensemble toward a prefigurative future which realizes itself through it."[20] Again, we see the logic of the practico-inert and its exigency as foundational in the formation of the collective. The latter is formed as a fleeting unity, through the compulsion imposed by the collective object, that establishes limits and demands on the collective, and then introduces the basic social experiences of competition, alterity, and inessentiality.

4.3 SYNCHRONIC SERIALITY

Although "limited" and "superficial," the example of the bus queue creates a space for understanding the complexity of real material conditions. Each collective, at each queue, is part of a larger structural system that has both lateral and vertical components. Laterally, each particular queue is a stop on a route that further widens the scope of the collective. Sartre refers to this as the "inert conducting medium" of inertia. This is the lateral relation of serial collectives dispersed throughout a given practico-inert field in so far as they are united indirectly. So, while the bus queue is an example of a direct serial gathering, and the radio broadcast is an example of the indirect gathering, the lateral inert conducting medium combines the two.

For example, the members of the bus queue are not only directly gathered in relation to the collective object in their diachronic experience, but they are also united (fleetingly) to others within the broader public transportation system. Thus, diachronic seriality takes place both directly (in relation to presence) and indirectly (in relation to varying degrees of absence). In this sense, not only are the individuals within a given collective serialized, but the collective itself is serialized, as it is part of a larger diachronic serial process. One's place in a particular queue is further dependent on the other individuals in other collectives that are united by the collective object—the bus on this particular route. Therefore, scarcity is magnified in a broader milieu. This scarce bus-milieu becomes a field of indeterminacy. There is no way of knowing how busy it is, or how busy it will be, at various points along the route. Competition becomes intensified as quantity increases across temporal zones. Interchangeability magnifies as the route is enlarged to include greater density of the population. And inessentiality becomes more embedded as the number of potential replacements is increased. All of this leads to a system of alterity writ large.

Synchronically, one's place in the bus queue is part of a massive economic, civic, political, and cultural machine. Not only are individuals and collectives in a particular queue united with others in a large lateral relation by a collective object, but each individual, each collective, and the aggregate of them all, along a particular route, throughout a particular day, and over the course of the life of the public transport system, also share a deeper "identity" as members of a systemic institutional logic. The collective object (ex. the bus) is itself a particular appendage of a large complex body of socio-economic relations. Other appendages include (but are by no means limited to): the other buses on the same route; other buses on the various intersecting and parallel routes; the management team who draws the routes; the city planners and legislators who approve the routes and determine the areas that are best suited for service; the commercial lenders who provide the business loans for the transport company; the banks who support the lenders; the civic authorities who determine subsidies for the transport company providing a public service; the insurance company that covers the corporation in case of accident and injury—examining the tangled web of structural relations continues *ad infinitum*. The point is this: there is a synchronic—i.e., structural—component that needs to be understood under conditions of seriality as integral to the experience of social life. This component is the synchronic logic of seriality.

4.3.1 Objective Spirit:
The Medium for the Circulation of Significations

If the diachronic logic of seriality is abstractly defined by its *temporality*, the synchronic logic of seriality must be understood in its *atemporality*. That is, synchronic logic reveals the intensive variations of structural complexity that impinge on individuals in serial conditions at each moment of lived experience. The extent of this structural complexity is immense, but suffice it to say that it includes the entirety of the relations that constitute the practico-inert field that unites the collective or indirect gathering. Sartre calls this structural complexity "objective spirit."

Introduced toward the end of *CDR*, objective spirit refers to class-being in a Marxian sense. Engaging a passage from *The German Ideology*, Sartre says that

> [Individuals] find an existence already sketched out for them at birth; they "have their position in life and their personal development assigned to them by their class." What is "assigned" to them is a type of work, and a material condition and a standard of living tied to this activity; it is a fundamental attitude, as well as a determinate provision of material and intellectual tools; it is a strictly limited field of possibilities.[21]

Again, Sartre appeals to the notion of destiny in relation to the demands placed upon workers in a field of limited possibilities. "Objective class spirit" is therefore the structural condition that predestines class life.

Sartre's use of "objective spirit" would continue in his psycho-biographical work on Flaubert, *The Family Idiot* (hereafter *FI*). There, he defines objective spirit as "nothing more than culture as practico-inert." He would continue on to say, "The Objective Spirit represents culture as practico-inert, as the totality to this day (in any day) of the imperatives imposed on man by any given society.... For the Objective Spirit tells us, contradictorily but imperatively, who we are: in other words, what we have to do."[22]

It is important to note that Sartre's use of objective spirit has more resonance with Dilthey than Hegel. It is worth quoting Elizabeth Butterfield in length on this point:

> Dilthey was critical of all constructionist approaches, from Comte's sociology to Hegel's philosophy of history, because he was opposed to the project of imposing an inhuman order onto human history by means of artificial constructions. In order to remove its idealist connotations, Dilthey redefined Objective Spirit in terms of concrete human expressions. Objective Spirit, he claimed, is constituted by both simple expressions, like the wind of an eye, and expressions that exist on a larger scale, such as language, customs, styles of life, the state, law, morality, economic systems, and science. In Dilthey's work, Objective Spirit also includes those human expressions that Hegel had included in Absolute Spirit: philosophy, art, and religion. When Dilthey used the term Objective Spirit, it did not designate any sort of ideal collective consciousness of a people; rather, he used the term to refer to the concrete collection of expressions that form a unity of context, like a "community of ideas."[23]

In this sense, objective spirit is like a "Big Other"—the grand practico-inert that stands over history and that imposes itself upon the individuals within it. It is not an immaterial power guiding history, nor is it to be conceived as a group consciousness. Rather, it is the complex synthesis of the totality of praxis that has been stored in the practico-inert field. This includes all its laws, codes, cultural norms, political histories, economic theories, religious expressions, legal formulations, business models, etc.—and all the variegating complexities that each of these expressions of history represent. What matters for Sartre is that, "the word 'spirit' is shorn of its spiritualistic associations so that it simply means a *medium for the circulation of significations* [emphasis added]."[24]

4.3.2 Objective Spirit:
Language, Thought, and the Structure of Inhumanity

This is where Sartre's renewed understanding of language has bearing. For Sartre, in *CDR*, "words are matter."[25] They are practico-inert totalities that (in)humans use in totalization as they interiorize the cultural field (objective spirit) and then re-exteriorize a modified cultural field (objectifications of spirit). As Butterfield states, "Language always refers to the entire context of meaning, and for this reason, Sartre claims that when we read words we are actually swallowing society whole."[26] She would continue, "As the collection of human expressions in the world, Objective Spirit can be understood as a human creation. It constantly develops and changes, further enriched everyday by new expressions and creations of meaning. Each new action, when added to the collection, alters it slightly."[27] This process of swallowing society whole and then altering it in "each new action" is what brings together both the diachronic and the synchronic.

Between objectifications of spirit, there is a temporal movement that separates the two (and that unites them in a relation of synthetic disjunction). What matters most is that the complex structural condition that is objective spirit is understood as the serial force that conditions each moment in concrete material life. Therefore, as language is imposed on individuals as a mediatory practico-inert network, it must also be taken up and expressed as praxis. This taking up and expression however cannot be understood as a free human action. Because language is conditioned by objective spirit, the words that are used are appropriated from the practico-inert field (conditioned by the milieu of scarcity) and then expressed in ways that themselves are conditioned by the limiting power of the totality that is objective spirit. So not only do words have inherent limitations, but the limiting possibilities that are presented by objective spirit ensure that life under serial conditions will remain *inhuman*.

This is not to say that there is a conscious awareness of this inhumanity in the interiorization and exteriorization of objective spirit. On the contrary, the radical unconsciousness of this inhumanity is a prerequisite for life under serial conditions. In lived experience (*le vécu*), there is a necessary unconscious comprehension of psychic life, as the latter is a totalization.[28] And this unconscious comprehension is what gives identity to those who are united in inhumanity by objective spirit. Kenneth Anderson frames this comprehension this way: "We are united to others by inter-individual structures of materiality, the most fundamental of which is signification, the most concrete and universal of which is language. A profound comprehension underlies the incommunicability and alienation accompanying the reality of language as an external public institution."[29] This "profound comprehension" is what Anderson refers to as a "pre-linguistic reciprocity." Therefore, not only are individuals themselves alienated in relation to objective spirit, but they are structurally alienated in relation to Others. This is because, under serial conditions, communication in any real sense is impossible as the expressed ideas are "not presented as the determination of language by the individual himself, but as his *other* opinion."[30] That is, the ideas that are expressed have been conditioned by exigencies predestined by objective spirit.

This is not to reduce objective spirit to language, but to give its most profound instantiation. Objective spirit is the entirety of culture at any given moment, at every given moment, that impinges upon individuals and predestines their lives. Therefore, synchronic seriality drastically diminishes any notion of freedom under serial conditions. As objective spirit conditions praxis, inhumans appropriate those conditions as their own, creating identities in the process that have been externally determined by praxis that is not their own. This is the return of stolen praxis that we introduced earlier that conditions lived experience through the exigent limits and demands of the practico-inert field. Words are spoken. Thoughts are thought. Activities are enacted. But all these expressions of life are no more notions of free human expression than the steps of the oxen under its yoke.

Diachronic seriality presents a temporal logic of alienation that is only deepened and complicated by the addition of synchronic serial logic. The result is the elaboration of two dimensions of alienation that dehumanize the anthropological predicament to the hilt. But there is yet one more link in the logical chain of seriality that needs to be connected before the depths of the human predicament can be made intelligible. It is the admixture of the diachronic and synchronic into a grand synthesis of serial complexity. In passing, Sartre refers to this as "Infinite Seriality."[31] However, he does not explore the implications of this convergence as a formal notion. Therefore, in order to better understand the full extent of serial logic, it is crucial to investigate the interpenetrative effects of the lived experience that compose Infinite Seriality; this is what is being termed here *Kaironic Seriality*.

4.4 KAIRONIC SERIALITY

The term Kaironic Seriality is not a term used by Sartre himself. It is a term that the author derives from a close reading of Sartre's often ambiguous references to the social experience of seriality. In the abstract, this manifold experience can be divided into diachronic and synchronic modes. However, in lived experience, seriality is a constitutive pluridimensional field of alienation that impinges on inhuman bodies at infinite levels of interpenetrating variation. Kaironic Seriality is our effort to make the latter intelligible. Therefore, to understand its usage in the present project, it will first require us to understand the etymology behind its construction. Then we can look to *CDR* to see how and in what ways seriality is "Kaironic."

4.4.1 Kairos: *The Opportune Time to Act*

There are three layers of meaning to *kairos* that are most pertinent in relation to Sartre's formal investigation into seriality. Two are theological and the other more properly philosophical, although the former two are also reproduced within the philosophical. The theological meanings pertain to the apocalyptic time of the Messianic Event, whereas the philosophical meaning pertains to the invocation of prescriptive action. Taking these two meanings together, Kaironic Seriality should be understood as enunciating the impossibility of life and heralding the ever-present potency of the apocalypse to irrupt from within the conditions of Infinite Serial alienation.

In the theological sense, *kairos* relies upon an ontology of peace. Restoring the world to rights is based on the assumption that the world was created in peace and that the ground of material reality is therefore peace *in se*. However, this peace has been disrupted, antagonism has been introduced through sin.

Philosophically, this ontological assumption is discarded. This is why our investigation of *kairos* moves from the descriptive to the prescriptive. The descriptive presumes that action in the opportune moment is known: it is meant to bring the world back into a peaceful relation with God whose law has been written on the hearts of men. But philosophically, there is no preformed ontological necessity that discloses precisely how to act. Thus, there is an openness and sensitivity to context that characterizes the prescriptive understanding of the kaironic moment.

Historically, the term *kairos* emerged in distinction to *chronos*. It is first found in the theory and practice of rhetoric, designating the "proper time," or "opportune moment" for an action. As Janet Atwill writes, "Kairos signifies, on the one hand, the exact or critical time, season, opportunity, but it can also mean advantage, profit." She would continue, "In mythic accounts . . . the opportune moment may be a matter of waiting for a god to fall asleep or turn his back."[32] Such a moment is opportune because the material conditions have created a space wherein acting becomes right. And what is more, the right action is not ambiguous, but is known by those in the situation who are at an advantage that was not present prior.

The term derives its significance from the Sophists who made it their responsibility to be able to exhort and intervene when the time was right. Protagoras is credited as being the first "to expound the importance of the right moment [*kairou*]."[33] Later, Aristotle would articulate the importance of knowing the right time to speak:

> Making the audience attentive is a feature common to all parts of a speech, if there is need of it [at all]; for these remedies are sought everywhere, not just when beginning. Thus, it is ridiculous to amass them at the beginning, where all listeners are most paying attention. As a result, whenever there is an opportunity, one should say [things like] "And give me your attention, for nothing [that I say] pertains more to me than [it does] to you" and "I shall tell you something strange, the like of which you have never heard."[34]

In a very simple sense then, in its historical emergence, *kairos*, as distinct from *chronos*, was a *qualitative* rather than *quantitative* temporal designation denoting an opportune time to act. In rhetoric, this meant being aware of the appropriate time to wield one's learned skills of articulation and persuasion to affect an audience toward desired ends. While we are not reproducing the rhetorical sense regarding a single speaker knowing how to rouse an audience, our usage of Kaironic Seriality does echo the importance of knowing when and how to act. In effect, it is a call to arms. This will be particularly important when we get to part II. But without getting ahead of ourselves, if we are to make the logic of Kaironic Seriality intelligible, we must understand the theological and philosophical resonance of *kairos* itself.

4.4.2 Kairos: *A Theological and Philosophical Story*

This account is by no means an exhaustive engagement of the complex history of the concept *kairos*. As with chapter 1's discussion about the separation of *logos* from *mythos*, we are establishing a general conceptual narrative to give a sense of the term *kairos*; particularly the sense that most resonates with our development of "Kaironic Seriality."

Theologically, *kairos* is used in various ways. In the New Testament, Jesus declares that, "The *kairos* is fulfilled, and the kingdom of God is at hand."[35] This time of which he refers is the culmination of Jewish Messianic expectations. Jesus's ministry, then, can be seen as the self-proclaimed material instantiation of the kingdom of God. Of course, this does not mean that the kingdom is fully revealed. It is proleptically revealed, both now and not-yet. Thus, there is a dual tension that must be maintained in this use of *kairos*. The kingdom is both now-here and nowhere. There was still work to be done in order to bring the Earth to rights and create the single people of God promised in the Abrahamic Covenant. That said, we ought not view this dual sense as referring exclusively to a chronological notion of a future fulfillment of the Abrahamic Covenant. It was the events that would lead to the death of Jesus that would cause the early Christian church to consider the eschatological meaning of Jesus' proclamation more fully, ultimately giving the futural sense more value over that which was already instituted in the life and ministry of Jesus. This is not to say that the "now" element of the kingdom was erased, but rather to note how the emphasis shifted, from the utterances of Jesus, to early theological formulations of Paul and then among the early Christian community who wrestled with both.

In the third century, the early Christian theologian, Origen of Alexandria, sought to articulate a meaning of *kairos* that encapsulated both values equally. For him, "*kairos* denotes a quality of action in time, when an event of outstanding significance occurs . . . a moment of time when a prophecy was pronounced . . . when a prophecy is fulfilled."[36] This is when *kairos* begins to take on an apocalyptic intensity, one that would become the focus of post-Messianic expectation; a sort of post-Messianic Messianism. However, the Church rapidly sought to quell this qualitative sense of *kairos* in order to maintain stability and institutional legitimacy over the *eschaton* as such. That is, the Church viewed itself as the fulfillment of this second meaning that was instituted by the incarnation. And only through the sacramental system would the *eschaton*, or the *kairos*, be realized. As Koselleck notes, "A ruling principle of the Roman Church was that all visionaries had to be brought under its control." This requirement to control the prophetic imagination was because, "The Church is itself eschatological. But the moment the figures of the apocalypse are applied to concrete events or instances, the eschatology has disintegrative effects."[37] These disintegrative effects are precisely what occurred with the Protestant Reformation and the subsequent rise of the nation state, culminating in the market system as conditions of new forms of salvation that preclude the futural eschaton from ever coming, since this future fulfillment would mean the end of capitalism and/or the state.[38]

Philosophically, this dual sense of the now-here and nowhere of *kairos* is articulated by Nietzsche's Zarathustra. Philip Goodchild articulates this well when he pens the following:

> I have not endeavored to write about his world, I have written about something outside, something future—a menace, a nightmare—but one that rapidly encroaches upon this world, that fills its interstices, that mediates its relations. I have written of the universal solvent that flows across our surfaces, into our pores, our gaps, our distances, our hesitations, and intervals. I have written about the power that has no time or place of its own, but remains forever to come—and yet its gravity is real and absolute.[39]

This Nietzsche-inspired poetic tells of a future hope, a hope for a time to (forever) come. This "time" must not be read as pertaining to *chronos*, but rather to *kairos*. It is an epoch, an Event, one that initiates a shift in piety, if you will. It is the *kairos* of the Overman.

Nietzsche considered himself an untimely philosopher. As such, his thought was an affront to the dominant pieties of the day. This is the reason his ideas have been viewed as such a threat to the religious establishment. However, his negativity toward religion and metaphysics (particularly the Lutheran Christianity of his geo-historical context) must not color our interpretation of Nietzsche as a "nihilist."[40] Such would be a gross misinterpretation. After all, it was the nihilism of Christianity and dogmatic Platonism that replaced the density of life, nature, and history with pity and weakness and with arid, grammatical inflation that is the true *Nihilism*. Resisting the nihilist reading of Nietzsche then, we must view him as a pious *thinker of the impious*. In other words, his refusal of Christianity and metaphysics is not the affirmation of the *nothing*—it is the affirmation of the *nowhere/now-here*.

To say that Nietzsche espoused an *eschatology* may in itself be impious among Nietzsche scholarship. But the truly Nietzschean act would be to confront the canon of scholarship in order to stimulate thought. Thus, one ought not to be resistant to terminology merely for its accepted, canonical reception among the majority. Therefore, re-appropriating the term "eschatology" outside the preconceived bounds of metaphysical dogmatism and in direct contradistinction to such preconceptions might actually clarify Nietzsche's future hope as a type of apocalyptic vision.

4.4.3 Kairos: *Now-Here/Nowhere*

Nominating Nietzsche's eschatology as the *nowhere/now-here* is an intentional play on the traditional eschatological formula of the *now-and-not-yet*. As mentioned in subsection 4.4.2, this eschatological formula celebrates the initiation and partial realization of the kingdom. For Christian theology, this now/not-yet tension is both the hope for the future fulfillment of God's divine intervention and also a challenge to reposition oneself and the Christian community as participants in this divine intervention.[41] In contrast, Nietzsche's *nowhere/now-here* does not derive impetus from extrinsic sources. There is no "divine life" to which participants of life, nature, and history must correspond. There is only the active flux of immanent life that equips and determines possible futures to come.

The "now-here" dimension of Nietzsche's eschatology is the immediate presence of immanent life. Corresponding with Sartre's sentiment that "man makes history to the extent that history makes man," Nietzsche believed that human beings were both products of fate and creators of life. As Keith Ansell Pearson explains, "Although fate is nothing other than a chain of events, as soon as we act we create our own events and come to shape our own fate."[42] This means that there is no future point from which humanity must derive its present purpose. There is no external totality that can give meaning to life. Instead—life *qua* activity is meaningful. This means that there is a profound and literal sense that the *eschaton* is *now-here*. The flow of received energy that constitutes life is only to be affirmed *as is*. And in this affirmation of life, humanity is able to create itself without viewing life—to any degree—as instrumental.

Although the Christian legacy has long sought to derive human solidarity from the universal commonality of the *imago dei*, such a formula is entirely instrumental. For instance, "Radical Orthodoxy" philosopher and theologian John Milbank asserts, "As theology puts it, we are to love people because—and even only insofar as—they display the image of God." He continues on by claiming that this universal commonality is "unique and particular."[43] The significance here is that, for Milbank, only that which is "unique and particular" can provide real value as it "stands out" in marked contrast to the ordinary.

Questions arise however: Is he trying to derive the "unique and particular" from the universal? And in the process, is he not merely reducing the value of immanent life to a derivative? No doubt, his answer would be that he is not viewing human life in *instrumental* terms, but in *participatory* terms.

However, is he not always-already betrayed by the very framework within which he works—namely, the Onto-Theological orientation of thought? Anticipating Milbank's (and the entirety of orthodox Christianity's) *apologia*, Nietzsche wrote the following:

> To love mankind *for God's sake*—this has so far been the noblest and remotest sentiment to which mankind has attained. That love to mankind, without any redeeming intention in the background, is only an *additional* folly and brutishness, that the inclination to this love has first to get its proportion, its delicacy, its grain of salt and sprinkling of ambergris from a higher inclination: — whoever first perceived and "experienced" this, however his tongue may have stammered as it attempted to express such a delicate matter, let him for all time be holy and respected, as the man who has so far flown highest and gone astray in the finest fashion!⁴⁴

Therefore, a Nietzschean response to Milbank would be that loving others "for God's sake," regardless of any qualification (i.e., appeals to participatory ontology or the universal commonality of the *imago dei*), is folly because appealing to "higher inclinations" only misdirects human attention (i.e, piety). Instead, Nietzsche's impious piety leads him to a rejection of transcendence as such in favor of a radical affirmation of life; the resultant process being that humanity is able to create itself and recreate itself through endless valuation.

Without transcendence governing an open process of transvaluation, the *eschaton* must also be viewed as *nowhere*. Prolepsis is the idea that best encapsulates the nowhere's relation to the now-here for the precise reason that Nietzsche's future humanity is always *virtually* existing before it *actually* does—this is the untimely character of his philosophy. What this anticipatory notion signifies is that immanent life is both the *condition* and the *hope* of Nietzsche's apocalypse. His doctrine of the "eternal recurrence of the same" is his shorthand for this hope.

> [W]e have to put the past—our past and that of all humanity—on the scales and also outweigh it—no! this piece of human history will and must repeat [*wiederholen*] itself eternally; we can leave that out of account, we have no influence over it: even if it afflicts our fellow-feeling and biases us against life in general. If we are not to be overwhelmed by it, our compassion must not be great. Indifference needs to have worked away deep inside us, and enjoyment in contemplation, too. Even the misery of future humanity must not concern us. But the question is whether we still want to live: and how!⁴⁵

Baffling as this doctrine may be, eternal recurrence is as crucial to Nietzsche's corpus as are the concepts "will to power" and "transvaluation of values." For, eternal recurrence is the fate that articulates life, nature, and history—it is its motor and its *schema*.

With the latter in mind, eternal recurrence must not be understood as either stasis or bland repetition within a linear conception of time. In many ways, East Asian or Indigenous Australian understandings of cyclical time may actually provide us with the best analogy of what Nietzsche was expressing. This is because eternal recurrence "has a 'transforming effect' not through the creation of any new energy but simply by creating 'new laws of movement for energy.'"[46] This is the dialectical logic that Lévi-Strauss sensed in the holism of the "savage mind," and that we addressed in chapter 1. And it is this latter possibility of recreation that enables human beings to order themselves differently—both as singular assemblages of forces and as a group.

Although this fate is daunting for humanity, it must also be understood as the greatest test of human resolve. As creature-creators, acting within the conditions of fate that precede us, we inherit all the possibilities of life with which we are responsible to create—endless valuation. To whom are we responsible? Ourselves and none other. And it is this mantle of responsibility that humanity must take up in order to create itself as more-than-human—the Overman. Thus, the future of "man" is a "man of the future," one that is a result of humanity's continual creation and recreation of values. In this sense then, in the sense of a reconstitution of humanity as such, is Nietzsche's eschatology to be understood; for, the conditions of life are always *now-here* and *nowhere*—the affirmation of life and the Overman:

> This man of the future, who in this wise will redeem us from the old ideal, as he will from that ideal's necessary corollary of great nausea, will to nothingness, and Nihilism; this tocsin of noon and of the great verdict, which renders the will again free, who gives back to the world its goal and to man his hope, this Antichrist and Antinihilist, this conqueror of God and of Nothingness—*he must one day come*. But what am I talking of? Enough! Enough? At this juncture I have only one proper course, silence: otherwise I trespass on a domain open alone to one who is younger than I, one stronger, more "*future*" than I—open alone to Zarathustra, Zarathustra the godless.[47]

4.4.4 Kairos *and Prescriptive Action: The Time Is Now*

So while Nietzsche's conception of the nowhere and now-here is illuminating as a synthetic understanding the first two senses of *kairos*, the articulation of this "day to come" is still unclear. That is, the necessity of this "conqueror of God and of Nothingness" needs to be understood in its material manifestation as irrupting into the *now*. And this is why the term Kaironic Seriality has use in relation to diachronic and synchronic seriality. For, whereas the diachronic and synchronic remain at the level of description, Kaironic Seriality also implies prescription. It implies that the time to act is now, so there must be an act. In this way, it mediates between the diachronic shift from collective object to collective object and the synchronic structuration of objective spirit that conditions these diachronic shifts.

Analogously, we might say that *kairos* acts as the shifter or the invocation between the semiotic (synchronic) and the semantic (diachronic). According to linguist Émile Benveniste, speaking is formally impossible. This is because language is divided into the semiotic and the semantic. The semiotic are names/signs and the semantic is discourse (*logos*). In the semantic, we enter the mode of signification proper of discourse. Discourse is not the sum of signs. Rather, it is the global sense which realizes itself in signs. So, how is this paradox of the formal impossibility resolved in material speech? In a sense, this has to do with the invocation, the call to act.

Benveniste refers to this invocation as "enunciation." Enunciation is what makes it possible for each person to express his or her subjectivity. Through the use of "deictic indicators" (I, you, etc.), one is able to designate him/herself as participating in the inter-subjective discourse: "Language is possible only because each speaker sets himself up as a *subject* by referring to himself as *I* in his discourse."[48] The power of the deictic indicator therefore is precisely in its bridging the gap between the semiotic and semantic, the synchronic and the diachronic, as it enacts a performative utterance.

Deleuze refers to these indicators of enunciation as "pragmatic factors":

> Besides studying the structures of language, linguistics has had to address a whole semantic domain that does not result from these structures and keeps them open indefinitely. But increasingly, this affirms the importance of pragmatic factors, which are not outside the language, or secondary, but which are *internal variables, agents of enunciation* with which languages or change occur. [Emphasis added][49]

These internal variables are intensive variations that produce effects precisely in their shift in relations of degree and intensity. The effects they produce are the signs of language. So, whereas Benveniste identifies the locus of enunciation with the I or You, Deleuze refers to pre-individual variations. The importance of both, however, is in how language is able to overcome its formal impossibility: in transversing the diachronic and synchronic.

Passing from virtuality to actuality, then, is the problem that Kaironic Seriality corresponds to. If seriality were only understood in diachronic and synchronic terms, the movement of totalization would have no way to speak about concrete seriality. It would remain purely at the formal level. But seriality is not an immaterial formal concept, even though its logic must be understood as such in the first instance. As part of the living logic of action in *CDR*, the logic of seriality must also have a lived component. In other words, how are the formal and logical conditions of serial life mediated by the practico-inert field embodied in concrete praxis? And what is more, could it be possible that this embodied experience of seriality produces the conditions of its own dissolution? Or once more, as an analog to the discussion above on Deleuze and Benveniste (a point to which we will return in chapter 5), are there internal variables and/or agents of enunciation embedded within infinite serial existence that can still speak? And if so, what would it mean to declare that "the time to act is now"?

To summarize our conceptual narrative, if *kairos* designates the opportune time to act, the issue becomes how to enact this moment. And if *kairos* also indicates a dual sense of both *now* and *not-yet*, understanding how to attune ourselves to the opportunity of the moment in order that we act is paramount.

We can borrow a term from Pierre Bourdieu here to help frame our response. He refers to knowing the right moment as the "embodiment" of an art. It is not something one has, but something one is. Only this embodiment "makes it possible to appreciate the meaning of the situation instantly, at a glance, in the heat of the action, and to produce at once the opportune response."[50] As we will discuss in the next chapter, Sartre describes the embodiment of the art of the opportune response to seriality through the logic of the group in the wake of the apocalypse. However, we cannot fully appreciate the logic of this rupture if we do not understand the perpetual presence of the threat of the Impossible insofar as it constitutes inhumans entirely in their social relations. This is what we address next.

But first, to sum up the relation of the above discussion of *kairos* in its relevance to the logic of seriality: 1) *kairos* describes the age of pluridimensional seriality; 2) it heralds the opportune moment and a sense of the perpetual presence and absence of the apocalypse; and 3) *kairos* also calls for the embodiment of the proper action under particular conditions. Therefore, Kaironic Seriality is a useful concept in that it encapsulates the complexity of the opportune moment whereby the apocalypse can break forth under extreme conditions of serial alienation (i.e., the Impossible).

4.4.5 Kaironic Seriality: Variegating Serial Existence

Let us readjust our focus toward the concerns within *CDR*. Although Sartre does not use the term "Kaironic Seriality," he hints at its meaning. Referring to collective and basic sociality, Sartre claims that he had to simplify matters to make the formula of seriality intelligible. And while simple collective structures do exist diachronically, life in concrete material conditions is more complex. What Sartre calls a massified dispersal of serial conditions is what is encompassed in the descriptive component of Kaironic Seriality. This massified dispersal is made up of "complex chains and polyvalent systems," through which multiplicities change position, making new connections and establishing new orders of relation within the varying dimensions of complex chains and polyvalent systems themselves.[51] In other words, as individuals move through their daily lives, they engage in an endless repetition of connectivity with various serial contexts—both diachronic and synchronic.

A woman in a bus queue, for example, is serialized in relation to the direct collective object, the indirect series, the structure of the public transportation system, and all the complex layers and dimensions that constitute objective spirit in each contracted moment. This massified dispersal compresses down on *inhuman* bodies, creating a monstrosity of alienation that mediates all social relations under conditions of scarcity in real history—this is the *concrete universal*. Every new temporal expression of totalization creates a new network of massified dispersal, shifting individual components in and out of a network of serial alienation, with some serial elements dropping out of the network and others entering it, creating new experiences of alienation.

As the network of alienation is reordered in its constant state of flux, serial powers also increase and decrease in intensity. For example, a person's religious commitments will shift depending on her proximity to particular persons and locations or depending on the day of the week. Likewise, when a lawyer leaves her office for the day, she leaves behind certain direct series and collective objects and picks up new ones as she gets into her car, fills her gas tank, and meets friends for after-work drinks; all the while retaining her serial identity as a lawyer (as well as a lover, a daughter, a Muslim, a runner, a Democrat—and all these to varying degrees of complexity and intensity depending on her position within the shifting network of serial variation). This results in a *variegating serial existence*. That is, Kaironic Seriality is not to be understood in homogenous terms. It may be acceptable to speak of it as hegemonic, but only if it is understood that this hegemony is itself more akin to a shifting network of power relations than a static web.

4.4.6 Kaironic Seriality:
The Differential and the Impossibility of Impossibility

Sartre calls the total field of seriality "Earth." It is the "Elsewhere of all Elsewheres," or even better "the series of all series of series," which he says will "either crush me or ensnare me."[52] There is a hint of irony in referring to the total field of seriality as "Earth," but only in the sense that it recalls feelings of absurdity. Sartre's point is that life on Earth is lived in paralysis, practical impotence. In his words, "[All] men are slaves in so far as their life unfolds in the practico-inert."[53] Freedom, then, in this context, is a pipe dream. It has nothing to do with any possibility of "freedom of choice." Rather, freedom under Kaironic Serial conditions is only "the necessity of living these constraints in the form of exigencies which must be fulfilled by a *praxis*."[54]

But there is still a sense in which individuals bear a uniqueness in Kaironic Seriality. And this uniqueness is what hints at the possibility of breaking the yoke of Infinite Seriality. This is where the second sense of *kairos* becomes relevant. Kaironic Seriality does not only describe the time or age in which we live, but it also indicates the source of its own overcoming. If life were merely dominated by a homogenous monstrosity, then there would be no hope for novelty. The famous maxim, "The master's tools will never dismantle the master's house" would ring unquestionably true.

In fact, we can take it one step further and suggest that an awareness of and desire for an alternative is an indication of a gap within the hegemonic logic of Kaironic Seriality itself. For, if "this is water," then even the notion of breathing without gills would be nonsensical. But precisely because "life is a perpetual (horizontal and vertical) re-totalisation,"[55] the dialectic creates space for novelty to emerge through the irruption of "differentials." In other words, within the structures of Kaironic Seriality's dominant logic exists the flows of life from which freedom can break forth. Elizabeth Butterfield signals the way forward:

> There is both similarity and difference in the way individuals internalize the external. The external practico-inert structures which are internalized are stable enough to allow the use of concepts such as the "spirit of the generation," a certain "French attitude," or the "Catholic mindset," for example. Yet, at the same time, each individual internalizes these entities from his or her unique position, and an individual's perspective on the greater Objective Spirit cannot be replicated. . . . An individual's expression always reflects the particular "spin" of his or her unique understanding and perspective.[56]

This unique spin is what Sartre refers to as "the differential." Yes, objective spirit conditions each moment in a common way. After all, it is the entirety of culture objectified in a monstrous practico-inert field that is mediated in a social milieu. So there are limited possibilities in the objective material life of individuals. They are predestined. However, the returned praxis that haunts life in the present and demands that life be lived according to the dictates of Kaironic Seriality can cause a break. This is the impossibility for Sartre. It becomes "impossible that this should continue; it is impossible that it should be unchangeable; it is impossible that there should be no way out, that I should continue to live like this."[57] And with a resounding, "No!" the tyranny of Kaironic Seriality can and must be contested.

As the common condition is interiorized, a transformation takes place which creates a space for freedom to emerge. This is not to suppose that freedom *will* emerge. For as Nina Power rightly states, "For Sartre, it is eminently possible to live 'serially' . . . and never have an experience of humanity."[58] But it is to signal that the hegemonic control of Kaironic Seriality is not without its own dissonance. In fact, Kaironic Seriality contains its own internal contradictions. As the shifting network of Kaironic Seriality creates new connections and deepens intensities of alienation lived on "Earth," unconscious exigencies of resistance (rather than serial exigencies) begin to form when a chord is pricked, through the unique "spin" of totalization. Perhaps this prick is better understood as a spark—*a spark of life*.

This spark is the source of freedom that emerges within the opportune moment of life lived in Kaironic Seriality. As the latter expands its constitutive control over life, so too does the pressure it exerts, making the opportune moment a perpetual virtual fact of Kaironic Seriality. In a sense then, the logic of Kaironic Seriality both describes the times as being thoroughly conditioned by pluridimensional mediatory relations (i.e., the practico-inert field) and infused with a corresponding variegating experience of social alienation (seriality), and it also describes the *necessity* of "humanity." Not that this necessity is experienced by all, but that this necessity is always looming, always constitutive of the process of totalization itself. The time to act is always *now* because of the compression of seriality, which perpetually creates a situation of impossibility. However, becoming more aware of this impossibility is another issue, one that will concern part II. For now, we only need to reiterate that it is never not a moment that requires action and that the spark for this action is the result of the logic of seriality.

4.4.7 Kaironic Seriality: It Is Never Not the Time to Act

Before examining the logic of this spark, an example will be helpful to clarify the logic of Kaironic Seriality. In the middle of 2015, as the Supreme Court of the United States was preparing to rule on *Obergefell v. Hodges*, a large cohort of American Evangelicals compared the looming legalization of gay marriage to the rise of fascism in Nazi Germany. Then-president of the Southern Baptist Convention (SBC), Dr. Ronnie Floyd, charged SBC disciples by declaring that "this is a Bonhoeffer moment for every pastor in the United States." At the time, Bonhoeffer scholar Stephen R. Haynes wrote a concise article arguing that such a designation is a radical distortion of the Bonhoeffer legacy, one that serves the presuppositions of the Evangelical political narrative more than any faithful rendering of Bonhoeffer's own outlook.[59]

The article is a cursory introduction into the life of the pacifist theologian turned attempted Hitler assassin, Dietrich Bonhoeffer, who was arrested by Nazi forces in 1943 and subsequently executed after an investigation revealed his involvement with the failed 20 July Plot. The primary point of Haynes's article was singular: to re-situate Bonhoeffer's legacy, wresting it from the pious hands of individualist religionists to set it free in the ethico-theo-political arena where it belongs. Quoting Bonhoeffer from his 1933 essay "The Church and the Jewish Question": "[The] church has an unconditional obligation to the victims of any ordering of society—even if they do not belong to the Christian community."[60] What Bonhoeffer does not say is that "The church has an unconditional responsibility to convert individual souls for the Kingdom," or that "The church has a responsibility as moral arbiters of world politics." What Bonhoeffer does say, repeatedly, is that a truly costly discipleship is one in which the Christian community treads the narrow path of social life by aligning with those who are the "weakest and most defenseless brothers of Jesus Christ."[61]

Foreshadowing the Liberation Theology movements that would emerge in the 1950s and '60s in Latin America and that would take on various forms up through the present day, Bonhoeffer's theology, his gospel, was necessarily ethical and social. His ministry was directed toward social malaise in the material world. Aligning God with the suffering man on the cross, Bonhoeffer believed that God allowed himself to be "edged out of the world."[62] As such, a faithful Christian witness is one lived in solidarity with the weakness of suffering humanity, not in the vindication of personal piety through theurgic practice. Combatting the German Christianity of his day, Bonhoeffer was appalled at the self-indulgence of private religion. This is why Haynes was compelled to challenge the hyper-individual sensationalism of the Evangelical misappropriation of Bonhoeffer when faced with what they saw as a threat to the moral laws of God. To claim that it was a "Bonhoeffer moment" in 2015, as a reaction to the perceived moral decline of American culture, is to misunderstand the logic of the original "Bonhoeffer moment."

One year later, an historical moment stoked the flames of fear in such a way that the call for the opportune moment resurfaced. This time, however, Haynes himself was wielding the image. Although far from a clarion call, Haynes wrote a follow-up article entitled, "Has the Bonhoeffer Moment Finally Arrived?"[63] Haynes implies that the election of Donald Trump as president of the United States might just be a more accurate context in which to apply the kaironic designator. A stimulating article, Haynes doesn't lavish energy debating Trump-Hitler comparisons (in fact, he outright states, "Trump is not Hitler"). Instead, he illuminates a common *structural tendency* between Bonhoeffer's historical *kairos* and the present.

This tendency is a broad logical paradigm that emerges in a milieu of crisis. As Haynes states, "[We] cannot forget that [Trump] came to power reiterating promises that appealed to the most racist and xenophobic elements of the American electorate, promises that have instilled anxiety and fear in millions of Americans." Thus, it is the potential threat of racist and xenophobic rhetoric become policy and vigilante action that kindles Haynes's exhortation to embrace "our responsibility to those under threat." For Haynes, the logic of a Bonhoeffer Moment requires that there be an immanent threat to life; in particular, to those who are marginalized, under-represented, oppressed, threatened.

This is all well and good as a rhetorical device to stimulate the hearts and minds of liberal Christians with predilections for social justice. But Haynes's exhortation would benefit from both a deeper analysis and a broader appeal. This is not to suggest that there is no use-value in this type of Social Gospel. Surely there is. We also must not disregard any affective pull through the deploy of Bonhoeffer's legacy. Rather, it is to suggest that, as was noted above with regard to Milbank's Onto-Theological instrumentalism, there is a restricted and restricting logic at play that stifles the potency of social solidarity percolating on the surface of any given social context. To truly engage in effective social action there must be an appropriate awareness of the material conditions that produce crises, as well as a narrative that can rouse a large swathe of participants.

In a *Boston Review* article, Ronald Aronson argues that there must be both a warm *and* cold stream that characterizes liberatory politics.[64] The warm stream is akin to subjective affects, motivation, and transformation, whereas the cold comports itself toward the analysis of objective material conditions. Aronson suggests that both of these streams lost their impetus in previous decades, but that the Occupy movements and the Bernie Sanders campaign during the 2016 election cycle in the United States signal a spark to life of the streams of transformative social praxis. In particular, it is a nascent future-oriented hope that Aronson finds so promising. Although not clearly defined, this "New Politics of Hope" indicates a site for growth that must not be downplayed. The germinal seeds of a revolutionary logic are at play—it is our responsibility to bring them to flower.

Toward this end, we must seek a dispositional re-orientation; one that is able to palpate the surface of simmering liberatory praxis and that also has a sensitivity to objective conditions. To appeal to the former requires a concern for subjectivity; to the latter, patience in analysis. This is what Haynes's article misses. His focus is squarely on a limited, pre-defined understanding of the "warm stream." Yes, he does feign at analysis by referring to a material crisis in an attempt to draw a through-line to the contextual conditions that led to Bonhoeffer's resistance. However, to speak of a particular Bonhoeffer moment is to romanticize or fetishize a cultural phenomenon. This tends to drudge up dramatic popular responses more than vigilant engagement. More egregiously, in the context of this chapter, it also implies that there are moments which are not "Bonhoefferian." Beyond being insufficient from an analytical perspective, the concern is that this lays the tracks for self-legitimized complacency, which must be resisted. Not to proffer an alternative fetishized mantra of perpetual revolution, but because attunement to material conditions reveals the perpetual state of crisis under the conditions of Kaironic Seriality.

Further, the problem with the type of appeal exhibited by Haynes is that it actually *ignores* the perpetual, intrinsic crises of serial existence. As such, any appeal to a particular moment only offers reactionary solutions to a given situation, rather than active engagement. The point is not to dismiss Haynes or those of his ilk (especially considering the small sample size and formal restraints of an opinion piece). Rather, this criticism is to force the conversation into deeper realms of emancipatory political thought and engagement. Toward this end, it would be better to speak of the warm stream and the cold stream as being refracted through one another. Material conditions and subjectivity must be seen as co-inhering—as co-constituting tendencies that can only be understood in their relation to one another, as two factors contributing to the present holistic *mise-en-scène*.

Here is where we come full circle: it is never *not* a Bonhoeffer moment. That is, there is always an immanent threat looming, haunting us with destruction: destruction of values; destruction of freedom; destruction of equity; destruction of flourishing; destruction of hope; destruction of creativity; destruction of the very potential of Life. In the words of Sartre, we are perpetually threatened by the *Impossible*. And it is being properly attuned to this monstrosity, through the embodiment of an art, that will overcome the romanticism that Haynes (et al.) espouse. There are no special moments that require awakened activity. There is only a permanent state of crisis that requires endless vigilance, engagement.

This is not to suppose that there are no geographical or temporal sites that require particular attention. Certainly there are contracted points of pressure within this matrix of crises. But these points are better understood as indicators that show us exactly where to direct our forces. They are groans echoing out for the opportune response. They heighten our sensitivity so that we can properly focus our attention elsewhere, to different locales and times. But the logic of the Bonhoeffer moment persists. Under conditions of Kaironic Seriality, there is never a time for complacency or rest. The threat of the Impossible ensures that life is stifled—we are *inhuman*, in Sartre's words.

But this inhumanity also bears the emergence of humanity through the spark of the differential. We can transform our situations. In fact, there's a sense in which we must—the descriptive analysis of crisis also contains the prescriptive invocation to act. By attuning ourselves to the perpetual threat of the Impossible, the impossibility of Impossibility wakes us from our slumber. We no longer unknowingly embody crisis but feel it as a disease. Sparked to life, we can create afresh, both the warm and cold streams. Refusing to stay neutral on a moving train, we can engage in transgressive praxis that experiments with our material conditions and ourselves. We can create new humanisms—that is, new logics about what being human might become. We can build new structures. And more than anything, we can stand in solidarity with those who similarly feel this threat. As Alain Badiou once remarked, for Sartre, "there was always *some* war to be fought."[65] But understanding how this spark-to-life skirts the destiny of serial repetition by becoming a blaze of vitality requires an investigation into another type of logic altogether: the logic of the group.

NOTES

1. Sartre, *CDR*, Vol. 2, 152.
2. Sartre, *CDR*, 55.
3. Ibid., 668.
4. Ibid., 667.
5. William Connolly, *A World of Becoming* (Durham, NC: Duke University Press, 2011), 97.
6. Sartre, *CDR*, 267.
7. Ibid., 266.
8. Klockars, *Sartre's Anthropology as a Hermeneutics of Praxis*, 128.
9. Thomas Flynn, "Sartre and the Poetics of History," in *Cambridge Companion to Sartre*, ed. Christina Howells (Cambridge: Cambridge University Press, 1992), 236.
10. Ibid., 236.
11. Fox, 72.
12. Sartre, *CDR*, 288.
13. Ibid., 713.
14. Flynn, *Sartre and Marxist Existentialism*, 98.
15. Sartre, *CDR*, 259.
16. Ibid., 265.
17. Ibid., 270.
18. Robert Doran, "Sartre's Critique of Dialectical Reason and the Debate with Lévi-Strauss," *Yale French Studies*, no. 123 (2013): 47.
19. Sartre, *CDR*, 295.
20. Ibid., 551.
21. Ibid., 232. The passage he quotes is from Karl Marx, *The German Ideology* (Moscow: 1964), 69–70.
22. Jean-Paul Sartre, *The Family Idiot*: Volume 5, trans. C. Cosman (Chicago: University of Chicago Press, 1987), 47, 48.
23. Butterfield, 49.
24. Sartre, *CDR*, 776.
25. Ibid., 98.
26. Butterfield, 51.
27. Butterfield, 54.
28. Jean-Paul Sartre, "The Itinerary of a Thought," in *Between Existentialism and Marxism*, trans. John Matthews (London: Verso, 2008), 41.
29. Kenneth Anderson, 270.
30. Sartre, *CDR*, 301.
31. Ibid., 670.
32. Janet Atwill, *Rhetoric Reclaimed: Aristotle and the Liberal Arts Tradition* (Ithaca, NY: Cornell University Press, 1998), 57.
33. Ibid., 58.
34. Aristotle, *On Rhetoric: A Theory of Civic Discourse*, trans. George A. Kennedy (New York: Oxford University Press, 2007), 234–35; 1415b.
35. Mark 1:14.
36. Reinhart Koselleck, "Crisis," trans. Michaela Richter, *Journal of the History of Ideas*, 67, no. 2 (2006): 360–61.
37. Reinhart Koselleck, *Futures Past: On the Semantics of Historical Time*, trans. Keith Tribe (New York: Columbia University Press, 2004), 13.
38. Konings, *The Emotional Logic of Capitalism*.

39. Philip Goodchild, *Capitalism and Religion: The Price of Piety* (London: Routledge, 2002), xv.

40. See John Milbank, *Theology and Social Theory: Beyond Secular Reason* (Oxford: Blackwell, 2006), 278–91, for a detailed defense of the claim that Nietzsche and post-Nietzschean philosophy espouses a "single nihilistic philosophy."

41. See, for example, John Howard Yoder, *The Politics of Jesus* (Grand Rapids, MI: Eerdman's, 1994).

42. Keith Ansell Pearson, "A Dionysian Drama on the 'Fate of the Soul': An Introduction to Reading on the Genealogy of Morality," in Christa Davis Acampora, *Nietzsche's On the Genealogy of Morals: Critical Essays* (Lanham, MD: Rowman & Littlefield, 2006), 27.

43. John Milbank, "Materialism and Transcendence," in Creston Davis, John Milbank, Slavoj Žižek (eds.), *Theology and the Political: The New Debate* (Durham, NC: Duke University Press, 2005), 399.

44. Friederich Nietzsche, *Beyond Good and Evil*, trans. Helen Zimmern (Mineola, NY: Dover Publications, 1997), 42.

45. Nietzsche, *KSA*, 9:11 [141], quoted in Pearson, "A Dionysian Drama on the 'Fate of the Soul,'" 37.

46. Ibid., 37.

47. Friedrich Nietzsche, *Genealogy of Morals*, trans. Horace B. Samuel (Mineola, NY: Dover Publications, 2003), 66.

48. Émile Benveniste, "Subjectivity in Language," in *Problems in General Linguistics* (Miami: University of Miami, 1974), 224.

49. Jeanette Colombel, "Deleuze-Sartre: pistes," in *Deleuze épars: approches et portraits*, ed. by André Bernold and Richard Pinhas (Paris: Hermann Éditeurs, 2005), 40.

50. Pierre Bourdieu, *The Logic of Practice*, trans. Richard Nice (Stanford, CA: Stanford University Press, 1980), 104.

51. Sartre, *CDR*, 277.

52. Ibid., 324.

53. Ibid., 331.

54. Ibid., 326.

55. Ibid., 75.

56. Butterfield, 65 and 67.

57. Sartre, *CDR*, 329.

58. Power, "From Theoretical Antihumanism to Practical Humanism," 118.

59. Stephen R. Haynes, "The Bonhoeffer Moment Is Here: Now What?," July 5, 2016. Huffington Post, http://www.huffingtonpost.com/stephen-r-haynes/the-bonhoeffer-moment-is-_b_7731324.html.

60. Dietrich Bonhoeffer, "The Church and the Jewish Question," in Dietrich Bonhoeffer, *No Rusty Swords: Letters, Lectures and Notes, 1928–1936*, ed. and with an introduction by Edwin H. Robertson, trans. Edwin H. Robertson and John Bowden, Volume 1, *Collected Works of Dietrich Bonhoeffer* (New York: Harper, 1965), 225.

61. Haynes, "The Bonhoeffer Moment Is Here."

62. Dietrich Bonhoeffer, "Excerpts from Letters and Papers from Prison," http://www2.kenyon.edu/Depts/Religion/Fac/Suydam/Reln220/Bonhoefferex.htm.

63. Stephen R. Haynes, http://www.huffingtonpost.com/stephen-r-haynes/has-the-bonhoeffer-moment_b_13275278.html.

64. Ronald Aronson, "A New Politics of Hope," excerpted from *We: Reviving Social Hope* (Chicago: Chicago University Press, 2017), http://bostonreview.net/politics/ronald-aronson-new-politics-hope.

65. Badiou, *PP*, 17.

Chapter Five

Freedom and the Logic of the Group

"The transformation therefore occurs when impossibility itself becomes impossible, or when the synthetic event reveals that the impossibility of change is an impossibility of life. The direct result of this is to make *the impossibility of change* the very object which has to be transcended if life is to continue."
—Jean-Paul Sartre [1]

We concluded the previous chapter not only by suggesting that Kaironic Seriality describes the age of seriality in its monstrous hegemonic influence, but also by noting the prescriptive invocation to act. Borrowing terminology from Bourdieu, we mentioned that in order to act it requires the embodiment of an art; one that would be properly attuned to the needs of the *kairos* and that would emerge with an opportune response. This chapter is an investigation into Sartre's effort to describe this response.

We being with praxis, a term that is fraught with confusion because of the scholastic reading of Sartre as an existentialist. Section 5.1 presents praxis as the logic of (in)human activity. Eschewing the orthodox reading of Sartre's prioritization of individual praxis, we present the hypo-logical concept that defines praxis as a dialectical abstraction of totalization in the practico-inert field. The point here is that any sense of voluntarism is eradicated as Sartre shifts his thinking toward a structural and historical theory of mediation.

Section 5.2 is a speculative engagement with Sartre's understanding of the Apocalypse. Derived from Malraux, the apocalypse is a moment of subjective irruption. That is, it is a tear in the fabric of Kaironic Serial hegemony, and the institution of the process of humanity. We engage with Alain Badiou and Gilles Deleuze and their respective theories of the Event/event. While not retrojecting their unique ideas back into *CDR*, instead we show how each was influenced by different dimensions of Sartre's philosophy of the Event. By the end of the section, the goal is not to establish what the apocalypse is *per se*, but to establish under what conditions the apocalypse is actualized.

The rest of the chapter investigates the variant iterations of the group explored in *CDR*. We begin in section 5.3 with the group-in-fusion as the practical ensemble characterized by *mediated praxis*. Section 5.4 turns to the pledged group which introduces a permanence through swearing an oath, which in turn shifts the mediation from praxis *per se* toward *pledged-praxis*. Section 5.5 focuses on the *mediated capacity* of the life of the organization and then section 5.6 examines the post-eventual ensemble known as the institution, which is characterized by *mediated function*. These iterations will come to be understood as formal abstractions that reveal various logics inhering within concrete material life. That is to say, it is better to view these iterations not so much as actual social ensembles but as formal abstractions regressively extracted from an examination of the dialectical flow of totalization. This does not preclude the possibility that ensembles might form along similar lines, or that even historically they haven't already. Rather, the point of the regressive investigation into the logics of group formation is to reveal under what conditions praxis becomes human, and why. And what is more, to further understand how it is that we are to make sense of the relation between seriality and freedom in light of the logic of the apocalypse.

5.1 PRAXIS, THE LOGIC OF (IN)HUMAN ACTIVITY

No discussion of freedom can take place without first investigating Sartre's understanding of praxis *as freedom*. In *CDR*, praxis is defined as "man—man making himself in remaking himself."[2] There is a productive self-referentiality in this maxim. (In)humanity for Sartre, makes itself in the continual process of remaking itself. There is an unceasing activity that is fundamental to the project of praxis. Praxical life is never settled. There are no moments of stasis in any real sense. Of course, abstractions can be made, snapshots can be taken, but these are only useful for particular conceptual ends (ex. as moments within the broader dialectical investigation itself). As such, praxis must be understood as both formal abstraction and lived.

5.1.1 Praxis: The Autopoetic Process of Totalization

The difficulty in this is that by speaking and writing about a process that is in perpetual flux, the very investigation itself can be seen to be an abstract reduction. This goes to the heart of one of Lévi-Strauss's criticisms of *CDR*: that Sartre uses analytic reason in his investigation of dialectical reason. The retort, of course, is that Sartre is not employing analytical reason (although *CDR* is a "regressive *analysis*"). Rather, *CDR* is a moment of the dialectic itself. Keeping in mind the Paradoxico-Critical orientation, this means that

CDR is a self-referential productive paradoxical and critical exploration of the dialectic, as well as an investigation into the grounds of the dialectic. Therefore, it must be perpetually upheld that what Sartre is attempting to investigate (*expérience*) are the formal conditions of an ever-flowing process of becoming. That is why he employs the term praxis (which in itself is a term that inherently includes a notion of movement) to define the (in)human.

With this, Sartre retains some consistency with his earlier formulation of the for-itself. Correspondingly, the practical project of praxis also works "for itself." That is, praxis creates itself in the perpetual recreation of itself. However, this self-creation must not be understood in any primary sense as it was with the for-itself. Self-creation here is better understood as the autopoetic process of *totalization*. What this means is that autopoesis is not understandable apart from considering its relation to the situation, which itself is both praxis and inertia. Therefore, what praxis implies is also anti-praxis—and vice versa. The autopoetic process of totalization is the effect of the "differential" that was mentioned in the previous chapter. It is the "unique spin" that praxis enacts in the totalizing activity. The point being this: the autopoetic process of praxis making itself by remaking itself is not a dualistic conception whereby praxis is separate in any ontologically meaningful sense from the material condition in which it is embedded. Rather, the auto-transformation is an *effect of totalization*, which, as dialectical movement, can never be purely understood in terms of isolated components. This is why it is better to speak of praxis as being a formal and lived notion, rather than an individualistic and autonomous characteristic.

5.1.2 Against the Primacy of Individual Praxis

Opposed to this idea is the dominant interpretation of praxis supported by thinkers like Raymond Aron and Thomas Flynn, who see a *primacy of individual praxis* in *CDR*.[3] For Flynn, it starts with the idea that, "Praxis, like consciousness, is ontologically free."[4] Retrofitting praxis into the for-itself schema, Flynn takes praxis to have a primary ontological status as a negating (i.e., transcending) activity. This is why he states that the subtitle for *CDR* could be "An Essay on Social Ontology." Like in *BN*, what Flynn sees Sartre doing in *CDR* is discussing "the nature and functions of the basic kinds of social being."[5] Therefore, praxis replaces the for-itself in content but not in form. As he sees it, praxis is a negating, transcending, free ontological activity that mirrors the ontological activity of (what he calls) the intending "productive void" that is consciousness in *BN*.

The problem with this is twofold: first, praxis is not free in the same way as the for-itself. As we expounded in the previous chapter, praxis is predestined. Its "freedom" is therefore a conditioned freedom that is rooted in the mediatory relation between the practico-inert and praxis. That is, the limited field of possibilities, as presented in Kaironic Seriality, limits the "freedom" of praxis by determining what this very freedom might mean. To speak of praxis as being "ontologically free" is to claim a foundational purity that is absent in Sartre's understanding of mediated praxis in *CDR*. There is only a simple, abstract notion of praxis-as-free in the early stages of Sartre's development. As his investigation develops, however, this abstraction is itself complicated and transformed as he shifts from the simple to the complex material realities of the underlying logic of praxis. Therefore, praxis is better understood as being *conditionally free in situations that are not of its own choosing*.

The second oversight in Flynn's reading is that praxis is not an *ontological* fact but a *logical* one. *CDR* is not an investigation into the ontology of praxis or social ensembles. It is a theory of the formal and logical conditions of lived experience. It is not concerned with "the nature and functions of the basic kinds of social being," as Flynn supposes, but with investigating practical ensembles in order to extract formal concepts that make them intelligible. This is a different project. The project Flynn presumes is phenomenological, whereas the reading we espouse is transcendental. And while the two are not necessarily mutually exclusive, prioritizing the transcendental method over the phenomenological is preferable in that it illumines the path beyond a Constructivist divide between praxis and its material conditions, toward a Paradoxico-Critical dialectical reason.

Flynn hints at such an approach when he quotes Sartre avowing that praxis is "entirely dialectical: its possibility and its permanent necessity rest upon the relation of interiority which unites the organism with the environment and upon the deep contradiction between the inorganic and organic orders, both of which are present in everyone."[6] However, Flynn quotes this passage to support the primacy of labor, without realizing the shift toward the end regarding the univocal interior relation between organism and environment, between the organic and inorganic *orders*. This is not a mundane choice of word, for Sartre. "Orders" implies a pluridimensional cross-pollination that deconstructs the binary relation that Flynn has to suppose by giving primacy to praxis (no matter how much he tries to embed it within dialectical language). Further, the notion that these orders are present within everyone gives us insight into Sartre's anthropology in *CDR*: namely, praxis is theory of multiplicity with orders upon orders. This is further supported by calling back to our discussion in chapter 1 where Sartre referred to subjectivity in the Rome lectures as a system of interiority.

Thus, where Flynn sees *CDR* as an extension of the ontological project in *BN*, we prefer to read it as a dialectical transfiguration of Sartre's phenomenological method. It is precisely because Sartre does not give primacy to individual praxis in *CDR* that our reading has validity. Therefore, we defend the thesis that *CDR* is not, in fact, an essay on social ontology, but an investigation into the conditions of any potential future social ontology. This is what Sartre means when he refers to it as a prolegomena to any future anthropology.

This does not mean that ontological considerations must be withheld. What it does mean is that such considerations can only come after the formal investigation has been undertaken without first assuming the basis as being ontological. In his earlier writings, consciousness is understood as ontologically free because Sartre's understanding of consciousness was methodologically rooted in an individualistic conception of the human. Therefore, his basis was predetermined by his Cartesianism. Praxis, however, is a multiplicity, it is embedded, and it is expressed as totalization, which means that—formally—praxis is first and foremost the logic that explains (in)human activity in history. This is how we must understand the basis of praxis. *Praxis is the logic of (in)human activity as a system of interiority*. This is where an investigation into freedom must begin.

But this logic of (in)human activity cannot be considered in isolation. As was investigated in the previous chapter, praxis is embedded in an age of seriality. And this serial conditioning radically limits any possibility for freedom. Under serial conditions, praxis is mediated by the practico-inert. The result is that one is alienated from oneself and from Others. However, through the "differential," as praxis interiorizes its situation in totalization, a space is opened up for genuine freedom. In isolation, the differential is meaningless. It is only when this differential is able to spread in a group setting that it can become a free (common) praxis. This spreading is the upsurge of affective antagonism emerging from within Kaironic Seriality. And this affective antagonism is the logic of group praxis that will be investigated throughout the remainder of part I.

5.2 THE APOCALYPSE

As early as 1946, Sartre began exploring the group logic that would be fully developed in *CDR*. In his essay "Materialism and Revolution" (*MR*) Sartre states, "It is precisely in becoming revolutionaries, that is, in organizing with other members of their class to *reject the tyranny of their masters*, that slaves best manifest their freedom [emphasis added]."[7] What is most notable about this quote for present purposes is the notion of antagonism that Sartre states best manifests freedom. This is an idea that would follow him for the rest of his political career and that would influence later thinkers such as Fanon and Badiou.[8] Freedom is the rejection of control from *without*, which in turn instigates a free action from *within*. This is the shift from *compelling* to *impelling*. However, a problem immediately arises: how can free praxis impel if the Sartre of *CDR* eschews individualistic notions of freedom? How are we to understand freedom if there is no ontological primacy of individual praxis, as the interpretations of Aron and Flynn claim? That is, how can Sartre maintain a notion of freedom that is both committed to subjectivity and that is consistently materialist? To understand this requires an investigation into Sartre's notions of the apocalypse and the group-in-fusion.

5.2.1 Organizing the Apocalypse

Apocalypse, for Sartre, is not to be understood in terms of *chronos*, as some future cataclysmic event. Rather, the apocalypse is the revealing or appearing of the novel—it is much more akin to the *now* component of *kairos* that we developed in chapter 4. Sartre derives the term from André Malraux's novel on the Spanish Civil War, *Days of Hope*, in which the characters are torn between the dire reality of their situation and the undeniable hope they know to be delusional.[9] They describe this ambiguity as an "Apocalypse of fraternity." Malraux continues: "[The] apocalyptic mood clamours for everything right away. . . . [But] it's in the very nature of an Apocalypse to have no future. . . . Even when it professes to have one."[10] This is a hope against hope, a hope that lays one bare to the situation. In this hope, there is both resilience and defeat. As Officer Garcia ruminates, "Apocalyptic fervor is ingrained in every one of us, and there's the danger. For that fervor spells certain defeat. . . . Our humble task . . . is to organize the Apocalypse."[11] This is perhaps the best definition of the productive tension between Kaironic Seriality and the apocalypse that one could hope for. It also recalls our attention to the perpetual hope embedded with the Sartrean project that we mentioned in chapter 2 when distancing the present project from the pessimistic readings of *CDR*. By invoking Malraux's use of "Apocalypse," Sartre expresses an unwavering commitment to hope despite—or perhaps precisely because of—dire circumstances. Therefore, echoing officer Garcia, we must see *CDR* as largely concerned with *organizing the apocalypse*.

There is a double movement in the apocalyptic moment: 1) negative and 2) positive. The negative movement is the dissolution of seriality. The positive movement is the transformation of subjectivity. Again, these two notions are only abstractly separate. In reality, they are simultaneous moments of dialectical totalization. As Sartre states, the apocalypse is "the dissolution of the series into a fused group."[12] Here we see that Sartre does not equate the apocalypse with the group-in-fusion, but rather characterizes the apocalypse as the trigger that opens up a space for the group to be possible. It is the condition that is required for group praxis to emerge. But what exactly is the apocalypse? How does it function? And from whence does it come?

The apocalypse is best understood as the initial break in Kaironic Seriality. As was discussed above, Kaironic Seriality is not a monolithic whole. There is an inherent dissonance within Kaironic Seriality. This dissonance is the differential that occurs in totalization when objective spirit (or the practico-inert more generally) is interiorized and given a unique spin. Objective spirit is common for all *as objective*. However, when appropriated by individuals (who are themselves uniquely compressed by serial conditions based on the variations of intensities of material relations impinging upon them at any given/every given moment), objective spirit is transformed through praxis. The multiplicity that inheres within the massified dispersal of Kaironic Seriality ensures that from objectification to objectification a mere repetition of the same is resisted and that novelty can emerge.

One way of thinking about the apocalypse is that it is a tear in the fabric of both diachronic and synchronic seriality—the synthesis of which Sartre calls "Infinite Seriality."[13] Remember that "Infinite Seriality" is the descriptive component of the more complete concept that we developed in chapter 4 as Kaironic Seriality. Thus, the apocalypse is understood as the space opened up by the differential writ large from within any synthetic serial context. That is, the apocalypse is the intensification of the differential—the spark of life become combustible and contagious. As the impossibility of continuing to live life under Kaironic Seriality becomes more deeply felt, the fact of apocalypse becomes more actual. The virtual potency for apocalypse is always there in Kaironic Seriality; people are thoroughly exploited; they are inhuman—this is the moment!

5.2.2 The Apocalypse: Unconscious Comprehension and Subjectivity

However, there is a lack of awareness of this alienation. To some degree it may be understood. But this *apprehension* is not *comprehension*. Apprehension can still be repressed by the compression of serial forces. This is how false solidarity arises, how social *identities* and class *identities* are constituted. They are genuine actions by individuals with genuine concerns, but they are not transformative. Comprehension only arises once the Impossible becomes *impossible* through a radical irruption of common antagonism against seriality.

In the preface to Fanon's *The Wretched of the Earth*, Sartre details how the colonized have reached this *comprehension*:

> Terrified, yes. At this new stage colonial aggression is internalized by the colonized as a form of terror. By that I mean not only the fear they feel when faced with our limitless means of repression, but also the fear that their own fury inspires in them. They are trapped between our guns, which are pointing at them, and those frightening instincts, those murderous impulses, that emerge from the bottom of their hearts and that they don't always recognize. For it is not first of all *their* violence, it is ours, on the rebound, that frowns and tears them apart; and the first reaction by these oppressed people is to repress this shameful anger that is morally condemned by them and us, but that is the

> only refuge they have left for their humanity. Read Fanon: you will see that in a time of helplessness, murderous rampage is the collective unconscious of the colonized.[14]

Here, we encounter two themes that have previously appeared in our investigation: 1) compression from without, and 2) the differential. But here Sartre takes the discussion one step further. Now, the differential is common. This is our first glimpse into the logic of group fusion. Yes, there is still an external threat, under which it is impossible to continue living. But more than that, there is the *internal fury* that is inspired by this impossibility. And this internal fury is what becomes contagious, what becomes the "collective unconscious" of common praxis.

Therefore, the apocalypse is the moment of irruption whereby individuals, in a novel sense, comprehend the impossibility of living the Impossible any further. As noted in the quote from *The Wretched of the Earth*, this comprehension is unconscious. This is because what is actually taking place is a subjective transformation. There is a shift from inhuman to human. As Sartre would later state in "The Itinerary of a Thought," subjectivity is "the small [gap] in an operation whereby an interiorization re-exteriorizes itself in an act."[15] This gap is the differential that was noted in the final pages of the previous chapter. It is also what was analogously described when discussing the performative capacity of Benveniste's "deictic indicators" and the intensive variations of Deleuze's "pragmatic factors." Now, it can be classified as subjectivity itself. In other words, subjectivity, as the gap between interiorization and exteriorization, is the differential.

The moment of totalization whereby praxis interiorizes and then re-exteriorizes objective spirit and uniquely appropriates the latter by transforming it in novel objectification(s) is subjectivity. And this subjectivity under apocalyptic conditions is the root of freedom. Therefore, the apocalypse is the first moment of genuine subjective constitution in the creation of the human, coming to life out of conditions of previously indomitable inhuman serial existence. Thomas Flynn refers to this as the awakening of the "dormant seed of organic praxis in the humus of seriality."[16] While he doesn't talk of subjective constitution, what he is describing is the same awakening, the awakening of the power to truly, and for the first time, *act*. This logic will become clearer and more defined by investigating the group-in-fusion. But first, a question regarding how and when this apocalyptic Event breaks forth needs to be briefly discussed in relation to praxis and the logic of the group.

5.2.3 Apocalypse: The Event—Badiou

In the previous chapter, the term *kairos* was explored in relation to the compression of Infinite Seriality to produce the effects of its own dissolution.

Termed "Kaironic Seriality," the argument was made that inhuman life is perpetually conditioned by historical circumstances that impinge upon it in such a way as to make living as inhuman itself impossible. The chapter concluded by suggesting that it is never not the opportune moment to act in antagonism to Kaironic Seriality. However, articulating *how* to act remains a problem. That is, what is the actual experience of an Event like, and can one be forecasted or even consciously created?

According to Alain Badiou, Sartre's theory of the group describes a "multiplicity of individuals whose unity is a passive synthesis."[17] What is more, Badiou claims that because Sartre's subject only emerges in antagonism to seriality, "[The] human is nothing more than the dissolution of the inhuman."[18] This infra-politics between flashes of humanity that emerge under historical circumstances of passive synthesis is, thus, insufficiently political. For his own part, the early Badiou wants to think the continuity of politics through the moment of the Event and into the preservation of subjectivity in the political party. Sartre's purely subtractive humanism, therefore, is incapable of being truly affirmative and creative, in Badiou's eyes. Thus, what Badiou wants is to develop a theory of the political subject that is not merely an historical and revolutionary agent, but one that is political and consistent.

Commenting on Badiou's indebtedness to Sartre, Brian Smith criticizes the ontological status of Sartre's theory of practical ensembles.[19] For Smith and Badiou, it is Sartre's persistent commitment to the in-itself/for-itself phenomenological ontology of *Being and Nothingness* that prevents *CDR* from grounding a properly materialist political subjectivity.[20] As Smith states at the outset of his essay on Badiou and Sartre, Badiou finds Sartre's philosophy of the Event (i.e., apocalypse) useful, but only up to a point.[21] Badiou's early fidelity to Sartre is primarily focused on revolt and group formation under aleatory historical conditions. He quotes Sartre on the reasons for the revolt: "[There] has to be a conjunction of historical circumstances, a definite change in the situation, the danger of death, violence."[22] This focus on chance will be carried over by Badiou in his own development of the group subject.

However, the ontological assumption of the imaginative structure of the for-itself is problematic for Smith because Sartre's group formation can only ever end up with a "group of subjects rather than a group subject."[23] The stakes of this are crucial for Smith and Badiou. Without a group subject, political action cannot be sustained. Dissolution into seriality is inevitable as the competing projects of free for-itselfs transcend one another in imaginative conflict. Badiou's solution is to preserve the *chance* of the historical contingency of the aleatory but without preserving the phenomenological ontological structure of the for-itself.

In *Theory of the Subject* (*ToS*), Badiou elaborates on this rejection of individual praxis in favor of a "subject effect."[24] This subject does not preexist its own formation, but creates itself out of contingent historical circumstances. Thus, what Badiou most transposes into his own work from Sartre, up through *Logics of Worlds* (*LoW*), is that he is a philosopher of the decision.[25] Badiou agrees with Sartre that hyper-organicism is problematic, but both he and Smith misread the conditionality of the logic of the group. That is, Smith claims that, "[Badiou] thinks that there is more to the idea of a group subject motivated by unconditioned activity than Sartre allows for." He continues, "[The] theme of unconditioned activity . . . is central to all Badiou's later work. . . . This move on Badiou's part is a move to affirm the second form of freedom, which creates a subject in response to a chance event. This, for Sartre, is always hypothetical or impossible, existing only at the margins of human existence." And then Smith would conclude this section with, "The existence of the fused or unconditioned group must be extended beyond the finite bounds of its appearance and first struggle."[26]

Although Smith is elsewhere critical of Badiou's philosophy of the subject,[27] his following of Badiou's lead through *ToS* peppers his reading according to the ontological and normative hermeneutic that we have been critical of through this project. Without rehashing that argument here, what is most important for this section is the notion of conditionality in the logical construction of the group's collective unconscious. Smith, following Badiou, criticizes Sartre for remaining committed to the individual praxis and imaginative structure of the for-itself. Badiou is happy to flesh out the decisionism that he admires in Sartre's existential thrust, but he underemphasizes the perpetual presence and conditioning of material conditions according to the logic of seriality (as Kaironic Seriality).

To respond, in the first place, the emergence of the group is not unconditioned. It is precisely conditioned by the compression of exigencies within Kaironic Seriality, which perpetually threatens inhumanity with the Impossible (i.e., that there is no alternative). To think of group formation in terms of decision is to impose a recognition onto an unconscious pattern formation. Yes, there is an irruption of freedom as the spark of the differential spreads through mediated praxis, but to speak of this in terms of decision or unconditionality is to remove this process of subjectivization and group formation from the conditions under which it emerges, which is precisely what the investigation into the logic of the group is most centrally concerned with.

The second point pertains to the persistence of Kaironic Seriality that ensures that it is always the condition for the spark to ignite. This means that the "existence of the fused group" is not beholden to a fleeting moment as in the ontological readings of *CDR* but can be understood as explaining the logic of *how* seriality is dissolved under conditions of Kaironic Seriality.

And the third point, for now, is to note that the logic of the group cannot be reduced to its phenomenal circularity from group to series but must be understood in its logical form as a way of making intelligible group formation in the first instance.

Badiou's reading of Sartre is both critical and sympathetic. He admires the chance emergence of the group out of the apocalyptic Event. This continues through all of his works. However, his early admiration for the aleatory historical circumstances shifts slightly. After *ToS*, Badiou focuses less on the historical circumstances and more upon the flash of the unconditioned. In *Being and Event*, Badiou would assert, "Man is *not* a political animal: the chance of politics is a supernatural event."[28] This reference to a "supernatural event" distinguishes Badiou's theory of the subject in that the Event is not a conditioned passive synthesis arising from the dissolution of historical serial conditions. Rather, the Event must be understood as unconditioned and ahistorical. What he admires in Sartre's theory of the apocalypse and the group is that an irruption creates a novel Event. However, contra the position argued in this project, for Badiou, Events are unconditioned, ahistorical, and *rare*; which, in turn, means that subjects are themselves rare emergents.[29] This does not mean that we are supposing that full human subjects, in the Sartrean sense, aren't rare in their actuality. Rather, the developing point is that structurally the logic of *CDR* differs from Badiou's project in that the logic of subjective constitution is not something "supernatural" or "rare." Rather, the conditions of subjective constitution are ubiquitous, and ultimately the degrees of subjectivity shift and vary depending on the confluence of forces impinging on a given body within a pluridimensional lived existence. This goes to the heart of the different orientations between Badiou (Generic) and Sartre (Paradoxico-Critical) that we established in chapter 1. As such, the logic of the group will not be understood as a unique phenomenological event, but rather will articulate the virtual potential for subjective constitution to emerge under conditions of Kaironic Seriality.

5.2.3 *Evental Logic: Badiou and/or Deleuze*

The debate that is underlying this formulation of the Event as we tend toward an elaboration of the logic of the group can be situated between the ideas of Alain Badiou and his bête noire Gilles Deleuze. James Williams has neatly outlined the differences between Badiou and Deleuze pertaining to their uses of "Event" (see Table 5.1).[30]

While it would be anachronistic to squarely situate Sartre's logics of the apocalypse and the group within either column, a reverse engineering of Badiou's and Deleuze's work in relation to Sartre would be more productive. That is, both Badiou and Deleuze have claimed some semblance of a Sartrean lineage.[31] With moments of criticism and praise disbursed throughout

Table 5.1.

Badiou	Deleuze
Rare	Ubiquitous
Come from the excluded part	Processes of becoming
Related to truths	Prior to truths
Logical unfolding	Non-logical
Organizing and ordering moments	Experimental, creative moments
Unfolding and decision	Interrelated in complex ways

their oeuvre[32] and with direct statements claiming indebtedness to Sartre's investigation into the group logic,[33] bringing Badiou and Deleuze together might elucidate a common source in *CDR* that will help interpret a more nuanced reading of the logic of the group than is generally espoused.

As Williams explains, Badiou's theory of the Event is based on his essentially binary ontology:

> We either have a well-ordered and consistent structure that admits of no events, or we have a line of militant moves from point to point that are generated by a named event and a corresponding truth (such as "all men are equal") that can never appear as such, even within the new structure that emerges with the militants and that will eventually disappear with them. There is therefore always a series of radical oppositions at work in his philosophy, such as the pure philosophical one of event and state or the derived political ones of reactionary and militant.[34]

This means that, for Badiou, there is the non-Eventual state of affairs and the post-Eventual state of affairs. This is essentially a logical binary causal relation that depends on the status and emergence of an Event, which in turn produces a binary state of affairs.

In *Logics of Worlds* (*LoW*), Badiou articulates the non-Eventual states of affairs in terms of transcendental coordinates that condition phenomenological life lived within an infinite plurality of worlds. These worlds are composed of infinite relations of identity and existence that things hold in relation to others.[35] The degree to which these identities appear is based on the intensity of relations that compose the particular network of relations, ranging from minimal to maximal appearance. The minimal appearance is the "inexistent," whereas the maximal is "absolute." The inexistent object is not to be understood as ontologically non-existent. Rather, the inexistent, or minimally apparent existent, exists *as though* it were not there. It is a real object but it is a situated void. It is a parallel at the ontic level of the void at the ontological level. As such, it is a function of a particular ordered world and therefore can be brought to greater or maximal existence. An example of an inexistent would be any subaltern person or group within a given world. Thus, the task for politics is to understand how such persons and/or groups are able to gain maximal existence. The point of the Event in relation to this is the introduction of that which is not always-already situated in the world (or in any world) to allow for a truth to emerge that will absolutize the inexistent.

If the Event were understood as the reorganization of these relations of appearance, then the world would merely be reordered, without actually transforming the status of the relation between inexistents and existents. But through the irruption of the Event, the transcendental coordinates themselves that condition phenomenological worlds are eroded.

What emerges in relation to the Event is the subject. As mentioned above, in *ToS*, the subject is understood as a "subject effect." It is constituted through the Event itself, in naming the Event, and holding fast to it (i.e., fidelity to the Event). But the subject must not be understood as an object. The subject is not of the order of relations or identities of the world. An object is any entity that both appears and exists and is defined by a place/identity in a world. A subject, by contrast, is not just an object—it is in the world but not of the world.

Similar to Sartre, there is a negative or subtractive sense that defines the subject in Badiou. The subject emerges in relation to the dissolution of the transcendental coordinates of the world (similar to the dissolution of relations within the pluridimensional field of Kaironic Seriality) as the subject becomes less and less identified by the divisions of the world. The subject essentially dis-identifies with the world. However, and this is key, the subject is not a person *per se*. Rather, it is a position in the world. And anyone can occupy it. The subject then is not a worldly being *plus* a surplus of political activity. The subject is a subtraction from a place in the world insofar as it occupies the position opened by the Event.

For Deleuze, there is a distinction that needs to be drawn between events and the capitalized "Event." As Williams notes, Badiou overlooks this subtle distinction when criticizing Deleuze in *LoW* and ends up missing something of central import: namely,

> [All] events communicate in one Event where communication is not in terms of set meanings but in terms of processes. Events set each other in motion with no limits in principle; they therefore communicate in one great Event constituted by this multiple, mobile and ever-changing series of relations. It can therefore be argued that this latter Event should not be thought of as the "One" but rather as a multiple that cannot be represented as a unity or identity; the Event is in the communication of all events rather than in their collection or as their essence.[36]

What this means is that there is a sense in which each event communicates with one another and that these communications are not reducible to or extrapolated into an overarching singular Event. Rather, they are various sense-instantiations or expressions of unique communication of the unfolding of Life itself.

This highlights the difference between Badiou's essentially binary ontology and Deleuze's univocal process ontology of difference. For, Deleuze's events are articulations of the unfolding of Life insofar as Life is expressed to varying degrees of intensity and appearance across an immanent plane. As such, an event is any shift in intensity between actual relations or virtual potencies. This is not to suggest that events are themselves meaningful, but that rather meaningfulness itself is conditioned by the prior shift in intensity (i.e., an event). It is this pre-subjective intensive variations that we discussed previously as Deleuze's "pragmatic factors." Now we understand more fully how Deleuze articulates overcoming the formal impasse of language that Benveniste presents. It is precisely in that language is itself an effect of the multiplicity of events, which are themselves forever excessive of the limits and demands imposed by practico-inert field that is language. Events, therefore, are not "supernatural" (however one is to take this metaphor). They are the ever-present expression of processes of becoming that can be articulated in actuality or virtuality.

This means that events are ubiquitous. They do not come from outwith a world. They are not the unconditioned. They are instead better understood as the actual conditions of any effect or shift or change in a world (or more precisely any existing field). This is because Deleuze's plane of immanence is continuous. This is not to say it is consistent, but rather to note that events initiate shifts from within an already existing paradigm of potency—think Paradoxico-Critical orientation. The event is the shift in that univocal field of difference itself. For Badiou, this is precisely why Deleuze's micro-revolutions are not sufficient to introduce novelty or change. An Event, for Badiou, must break with the relations of any phenomenological world if it is to have a real impact on material reality. This is also why Peter Hallward can remark that Deleuze's philosophy is not able to theorize the introduction of the novel, but merely rests at the level of a type of mysticism "that leads forever out of our actual world."[37]

These readings fault Deleuze on two fronts: 1) for reproducing the transcendental coordinates of phenomenological reality and 2) escaping the actual material inexistences in favor of potential transformations at the local and non-subjective level. To sum up Badiou's position on the world-event structure:

> We begin with the underlying ontological components: world and event, the second introduces a rupture in the presentational logic of the first. The subjec-

tive form is then assigned to a localisation in being that is ambiguous. On the one side, the subject is but a set of elements of the world, and therefore an object of the scene where the world presents its multiplicities; on the other side, the subject orientates that object, in terms of the effects it can produce, in a direction that comes from an event. The subject can therefore be called the unique known form of thinkable "compromise" between the phenomenal persistence of the world and its evenemental [*événementiel*] reshaping.[38]

There is, thus, a redoubling of sorts. As the subject emerges in fidelity to the Event, it must then bear witness to the truth of that event in the world by turning the truth back onto the world to reconstitute it anew. In a sense, the Event becomes the only source for new potential truths to be instituted in any given/all potential world(s) that would otherwise reproduce itself/themselves without change.

The Deleuzian position theorizes the complete opposite. That is, change is all there is. "Worlds" (or transcendental fields) are cut through with processes of transformation at every stage; and these transformations are expressed in varying degrees of intensity. A given state of affairs is the individuation of this expression of intensity. In Williams's words, a given "state is undergoing events, introducing novelty and stress into it at all times and in all parts where there is a change in intensity in the state."[39] Therefore, any change in actual relations or virtual potency are focal points of events. And these events cut through the interrelations between a given field and the various "worlds" that intersect with it. What this results in is a theory of pluridimensional interpenetrating conditions of relationality, much like how we have articulated life lived in Kaironic Seriality.

And this is where we can begin to see the Sartrean resonance in both Badiou and Deleuze (see Table 5.2). Badiou takes from Sartre the moment of rupture and the intensity of its measured effects; Deleuze expands on Sartre's notion of the transcendental field that creates the conditions for the rupture to take place. Badiou develops a theory of the subject that is necessarily related to the Event; Deleuzian events are pre-subjective and create the conditions

Table 5.2.

Badiou	Deleuze
Rupture and its effects	Transcendental field that creates conditions for rupture
Theory of the subject related to the Event	Events create the conditions of subjectivity
Events are novel reorganizing and reordering moments of worlds	Events are expressions of creativity and experimentation in unfolding fields in the process of becoming

out of which subjectivity itself is individuated. Events for Badiou are novel reorganizing and reordering moments of worlds; Events for Deleuze are expressions of creativity and experimentation in unfolding fields in the process of becoming.

5.2.4 The Logic of the Apocalypse

What this means for the present project is that both Badiou and Deleuze can help us construct the logic of apocalypse through their divergent theories of the Event/events. Shortly after Sartre's death, in a letter to his friend Jeannette Colombel, Deleuze wrote,

> The "situation" is not a concept among others for Sartre, but the pragmatic element that transforms everything, and without which concepts have neither meaning nor structure. A concept has no structure or meaning as long as it is not situated. The situation, is the functioning of the concept itself. And the richness and novelty of Sartrean concepts derives from this point, they are the expressions of situations, at the same time as situations are assemblages of concepts.[40]

This elaboration of the co-constitutive relation between Sartrean concepts and situations summarizes nicely why we reject Flynn's (et al.) reading about the primacy of praxis. As Deleuze reads Sartre, we can follow by saying that Sartre's "situations" are analogous to Deleuze's "pragmatic factors."[41] They transverse the structures of language and philosophical concepts that condition a given milieu. Referring back to the brief mention of Émile Benveniste in chapter 4 on Kaironic Seriality, we can say that, for Deleuze, Sartrean situations are akin to enunciation. They are what bridge the gap between the semiotic and semantic, or between the synchronic and diachronic—they are the invocation of *kairos*.

So perhaps we might say: the situation is what brings things to life. As Deleuze says, pragmatic factors (situations) are "internal variables, agents of enunciation with which languages or change occur. [The situation] traverses [language structures and philosophical concepts] through and through, it determines their new divisions and their original content."[42] This is what reveals the logic of the apocalypse: it is the irruption of hope from within the invocation of Kaironic Seriality, whose conditions are ever-present, as the shifting field of material relations tells the story of novel evental creation. This does not mean that every apocalypse is a revolutionary storming of the Bastille in actual historical terms. Rather, the example of the Bastille has use-value insofar as it illuminates the pragmatic factors that are enunciated in the imperative, "To the Bastille!" Thus, what we can extract from such an Event is that situations are fluid landscapes of becoming that contain internal variables whereby upsurgent flashes of creation and Life (i.e., freedom) can be actualized.

At this stage of the investigation, while we may not be able to say, "this is the apocalypse," we can say that the time of the apocalypse is always *now*. Rather than delineating what the apocalypse is or where it has been, what we have established is a formal frame for identifying how and why the apocalypse can be actualized. This means that the logic of the apocalypse articulates humanity's potential to be actualized at any point. It is reproduced in totalization and mineralized into the practico-inert field. Just because there is inertia does not negate the praxis embedded therein. It is dormant, as Flynn notes. It must be awakened if freedom is to become actualized. And this is why understanding the logic of the group is crucial. For, it articulates the formation of praxis-in-common under conditions of Kaironic Seriality that enact the invocation of the situation. This is the beginning of developing the embodiment of an art of the opportune moment. Understanding this logic is then crucial if we are going to develop an orientation that will allow for the potential of liberatory praxis to become better attuned to Kaironic Seriality so that prescriptive enunciations can palpate the surface of actual life to release the flows of virtual evental creation.

5.3 THE LOGIC OF THE GROUP-IN-FUSION: MEDIATED PRAXIS

The group-in-fusion is the differential becoming common. His action becomes my action; her subjectivity, my subjectivity. There is a telepathic and empathic connectivity that unites each through a common action. It is the unconscious, affective reciprocity of the emergent translation of the differential between participants who have been united through the apocalypse.

5.3.1 Contagion and Affect

The use of "telepathy" is not meant to refer to some supernatural, extrasensory perception. Rather, it is a concrete, material contagion of affectivity. Had Sartre understood mirror neurons, he may well have ventured to explain how the occurrence of group fusion has a biological substrate. For present purposes, that is inconsequential (although, we will return to this in chapter 8). What matters is that group fusion is a concrete, material, and common contagion.

Similarly, the use of "empathy" does not refer to the common notion of feeling compassion for another. It refers not to cognitive empathy but tends toward what psychologists refer to as affective empathy (with some minor points of divergence). Cognitive empathy refers to a role-taking approach where "an empathic person can imaginatively take the role of another and can understand and accurately predict that person's thoughts, feelings, and actions."[43] Affective empathy, by contrast, is a "vicarious emotional response to the perceived emotional experiences of others."[44] Whereas the former is a conscious recognition of the other's feelings that entails an element of predictive accuracy, the latter includes the immediate sharing of feelings.

The risk of affective empathy, according to neuroscientist Matthieu Ricard, is that without maintaining a separation between self and other in the role-taking distancing of cognitive empathy, one might risk "emotional contagion." Emotional contagion is the automatic feeling of an "other's emotion without knowing that he or she is the one who provoked it, and without being really aware of what is happening to me."[45] This is what he argues exists in animals and young children. It is characterized by a lack of control or conscious directedness *per se*. It is simply the contagious spread of an impulse. While we are employing the use of both contagion and empathy to describe the effect of the differential writ large to articulate the logic of the group, this is not to suppose that the spread of subjectivity through shared praxis is the undirected spread of impulsive *feelings*. It would be better to speak of the affectivity of the group logic as being prior to feelings, so understood.

Cognitive scientist Antonio Damasio refers to feelings as the shadow of emotions.[46] He corrects the commonly expressed interchangeability between feelings and emotions by drawing a distinction between awareness and unconscious stimuli:

> In everyday language we often use the terms interchangeably . . . but for neuroscience, emotions are more or less the complex reactions the body has to certain stimuli. . . . This emotional reaction occurs automatically and unconsciously. Feelings occur after we become aware.[47]

It is this definition of emotions that we are interested in. That is, affective empathy is less about feelings than about an automatic and unconscious stimuli. This skirts the problems of emotional contagion as defined by Ricard, as common praxis does not, in the first instance, pertain to feelings. Similarly, the orthodox psychological definition of affective empathy is also too closely related to what Damasio identifies as feelings. Thus, the deployment of empathy here refers to a contagious, affective (i.e., unconscious and automatic) vicarious experience of a common goal. Granted, Sartre did not have the tools of neuroscience at his disposal. However, his investigation into the fusion of the group and the descriptions he uses fit nicely—analogously, if nothing else—within the definition of affective empathy and the structure of emotions derived from Damasio. This does not mean the logic of the group is "irrational." No, as Sartre makes clear, the logic is intelligible.[48] But this intelligibility is not based on a rational choice of calculating participants. It is not Game Theory. Rather, the fusion takes place at the affective level.

5.3.2 Subjective Constitution and Comprehension

Gavin Rae suggests that the group-in-fusion is a rational formation based on the idea that,

> [Each] individual recognizes that the other: 1) has the same end as she does; and 2) is crucial to the attainment of their common end. This ensures that each individual recognizes that the activities of the other are crucial to the attainment of their shared common goal.[49]

While it is patently the case that each end is common and that a *comprehension* of this is crucial to the condition of the group fusing in the first place, it is not the case that this comprehension is a "recognition." Such an idea is a derivative. That is, this idea of recognition is only valuable *after* first understanding the logic of the fused group in the establishment of ways to apply this logic. Because Kaironic Seriality conditions all thought, all recognition is really a mis-recognition. There needs to be a shift in the very logic of cognition to allow for recognition to be comprehensible. This is why Sartre elaborates the logic of the apocalypse as the condition for the fusing of the group. Thought must be sparked to life first, then shared. Only after *might* we be able to speak of recognition. But this is not something we can presume is guaranteed. Therefore, we must understand that the initial fusing of the group takes place at the unconscious level and is only recognized (at first anyway) through a form of serial reason (keep in mind that this issue pertaining to mis-recognition and recognition will be a central theme of part II).

Thus, in the activity of the group-in-fusion, as analyzed by Sartre, there is no "recognition." There is *comprehension*, but only as this comprehension is understood non-thetically. Therefore, it seems that Rae's mistake is that he is using phenomenological language to describe a formal materialist activity. Furthermore, Rae is neglecting the logic of the apocalypse and the group-in-fusion as a moment of subjective constitution through the dissolution of Infinite Seriality. This ensures that his reading of *CDR* remains at the phenomenological and ontological level, rather than the formal and hypo-logical.

But this idea of subjective constitution needs to be given substantive meaning. In the apocalypse, subjective constitution is limited to a conception of the emergence of praxis in common. The apocalyptic subject is merely a "disintegrated individual."[50] This means the grouping of disintegrated individuals have no substantial being. What needs to be understood, therefore, is how subjectivity is common and how concrete subjectivity is not lost in hyperorganicism or collective consciousness. According to Flynn, it is "the ontological primacy of praxis [which] saves Sartre from Hegelian 'hyperorganisms' and even, he sometimes insists, from Durkheimian 'collective consciousness.'"[51] What this seems to imply is that the ontological primacy of praxis is an atomization of free individual praxes that come together consubstantially in activity, united by the interstices of mediated reciprocity (through the "mediating third"). The problem with this is that the group is not atomized. There is no "ontological primacy" of free individual praxis. There is only a formal logic of praxis in *CDR* that reveals to us the conditions under which common praxis might emerge.

The primacy of free individual praxis is an abstract formulation that provides a framework for an investigation into a Constructivist social ontology. As such, it does not explain the conditions for the commonality in group fusion. In seeking to protect Sartre from hyperorganicism, Flynn makes the opposite mistake by atomizing the praxical logic. Instead, Sartre walks a fine line between the two, refusing to reduce group praxis to an atomistic theory of social formation while simultaneously resisting hyperorganicism and collective consciousness. The result is that the group-in-fusion is connected through the "fusing" of empathy and the differential. It is therefore an affective logic of differential common action—a disjunctive synthesis. As Mark Poster states, "Since it has no ontological status, the group can persist only through the commitments of its members."[52] And as has been shown, these commitments, as common, are impelled by a "collective unconscious" that has been instigated by the external pressure of Kaironic Seriality and by the internal fury of those who comprehend it in its impossibility. This is what the Sartre quote at the beginning of this chapter refers to: transformation occurs when the impossibility of life is comprehended as itself being impossible. What needs to be explained now is the mechanism that enacts this transformation toward common subjectivity under material conditions.

5.3.3 *The Logic of the Group-in-Fusion*

As has been outlined above, in Kaironic Seriality, inhumans are overdetermined by the practico-inert field. Therefore, inhuman relations of conflict and alterity abound. However, in the apocalyptic upsurge, there is a shift from negative mediation through the practico-inert to positive meditation through common praxis. Sartre puts its succinctly: "[the] mediator is not an object, but a *praxis*."[53] What this means is that, in the apocalyptic constitution of subjectivity, by the common comprehension of the impossibility of living in Kaironic Seriality, praxis is united internally through an empathic connection. This empathic connection becomes the mediation of the group-in-fusion. Wilfrid Desan puts it nicely when he states that in the group we understand "the Other as a dimension of our own life."[54] No longer are *inhumans* mediated (and alienated) by the practico-inert field. Instead, *human subjects* are constituted and united through their shared praxis in opposition to the practico-inert field itself. In Sartre's words, the group "produces itself in and against the practico-inert field."[55] Here, again, we see the autopoesis of praxis. The group "produces itself." And as before, this autopoetics is an effect of totalization. The group totalizes itself in its common praxis and thereby shifts the ternary relations, from mediation through the practico-inert field to mediated praxis, and in the process creates a field of empathic subjects who are common insofar as each has the same unconscious fury as the next. This is the basis for building up subjectivity within the group. However, in the moment of the group-in-fusion, this subjectivity is still in its germinal stage. It will progress as the group accomplishes its goal, stratifies into established functions, and organizes. This will be covered in the coming sections.

For now, we must make sure we understand the logic of the group-in-fusion. This dense passage from *CDR* will guide us as we make this logic explicit:

> [The] objective of the third party produces itself for him as a *common* objective, and the plurality of epicentres reveals itself to him as unified by a *common* exigency (or *common praxis*), because it *decodes* serial multiplicity *in terms of a community which is already inscribed in things*, in the manner of a passive idea or a totalising destiny.[56]

In this obscure passage, Sartre indicates how the logic of the group-in-fusion is able to 1) uphold a robust notion of concrete praxis; 2) explicate the reason subjects are united in common praxis; 3) describe how subjective constitution takes place from within Kaironic Seriality; and 4) suggest how common praxis resists hyperorganicism or collective consciousness.

First, Sartre upholds a robust notion of concrete praxis in that the third party is understood as self-producing a common objective among a field of other third parties—i.e., "epicentres"—who also self-produce this common objective. That is, each acts commonly on the group itself, creating the group itself, as each is mediated by the praxis of an other (or all others). There is no dissolving of praxes into one another. Rather, mediation is maintained as the unifier and preserver of concrete praxis. Second, mediation also explicates the reason subjects are united in common praxis: exigency. Material conditions either compel or impel action. In the milieu of scarcity, under practico-inert conditions, Infinite Seriality compels praxis through radical exigency, as both diachronic and synchronic limits and demands are synthesized and imposed onto contracted nodes within the social context. But in antagonism to Kaironic Seriality, destiny is transformed from pre-determination to common freedom in relation to a common exigency/praxis. This exigency ensures that the group is practically realist, for their response to the material situation that threatens them with impossibility is based on concrete material conditions, with the result being that transformed concrete material possibilities are therefore opened up.

What is more, third, by opening up these possibilities, subjective constitution is sparked to life as serial multiplicity is decoded and the inert community "which is inscribed in things" is resuscitated through mediated reciprocity. This resuscitation is possible because of the return of stolen praxis that is inscribed in the mediating practico-inert field. This mineralized praxis has both counter-final and differential elements in it. As has been thoroughly discussed, the counter-final elements of the material ensemble are what lead to seriality. However, so as to not ignore the complex intensive variations of totalization, it must be kept in mind that in the interiorization-exteriorization of the practico-inert field, there is a displacement of previous flashes of humanity. It just so happens that the practico-inert field exerts a more observable influence as its reserves grow exponentially greater than those of the differential, and because the logic of Kaironic Seriality conditions thought to seek its expression. Nevertheless, the point in discussion here is that even under such conditions, Sartre elaborates the logic of how the group-in-fusion makes intelligible the upsurge of humanity in antagonism to the monstrosity of Kaironic Seriality. And his final point is that the logic of the group-in-fusion is able to skirt the pitfalls of hyperorganicism or collective consciousness through common exigency insofar as this common exigency is affective and unconscious.

The remaining problem, for Sartre, is that the group is not a permanent social ensemble. It emerges in a situation that requires an immediate response, but once the goal has been reached, once the common affective exigency settles, the constitutive life of the group-in-fusion ceases. When the group-in-fusion meets its objective, it will dissolve *as such*, and the group that met its objective will be "united only by a past action" which is "engraved in their Being." This can (but not necessarily will) lead to a "desire to exploit it for their own purposes or in support of a particular policy."[57] What is certain is that the group cannot go back to the previous state of affairs, and the members of the group seek to preserve the past experience of freedom. As he would continue on to say, "The fused group should therefore be characterised as an irreversible and limited process: the reshaping of human relations by man had temporalised itself in the practical context of a particular aim and *as such* would not survive its objectification."[58] That said, it must be understood that there is a sense in which the potency of the group-in-fusion's common praxis will be preserved in the remaining members. It is mineralized in the pledge and in the very goals and activities of the organization. It is important to remember that the practico-inert is the *practico*-inert. And this crystalized praxis is preserved in a minimal sense, as a common past that once was radical freedom-in-action.

As such, there is a nostalgia that can come to characterize group action and organization after the group begins its fall back into seriality. But, the affective and constitutive logic of the group still resonates, although at a low hum. In this way, the social milieu, even the serial milieu, is not a mere fall back into a previous situation of impossibility (of course, we are speaking logically here, not temporally). It is not a repetition of the same. Rather, the group really has transformed human relations, human subjectivity, and the social landscape in a concrete and definitive way. Plus, beyond this, there is a sense in which the pledged group and the organization are still impelled by free, common exigence. But understanding the extent of this residual freedom requires further exploration.

5.4 THE LOGIC OF THE PLEDGED GROUP: MEDIATED PLEDGED-PRAXIS

After the irruption of the apocalypse and the emergence of the fused group, the remaining ensemble is what Sartre calls the "surviving group." The surviving group is the ensemble of subjects who were fused together in affective antagonism to the Impossible. Under the monstrous dominance of Kaironic Seriality, they were inhumans, living in impossible situations of exigence. Through the experience of shared exigency in mediated praxis, and by the opening of the space for freedom and novelty to emerge through the differential, subjective constitution began to create *human* existence. Quite literally, a new people are emerging.

However, the affective fury that fused the group in the first place is not a permanent condition. If the fused group accomplishes their common aim (whatever it might be), there is a settling of the exigent field. That is, the compression that made the impossible conditions of life in Kaironic Seriality impossible to continue living has been loosed. The common spark of life that spread to each, as common to all, blazed hot and far, but its oxygen supply—its imminent violent foe—has become less potent. This is the crucial moment in every revolution's wake. Once the enemy has been defeated, how can the crowd instill a permanence that refuses the past and that remains faithful to the common freedom of the subjects in the group? Enter the pledge.

5.4.1 Mediation Through Pledged-Praxis

For Sartre, the pledge is the action of the group to preserve itself in its freedom. It does this by swearing an oath to ensure that the group's commonality will not dissipate. Nina Power puts it thusly:

> Sartre needs to show how the group, in order to maintain itself and persevere in action, must interiorise the passivity of the practico-inert in activity (and

also interiorise a certain kind of inhumanity). It is not freedom that threatens the newly formed group but its collapsing back into seriality. This is the path that leads the group-in-fusion to form what Sartre calls a "pledged-group."[59]

What Power highlights is the *way* Sartre indicates how to preserve freedom in a material world that is constantly threatened by the dominance of seriality, under conditions of scarcity.

While it *is* the case that Sartre does seek to explain the logic of the perseverance of the group under the constant pressures that come from without, it is *not* the case that the group interiorizes "the passivity of the practico-inert in activity." At least not exclusively. Rather, the group seeks to interiorize *pledged-praxis*, which has characteristics of inertia, in that it is the introduction of permanence into mediatory group life, but also praxis in that it is a self-imposed mediation of positive reciprocal relations. What he presents is another shift in the locus of exigency. "Exigency, in this context, has the same characteristics, but it is the [pledged] agents themselves that are inorganic inertia [rather than the practico-inert or the free praxis of the mediating third]."[60] So, mediation has shifted from the practico-inert (under conditions of seriality), to praxis (in the group-in-fusion), to now mediation through pledged-praxis.

The difference between pledged-praxis and the practico-inert is that the former is the perpetuation of the logic of emergent *human* life, whereas the latter articulates the logic of the stored labor of *inhuman* life under basic serial conditions. In other words, pledged-praxis is the effect of transformed subjects who have emerged under conditions of apocalyptic novelty. In this way, pledged-praxis, as the mediation of the pledged group, ensures that the group will not simply fall back into the previous state, but will continue its totalizing dialectical movement. This does not mean that there is no sense in which seriality is not present in any capacity. On the contrary, seriality is always present as the necessary compression against which the group forms itself (and sustains itself). Further, seriality is intensified by the intentional self-imposition of stasis in the pledge.[61] But this isn't a complete reversion into a serial state. Rather, it is the group's attempt to remain free perpetually.

5.4.2 *Nostalgia and the Imagined Future*

The group attempts to remain free perpetually in two ways: 1) The group comes to see itself in its past victory and 2) the pledge is a guarantee against the future.[62] In other words, the pledge is essentially *nostalgic* and *imaginative*.[63]

The immediate threat is no longer present, but is imagined as a threatening absence that still looms. Sartre puts it this way:

> In absence, the new differentitations are, of course, determined in close relation to the totality of objective circumstances. Nevertheless, the group determines itself in accordance with a future unification (unification through the return of the enemy) and a past unity (its group-being as transcended past, or, in other words, its practical reality in so far as it *has been*, and in so far, as it has objectified itself in materiality).[64]

It is this two-way movement that prevents the pledged group from being a pure passive activity. If they were characterized exclusively by nostalgia, they would be a passive community externally united by an inert image. Likewise, if they were purely future-oriented, they would be united by a Utopian Ideal that is literally "nowhere," which would make the ensemble crudely idealist. But Sartre must maintain the realism of the group. Therefore, the pledge is nostalgic and imaginative, while autopoetically attempting to maintain its presence in concrete, material conditions of de-alienating exigence.

However, if Sartre can be faulted anywhere with regard to his investigation into the logic of the pledge, it is most strikingly with this latter notion. That is, he is insufficiently realist in his investigation and development of the logic of the pledge. The group-in-fusion is eminently realist. In fact, they are driven exclusively by the realism that breaks forth under the pressures of a system that seeks to hide the truths of the real exploitative conditions of life in Kaironic Seriality. The pledged group, however, by virtue of looking backward and forward, perpetuates an idealist tendency by creating itself through memory and imagination. Sartre states that the pledge brings "the future group [to the] present community as the limit to all possible transcendence [dépassement]."[65] In this sense, the pledged group creates itself in the present by bringing this future image into the present, and as a result introduces new limits and exigencies that are conditioned by projected future praxis. This means that the pledged group is constituted by the mediatory functions of a future image and the exigencies contained therein.

This does not mean that the logic of the pledged group is somehow deficient or useless. There is still value in understanding it, particularly in relation to the entire logical chain of the group. But it does need to be kept in mind, so that the gaps in his logical framework can be filled in to make any application of it more complete, and therefore more effective and applicable.[66]

5.4.3 Terror

Yet, the core of the pledge is still to be explored. And this is the true bedrock of the logic of the pledge. Because, yes, in one sense, the pledge is the desire of the group to maintain itself in freedom, but really, even this desire is itself a derivative founded upon *fear*—or as Sartre says *terror*. Terror comes to the pledged group, in the present, through the fabrication of the future image. This future image is of the foe returning. Although not an imminent threat, the fear of its return is felt by the group through the creation of the future image. They can never return to the previous state. Therefore, they are bound together in their shared anticipation of the next wave of violence. And knowing full well that they have already been successful once, they are confident that they can be successful again. This is the paradox of the pledged group: they are united by their past victory and by their future fear.

However, the intelligibility of the terror of the pledge requires one more nuance. It can only be revealed in what Sartre calls "fraternity-terror."

> [This] is precisely what the pledge is: namely the common production, through mediated reciprocity, of a statute of violence. . . . To swear is to say, as a common individual: you must kill me if I secede. And this demand has no other aim than to instill Terror within myself as a free defence against the fear of the enemy.[67]

Here what we see is that the pledged group becomes its own immediate objective by instilling terror upon itself. Thus, the logic of the pledged group cannot be understood without incorporating a robust notion of the logic of fraternity-terror.

In reference to the past (whether the imagined or actual past is of no real consequence to the formal structure of this activity), the group is aware of its success and must declare to never go back to the pre-group state. Looking forward, the group anticipates the return of the foe, or the attack of another, and galvanizes around an anticipatory fear. And in the present, based on nostalgia and the future image, fear permeates the group; fear that one will secede, fear that *I* will secede. The exigency of the pledged group therefore ultimately becomes an exigency based on fraternity-terror.

Badiou reads the pledge as "the point where the possibility that the group might disperse has been internalized." This seems correct. However, he continues, "As everyone is the third party for everyone else, he fears the *dispersed solitude* that is both the others' doing and his own doing. It is not enough for reciprocity to be *immediate*. It requires a stable mediation. It is the oath that allows everyone to commit themselves to remaining the same [emphasis added]."[68] Exposed here is Badiou's phenomenological ontological reading of the in-itself/for-itself projected into the logic of the pledged group.

It does not seem accurate to state that one fears "the dispersed solitude that is both the others' doing and his own doing." Nor does it fit within the schema of the group logic to claim that reciprocity in the group is "immediate." The fear is first and foremost conditioned by the fear of the Impossible, the imminent foe that could return from outside the group. That interiorized future threat ensures a heightened state of awareness and anxiety within the relations of the group. But it does not threaten the members of the group with solitude. There is no isolated individual for the Sartre of *CDR*. Serial relations are not characterized by solitude, but rather, mimetic rivalry, alterity, and interchangeability, all of which are social phenomena. The "solitude that is both the others' doing and his own doing" rings much truer with the structure of inter-subjective conflict in *BN*.

The same tendency can be seen in Badiou's assumption that in the group "reciprocity is immediate." In the group, mediatory relations still abound. They have shifted from the serial mediatory relations conditioned by the practico-inert field, but relations between members of a group are not immediate. They revolve around the ubiquity of the mediating third. Yes, Badiou is right that the oath must be sworn to clearly demarcate who would be a traitor and to impose a permanence onto the group to prevent such treason. But as Sartre makes clear, "Suspicion appears within the group not as a characteristic of human nature, but as the behaviour appropriate to this contradictory structure of survival: *it is simply the interiorisation of the dangers of seriality* [emphasis added]."[69] Again, Sartre explains how the threat that constantly imposes itself is seriality. This is what leads to fear and suspicion. It is not the potential of the group to become atomized individuals.

Suspicion enters the frame because of the pervasive presence of seriality as introduced through the practico-inert; in this case, the inertia introduced by nostalgia and the future image. Pietro Chiodi echoes this sentiment when he comments that the members of the pledged group swear that s/he will never become other *through self-imposed fraternity-terror*—what he calls, "reflexive fear."[70] There is no imminent enemy that organically unites the group in commonality, so they must manufacture fear (i.e., create a fear-image). This is the reason why Sartre says the pledge is a "creative act" whereby the pledged group creates itself in common.[71] However, this creative act must not be understood as the pure expression of some type of artistic freedom (or the embodiment of an art of opportune action, for example), but rather as the self-imposition of nostalgia and fear, which in turn mediates the pledged group in relations of fraternity-terror.

5.4.4 Sartre, Badiou, and Institutional Fidelity

Perhaps the reason Badiou reads Sartre the way he does (besides the ontological differences) pertains to Badiou's notion of "institutional fidelity."[72] For Badiou, the Christian Church serves as a model of this. As he says, "the Church [was] the first institution in human history to aspire to universality" by clearly demarcating the line between orthodoxy and heresy.[73] Through fidelity to the Christ-Event, the Church was able to bring into existence that which was previously inexistent, by establishing itself in relative fraternal order.

Of course, fidelity *as such* does not necessarily relate to the theological. Stripped down, fidelity pertains to the constitution of a political subject. "[To] become a political subject is to be constituted in relation to an event . . . as the bearer of a truth process who is called upon to maintain an enduring fidelity to the event and its commands."[74] We covered this idea above in section 5.2 on the Apocalypse. But in that section, our concern was on the status and efficacy of the Event itself in constituting subjects. Here, what matters is the notion of fidelity that preserves that which has been made existent. What matters is that the institution becomes the "husk" which contains the enduring fidelity to the "event and its commands."[75] As such, the party or the Church for Badiou are subjective. As Power explains:

> Badiou is very close to Sartre on this point (although for Sartre there is no question of "the party" preserving the initial moment of revolt)—the ossification of force into institutions is not the framework that preserves the initial moment of novelty: here we see why Badiou must maintain the centrality of the "subjective"—structures and organization are not enough *if their participants are not gripped* by the motive force that catalysed their initial movement.[76]

It is the last sentence that is most illuminating when comparing Badiou's notion of fidelity to Sartre's logic of the pledge. For both, the members of the group must be "gripped" by the catalyst that fused the group/subtracted the subject.

However, for Badiou, that which binds the political subject is not fraternity-terror but fidelity. Institutions themselves are not sufficient to constitute political subjects. This is why political parties, or anarchist collectives, or parachurch communities *as such* are not the bearers of subjectivity. They can still be conditioned by the transcendental coordinates of a world (in the language of *LoW*). It is only those institutions that hold fast to the Event that are marked by subjectivity insofar as they preserve the "event and its commands." This does not mean that political subjects will endure forever. No, Badiou shares Sartre's concern for the tendency of revolutionary fervor to dwindle.[77] However, the very constitution of the institutional subject for Badiou is quite stark in contrast to the pledge in that there is no necessary introduction of seriality into the very life of institutional fidelity itself.

For Badiou, the relations of phenomenological worlds decrease or increase to varying degrees of intensity. As a political subject emerges, the world in which the subject acts has not been completely transformed. Therefore, new inexistences will always need to be brought to existence. Badiou does theorize the existence of a world where no future political action is required—the atonic world. However, this world is not common, and is not one transformed by the over-saturation of political subjectivity but is wrought by the transcendentals which stifle any possibility for decision whatsoever[78]; in the least, it is not a world with which we are concerned in the present investigation. With that, what must be stated is that, for Badiou, worlds will always introduce new sites, or points, that require further subtraction. However, there is a purity that characterizes the constitution of political subjectivity that is absent in Sartre.

For Sartre, the pledged group is constituted precisely on the basis of the introduction of the fear-image. This means that seriality is part of the pledged group's very existence. This is not to overstate the point. The pledged group is not *merely* a serial grouping. Remember, they are mediated by pledged-praxis. However, if we are to understand the logic of the pledged group, particularly in contradistinction to Badiou's concern for "institutional fidelity," the constitutive centrality of seriality must be emphasized.

5.4.5 The Pledge's Practical Function

As was mentioned above, in the pledged group, mediation is via pledged-praxis. This pledged-praxis is now understood in relation to nostalgia, the future, and fraternity-terror. But Sartre also wants to make it clear that the pledge serves a practical function. That is, the pledge is a "practical device" and a "regulatory praxis."[79] It is rooted in the idea that trust is a delicate social modulator that requires some grounding for its legitimation. Thus, with the eradication of the previous forms of legitimacy and their promises of trustworthy reciprocity (which turned out to be negative reciprocity as conditioned by the practico-inert field), there must be a new fabrication of the grounds of legitimate reciprocity. "Fabrication" is of course not meant to imply arbitrary construction. It is certainly necessary (in its contingency, of course). But this fabrication must be created anew, by a new human logic, a human logic that has been constituted under different conditions than the inhuman logic that constituted the constellation of legitimacies of serial existence.

Sartre is seeking to maintain his realism here. The usefulness of the pledge is rooted in real fear in the present. The group really is under constant threat. Kaironic Seriality is the logic that declares that humanity is impossible. Therefore, the pledge is useful insofar as it practically regulates the group by instilling a permanence through the rousing of affects and the creation of new grounds of legitimacy. From affect to affect, the group creates itself through various phases and degrees of mediation. In the logic of the group-in-fusion, humans are resuscitated through the irruption of the apocalypse, which sparks subjective constitution; the spark spreads and subjects are made in common, through common exigence. They are empathic individuals working in common toward a common objective. The logic of the pledged group is rooted in fear: fear that the past might return; fear that alterity might return through dissidence; fear that another foe will come. Therefore, it is affect—affect as sparked and affect as roused—that serves as the motor for group logic in the fused group and pledged group. In the organization, however, as stratification sets in, group members begin to take on particular roles. The next step in the logic of the group, therefore, is organized affect in the form of *mediated capacity*.

5.5 THE LOGIC OF THE ORGANIZATION: MEDIATED CAPACITY

There is some debate in the secondary literature regarding the re-introduction of seriality in Sartre's investigation into the logic of the group. It centers around deciphering at which point in the stratification of the group seriality comes to dominate, turning the group into a serial gathering. For some, the pledge reintroduces inertia and thereby, through the establishment of permanence, initiates a shift toward serial existence. For others, it is not until the organization that seriality becomes constituent. And yet still, for a select few, who have become more prominent in recent years, the organization is the ideal social gathering, with the institution being the phase where the alienating power of seriality has returned. Kristian Klockars explains the intricacies of this nuanced debate:

> But exactly where is the "turning point"...? Does the main dividing line go between the group-of-fusion, which is defined purely in terms of praxis, and the pledged group, which introduces terror (sanctions) into the human relations? Or does it go between the organised group, which constitutes non-hierarchically organised long-term projects, and the hierarchical institution, which introduces subjugating leadership? The answer to this difficult question depends on whether one chooses to emphasise *purity of form and anarchism*, on the one hand, or *concreteness and the possibility of an ideal society*, on the other, as the major ingredient of Sartre's ethical thinking. That is, in the first case, already social organisation would be seen as a first step toward alienation, whereas in the second case, one would imply that Sartre believed in the value of a common organisation (at least as a first step toward an ideal society).[80]

5.5.1 The Turning Point: The Introduction of Seriality into the Group

Nina Power is a theorist of the first grouping, that the pledge initiates the introduction of seriality. She states that, in the pledge, the group interiorizes "the passivity of the practico-inert in activity."[81] Her reading is based on the valorization of the moment of irruption in the apocalypse and the ordering of the group-in-fusion. For her, this mode of the ensemble best encapsulates freedom in the group's immediate antagonism. As she states, "Group activity is simply the pure moment of revolt, for however brief a period."[82]

Thomas Flynn represents a more modest position. For him, the pledge does not introduce passivity because the pledge is self-imposed. Therefore, "praxis remains primary."[83] Elsewhere, Flynn would write, "The artificial (*factice*) inertia of the pledge forms the apex of [Sartre's] social dialectic in terms of freedom-necessity and yields the 'common individual' (group member as such) as the effective positive agent of history."[84] For Flynn, the pledge only imposes an "artificial inertia" upon the members of the group. As such, the pledged group maintains its freedom as each member becomes "the effective positive agent of history."

More recently, Gavin Rae has suggested that, in fact, for Sartre, the organization is the mode of group formation that best stimulates freedom. He argues that, "while the group formations called the series and the institution constrain the individual's practical freedom, the open, democratic group formations called the group-in-fusion and, in particular, the organized group, enhance the individual's practical freedom."[85] It is the "in particular" that is most interesting in his reading of *CDR*. For Rae, the organization is the group most apt to enhance practical freedom. In fact, he even suggests that individuals ought to seek out joining groups that are ordered in the vein of Sartre's organization in order to best experience practical and political freedom.[86]

The confusion surrounding the "turning point" (as Klockars called it) can be understood in light of two general causes; the first of which is endemic to the text itself; the second stemming from the common method of reception of *CDR*.

First, Sartre was somewhat ambivalent when detailing the point at which seriality would come to exert a dominating influence over the logical chain of the group. At times, he does speak of inertia entering the group through the pledge.[87] And he appears to suggest that there is a negative effect of the pledge imposing a "being" onto the spontaneous freedom of the surviving group.[88] However, as was covered in the previous section, he also insists that freedom is made common and that the mediatory relationship of the pledged group is a pledged-praxis, not the inertia of the practico-inert exclusively. Further, Sartre seems to divide his four logical modes of the group into two divisions: the "fused and pledged, organisational and institutional."[89] This division places the fused group and pledged group in the same simple category and places the organization and institution in the other. However, does this two-part division mean that the first groupings are the bastions of freedom, whereas the second are ensembles of alienation? Rae has argued quite convincingly that such is not the case.

This leads us to the second cause for confusion surrounding the "turning point." If *CDR* is read as a text of social ontology, or similarly, if *CDR* is read as espousing a normative vision for the ways social groupings ought to be arranged, then the debate ought to be framed as it has been historically. However, this normative reading misses the intended purpose and heuristic vitality of the text as a regressive analysis of the conditions of praxis. As has been argued throughout the present book, *CDR* is an investigation into the formal conditions of structural and historical anthropology. That is, *CDR* is investigating, first, the logical underpinnings of abstract social groupings, only to subsequently compound these logical abstractions in deeper levels of pluridimensionality in light of concrete, material conditions. The result is that Sartre develops a logic for making the conditions of history intelligible. He is not engaged in normative ascription. Nor is he seeking to develop a theory of how groups are actually ordered (at least not necessarily so).

Therefore, the debate over the "turning point" is taking place at the wrong site of discourse. It ought rather to be centered around the reasons seriality enters at certain points; and to what degree; under what conditions; resulting in what effects. Likewise, the investigation of the various modes of group life ought to reveal the logic of these various stages insofar as each phase presents different and specific ways in which subjects are united in relation to Kaironic Seriality. This helps explain Sartre's ambivalence when investigating each mode of the group. For, *each mode of the group is itself an unfolding moment of totalization that is rife with complex relations of varying degrees of seriality and freedom.*

5.5.2 The Logic of the Organization: Distribution of Tasks

With the interpretative space now cleared, the logic of the organization will be more clearly understood. As Sartre makes it clear, his purpose in exploring the dialectical rationality of the organization is to investigate the way(s) in which organized action is praxis. That is, is it common? To what extent? How does it differ from mediated praxis and mediated pledged-praxis? In what way(s) is affect organized?[90]

These questions are summed up in the following quip: "Organization is a distribution of tasks."[91] This is the basic intelligibility of the organized group. In the organization, stratifications become more clearly defined and roles settle. In the group-in-fusion, individual roles aren't pre-established. One member acts instantaneously in light of his or her position under conditions of imminent threat. In the organization, by contrast, tasks are distributed in three ways: 1) based on the capacities of the individual members of the group, 2) based on the requirements of the individual tasks, and 3) based on the group's overall objective. Sartre uses the example of a soccer team to illustrate this.

With a soccer team, each player has a particular task. This task is assigned based on the skill set of the player; in relation to the other players on the team; in relation to the players on other teams; in relation to the rules of the game; in relation to the expectations that each position demands; and in relation to the historical development of the totality of soccer as a sport—all for the purpose of winning.[92] Each position creates exigencies that praxis must act in accordance with by interiorizing this exigency and then enacting exigencies (ex. training, diet, practice, etc.) that best accord with the function of that role within the common goal of the team.[93] In this sense, there is both limit/demand and praxis. And the organization (i.e., the soccer team) functions best (i.e., wins) when the players are fulfilling their roles to the best of their abilities.

There is another dimension to the logic of the organization that needs to be highlighted. This is the way in which the group acts upon itself. As has been discussed throughout this chapter, the apocalypse is the notion of the process of subjective constitution being instigated. Once inhumanity has been dissolved and the spark of life has become contagious, the logic of the construction of humanity itself takes various forms. In the organization, this logic is understood as "[the] group defines, directs, controls and constantly corrects the common *praxis*; it may even, in some cases, *produce* the common individuals who will realise it (through technical education, for example, etc.)."[94] This is the further explication of the ways in which subjectivity is autopoetic in common praxis. For Sartre, the differentiation of the organized group is of little importance because its appearance is "immediately intelligible." What is important is precisely "the relation between *the action of the group on itself* and *the action of its members on the object*."[95] In other words, what becomes central for Sartre is the relationship between two modes of common exigency: one internally directed and the other externally directed.

As the organization acts on itself, it perpetually recreates itself in its desire to achieve a common goal. This is crucial to understand: the internal exigency is the shared freedom of the dispersed functions as the organization transcends one moment of common praxis in its perpetual totalization toward future common exigencies. In this way, the organization preserves its freedom. It is not driven by inertia coming from without but impelled by a deepening of autopoetic exigencies. Therefore, as the organization works on itself, it constitutes new arrangements of subjectivity. And at the same time, the shared capacities of the ensemble of perpetually created subjects work together to accomplish shared objectives. These two aspects of organizational logic provide the way forward for both micro- and macro-political thinking, which will be the primary subject of part II.

In this way, Gavin Rae's positive reading of the organization is most close to the logical analysis that is presented here. While his suggestion that one ought to seek membership in social and/or political organizations falls prey to the ontological and normative interpretive problems highlighted throughout, the emphasis he places on the organization's capacities to perpetuate freedom charts a useful trajectory. Similarly, Klockars suggests that Sartre "has in fact given us . . . an example of an ideal social formation: the (organised) group."[96] Instead of this type of normative judgment, it is better to state that Sartre has developed a logic of the organization that demonstrates the ways in which social stratification can maintain freedom by *mediating capacities* through the organization of affects in relation to a common objective.

With that, there is still one mode of group life that needs to be explored: the institution. For Sartre, the institution is logically posterior to the organization because of the proliferation of alterity due to "systems of composite reciprocities." Sartre refers to the organization as a "regulated heterogeneity."[97] This is based on the enrichments and determinations of exigent limitations and demands. For example, an organization may have become united by the pledge, and hence from the perspective of the self-imposition of the pledge, each member was granted an equal status before the constitutive image. But not all the members of that organization will ultimately have all the same capacities, desires, functions, skills, concerns; nor will they belong to the same age group, social class, political organization, etc. The result is that heterogeneity comes into the organization—in fact, defines the organization. And this heterogeneity is the basis for the reintroduction of alterity. As the "task becomes more complicated and the volume of the group increases, systems of simple reciprocities are replaced by systems of composite reciprocities."[98] The result is that hierarchy is introduced, and institutionality serializes group life.

5.6 THE LOGIC OF THE INSTITUTION: MEDIATED FUNCTION

The logical chain of group life proceeds from mediated praxis, to mediated pledged-praxis, to mediated capacity, to, finally, *mediated function*. In the institution, what Sartre identifies is the logic of "the systematic self-domestication of man by man."[99] Affect becomes impotent as the subjects in the institution are declared inessential in relation to the essentiality of the institution. In fact, the subjects become the means to perpetuating the essentiality of the institution.[100] This is, of course, the radical inverse of the logic of the group-in-fusion. The logical cycle has come about-face. The common action through the distribution of tasks that characterized the mediated capacity of the organization is discarded for pure, repetitive *function*. Sartre states that, in the institution, "[Freedom], conceived as a common transcendent subject, denies individual freedom and expels the individual from function; function, positing itself for itself, and producing individuals who will perpetuate it, becomes an *institution*."[101]

There is still a sense in which Sartre discusses freedom in relation to the institution. However, this freedom is no longer the shared spark of life of human subjects in mediated reciprocity. Rather, freedom belongs exclusively to what Sartre calls "the sovereign." The sovereign need not be understood as an individual *per se*. Rather, the sovereign is better understood as the dominant logic that withholds the freedom of the institution from the inessential component parts.[102] It can be an individual, a gathering of individuals, or a set of abstract ideas. Thus, "freedom" is an ironic turn of phrase to denote the source of potency in the institution. For Sartre, the cause of the institution is "greater than all of [the members]" and "there is only one freedom for all the members of the [institutionalized] group: that of the sovereign."[103]

Clearly, what has been re-introduced at this stage is the dominance of seriality. In the institution, subjects are "united" through shared alterity. Each functions as a cog in the institutional wheel, serving the purposes of the institution. However, the logic of the institution is not identical to the logic of the collective. In the collective, inhumans are mediated by the practico-inert. But in the institution, subjects are mediated by a shared commitment to the logic of the institution itself. In other words, they are mediated by the self-domestication of their pure functionality in service of the sovereign. The difference lies in the logical causal chain. That is, under the conditions of simple abstract seriality in the collective, as mediated by the practico-inert field, the bodies "united" are inhuman through and through. In the institution, the subjects are the remnant of those who have been transformed through the various stages of the group. The result is that, formally, the subjects in the institution bear a level of humanity within (regardless of how suppressed by institutional dominance) that was absent in the formal abstract investigation of life lived under the compressed conditions of Infinite Seriality. So, although the institution is the model of group life that reintroduces the idea of the dominance seriality, for Sartre, there is a crucial difference between the institutional logic and the logic of the series.

That said, by reintroducing seriality at this stage of development, Sartre has brought his investigation to the end of its logical spiral. His foray into the formal conditions of structural and historical anthropology has revealed a set of logical constructs that make the conditions of social life under historical conditions of scarcity intelligible. They are not absolute facts. Nor are they universal logical principles. Rather, they are practical devices that themselves are part of the totalizing flow of history. But they are still conceptual abstractions.

In order to better understand concrete material existence, it needs to be reiterated that at each given moment, at every given moment, dispersed everywhere around "Earth," these varying modes of social life intermix in a massive cross-contamination of complexity. Any ensemble that emerges, therefore, will never fully eradicate the entirety of the influence of Kaironic Seriality that impinges upon its various members. There may be a sense in which the antagonism is directed to a particular intense expression of this seriality, and that the ensemble successfully eliminates that particular threat. However, each body in the ensemble, each node within the larger network of the social field, will still retain varying degrees of serial alienation within. This is why Sartre refers to the monstrosity of seriality as *Infinite* Seriality.[104]

The persons in the group-in-fusion, while "free" in relation to the immediate threat that fused them in the apocalyptic moment, are still part of various institutional systems that persistently impinge upon them throughout the duration of the apocalyptic Event. Likewise, according to the logic of the organization, there will be varying levels of seriality that will define an individual member outside the scope of the task of the organization. So, in reference to the task of the organization, the subject might still be living according to a de-alienated logic, but with respect to the entirety of her life, she will still be influenced by Kaironic Seriality (to varying degrees of intensity and actuality).

Sartre was keenly aware that seriality was a persistent monstrosity. He knew that group irruption was not sufficient in itself, in its particular uprisings (even its multiple uprisings) to create a socialist revolution around the globe. However, this was his ultimate hope: that a socialist revolution would take hold. And this is how we must understand his investigation into the conditions of History: in light of the persistence of seriality, even through the many revolutionary uprisings, how can there be a global effort to effect a transformation of life in such a way as to make global socialism possible? In other words, his ultimate desire to discover and find the one meaning of History was to serve as a tool in the hands of humans (however they come to be created) to create society as a work of art.

This prepares us for part II, wherein the investigation will examine the power of the imagination to effect this Sartrean vision. Eschewing the normative and ontological readings of *CDR*, part II will proceed by developing what we will call an imaginative logic of action based on the investigation into the formal and logical conditions of history as outlined above.

NOTES

1. Sartre, *CDR*, 350.
2. Sartre, *CDR*, 329.
3. Flynn's reading of the "primacy of praxis" is perhaps the most influential interpretation of praxis in *CDR* and has influenced readers from Butterfield, to Fox, to Dobson, to Heter. Really it is the dominant view in *CDR* reception.
4. Flynn, *Sartre and Marxist Existentialism*, 104.
5. Flynn, *Sartre: A Philosophical Biography*, 335.
6. Sartre, *CDR*, 90.
7. Jean-Paul Sartre, "Materialism and Revolution," in *Literary and Philosophical Essays*, trans. Annette Michelson (New York: Collier Books, 1962), 245.

8. Fanon's indebtedness to Sartre is well-documented, whereas Badiou's has only more recently come to light, particularly in the work of Nina Power. In her PhD thesis "From Theoretical Antihumanism to Practical Humanism," which she defended in 2007, she quotes an interview where Badiou states, "I must say that in effect [my] notion of event finds its genesis . . . in the descriptions of the group-in-fusion, and particularly all the episodes of the French Revolution interpreted by Sartre in this way." Power would comment, "Whilst both are concerned with an analysis of collective political events, Sartre in effect primarily describes the moment of rupture, whereas Badiou's emphasis is on the way in which the collective subject holds true to a political event, and indeed, is actually constructed by it" (185). While this is the most accepted reading of Sartre's notion of the group-in-fusion, this project will indicate that, in fact, Sartre does theorize the construction of the political subject with his group logic in *CDR*—one might even be tempted to suggest that this is the most basic step in the logic of group formation that progresses through the fused group through the organization. This will be developed throughout this chapter and in part II more broadly.

9. Sartre, *CDR*, 357.
10. André Malraux, *Days of Hope* (London: Penguin, 1970), 100 and 102.
11. Ibid.
12. Sartre, *CDR*, 357.
13. Ibid., 670.
14. Jean-Paul Sartre, "Preface," *The Wretched of the Earth*, trans. Richard Philcox (New York: Grove Press, 2004) lii.
15. Sartre, "The Itinerary of a Thought," 35.
16. Flynn, *Sartre, Foucault and Historical Reason*, Volume 1, 124.
17. Badiou, *PP*, 19.
18. Ibid., 31.
19. Brian A. Smith, "Badiou and Sartre: Freedom From Imagination to Chance," in *Badiou and Philosophy*, ed. Sean Bowden and Simon Duffy (Edinburgh: Edinburgh University Press, 2012).
20. Badiou, *PP*, 19.
21. Smith, "Badiou and Sartre: Freedom From Imagination to Chance," 203.
22. Sartre, *CDR*, 401.
23. Smith, "Badiou and Sartre," 204.
24. Alain Badiou, *Theory of the Subject*, trans. Bruno Bosteels (London: Continuum, 2009), 154, 300.
25. Alain Badiou, *Logics of Worlds*, 404–405.
26. Smith, "Badiou and Sartre," 213–14.
27. Brian Anthony Smith, "The Limits of the Subject in Badiou's Being and Event," *The Praxis of Alain Badiou*, 71–101.
28. Alain Badiou, *Being and Event*, trans. Oliver Feltham (London: Continuum, 2005), 345.
29. Alain Badiou, *Conditions* (Paris: Seuil, 1992), 234, note 41.
30. James Williams, "If Not Here, Then Where? On the Location and Individuation of Events in Badiou and Deleuze," *Deleuze Studies*, 3, no. 1 (2009): 101–102.
31. Badiou's indebtedness has been cited throughout. See Deleuze, "He Was My Teacher," in *Desert Islands and Other Texts 1953–1974* (Paris: Semiotext(e), 2002), 77–80.
32. Again, Badiou's relation to Sartre is well known. Deleuze's, however, has been treated with less nuance. Most disregard Deleuze's interest in Sartre as a teenage infatuation. See, for instance, François Dosse, *Gilles Deleuze et Félix Guattari: Biographie croisée* (Paris: Éditions La Découverte, 2007)]. However, for an example of Deleuze's enduring praise for Sartre, see his letter to friend Jeanette Colombel shortly after Sartre's death: "Deleuze-Sartre: pistes," in *Deleuze épars: approches et portraits*, ed. by André Bernold and Richard Pinhas (Paris: Hermann Éditeurs, 2005). And also reference footnote 2 in his final essay "Immanence: A Life" where he credits Sartre for his early exploration of a pre-personal transcendental field as early as *Transcendence of the Ego*. Gilles Deleuze, "Immanence: A Life," in *Pure Immanence: Essays on a Life*, trans. Anne Boyman (New York: Zone Books, 2001), 32, note 2.
33. See Gilles Deleuze and Félix Guattari, *Anti-Oedipus* (London: The Athlone Press, 1983), 256–57: "Sartre's analysis in the Critique appears to us profoundly correct where he

concludes that there does not exist any class spontaneity, but only a 'group' spontaneity: whence the necessity for distinguishing 'groups-in-fusion' from the class, which remains 'serial,' represented by the party or the State."

34. Williams, "If Not Here, Then Where?," 104.

35. Alain Badiou, *Logics of Worlds: Being and Event II*, trans. Alberto Toscano (London: Continuum, 2009), 118–40.

36. Williams, "If Not Here, Then Where?," 98.

37. Peter Hallward, *Out of This World: Deleuze and the Philosophy of Creation* (London: Verso, 2006), 164.

38. Badiou, *LoW*, 89.

39. Williams, "If Not Here, Then Where?," 113.

40. Colombel, 39.

41. Ibid., 40.

42. Ibid., 40.

43. Albert Mehrabian and Norman Epstein, "A Measure of Emotional Empathy," *Journal of Personality*, 40, no. 4 (1972): 525.

44. Ibid., 525.

45. Matthieu Ricard, *Altruism: The Power of Compassion to Change Yourself and the World* (Back Bay Books, 2016).

46. Antonio Damasio, *Looking for Spinoza: Joy, Sorrow, and the Feeling Brain* (London: Williams Heinemann, 2003), 29.

47. Antonio Damasio, int. Manuela Lenzen, "Feeling Our Emotions," *Scientific American*, https://www.scientificamerican.com/article/feeling-our-emotions/.

48. Sartre, *CDR*, 378.

49. Gavin Rae, "Sartre, Group Formations, and Practical Freedom: The Other in the *Critique of Dialectical Reason*," *Comparative and Continental Philosophy*, 3, no. 2 (2011): 193.

50. Ibid., 330.

51. Flynn, *Sartre and Marxist Existentialism*, 110.

52. Mark Poster, *Sartre's Marxism* (London: Pluto Press, 1979), 87.

53. Ibid., 377.

54. Desan, *The Marxism of Jean-Paul Sartre*, 65.

55. Sartre, *CDR*, 345.

56. Ibid., 367.

57. Ibid., 389.

58. Ibid., 390.

59. Power, "The Terror of Collectivity," 101.

60. Sartre, *CDR*, 426.

61. This is something that will be discussed further in part II. For now, it need only be kept in mind that the logic of group life is abstractly separated from, and intelligible only in opposition to serial life. The truth of the matter in concrete material life, however, is that there is no full separation between the two, and that, in fact, both are present at all times to varying degrees.

62. Sartre, *CDR*, 415, 419.

63. While both of the terms could be subsumed under the idea of "imagination," for present purposes, they will be kept distinct. As we progress to part II, the reasons for this will become clearer.

64. Ibid., 413.

65. Ibid., 420.

66. This is one of the tasks of part II.

67. Ibid., 431.

68. Badiou, *PP*, 25.

69. Sartre, *CDR*, 419.

70. Chiodi, 75–76.

71. Sartre, *CDR*, 437.

72. Badiou, *BE*, 214.

73. Ibid., 214.

74. Toula Nicolacopoulos and George Vassilacopoulos, "Philosophy and Revolution: Badiou's Infidelity to the Event," in *The Praxis of Alain Badiou*, ed. Paul Ashton, A. J. Bartlett, and Justin Clemens (Melbourne: re.press, 2006), 368.
75. Badiou, *BE*, 41.
76. Nina Power, "Towards an Anthropology of Infinitude: Badiou and the Political Subject," in *The Praxis of Alain Badiou*, ed. Paul Ashton, A. J. Bartlett, and Justin Clemens (Melbourne: re.press, 2006), 328–29.
77. Badiou, *BE*, 345.
78. Badiou, *LoW*, 420.
79. Ibid., 420 and 423.
80. Klockars, 133.
81. Power, "The Terror of Collectivity," 101.
82. Power, "From Theoretical Antihumanism to Practical Humanism," 95.
83. Flynn, *Sartre and Marxist Existentialism*, 110.
84. Flynn, *Sartre, Foucault, and Historical Reason*, Volume 1, 136.
85. Gavin Rae, "Sartre, Group Formations, and Practical Freedom: The Other in the *Critique of Dialectical Reason*," *Comparative and Continental Philosophy*, 3, no. 2 (2011): 183.
86. Ibid., 202.
87. Sartre, *CDR*, 419.
88. Ibid., 414.
89. Ibid., 686.
90. Ibid., 445–46.
91. Ibid., 446.
92. Of course, matters are complicated when varying levels of economic, political, social, or cultural factors are included.
93. Ibid., 450.
94. Ibid., 447.
95. Ibid., 448.
96. Klockars, 185.
97. Sartre, *CDR*, 463.
98. Ibid., 479.
99. Ibid., 606.
100. Ibid., 600–601.
101. Ibid., 600.
102. Sartre would explore this notion of the sovereign to great detail in Volume Two through the person of Stalin and the logic of Stalinism. See Alberto Toscano's excellent article "Sovereignty and Deviation: Notes on Sartre's Critique of Dialectical Reason, Vol. 2," *Crisis and Critique*, 3, no. 1 (2016): 280–99.
103. Ibid., 621.
104. Ibid., 670.

Part II

Toward an Imaginative Logic of Action

If part I is the exegetical portion of the present investigation, let us frame part II as the speculative portion. Having investigated the logical constructions developed in *CDR*, the rest of this book will proceed in two ways. First, in chapter 6, Sartre's early phenomenological inquiry into the imagination will be briefly outlined. The purpose of this is to reveal the ways in which the imagination functioned for the early Sartre's general theoretical disposition. That is to say, the imagination will come to be seen as central to his understanding of consciousness and thus his phenomenological ontology. We will see the limits of his theory of the imagination for political praxis and will then make connections with other thinkers, and even the later Sartre himself, in order to suggest ways in which the imagination might be made politically relevant, even necessary.

The goal of this first step is to prepare for the development of what, in chapter 7, will be termed the "imaginative logic of action." The latter weds together Sartre's theory of the imagination in his early writings with the "living logic of action" in *CDR* as explored in part I. A key claim guiding this chapter will be that Sartre unwittingly develops a theory of praxis in *CDR* that supplements his earlier work on the imagination by infusing the latter into the logical constructs that were explored in chapters 3, 4, and 5 as a necessary constituent component. The imaginative logic of action will, therefore, come to be seen as the affective, active, and *imaginative* logical disposition that both constitutes human subjects and enables them to perpetually contest the serial forces that constitute our worlds.

Then in chapter 8 we shift to the second aim of part II. Once this logical disposition is established, we will muse on the ways it can contribute to the project of creating new humanisms and the perpetual creation and recreation of de-alienated society. We engage with a series of disparate theorists and concepts in order to supplement our Sartrean project with ideas that might fill in gaps or present robust conceptual frameworks that can aid in grounding an embodied art of contestation to Kaironic Seriality. And then in the final chapter of this book, we turn toward a speculative proposal for both understanding and contesting the hegemonic logic that constitutes serial life in late-capitalism: the serial logic of neoliberalism. We do this by understanding the stakes of the present investigation in light of pressing concerns that have consumed socialist philosophy since Marx. Particularly, how can praxis become translucid to itself, in order to induce liberatory action, when the serial logic of neoliberalism constitutes inhuman neoliberal subjects who are thoroughly conditioned by false consciousness (i.e., serial reason)? As Kaironic Seriality indicates that it is the never *not* the opportune moment to act, we will suggest how it is that the serial logic of neoliberalism must be understood as both suppressing freedom and serving as a potent condition for its actualization.

It must be granted that this is a creative reading and application of Sartrean concepts, but one that is thoroughly rooted in exegesis. Therefore, fidelity *and* creativity will guide the rest of this project.

Chapter Six

The Logic of Poetic Imagination

"By and by, we learn to prefer the closure of constraint to the openness of context. We are progressively trained to refuse the gift of imagination, to stay in touch with reality, as we are wont to say. We learn to mistrust and resist the lure of the merely imaginary in favor of the really real."

—Matthew Ally [1]

To begin our speculative construction of the imaginative logic of action, we turn our attention to some of Sartre's earliest writings. Perhaps a novelist and playwright in spirit more than a philosopher, Sartre prized the imagination's productive capacities. In the theater, famed acting coach Sandy Meisner is noted for declaring that acting is "living truthfully under imaginary circumstances." We might alter this along Sartrean lines by saying the same about lived experience. Thus, resisting our mistrust of the imagination by resituating it as a central constitutive component of lived experience is the undercurrent of the foregoing pages.

As Sartre would recount toward the end of his life, "I believe the greatest difficulty [encountered in my research for my Flaubert study] was introducing the idea of the imagination as the central determining factor in a person."[2] Although the present project is not the space for an exposition on what is surely another under-read and under-appreciated text, this reflection indicates a central tenet of Sartre's philosophical motivation: the imaginary is the central determining factor in a person. What this means, what it implies, and how it fits into the construction of an embodied art of liberatory praxis is what we will begin to explore now.

Toward that end, section 6.1 presents an overview of Sartre's early development of a phenomenological theory of the imagination before exposing the limits of the imaging consciousness in the construction of a political project. Then, we work toward establishing the central, constitutive role of the imagination as a moment of praxis. The imagination must not be understood as *related to* praxis, but rather a dialectical moment *of praxis in totalization*. We attempt to articulate this by demonstrating how the image functioned in Sartre's early phenomenological writings and how it might therefore be able to teach us how to develop a forward-looking approach toward liberatory praxis.

Then in section 6.2, we explore a new logic of the imagination; one that builds on the architecture of section 6.1. Making a distinction between thinking Utopia and utopic thinking, this section articulates the three functions of the imagination as 1) a moment of praxis, 2) as the transcendental condition of the project, and 3) as the site of the perpetual creation of novelty. We bring Sartre into dialogue with Charles Taylor and John Sallis, distancing ourselves from the former's "social imaginaries," but drawing inspiration from Sallis's notion of the "force of imagination." However, whereas Sallis's account of the imagination is found to contain an insufficient theory of materiality, after examining the logic of his poetic imagination, we begin to sketch the outlines of the imaginative logic of action.

6.1 THE USEFULNESS AND LIMITS OF SARTRE'S IMAGING CONSCIOUSNESS

6.1.1 The Image and the Real

In *The Imaginary* (hereafter *PI*), Sartre outlines a phenomenological theory of the imagination. Viewed in terms of intentionality, the imagination is not a supplement to consciousness, the image is not in consciousness, but rather imagination is a type of consciousness—an "imaging consciousness."[3] As such, it is always directed toward an object. Thus, the object of the image is not the image itself, but that "real thing" the image presents.

In the case of non-fictive objects, there is an actual material object that is sought by the imaging consciousness. Being both present (as an object of the image) and absent (as not physically present), the object of the image is "intended" by the spontaneous emergence of the imaging consciousness. In fact, both the image and the imaging consciousness arise together—they are understood as co-constituting,[4] with the image being the relation between the imaging consciousness and the object intended.

But it must be remembered that the image is not an existent for its own sake—it is only an *analogue* of the real object sought. As such, it is deemed *irreal*. "Without doubt it is present but, at the same time, it is out of reach. I cannot touch it, change its place: or rather I can indeed do so, but on the condition that I do it in an irreal way . . . to act on these irreal objects, I must duplicate myself, irrealize myself."[5] Thus, the real desire, the ultimate desire, is to realize the material object in perception. Of course, the latter is impossible. Therefore, there is a deferral of desire/intentionality from the real toward the irreal.

This process is both satisfactory and frustrating: satisfactory because the object is partially presented in its absence as a phantom which gives minimally that which the real could give infinitely; and frustrating because the image is an already constituted irreal existent that will only play at satisfying desire—because it has no autonomous capacity, it teaches nothing, and it is finite insofar as it is a product of the intending imaging consciousness.[6] The result is that consciousness is constantly surrounded by phantom objects, which provide us with a "perpetual evasion . . . [from] our current condition, our concerns, our boredoms; they offer us an escape from all the constraints of the world, they seem to be presented as a negation of the condition of being in the world, as an anti-world."[7] In other words, they provide an escape from that which *is*.

However, this "anti-world" is a world constituted by inert, irreal objects that can do nothing by themselves; therefore, any attempt to base *praxis* off such a world will only provide episodic expressions of positive affect. The extreme of such an effort is what Sartre identifies in the schizophrenic.

> To prefer the imaginary is not only to prefer a richness, a beauty, a luxury as imaged to the present mediocrity despite their irreal character. It is also to adopt "imaginary" feelings and conduct because of their imaginary character. One does not only choose this or that image, one chooses the imaginary state with all that it brings with it. . . . This factitious, solidified, slowed down, scholastic life, which for most people is but makeshift, is precisely what a schizophrenic desires.[8]

For Sartre, what a schizophrenic desires is to bathe in the sea of fancy. This is not an ethical indictment but a descriptive analysis of the line of flight of the imagination when completely untethered from material exigence. That said, this does not diminish the centrality or the power of the imagination, but merely demonstrates how living in an "imaginary state" is a flight from reality, and thus hardly a mode that would provide the sort of real life liberation that so concerned Sartre.

In contrast to the image stands the real. The real for Sartre (in *PI*) is that which is given in perception. In *PI* (and as later developed in *BN*) it is the "in-itself." The in-itself has an infinite depth of being in relation to perception, as the latter is incapable of exhausting all being-in-itself has to give.[9] David Reisman explains how this is the case:

> One sees [an object] from a certain angle, but as something that would present other aspects if looked at from another angle, or touched or smelled . . . The material object . . . is constituted by the consciousness that apprehends it in

that it is given in perception only through an aspect, yet is an object of indefinitely many aspects.[10]

In Sartre's words: "Although an *object* may disclose itself only through a single *Abschattung*, the sole fact of there being a subject implies the possibility of multiplying the points of view on that *Abschattung*. This suffices to multiply to infinity the *Abschattung* under consideration."[11] He would continue on to say that although the appearance is finite, "in order to be grasped as an appearance-of-that-which-appears, it requires that it be surpassed toward infinity."[12]

While Sartre's phenomenological elaboration of the relation between consciousness and the in-itself is not the central concern for the present project, these quotes do at least explicate a key component for apprehending a common tendency between subjects (consciousness/praxis) and material exigency (in-itself/practico-inert). Namely, in Sartre's early work, that being which arises from the in-itself, the for-itself, has infinite freedom because of the *infinite possibilities of that being to which it relates and from whence it came*. Therefore, the real has infinite possibilities that both confront the subject as the site of viscous absurdity, and also offer potential for overcoming one's situation as one creates oneself by one's radical freedom for oneself.

In *CDR*, the real is still understood as materiality. However, the concept of materiality is refracted through the logic of the practico-inert field that sets the parameters of praxis through limits and demands, thereby alienating praxis from the finality of its project(s), and that limits the field of possibles through mediated exigencies—the return of stolen praxis. As the group seeks "to snatch from worked-upon material its inhuman power of mediation," it constitutes subjects according to mediated reciprocity in which each subject remains concrete but also concrete-for-others, and each other (i.e., mediating third) does the same. Therefore, the human, as constituted according to the logic of the group, is freed from the negative reciprocity that necessarily arises from the dialectical relationship between the project and the situation under conditions of serial alienation. As mentioned earlier, it is this process of de-alienation that most concerns Sartre.

If it is the case that life lived in Kaironic Seriality is a necessary result of scarcity and the dialectical relation between praxis and the situation, and if the image (i.e., the relation between consciousness and the intended object) only offers finite, momentary satisfaction and/or glimpses into that which might be, then in what way can the imagination aid us in constructing a broad social theory? Let me suggest that what needs to be explored is the way in which the imagination functions as a moment of praxis, as the transcendental condition of the *project*, and as the site of the perpetual creation of novelty. These three functions will be more fully explored in section 6.2. What inter-

The Logic of Poetic Imagination 163

ests us at the moment is establishing the frame that the imagination is not viewed as an *ad hoc* addition to praxis and its relation to the material, but that it is a constitutive component of praxis in totalization.

6.1.2 The Limits of the Imagined Future

Returning for a moment to *PI*, Sartre notes that there are two ways in which we can conceive of the future: 1) the living future and 2) the imagined future. The former is the "temporal ground on which my present perception develops, the [latter] is posited for itself but as *that which is not yet*."[13] The living future is part of real existence, which occurs with "present, past and future structures, therefore the past and the future as essential structures of the real are equally real, which is to say correlates of a realizing thesis."[14] But the imagined future is posited by oneself, for oneself, as an absence (a nothing, an unreality) that is desired.

In the case of the group, the pledge pertains to the imagined future in that it 1) recollects a past moment of reality and seeks to recreate the exigence of that moment by the positing of an image (nostalgia) and 2) posits a future foe that is not imminent (imagination). The problem is that while nostalgia and imagination can indeed actualize a small degree of the affective impetus of the past and can stimulate genuine feeling toward the future foe, it is not able to reach the *real* of those situations by virtue of the inert and irreal nature of the image. This is because nostalgia and the imagination alone only produce the "imaginary state" that Sartre associates with the schizophrenic's desires. Thus, by nostalgia and imagination *alone* (i.e., the pledge) the group will never be able to sustain itself and prevent ossification into seriality or alienating institutions.[15]

Referring to the time after the fusion of the group and at the beginning of the pledge process Sartre remarks,

> We may speak here of *reflection*, in the strictly practical sense: the group, waiting for the attack, looks for positions to occupy, divides itself so as to man all of them, distributes weapons, assigns patrol duties to some, and scouting or guard duties to others, establishes communication . . . and in this way, in the free exploitation of places and resources, it constitutes itself for itself as a group.

He would continue on to say,

> It is impossible to deny that [the group] *posits itself for itself* once it has survived its victory. Or, to put it another way, there is a new structure to be explained: *group consciousness*. . . . Furthermore, the problem of the *surviving group* . . . suddenly becomes connected for us with the problem of *being*, that is to say, of *permanence*.[16]

Seeking permanence, the group imposes an inert mode of mediated reciprocity from within. However, the pledge, as a reflective act of group consciousness, locks the group into a *statut* of permanence that does not allow the group to reshape itself freely. This is because, despite the pledge-image being constructed by autopoetic humans-in-becoming, the inertia that returns as the limits and demands of serial exigency, as well as the imposition of terror, operate through re-presentation. This act of re-presenting, understood on its own, is an activity of resistance to becoming. Thus, for Sartre, freedom is negated and necessity reigns.

This is the logic of the pledge from the perspective of the imagined future. We can see now why the pledge is locked in a tendential idealism; and we are also given insight into how the logic of the future image can be modified to escape this idealism. It is precisely in that the image, as a construct of praxis's own re-presentation of itself in the form of a pledge, circularly constitutes the pledged group according to its own prefabricated serial image. Thus, in order to avoid this mimetic serial tendency, there must be a way to conceive of the imagination as productive.

6.1.3 Toward Productive Fabulation

The only section in Volume One of *CDR* where Sartre engages the imagination is in the section "Totality and Totalisation." As was discussed in chapter 1, totality is a creation which is present in its entirety, whereas totalization is a developing material system. It should come as no surprise that Sartre classifies totality as "the correlative of an act of imagination."[17] This means that any totality is merely an *analogon*. Totalization on the other hand is the correlative of *praxis*; it is a perpetual dialectical ordering.

In his efforts to ground the intelligibility of dialectical reason, Sartre devises a theory of *praxis* that, at moments, is able to embody freedom. But this freedom is only momentary because once the group's objective has been achieved there is no longer an immediate and exigent situation that requires common *praxis*. The result is that the group must pledge itself, for itself, and to itself, by imposing inertia upon itself, in the form of a reflective act (i.e., an *analogon*). This *analogon* is set to remind the group of the possibility of the violent foe's imminent return. Structuring itself by an image of fraternity-terror, the group therefore negates its own free *praxis* in favor of a totality ("we *are* x"). Seeking to recreate the affective purity that arose initially at the moment of apocalypse, the pledged group views itself in its past victory by creating an image that will stir up the affective impression from that previous event. Successful in part, this effort is doomed to fail as the group permanently settles into this new order by serializing itself.

Therefore, what needs to occur in order to prevent this ossification is that the group needs to take a *progressive* approach and turn its gaze *forward* to the field of possibles. That is, the group must resist the urge to rest assured within the fraternity-of-terror and instead conceive of ways in which new events can be produced. That way, the non-reflective experience of the apocalypse might be perpetuated by the collective enunciation of the group.

Such *productive fabulation* would arise in situation and seek to surpass such conditions as it imagines and seeks to produce possibilities that are as yet impossible. The question arises: will such imagined futures *produce* the desired *result*? No, they won't. It is not the imagination that produces the apocalypse. Such is a spontaneous upsurge of non-reflexive praxis in situation. Nor does it produce a final result at all. The imagination's role is merely to create an image of that which is not yet in order to *motivate group action* through affective possibilities that arise therefrom. As stated in *PI*, at times, an image is created "for no other purpose than to arouse the feeling."[18] Of course, modifying the quote slightly in the language of our project, it is our goal to explore whether the imagination can rouse the unconscious affects of apocalyptic autopoesis. Attaching this to our investigation into the conditions for grounding dialectical reason, the imagination, therefore, is the essential first moment of *praxis* by which the *constituted group* envisions its next step in overcoming the conditions of scarcity and negative reciprocity. Then, through praxis, the situation is modified thereby creating new conditions that must be overcome.

The reason this forward-looking approach has validity is that the pledged group's primary error is in seeking to preserve that which once was, through the representation and reproduction of a past moment of pure freedom into a permanent state, whereas the desired approach would be one in which subjects arise out of a given set of exceptional circumstances and who continually create and produce new images. Therefore, creative imagining never settles and thus never ossifies into seriality and/or institutionalization. Of course, there will be moments when the group's particular task is accomplished, or when the apocalyptic moment ceases. But if scarcity is endlessly reproduced by the very conditions of Kaironic Seriality through totalization, then there will never be a shortage of situations of exigence that need to be *identified* and *transcended*.

This means that the group from one situation of exigence to the next is not the *same* as it was by virtue of the previous apocalyptic moment. The group must continually recreate itself in light of each given situation of exigence in order to resist ever settling into *being* x. There is an openness that must come to characterize the social order, one that connects both the material world and the imaginary. That is, human *praxis* must tether that balance between that which *is* and that which *might be*, with the hope that by being grounded in the former but simultaneously tending toward the latter a constant creation of affectivity will actually force the creation of the novel in new unforeseeable directions. In this way, we might call for a derealization of the political. Or, positively stated, we ought to revel in the imaginary with the hope that by the powers of the imagination we will be able to press the process of totalization into presently unforeseen situations that will allow us to appropriately respond as we seek universal liberation.

But precisely at this speculative point we encounter the limits of Sartre's imaging consciousness. The future image, as conceived from the perspective of *PI*, is not a sufficient concept for the actualization of such a project. The latter must be opened up to the real in order to have the efficacy that is required to fit a truly historical materialist logic of action, one that incorporates the unifying and affective power of the image, but that also remains grounded in material reality. And then, in line with the theme of this book, there must be an investigation into the dialectical logic that underpins such an imaginative project.

6.2 A NEW LOGIC OF IMAGINATION

Above it was stated that the imagination functions 1) as a moment of praxis, 2) as the transcendental condition of the project, and 3) as the site of the perpetual creation of novelty. It is these three functions of the imagination that must first be investigated in order to grasp the imaginative logic of action as developed in the forthcoming pages. The reason is that although Sartre's investigation into the imagination yields fruitful concepts that signal the way forward in a general sense, his development of the terms themselves must be supplemented in order to allow for a more robust conception of the imagination to attach to the logic of action as developed in *CDR*. Particularly, this section will focus on the ways in which the imagination is conceived in terms of its role as a *mediatory material exigency* within the larger social milieu.

6.2.1 Thinking Utopia or Utopic Thought?

Kristian Klockars falls into the normative and ontological trap by reading Sartre as a thinker of Utopia. He states that,

> Today Marxism can no longer be claimed to represent the mood of the times, nor does the kind of Utopian perspective Sartre seems to identify with have much to give. Quite the contrary, I consider the kind of political Utopianism that bases itself on images of ideal societies that appears to be *wholly* different in kind than our own a first step towards a dangerous "the end justifies the means" thinking. Today, perhaps more than ever, critical social theory needs to focus more on critical-normative issues, rather than Utopian ones.[19]

The two biggest problems with this reading of *CDR* is that Sartre is not basing his thinking 1) "on images of ideal societies" or 2) on images of ideal societies that are "wholly different in kind than our own."

The first point falls into the ontological and normative criticism that was outlined previously. To briefly recap, *CDR* is not concerned with developing normative ideals or social ontologies of possible social ensembles. His investigation into the various groups is a hypo-logical investigation into the formal conditions that make such ensembles intelligible. The second point is more pressing for this chapter. That is, Sartre is not proffering images of ideal societies that are "wholly different in kind than our own."

Even if we grant that Sartre is in fact developing images of ideal societies (rather than developing a logic that will aid in the construction of images to motivate action), the images that he investigates are in no way wholly different than our present state of affairs. In fact, it is the rigorous analysis of the formal conditions of society in Kaironic Seriality that is the earmark of his investigation. Klockars's error is that he neglects the enfolding, dialectical trajectory of *CDR*, which progresses from simple abstraction to complex and concrete dialectical abstraction. What is more, he fails to give proper attention to the status of *CDR* as a *prolegomena* to any future anthropology, the designation that Sartre explicitly employed.

The point being this: *CDR* investigates particular models of social ensembles, historical conditions, and anthropological forms in order to understand the logic that underpins praxis under serial and common conditions. The result being that his investigation is not "wholly different in kind than our own" social experience, for the investigation itself is precisely a regressive analysis of the forms of *this* social life in order to comprehend its constitutive logics further. Of course, Klockars's claim that Utopianism is dangerous must be heeded. As he notes, "The search for objective and normative moral principles and the positing of Utopian models of the ideal society share the dangers of becoming authoritarian."[20] In this much, we are all in agreement (Sartre included). However, this is why it is crucial to understand the imagination as a mediatory material exigency. And further, this is why we must make sure to open Sartre's understanding of the imaginary to a robust materialist conception of the imagination.

It must be made clear at this point that the present project is not in any way seeking to think Utopia (with a capital "U"). Utopian visions are trapped in the idealist tendency of the imagined future mentioned above. They are inert monoliths that stand above reality as transcendent Ideas. However, this is not to suggest that utopic thinking (with a small "u") *tout court* is necessarily subject to the same criticism. If the reader will indulge me some leeway to split hairs over capitalization, it might be said that the very thing this project proposes is utopic thinking. The difference, for our purposes, between thinking Utopia and utopic thinking is that the former is musing simply on the fantasy of that which is not (the "anti-world"), whereas utopic thinking is a logical disposition that surpasses the present state of affairs by aiming toward the not-yet. Utopic thinking is an optimistic comportment to the world. We might say that it is grounded by remaining true to the earth. Whereas thinking Utopia is concerned with re-presentation, utopic thinking is expressive and evental. Therefore, utopic thinking is not the mere construction of fanciful ideas that seem pleasant or equitable for their own sake, or even merely for the sake of those projecting them. Rather, utopic thinking is rooted in the actual conditions of concrete, material life. It derives its impetus from the field of material exigencies, while refusing to accept the present *statut*, and then aims toward that which is not yet in order to realize it. This is the type of thinking Sartre presents in *CDR*. His logic of action does not present a vision for Utopia; it is a framework for utopic thinking.

It is paramount that we grasp this distinction. The critique of dialectical reason is a critique of an approach to thinking. But not rationalist thinking in isolation from lived experience. Instead, it is a way of understanding thought as praxis. Which means that utopic thinking is not concerned with projecting rational ideas to which we can aspire (at least not in the first instance). Rather, it is concerned with structuring how productive thinking can proceed in the first place. For, if rational thought is conditioned by seriality, then all such future images will be adequately tainted by seriality. Whereas, if dialectical reason can be properly utopic (in the way we are using the term here), then the process by which such images are constructed themselves will be de-alienated. Comprehending how to do this is what we are endeavoring to do in this book.

6.2.2 Imagination as a Moment of Praxis

Ironically, in *CDR*, Sartre develops a theory of praxis that transfigures his earlier work on the imagination, albeit unwittingly. In *PI*, there are three ways that the real can be surpassed: affectivity, action, and imagination. These three cannot be separated in actual fact, but only in abstraction. Therefore, in lived experience, the productive activity of consciousness is simultaneously affective, active, and imaginative. In *CDR*, no longer viewing the human in phenomenological terms, these three abstractions still inhere in the (in)human project. Praxis, as the logic of (in)human action, includes all three elements in its totalizing activity. As Sartre would come to say, there is a "strict equivalence between praxis with its particular articulations and the dialectic as the logic of creative action."[21]

There are two things of note in this quotation. First, the *particular articulations* of praxis is referring to the differential, subjectivity. This is the spark of subjective constitution that was discussed in chapter 5. Second, praxis is equated with the dialectic *as the logic of creative action*. This means that praxis is understood as the logic of (in)humanity insofar as the (in)human project is essentially *creative*. As Thomas Flynn suggests, this unique activity—the particular articulation of subjectivity in praxis—is an act of the imagination.[22] Therefore, what Sartre develops in *CDR* is a materialist version of his earlier notion of the way consciousness surpasses any given situation.

The (in)human for Sartre, both transcends and invents its situation. Whereas in *PI* the imagination served as the solipsistic negating activity of individual consciousness in ontological freedom toward projects unique to a particular individual contra other competing projects, in *CDR*, praxis becomes a mediated activity of common imaginative negation in a milieu of scarcity. Thus, understood as a formal, synthetic abstraction, when we speak of praxis we must always speak of it in its three dimensions: as affective, active, *and imaginative*. To diminish the centrality of any of these dimensions is to neglect praxis as such. Thus, praxis is not only affective and active, but also—and most crucially for dialectical purposes—imaginative.

6.2.3 Transcendental Condition of the Project

The question remains, however, in what way ought we conceive of the imagination as mediatory? This must be answered in two ways. First of all, it is mediatory in its serial form. Second, it is mediatory, as common.

Serially, if praxis is stored in the practico-inert, and if praxis is affective, active, and imaginative, then the return of stolen praxis must contain the entirety of the logical structure of praxis in its alienating capacity. Therefore, inhuman life in Kaironic Seriality is mediated by the practico-inert in its pluridimensionality insofar as the practico-inert is the stasis of previous affective, active, and imaginative praxis. Therefore, in one sense, the imagination (as a moment of praxis), in Kaironic Seriality, is beholden to the exigencies of the practico-inert field. In another sense, the imagination is precisely the predestined inhuman praxis that is previously charted by the exigencies of the practico-inert field. And finally, the demands that are placed on inhuman praxis in Kaironic Seriality are partly characterized by their previous serial imaginative qualities that have been stored in the practico-inert through the past anti-dialectical relation between anti-praxis and the material condition. This means that the imagination, understood from the logic of Kaironic Seriality, is mediated through the practico-inert as part of the anti-dialectical activity of inhuman praxis.

This understanding of the imagination has resonance with Charles Taylor's development of the "social imaginary" in his monumental *Modern Social Imaginaries*. Comparing Sartre with Taylor on this point is useful in that the social imaginary also conditions and mediates social life. However, Taylor's concept is far too simplistic to offer the type of analysis that is required to grasp the depths of pluridimensional seriality. By bringing Taylor into dialogue with Sartre, it becomes clear just how valuable Sartre's heuristic is for understanding mediated social life in Kaironic Seriality.

Although not associated with alienation *per se*, the social imaginary, upon inspection, actually maps quite well onto the idea of serial imagination that was elucidated just above. For Taylor, "The social imaginary is not a set of ideas; rather, it is what enables, through making sense of, the practices of a society."[23] Elsewhere, he would write that the social imaginary is part of the "very formative horizon of my identity."[24] In other words, the social imaginary is the transcendental condition for social life. It is what makes possible the "practices of society." We could say that the social imaginary is the logic of Taylor's social theory.

However, unlike Sartre's investigation in *CDR*, Taylor's development of the social imaginary does not explore the various modes of pluridimensional experience. Rather, Taylor's conception of the social imaginary is an innocuous reading of the conditions that we have identified as Kaironic Seriality. This is not to claim that Taylor does not identify variations within his understanding of the social imaginary. As is the case, social imaginaries vary in many different ways. But what he neglects is an investigation into the varying logics that undergird these different expressions of the social imaginary. As Matthew Ally has pointed out, "The social imaginary possesses a certain recalcitrance to change—Sartre might call it quasi-being or inertia, Taylor might call it stability or integrity."[25]

This is the crux of the difference between Taylor and Sartre. For Taylor, the social imaginary, as a logical construct, is a neutral hegemonic conception of the ideological life of persons in communities. Sartre, by contrast, would identify the social imaginary as *objective spirit*, the Big Other that mediates life in Kaironic Seriality, and thus necessarily includes alienation as a result of life lived under such conditions. That is, Taylor's social imaginary is driven by a serial logic, one that he ignores in his examination of how social relations are mediated, identities are constructed, and how relational bonds are formed.

More positively, John Sallis presents a conception of the transcendentality of the imagination that fits well with the development of an imaginative logic of action. For Sallis, the imagination is the poetic activity that wonders excessively beyond nature as it is beckoned forth by the power of the elemental, namely the Earth and the Sky. Imagination is not a power of the subject. Rather it is in "excess of the self."[26] Like Sartre, Sallis understands the power of the exigency of material conditions. One is *drawn forth* toward the possible through the image, which is not a representation of the thing, but is rather the presence, occurrence, and locus of the thing.[27]

However, Sallis, following Aristotle and Heidegger, presents a conception of the imagination that is wedded to a conception of the elemental that is absent in Sartre. For Sallis, the imagination wonders excessively *beyond nature*.[28] Absent a critical theory of worked matter, it is the power of the elemental in its infinite depth that draws the imagination forward. This is the *force of imagination*. "*Force of imagination* names, not some capacity belonging to imagination, but rather the self-deployment of imagination itself at some site, indeed, as tractive, at some locus of presence."[29]

That said, the idea of wondering beyond nature is not entirely outside the purview of the logic of imagination that we are developing. Rather than speaking of nature, however, it is better to speak of the situation or the conditions in Kaironic Seriality. In this sense, a Sartrean inversion of Sallis's idea would be to speak of the force of imagination being drawn from the exigencey of the material situation that conditions and mediates social relations. In Kaironic Seriality, this mediation would lead to alienation and inhumanity, but would nevertheless still be characterized by the *force of imagination* that draws inhumanity toward the limits and demands of the practico-inert field. Therefore, along with Sallis, we can claim, "[Rather] than imagination belonging to the subject, the subject would belong to imagination."[30]

At this point, the logic of *serial* imagination is showing itself. But what of *common* mediated imaginative praxis? Sallis again provides a useful foray:

> Imagination can be otherwise deployed. Or rather, a certain impoverishment of imagination can come about, and the result can even be mistaken for imagination itself in its highest possibilities. When poetic imagination ceases to be poetic, it becomes mere imagining. This occurs, specifically, when the drawing is withdrawn from every matrix, when it ceases to bring about a draft in stone, on the shadable surface of a canvas, or in the sound of a voice. It becomes what one might call, in a very restricted sense of the word, a free drawing: lacking a matrix in which figuration could bring to manifestness some moment of the expanse of manifestation, imagination loses all connection with self-showing as such. In contrast to the disclosive artwork, it can only summon up mere phantoms.[31]

The final pages of *Force of Imagination* discuss the distinction between an effective poetic imagination and an impotent phantasmic imagination. The former is open to the elemental, the field of possibles, to exigency, whereas the latter is purely self-referential and self-derived. The phantasm is the images that merely perpetuates itself. It refuses to be sensitive to the beckoning of the exigent needs that saturate the field of possibles. As such, it can only create images that are static and closed off from the future, thereby recapitulating the past endlessly. This is the earmark of conservatism.

The poetic imagination, by contrast, is necessarily embedded in the milieu of exigency. It derives its potency from the demands of the elemental. Poetic imagination is therefore replete with capacity and potency. It is essentially impelled by the interiorization of these exigencies and then exteriorized into the field of perpetually reformed exigencies in a movement of dialectical totalization. Therefore, the logic of the poetic imagination must be contrasted with the logic of serial imagination, with the former according to the logic of the group and the latter according with the logic of seriality.

The differences, of course, between Sallis's understanding of the poetic imagination and a Sartrean imaginative logic of action are many. But where Sallis's logic of the poetic imagination is useful is precisely in its appeal to the creative activity of the imagination as it is impelled by the field of materiality that conditions subjective life and that forces imagination forward. In this sense, imagination is both the condition and the execution of action. In Sartrean terms, it can be said that a poetic imagination is the condition and enactment of dialectical totalization. Likewise, the distinction Sallis makes between poetic imagination and phantasmic imagining maps loosely onto the Sartrean distinction between freedom and seriality. The phantasmic imagining "ceases to be poetic," and as such it has no potency; it is impotent, in the Sartrean sense.

However, under conditions of commonality, according to the logic of the group, the mediatory activity of the imagination has specific characteristics that Sallis's account are unable to explicate. It can only be understood in its incorporation into the logical schema already sketched in chapter 5. Most importantly, what needs to be understood is the way in which the transformation of subjectivity in the irruption of the apocalyptic moment affects the imagination.

6.2.4 Site of the Perpetual Creation of Novelty

As noted above, praxis is affective, active, and imaginative. Conditioned by the logic of seriality, praxis is anti-praxis; as such, there is an impotence that characterizes the affectivity, activity, and imagination of inhumans. When the apocalypse breaks open the fabric of reality and initiates the subjective constitution of those whose praxis is mediated in common in the group-in-fusion, not only is there an affective and empathic connectivity that binds them in their common action, but their effort is shared in its creative expression as well. That is, their affective, empathic common praxis is imaginative at the same time.

Of course, making such distinctions is a theoretical abstraction for the purpose of understanding the logic that guides the action. In concrete, material life the mediation of affect, action, and imagination occurs simultaneously. Therefore, the differential of subjectivity that is sparked is ignited partly by the imagination, both from without, as the mediatory locus shifts from the practico-inert to the shared imaginative praxis of the members of the group, and from within, as the differential (i.e., subjective constitution) is transformed and given a new orientation toward the imaginative field itself.

Because of this transformation of subjectivity, utopic thinking becomes possible. That is, utopic thinking that is conditioned by a serial logic is nonsensical. Impotence reigns, and as such, thinking under such conditions will necessarily be (logically) impotent. The only logical conditions that prepare the way for utopic thinking are those that emerge under conditions of common praxis. As the group initiates the rebirth of human life, the imagination is resuscitated and reorientated so that the group will, by necessity, create imaginatively in its shared affective praxis. In this way, it can be said that group praxis is necessarily driven by a utopic logic.

But this utopic logic is not the mere creation of alternative ideals, as was Klockars's criticism of Utopia. Rather, this utopic logic is rooted in concrete, material conditions. As the group-in-fusion details a direct antagonism to an imminent foe, the actions of common praxis exhibit a utopic impetus in its violence. Once the foe is defeated and the pledge is sworn, the pledge-image is created as a self-imposed inertia that is both inert and dynamic. This pledge-image, as nostalgic and imaginative, mediates the members of the pledged group in commonality. As was noted in chapter 5, the pledge is not purely inert, but rather is the creation of human subjects, now understood as those whose upsurgent imaginative capacities have constructed a shared image to unite them in their desire for permanence. And, according to the logic of the organization, the imagination takes on an even larger role as social stratification sets in. Mediated by capacity, the freedom of the members of the organization is driven by the organization of affect in their perpetual recreation of themselves and in their common objective.

What this means for the foregoing pages of this project is that the logical constructs that were explored in chapters 3, 4, and 5 are now *infused with the imagination as a necessary, constitutive element*. Distinguishing between its impotent or poetic expression is crucial in elaborating how the imagination is central in constructing what is being termed here the "imaginative logic of action," and understanding how this logical disposition is useful for emancipatory political concerns in Kaironic Seriality.

While Sartre did not explicitly develop an imaginative logic of action, his project in *CDR* bears the latent information that this study palpates in order to release the potential benefits for developing social and political theories in the future. Moving forward, this investigation will now demonstrate how both seriality and freedom condition life in pluridimensionality. We will call that logic that is predestined by conditions of seriality the *serial logic of inaction*, and that logic that is conditioned by the freedom initiated by the apocalypse the *imaginative logic of action*.

NOTES

1. Ally, 325.
2. Interview with Michel Contat and Michel Rybalka, published in *Le Monde*, May 14, 1971, reprinted in L/S 119.
3. Jean-Paul Sartre, *The Imaginary: A Phenomenological Psychology of the Imagination*, trans. Jonathan Webber (London: Routledge, 2004), 7.
4. Ibid., 11.
5. Ibid., 125.
6. Ibid., 126.
7. Ibid., 136.
8. Ibid., 147.
9. Sartre, *BN*, xlxii.
10. David Reisman, *Sartre's Phenomenology*, 51.
11. Sartre, *BN*, xlvii.
12. Ibid., xlvii.
13. Sartre, *PI*, 182.
14. Ibid., 182.
15. This was discussed in chapter 5 when it was noted that the pledged group remains afflicted by an idealist tendency.
16. Sartre, *CDR*, 414.
17. Ibid., 45–46.
18. Sartre, *PI*, 142.
19. Klockars, 39.
20. Ibid., 177.
21. Sartre, *CDR*, 69.
22. Flynn, "Sartre and the Poetics of History," 228.
23. Charles Taylor, *Modern Social Imaginaries* (Durham, NC: Duke University Press, 2003), 2.
24. Charles Taylor, *Sources of the Self* (Cambridge, MA: Harvard University Press, 1992), 55.
25. Ally, 333–34.
26. John Sallis, *Force of Imagination: The Sense of the Elemental* (Bloomington: Indiana University Press, 2000), 21.
27. Ibid., 108.
28. Ibid., 220.
29. Ibid., 144.
30. Ibid., 145.
31. Ibid., 229.

Chapter Seven

A Tale of Two Logics

"[How] can he satisfy his needs without hurting himself, without reproducing, through his aspirations and satisfactions, his dependence on an exploitative apparatus which, in satisfying his needs, perpetuates his servitude?"
—Herbert Marcuse[1]

There are two modes of logic that will be explored in this chapter: the first, the *serial logic of inaction*, describes the conditionality of lived experience in Kaironic Seriality, whereas the second, the *imaginative logic of action*, explicates the logical framework under conditions of freedom. Neither of these designations are used in *CDR*. Rather, they are conceptual amalgamations derived from the findings of the present investigation. Their value is contained in their accuracy and deployment. Insofar as these terms remain faithful to a fresh explication of the logical constructs developed in *CDR*, as reconstructed in this project, they will come to be understood as accurate depictions of the logical underpinning of lived experience. Likewise, their deployment as logical concepts will prove valuable for social theory and future philosophical anthropological thinking as they each provide a robust framework for intelligibility, as well as equipping a forward-looking approach toward the field of possibles.

Section 7.1 constructs the framework for understanding the serial logic of inaction. Through the spread of serial thoughts and serial behavior, the logic of seriality will come to be articulated as a type of reason. This type of reason is characteristic of the living logic under Kaironic Seriality. But it is not merely a problem of deficient reasoning faculties or weak-mindedness that can be overcome simply through will or re-education or some exogenous approach. As Marcuse's question above suggests, the task must be to find a way to break the cycle of serial logic's constitutive and reproductive tendency. Therefore, in order to break the stranglehold of serial logic, we must formulate an alternative paradigm that is conditioned by the logic of the apocalypse.

Thus, in section 7.2, we develop a logic that is the speculative foil to the serial logic of inaction. If the serial logic of inaction is defined by serial thoughts and serial behavior, the imaginative logic of action is defined by free thoughts and free behavior. Of course, understanding what this means and to what extent this logical disposition can operate requires further elaboration. While we attempt to sketch a program for how to maximize the flow of the imaginative logic of action here, chapter 8 is the culmination of our present project. This section, therefore, presents the efficacy of the imaginative logic of action in relation to the competing efficacy of the serial logic of inaction. By the end, the reader will understand how both logics co-inhere within all the various nodes of the network of social life and will get a glimpse into a proposal for how to maximize the inexistence of freedom to as great a degree as possible.

7.1 THE SERIAL LOGIC OF INACTION

As was explored in chapter 4, seriality is karionic. Inhuman experience is the primary mode of social life in Kaironic Seriality. The depths of its infringement paint a bleak picture of the possibility of living freely, either individually or in community. Therefore, Kaironic Seriality must be understood as a formal, logical concept that makes this (seemingly?) dire *statut* intelligible. Further, it is a way of making intelligible the impossibility of living inhumanly by the invocation of the call that it is always the opportune moment.

7.1.1 The Logic of Serial Reason

The term Kaironic Seriality also does something else: namely, it reveals the depths of alienation to such an extent that the very rationality that governs inhuman life, and that is expressed in this impotent existence, is seen as the dominant mode of feeling, thought, and action. As Sartre states, "[It] is in the serial milieu and through serial behavior that the individual achieves practical and theoretical participation in common being."[2] In other words, social life in Kaironic Seriality takes place in the serial milieu and expresses itself as serial behavior. What is more, serial social life and serial behavior are governed by a logic that predestines life under such conditions. As Sartre makes clear, "[There] is a *logic* of the practico-inert layer" and as such there are "structures proper to the thought which is produced at this social level of activity; in other words, there is *a rationality* of the theoretical and practical behaviour of an agent as a member of a series."[3] This means that thoughts and actions under such conditions are circular and mimetic, reproducing the very serial logic that conditions thoughts and actions. What this leads to is a circle of self-flagellating serial tendencies.

This is what is meant by there being a serial logic that governs life under serial conditions. Members within any given series are complicit with the serial logic that predestines the exigencies of that situation. This complicity is not a moral concern, but a descriptive one. We might say that Sartre's notion of existential responsibility ought to frame our understanding of complicity. For, while it is structurally true that seriality conditions serial logic, this serial logic is also only lived through concrete (serialized) praxis. This doesn't absolve the latter from responsibility to the situation, even if this responsibility is not attached to a transcendent standard that imposes a system of debt/guilt. Rather, it is a responsibility to affirm the material conditions in which lived experience is always embedded so that understanding how the reproductive tendency of serial logic operates. By implication, being attuned to this complicity also illumines the cracks in the contingency of this operation.

If we broaden the implications of this serial operation in proportion with the monstrosity of Kaironic Seriality, the logic that predestines lived experience must be understood in relation to the polyvalent material exigencies that mediate social life in its pluridimensionality. Not to sound overly rhetorical, but there is no escape from this logic. It is the dominant power that makes life in Kaironic Seriality intelligible. All thought, behavior, social gatherings, political movements, etc., that are so conditioned, are serial; and as such, are predestined by the exigencies of the practico-inert field in all its various layers and dimensions of complexity.

One example that Sartre uses to give an idea of this formal conditioning is with regard to bourgeois respectability in the late nineteenth century.[4] For Sartre, respectability is a particular instantiation of what is being termed here the serial logic of inaction. Respectability was a "lay-puritan attitude to life."[5] It was the domination of culture over nature; the mortification of natural needs in favor of prizing sobriety, frigidity, constraint—in other words, being respectable. The bourgeois were distinguished by this particular identity marker. It is what separated them from the masses, the workers. But this artificiality was a serial construct that was imposed onto those who were born into the system, who then in turn interiorized this mode of objective spirit, and perpetually re-exteriorized respectability in new forms through the process of totalization. It was a "serial reason."[6]

As such, respectability was a practico-inert image that mediated social life in particular class arrangements. The result was that the individual actions undertaken by particular bourgeois were subject to the "*inert limitation and the guiding schema*" of one's comprehension of objective spirit. Again, as above, this comprehension is not necessarily conscious. In fact, more often than not, it functions as the unconscious lived reality of persons embedded within a particular mode of objective spirit. It must be granted that there are certainly occasions when there is clearly an awareness of living one's serial conditionality. It is not recognized as "serial," however. Rather, it is generally understood as a form of self-identification, group identification, or some combination of the two.

The point being this: respectability in the late nineteenth century functioned as a serial logic that *affected one's way of seeing and living in the world*. The result of this was that there could never be any real notion of "communication" under such conditioning. "There is nothing to communicate, since the same comprehension is present in everyone."[7] This is one way that Infinite Seriality limits the possibility for freedom. Under such conditions, there is not even communication. All thoughts, body language, words, inventions, social events—in short, *all signification*—are constituted alongside the serial ideology that predestines social life. Thus, communication is deemed mute. Like shouting into a mirror, it is the repetition of static ideas bouncing back and forth between inhumans who are, in effect, miming one another.

Of course, this examination is merely one minor investigation into the broader issue of Kaironic Seriality. But it does serve as a useful foray into the idea of how life is conditioned by a serial logic of inaction. For, with regard to bourgeois respectability, thoughts, words, and all action are impotent. One is unable to communicate in any real sense. Therefore, what occurs is a serial existence of the perpetuation of the same. Nothing really changes. Nothing really happens. Life is just a self-referential, self-perpetuating repetition of seriality.

7.1.2 The Fracturing and Reproduction of Serial Reason

Jonathan Crary discusses a similar phenomenon with respect to the contemporary info-tech landscape of late capitalist society. In a discussion about Bernard Stiegler's theory of the "homogenization of perceptual experience within contemporary culture,"[8] Crary suggests that there has been a large-scale "systemic colonization of individual experience . . . [by] the remaking of attention into repetitive operations and responses that always overlap with acts of looking or listening."[9] The result of this "entails a loss of subjective identity and singularity; it also leads to the disastrous disappearance of individual participation and creativity in the making of the symbols we all exchange and share."[10]

While Crary agrees with much of Stiegler's analysis, he differs by claiming that Stiegler focuses too much on the passive sphere of spectator receptivity. Instead, Crary notes that the current state of media requires participants to engage with the content by sharing, following, exchanging, and reviewing. The result is that he develops a dialectical logic that is very similar to Sartre's. It is worth quoting him in length:

> [Against Stiegler's] idea of the industrial homogenization of consciousness and its flows, one can counterpose the parcellization and fragmentation of shared zones of experience into fabricated microworlds of affects and symbols. The unfathomable amount of accessible information can be deployed and arranged in the service of anything, personal or political, however aberrant or conventional. Through the unlimited possibilities of filtering and customization, individuals in close physical proximity can inhabit incommensurable and non-communicating universes. However, the vast majority of these microworlds, despite their patently different content, have a *monotonous sameness in their temporal patterns and segmentations*. [Emphasis added][11]

What we see here is an explication of the dominance of Kaironic Seriality dispersed through a serial logic. The "parcellization and fragmentation" of the "fractured microworlds of affects and symbols" and the "monotonous sameness in their temporal patterns and segmentations" states precisely the way the serial logic of inaction functions. It is not a monolithic Idea without internal difference. It is not a mode of *ratio* separated from its constitutive, conditioning factors. Rather, it is a heterogeneous network of rationalities that have countless sites of variegating intensity that express themselves and that are enacted in many different ways; all the while being drawn by the dominant exigencies established by the practico-inert field, which in turn are re-constituted and re-inforced by this tendential serial operation. And the process repeats—*ad infinitum*.

However, for Sartre, there is both a commonality and a difference in seriality. That is, in reference to the collective object in diachronic serial relations, recurrence ensures a commonality of serial logic. Whereas in the structural network of synchronic seriality, there are layers enfolding within layers so that each individual body has various and thus unique institutional serial complexes impinging upon one. Some might be shared in a simple sense. But the particular complex, because of the uniqueness of each individual totalization, is specific to each body upon which it compresses and contracts. This field is the transcendental condition of social life as mediated by the practico-inert. It is what establishes how life is to be lived, what is to be believed, where individuals fit within a given society, and the entire plethora of social concerns in concrete, material existence.

But it is not merely an objective power. No, it must be kept in mind that every objectivity is the necessary condition for an interiorization. In this sense, Sartre speaks of the way "one makes oneself a bourgeois." Through interiorization, one appropriates the network of serial conditions, and every action, "every moment of activity is embourgeoisment."[12] Each individual in Kaironic Seriality does the same. In Thomas Flynn's words, it is "collective bad faith," and it is lived through the perpetual process of interiorization-exteriorization.[13] That is, the serial logic of inaction is what governs the process of totalization in Kaironic Seriality.

What we can learn from this is the way in which *inaction* is self-defeating as it produces its own alienation ("embourgeoisement"). As such, serial inaction is necessarily the reproduction of seriality within oneself and in the exterior field of objectification that serial inaction enacts. Flynn calls it a "deformation of praxis because of practico-inert mediation."[14] Serial logic prevents anyone under such conditions from doing anything other than reinforcing the monstrous powers of serial logic itself, and, therefore, unless there is direct antagonism to it, then there is a contagion that perpetually refabricates the serial logic. In this sense, we are all *responsible* for our participation in the perpetuation of serial logic.[15]

Crary states, "[Seriality] is the numbing and ceaseless production of the same. It is the weight of all the counterfinalities that inexorably act against our own intentions, our loves and hopes."[16] And this indomitable "weight" is what ensures that life lived in Kaironic Seriality is ultimately Impossible. With reference to the previous chapter, there is a sense in which the serial collective is engaged in an act of imaginative logic, but one that is limited by its complicity through interiorization of the serial conditions in which it finds itself; this is the phantasmic imagining that Sallis speaks of. It is an imaginative logic that is not sensitive to the exigencies of praxis, but that is rather beholden to the static inertias of Infinite Seriality. It does not yet recognize the opportunity of the *kairos*.

The group, on the contrary, uses a creative imagination, one that transforms the conditions in which it finds itself in order to intentionally recreate the world and aim toward future possibles of de-alienation. Apocalypse, then, creates the new in that it introduces possibles that weren't latent—but virtual—in the collective serial condition. What takes place is the introduction of a reality that wasn't merely potentially present in a latent state, but a new free creation of life and sociality that is not defined by alienation but by free communized praxis. Because of the irruption of the apocalypse, the imagination is freed (as is the rest of the human-in-creation). And as the individuals in the group become molten and share their mediated reciprocity, so the imagination is wrested away from the constraints of serial logic and a space is opened for a new logic to emerge.

7.2 THE IMAGINATIVE LOGIC OF ACTION

7.2.1 *The Realism of the Imaginative Logic of Action*

In *MR*, Sartre was interested in the development of a coherent philosophy that would free dialectical materialists "from the myth which crushes them and which hides them from themselves." In place of this myth, Sartre wanted to develop a philosophy that would be "superior to materialism in being a true description of nature and of human relationships."[17] Although it took him another decade to develop such a philosophy, the ideas of *CDR* are present, in germinal form, in the mid- to late 1940s.

The two most important aspects of this philosophy that he begins to explore in *MR* are 1) a commitment to the present situation and 2) a future-oriented praxis. As he states,

> What is needed is, in a word, a philosophical theory which shows that human reality is action and that action upon the universe is identical with the understanding of that universe as it is, or, in other words, that action is the unmasking of reality, and, at the same time, a modification of that reality.[18]

What he outlines here in bare bones is what would later become his notion of totalization in *CDR*: a dialectical philosophy of action that moves through the interiorization and exteriorization of the conditions in which one finds oneself thrown at each moment. But this philosophy must not be merely pragmatic in its activity. This is what he sees as the failure of the dialectical materialists. They do not have an accurate philosophy of the world *as it is*, and as such, are engaging in myth creation for the purpose of motivating action. This "pragmatic conception of truth will not do, for it is subjective idealism, pure and simple."[19]

Therefore, what he was seeking to explore, and what he would later develop in *CDR*, is a philosophical theory that is essentially realist. That is, it must be committed to the concrete truths of material life. It must not engage in thinking Utopia. In his words, "[The] revolutionary demands a philosophy which considers his situation, and, as his action has meaning only if it brings man's fate into question, this philosophy must be total, that is, it must produce a total explanation of the human condition."[20] This is why the dialectical relation between praxis and material conditions in *CDR* would become so crucial as the ground of his argument. In order to describe the revolutionary capacity of subjectivity, he had to construct a philosophy of the human that is essentially capable of revolution by its very existence. And this revolutionary capacity would be intelligible only by first understanding the conditions that mediate human (and inhuman) life. Then, and only based on such a realism, could one make the future orientation of praxis intelligible as it goes "beyond the situation in which [one] is placed . . . [as it aims] towards a radically new situation."[21]

The imaginative logic of action that is being developed here is the culmination of this philosophy. It is a way of comporting oneself to the world as it really is, in order to *analyze* it, *engage* with it, *connect* with it, and ultimately *surpass* it. Sartre scholar Matthew Ally states this perfectly when he notes that the task of Sartre's dialectical logic is to,

> *show* how everything is everywhere always at stake (a descriptive moment), in order to understand just *what* is at stake (an eductive moment) and *how* it came to be so (a regressive moment) and how it *comes* to be (a progressive moment), and all of this so that we might get a better grip on *a way forward* (a normative moment).[22]

The first four "moments" that Ally describes are placed in a necessary logical chain anterior to the "normative moment." They must be understood as the dialectical ground in order to avoid misunderstanding Sartre's method. Neglecting the robustness and nuance of Sartre's approach by jumping straight to normativity misses the comprehensive purpose of *CDR*, which is the *development of the grounding* for any future normative anthropologies. Once this grounding has been established, then there is a position from which projections toward the future can begin to build.

However, such construction must be aware of the logic that is guiding the project. Under Kaironic Serial conditions—insofar as the serial logic of inaction is guiding anti-praxis—there is an impotence of inaction and anti-dialectical reason that governs theory construction and the action that accompanies it, ensuring that the rationality coming therefrom will be frail and ultimately subject to the logic of the system that undergirds it. By contrast, an imaginative logic of action is the guiding logical form that *enables genuine theory construction and political and social engagement to flourish in a creative freedom of common praxis*.

Kristian Klockars voices a concern when he claims that Sartre's search for "*a comprehensive understanding of concrete reality*, and totalisation as a central notion of this ideal" is subject to the poststructuralist and postmodern skepticism provided by Foucault, Said, and Lyotard.[23] Klockars states that the contribution of these thinkers was to replace any notion of a total description orbiting a single center with that of a set of discourses and practices that focus on "discontinuities, transformations, thresholds and differences, and which rather 'would deploy the space of dispersion' than totalise."[24] Waging "war against the idea of totalisation," these thinkers are claimed by Klockars to have presented a criticism of all totalizing philosophies, of which Sartre was a signal figurehead.

The problem with this reading is that Klockars seems to be conflating "totalization" with "totality." Totality, of which Sartre himself is critical as being practico-inert, is the target of poststructuralist critiques and postmodern skepticism. Although the word "totalization" might be used at times by poststructuralists and/or postmodern theorists, the confusion is chalked up to the strange proliferation of the term in *CDR*. Totalization is a perpetual activity, aligned with praxis and processual flow. Totality is the static conception of *being* that is negatively aligned with the practico-inert mediator. Therefore, Klockars's conflation of totality with totalization and subsequent alignment of poststructural and postmodern criticisms with this conflation ultimately ends up being a straw man which neglects the nuance of Sartre's development of his dialectical logic as Paradoxico-Critical.

Although it is the case that Sartre wanted to eventually articulate a single meaning of history, this is not metaphysical speculation, or the institution of a metanarrative or a dominant "worldview." Rather, it is one meaning that is itself discontinuous. Or even better, it is the development of a logic that will enable *this* particular history to be intelligible in its pluridimensionality. This might still be an overly ambitious project that is lent to the skepticism of postmodern critique,[25] but it must be kept in mind exactly what Sartre was doing in *CDR*. He was seeking to understand the heterogeneity and pluridimensionality of concrete, material life by investigating the formal, logical constructions that make said life intelligible.

Engagement in the world, therefore, begins with a sensitivity to concrete materiality, to the situation. Embedded in the Impossible of Kaironic Seriality, the imaginative logic of action emerges in antagonism as the spark of life is initiated in the apocalypse. This logic is affective, active, and imaginative in all of its instantiations. That is, there is a commonality that is shared through mediated reciprocity as affectivity is dispersed and shared by a group logic. Likewise, it is enacted in the activity of the group itself, as the group logic is a living logic of action. And of course, it is imaginative—creative—as it freely surpasses the present *statut* in its perpetual transcending toward the future. And here we come full circle. The two general requirements of the imaginative logic of action are 1) a sensitivity to the present situation and 2) a forward-looking gaze.

7.2.2 The Imaginative Logic of Action: Sensitivity and a Forward-Looking Gaze

William Connolly speaks of the "seer" as one who "reads natural and cultural signs during fateful moments in modern life" and one who has "exquisite sensitivity to the world."[26] In this sense, those who are governed by an imaginative logic of action are *seers*. They are sensitive to the world as they are embedded in it, feeling the pressures of Kaironic Seriality that press them to extremes that can no longer be endured. Reality has been unveiled, the opportune moment perceived, an internal fury ignited, and the apocalypse brings to light a novelty that makes possible another reality. This means that seers are ones who sense the opportunity of the opportune moment of Kaironic Seriality.

This conception is not novel. The Marxist tradition has long viewed the revolutionary spirit as being guided by a similar sensitivity. In a passage from Engels's *Socialism: Utopian and Scientific*, we find the following:

> The growing perception that existing social institutions are unreasonable and unjust, that reason has become unreason, and right wrong, is only proof that in the modes of production and exchange changes have silently taken place, with which the social order, adapted to earlier economic conditions, is no longer in keeping. From this [from this dysfunctionality] it also follows that the means of getting rid of the incongruities that have been brought to light must also be present, in a more or less developed condition, within the changed modes of production themselves. These means are not to be invented by deduction from fundamental principles, but are to be discovered in the stubborn facts of the existing system of production.[27]

G. A. Cohen comments on this "optimistic" passage by claiming that, for Engels, the solution to the problem of asymmetrical property-power relations presents itself as necessary. It is only up to the socialist theorist to make the problem more felt so that revolutionary action can be taken.[28] This is the raising of class-consciousness leading to revolutionary praxis.

Without rehashing the problems associated with the "obstetric" metaphor of political practice that Cohen identifies in Engels's thought, what is curious is how the revolutionary disposition is essentially marked by an acute awareness of social contradictions: power is not equitably distributed; resources are not equitably managed; laws are enacted to ensure that access to power and resources remain restricted to certain types of societal actors; but curiously, the quality of value production does not accord with the quality of power, resource, or juridical management. Sensing these contradictions is both the result of being materially attuned and the source for overcoming these asymmetries. The question is *how*.

This is why the seer must also be driven by a forward-looking gaze. Contra Klockars's criticism that Sartre was a thinker of Utopia, the imaginative logic of action inspired by Sartre must, without hesitation, utilize utopic thinking. Alongside Herbert Marcuse's advocacy of an aesthetic ethos, the imaginative logic of action must not shy away from employing the imagination in the construction of alternative futures. This does not in any way suggest the elimination of the scientific character of critical theory. Rather, it means that

> Technique would then tend to become art, and art would tend to form reality: the opposition between imagination and reason, higher and lower faculties, poetic and scientific thought, would be invalidated. Emergence of a new Reality Principle: under which a new sensibility and a desublimated scientific intelligence would combine in the creation of an *aesthetic ethos*.[29]

This is the logic that must govern revolutionary praxis. The imaginative logic of action is deployed by seers who are sensitive to the real world, who refuse it, and who are motivated by an *aesthetic ethos*. As Ally states, it is "an orientation to the real refracted through the lens of the possible."[30] And because such persons have begun the process of becoming human through subjective constitution and the varying organizations of affect, praxis, and the common mediation of the two, they are driven by a logic that is creative and free. Only under such circumstances, only through the appropriation of such a logic, and only by the deployment of this logic can the cycle of serial logic be broken. This is the only hope for genuine action irrupting through "Earth." It is in the construction and deployment of an imaginative logic of action as it emerges in opposition to, and within the opportunity provided by, Kaironic Seriality under the threat of the Impossible.

7.2.3 Toward an Imaginative Logic of Action

At this point, however, it must be made clear that we are still working at the level of speculative abstraction. In lived experience, there is no way that the serial logic of inaction and the imaginative logic of action can be fully separated. What this means is that both inhere to varying degrees of intensity and in competing levels of efficacy within various (in)human bodies. Both logics exist simultaneously and in many ways feed off one another. Sartre himself states that "in every non-serial *praxis*, a serial *praxis* will be found, as the practico-inert structure of the *praxis* in so far as it is social."[31] This is not to claim that they exist in the same way, at the same time, thereby negating the qualitative differences between them. Rather, this is to state that the complexity of pluridimensional life ensures that the two logics can, and do, *insist* within the same contexts at the same time, competing for dominance.

If the scope of Kaironic Seriality is as thorough as has been suggested above, then even under moments of freedom in the apocalypse, there still remain levels of seriality that impinge upon the subjects who are antagonistic to it. Likewise, the logic of the group speaks of dissolving seriality in relation to the immediate threat, but not in relation to the totality of Kaironic Seriality. And in the wake of the apocalypse, since there has been an initiation of subjective constitution, even under new forms of seriality dominated by an institutional logic, there is still a remnant (at least) of the transformation that was sparked by the irruption of freedom. Therefore, it must be admitted that in concrete, material life, both the serial logic of inaction and the imaginative logic of action are present simultaneously in all contexts.

Therefore, the concepts developed, practico-inert objects constructed, activities undertaken, strategies envisioned, policies proposed, etc., need to be understood as complexes composed of both serial and free components. One is never entirely free. Nor is one ever entirely serialized. There is a sense in which humanity and inhumanity, potency and impotency, are present in bodies at all times. It is more a matter of which complex of forces is most expressed. This means that as praxis and anti-praxis work on matter (whether that be traditionally understood material objects or psychic ones), it does so only insofar as it is both compelled by serial forces and impelled by free motivations. This is because the context in which all activity takes place is conditioned by swirling fields of both practico-inert limits and demands and also by the virtual potency of the differential that is never diminished (despite how serialized it might be).

The goal becomes, therefore, not the wholesale replacement of one logic for another, but rather, the perpetual dissolution of the efficacy of the serial logic of inaction in the expansion of the efficacy of the imaginative logic of action. Sartre echoes this sentiment in this lengthy quote:

> [We] have supposed for convenience that the individuals who compose [the group] are *homogeneous*. . . . In fact, each comes to the group with a *passive* character (that is to say, with a complex conditioning which individualises him in his materiality); and this passivity—in which we should include biological as well as social determinations—contributes to the creation, even apart from seriality, of a hysteresis which is capable of occasioning a new *series*. For these and other reasons, the theoretical schema which I have sketched does not apply in reality: there are procrastinators, oppositionists, orders and counter-orders, conflicts, temporary leaders who are quickly re-absorbed and replaced by other leaders. But the essential point remains, through this *life* of the fused group (which is in fact only its struggle against death through passivisation): namely, if the group is really to constitute itself by an effective *praxis*, it will liquidate alterities within it, and it will eliminate procrastinators and oppositionists.[32]

Here, Sartre declares the real, concrete, material logic of the life of the group: it is the liquidation of alterity that is contained within it. In other words, Sartre was keenly aware that his accumulating investigation into the life of the group and the power of seriality were convenient abstractions that served the purpose of giving insight into the logics of freedom and alienation. This is what is meant when he says "the theoretical schema which I have sketched does not apply in reality." In the end, however, his investigation reveals that the two logics that explain and drive history *insist* (not *ek-sist*) in a complex agonistic relation of intensive variation.

This does not mean that Sartre was content to leave the discussion there. No, he was still the ever-optimist. And his concern, as it was in *MR*, was to construct a philosophy in order to equip revolutionary thought and action to actualize de-alienated life. But he needed to emphasize that this philosophy would only be understood as a logic that experiences itself, in and through the *praxis of struggle*, that is to say, antagonistic reciprocity . . . in *our* world (governed by scarcity). [. . . Dialectical logic] appears at the moment in which the group emerges from the oppressed series as a dictatorship of freedom. [. . . It] *is* the *praxis* of the oppressed in so far as they are common individuals rooted in a seriality of impotence.[33]

Therefore, as the serial logic of inaction and the imaginative logic of action battle for effective expression in a multitude of sites dispersed throughout the social milieu, there must be a war waged against seriality—from within. The imaginative logic of action is not exogenous. Rather, it is the epigenetic emergence of novelty within the interstices of dissonance contained within the network of power relations on "Earth." The revolutionary goal, therefore, is the maximization of freedom through the proliferation of an imaginative logic of action that erodes the conditioning stranglehold of Kaironic Seriality.

The question then remains: how does this happen? The next chapter will suggest two ways in which this erosion of Kaironic Seriality might occur. The ideas contained therein are not normative absolutes. Rather, they are speculative proposals that work within the imaginative logic of action that has been constructed thus far. In the end, this logic will itself become more clearly defined as it attaches itself to specific ideas that suggest ways in which revolutionary praxis will be foundationally supported. In the words of William Connolly, the task will be to "find ways to strengthen the connection between the fundamental terms of late-modern existence and positive attachments to life as such."[34] This will be done through an overarching motif that is being called the development of the *imaginative political subject*. This subject is one that is perpetually constructed through a totalizing relation to the imaginative logic of action, both being conditioned by it and by employing it.

NOTES

1. Marcuse, *An Essay on Liberation*, 4.
2. Sartre, *CDR*, 266.
3. Ibid., 266.
4. Ibid., 770–81.
5. Ibid., 770.
6. Ibid., 774.
7. Ibid., 777.
8. Jonathan Crary, *24/7: Late Capitalism and the Ends of Sleep* (London: Verso, 2014), 50.
9. Ibid., 52.
10. Ibid., 51.
11. Ibid., 53–54.
12. Sartre, *CDR*, 231.
13. Flynn, *Sartre and Marxist Existentialism*, 106.
14. Ibid., 105.

15. The idea that we are individually responsible in the dialectical totalization of this serial logic needs to be unpacked further. Of course, this is not the place for such an investigation, as the main purpose of this project is more foundational. That said, it must always be kept in mind that, for Sartre, the individual does not disappear in his materialism. Rather, the relation between the individual, the situation, and the social milieu are all cross-contaminating, ultimately inseparable in real, concrete, material life, but nevertheless each component functions by serving its purpose as moments of the dialectical logic.
16. Crary, 117.
17. Sartre, "Materialism and Revolution," 223.
18. Ibid., 229.
19. Ibid., 228.
20. Ibid., 226.
21. Ibid., 225.
22. Ally, 123.
23. Klockars, 17.
24. Ibid., 17.
25. This is precisely what Nik Farrell Fox explores in his book, *The New Sartre*. While he acknowledges that Sartre is a linchpin figure between the modernist and postmodernist traditions, he ultimately claims that Sartre was too wedded to his individualism to fully be understood within the postmodern ethos.
26. Connolly, 156 and 159.
27. Friedrich Engels, *Socialism: Utopian and Scientific* (London: Allen and Unwin, 1892), 75.
28. Cohen, 54–55.
29. Marcuse, 24.
30. Ally, 347.
31. Sartre, *CDR*, 266.
32. Sartre, *CDR*, 403.
33. Ibid., 804.
34. Connolly, 63.

Chapter Eight

Creating Society as a Work of Art

"[As] you know, for me there is no a priori essence; and so what a human being is has not yet been established. We are not complete human beings. We are beings who are struggling to establish human relations and arrive at a definition of what is human . . . we are seeking to live together like human beings, and to be human being. So it's by means of searching for this definition . . . that we will be able to consider our effort and our end. In other words, our goal is to arrive at a genuine constituted body in which each person will be a human being and in which collectivities will be not less human."

—Jean-Paul Sartre [1]

The above quote is the motor that will impel the rest of this investigation. "We are not complete human beings . . . we are seeking to live together *like* human beings and *to be* human being [emphasis added]." Therefore, an investigation into the imaginative logic of action in relation to the construction of *new humanisms* and the *perpetual creation of society* will illuminate conditions under which the above Sartrean quest is refracted through contemporary concerns.

The imaginative logic of action is what makes both the transcendental condition of freedom intelligible and what guides the effectiveness of said freedom. It mediates common praxis through totalization. In this task, there are two general dialectically related processes that pertain to subjectivity that will be explored in this final chapter. First, it will be crucial to understand that subjectivity is constituted in freedom. Second, we must examine how this process of subjectivization occurs. For present purposes, it is important to keep in mind that subjectivity refers to the condition and enactment of agency under conditions of group freedom (i.e., mediated group praxis), initiated by the affective spark of the apocalypse, in antagonism to Kaironic Seriality (recall the discussion on subjectivity and the differential from chapter 5). Since life in Kaironic Seriality is marked by *inhumanity*, there must be an investigation into the ways that *human* life might emerge through the process of subjectivization. The result will be that Sartre's call for a perpetual apocalypse will be dressed in new garb as it is refracted through the lens of this overall project.

We begin in section 8.1 by calling for the construction of new humanisms. Not humanism singular, but humanisms plural. The reason for this distinction is that the former is a practico-inert concept derived from serial reason, whereas totalization requires the perpetual creation of human logics. This sets up the next stage of development in section 8.2, where we discuss how this perpetual creation might take place through the perpetual withering of seriality. Through the perpetuation of micro-psychobiological shifts, subjective constitution is autopoetic as it contests the material conditions that impose seriality. This is not a complete idea about how seriality must be contested, but rather an example of one way in which seriality is withered while subjectivity is simultaneously able to be constructed in greater degrees of freedom. And then in section 8.3 we close the chapter by advancing Sartre's idea of the perpetual apocalypse. While he doesn't explain quite what he means when he muses that this is an appealing idea, what we can extract from his advocacy in relation to the project we are constructing is that this notion expresses a robust conception of the orientation that defines the imaginative logic of action as a perpetual disposition emerging from and contesting Kaironic Seriality.

8.1 CONSTRUCTING NEW HUMANISMS

If there is no transformation of subjectivity alongside a transformation of the conditions of life, then revolutionary activity will be incomplete. To aim toward one pole, to the neglect of the other, ensures that the transformation will be partial and that it will be predestined by the serial logic of inaction. The use of spatial metaphors here slightly betrays this process. To speak of "alongside" is, of course, metaphorical. And while there is a heuristic purpose in its use, the limits of language prevent speculative thought from truly reaching the facts of intensive variation that best characterize the relation between subjectivity and the conditions of life referenced here. We have employed various spatial metaphors and prepositional phrasing throughout, in order to create a sense of the internal relations expressed by dialectical logic. However, we are aware of the limitations of thought, particularly in a social context replete with the influences issued by analytical reason. That said, there must be a total effort, one that confronts all aspects of the diverse field of Kaironic Seriality, in order to allow the flows of a revolutionary logic to flourish.

8.1.1 *"Humanisms" Plural*

The first aspect of this total transformation that will be discussed here is with regard to the construction of new humanisms. To begin, we heed the call of Frantz Fanon: "For Europe, for ourselves and for humanity, comrades, we must make a new start, develop a new way of thinking, and endeavor to create a new man."[2] The creation of this "new man," however, must not be seen as the supplanting of a pre-existent *eidos* in favor of a new one. Instead, the creation of new humanisms must be essentially pluralist and open. This is the reason for using *humanisms* as opposed to *humanism*. The latter term is encased within a limiting and limited paradigm. It cuts short the polyvalence that makes up material life in real history, and instead offers a static vision of what could be. It also derives its theoretical strength from a serial vision, one that is not sensitive to the material exigencies of the real world.

The plural, humanisms, by contrast, is a concept that is more useful. As Nick Srnicek and Alex Williams write, it is an "empty placeholder that is impossible to fill definitively."[3] It contains within itself an openness that eschews philosophical, theological, political, and other historical logics that limit what might emerge through the creative interplay of various social forces, and instead leaves room for the upsurge of novelty through the proliferation of freedom in common praxis. It is a lived formal category, an historicized *a priori* that corresponds to the logic of totalization and praxis rather than totality and the practico-inert.

In the preface to *The Wretched of the Earth*, Sartre refers to the violence of the colonized and the emergence of subjectivity in this way:

> [Fanon] shows perfectly clearly that this irrepressible violence is neither a storm in a teacup nor the reemergence of savage instincts nor even a consequence of resentment: it is man reconstructing himself. . . . Once their rage explodes, they recover their lost coherence, they experience self-knowledge through reconstruction of themselves.[4]

It has been argued by Power and Flynn (among others) that *CDR* is unconcerned with subjectivity as such. Counterposing Badiou and Sartre, Power writes, "Sartre in effect primarily describes the moment of rupture, whereas Badiou's emphasis is on the way in which the collective subject holds true to a political event, and indeed, is actually constructed by it."[5] Likewise, Flynn is willing to concede only an inch with respect to subjective constitution in *CDR*: "The true 'subject' of history is the closely knit group, in the sense that only in the group does one overcome the passiveness and exteriority of the practico-inert and achieve a degree of mutual recognition among freedoms that Sartre visualizes as the 'reign of man.'"[6]

Ken Anderson argues to the contrary that *CDR* does in fact emphasize the way in which political and historical subjectivity is constructed: "The reintegrated organism projected through this disintegrated materiality would obviously not resemble the one appearing through serial isolation. But effecting this liquidation will require . . . not only change in the circumstances that constitute the practico-inert field, but also a *subjective transformation*." He continues, "*The revolutionary act is an expression of the dissolution of serial isolation in what Sartre terms a group-in-fusion* [both emphases added]."[7]

While Power is clearly right that Badiou's project is explicitly focused on subjectivity constructed through fidelity to the Event, it is not the case that Sartre primarily "describes the moment of rupture." In her view, "Sartre does possess a notion of a political subject." However, like Flynn, she equates Sartre's political subject with the historical group—in her case, specifically the group-in-fusion.[8] What is more, she would later modify her position and claim that Sartre does not in fact possess a theory of a *political* subject, but merely an *historical* subject.[9] This is because she follows Badiou's lead in criticizing Sartre's subject for being insufficiently structurally organized.[10]

Recall chapter 5 where we engaged with Badiou's and Smith's claim that Sartre's theory of the group is founded upon his phenomenological-ontological commitments to the in-itself/for-itself binary held over from *BN*. Power comes to a similar conclusion. For her, Sartre's historical subject is the result of the aleatory historical circumstances out of which it emerges. But this subject is not a political subject in that 1) it is not properly collective and 2) there is no political program or concerns motivating its formation. In fact, she would muse that Sartre's focus on novelty and discontinuity perhaps entail that "we should no longer refer to him as a Marxist."[11]

Similarly, Badiou claims that Sartre's theory of the group is essentially rooted in the framework of bourgeois revolutions and especially that of 1789. He refers, that is, to days of rioting in which there is no dialectic with institutional political forces and in which no people's party is present in the masses. From that point of view, fusion is a historico-revolutionary concept and not a political concept.[12] As such, for Power and Badiou, Sartre's "subject" is both politically benign and substantially vacuous.

However, to speak of it as being vacuous might not necessarily be a criticism. For as was suggested above, the idea of the human-in-becoming is better viewed as an empty placeholder to be perpetually filled in based on the particular circumstances out of which it emerges and toward which it is aimed in its praxis. In fact, Power criticizes Badiou for similarly theorizing a subject that is "strangely insubstantial."[13] She contends, "Badiou's desire to retain a notion of the political subject comes at the price of a certain emptying out of the concept."[14] Much like her reading of Sartre, Power notes that Badiou's relation to Marxism is tenuous. Communist, yes. But Marxist, perhaps not. She elaborates: "[In] terms of historical materialism's economic dimensions, it has also been argued that Badiou's analysis of politics does not commence or really engage with any fleshed-out description of capital;

indeed, the category of the economic as an analytic lens is largely absent from his work."[15] Again we see the resonance between Badiou and Sartre right at the same point where there is dissonance. Both Badiou and Sartre present a theory of the subject that is insubstantial and tenuously Marxist. This is because for Marx the subject is not a perpetually indefinable placeholder subtracted from historical conditions, whereas for both Sartre and Badiou, subjectivity is always related to the novel and to discontinuity.

However, whereas Badiou's subject is perpetually "beyond history," as Antonio Negri has remarked,[16] Sartre's subject is precisely historical. As such, Sartre's subject is not politically benign. It is always directed toward particular tasks, rooted in situations of exigence, and regressively made intelligible because of its embeddedness within socio-political conditions. Thus, the bifurcation between political and historical subject that Power articulates makes a division that ought not to be traced.

Further to this, as was explored in chapter 5, the moment of rupture, the apocalypse, is a crucial instigation of the spark of subjectivity. The logic of the group extends through its various iterations to reveal the organization and mediation of affect and praxis in the process of subjectivization. Thus, while it is surely the case that the logic of the group includes a notion of common subjectivity, Power and Flynn end up far too reductive. For, in line with Anderson, it is also the case that subjects themselves are structurally constituted as humans-in-common through the various logical formulae of the different group iterations. What this means is that there is both a sense in which subjectivity is grouped and individuated, political and historicized, with neither term predominant or exclusionary in relation to the other.

The other issue with Power's and Flynn's reading is that they are camping within the ontological and normative reading of *CDR* that we have already discussed above. When *CDR* is approached as a logic, as does Anderson, subjectivity becomes a paradigm that makes intelligible the effects of the group. This means that rather than speaking of a "true subject of history," it is better to speak of the process of subjectivization that is driven by the imaginative logic of action. For, remember, subjectivity is the differential, the gap between interiorization and exteriorization. As such, subjectivity, for Sartre, is a process. It is the gap in the activity of creative freedom that is enacted in totalization. This means that subjectivity is not a static term that defines what a human-in-construction might become. It does not define how "humanity" is understood *in se*. It is the logic that guides the creation of what humanisms might perpetually become, through the revolutionary act; the latter being both the expression of the new spark of life and the vehicle of subjective constitution. As Sartre himself states:

> [The] group statute is indeed a metamorphosis of the individual. And the practical moment of the actualisation of the powers constitutes him, in himself,

as fundamentally different from what he was on his own: adopted inertia, function, power, rights and duties, structure, violence and fraternity—he actualises all these reciprocal relations as his new being, his sociality.[17]

8.1.2 Historico-Political Posthumanist Humanisms

Loosely, it can be claimed that the Sartrean project of *CDR* has resonance with that of Martin Heidegger. Both men problematized certain received notions of humanity and subsequently sought to explore the conditions under which new conceptions of "the human" might emerge. While this is not the place to explore this in detail, a few cursory remarks to set the landscape will be beneficial.

Even though Heidegger's "Letter on Humanism" was written partially as a rebuttal to the Sartrean existentialism of "Existentialism is a Humanism," aspects of Sartre's project in *CDR* fit quite well into the Heideggerian framework. For Heidegger, "Humanism is opposed because it does not set the *humanitas* of man high enough." A few pages later, he writes, "So the point is that in the determination of the humanity of man as ek-sistence what is essential is not man but Being—as the dimension of the *ecstasies* of ek-sistence."[18] In these two passages, a central thrust of Heidegger's project is revealed. He wanted there to be an opening of Being to allow a more original and more "essential" idea of the human to be revealed. The early Sartre was unable to deal with this level of essentiality by remaining at the level of beings (as opposed to Being). Therefore, the for-itself, in-itself, for-others, and "man" (more broadly construed) in Sartre's early existentialist writings were second-order notions that had no grounding in Being that ultimately made them intelligible.

Power summarizes Heidegger's project in this way: "Heidegger undermines the term 'humanism' only to propose on a 'deeper' level its reclamation, posing the question of Man in a lateral way that evacuates the question of any primary or ontological political content."[19] In other words, Heidegger's concern was a "lateral" investigation into the Being of "Man" that would open a space in which a conception of the human could emerge that would be unsullied by political formulations.

This is precisely where Sartre differs, however. In the opening pages of *CDR*, Sartre is describing the task of the forthcoming tome. In the section titled "Scientific and Dialectical Reason," Sartre writes that, as a Marxist ideologist, his project is the "unveiling of being" and that this project presents itself as "an unanswered question as to the validity of this unveiling."[20] The overlap with Heidegger's project is clear and startling. What Sartre was setting out to do in *CDR* was investigate the unveiling of being and the meaning of being—the two poles of the Heideggerian project that was initiated in *Being and Time*. However, the difference lies precisely in that Heidegger's project, as shown by Power, sought to "[evacuate] the question of any primary or ontological political content," whereas Sartre's sought to pose the question of "Man" as primarily historico-political.

He states the question this way: "[Is] there a region of being where totalisation is the very form of existence?"[21] Of course, this "region of being" is concrete *praxis-as-totalization* (which will include both the absolute of praxis and the absolute of objective possibility in their dialectical spiraling *chaissé-croise*). Therefore, Sartre sets up the terms of his investigation in a Heideggerian-Marxian framework. He takes the intent of Heidegger and infuses it with historical materialism; the result being an investigation into the question of "Man" that is explicitly historical and political.

It is this political aspect that signals the increased distancing of Sartre's project from Heidegger's. As Elizabeth Butterfield notes, "[The] deconstruction of the human now requires a reconstructive moment."[22] What she develops throughout *Sartre and Poshumanist Humanism* is a reading of *CDR* that enables the concepts contained therein to reconstruct a posthumanist project that will appropriately respond to the socio-political demands of today. She uses *CDR* as a logic to equip posthumanist theorizing in the construction of potential humanisms after humanism's deconstruction in the post-Heideggerian and post-Nietzschean philosophical landscape.

If the Heideggerian project challenged the notion of the human on the grounds that all conceptions heretofore (since Aristotle) had merely been the second-order investigation of beings, and if Nietzsche waged an all-out war on transcendence, then emerging from the rubble of the philosophical agora must be projects that eschew both transcendent conceptions of humanity and those that fail to allow for a space in Being to be opened and then revealed. While Sartre's early work fits well within the Nietzchean paradigm, it is insufficiently Heideggerian. In *CDR*, he corrects this, but in an historical materialist framework.

Butterfield's project rightly takes the logic of *CDR*, in both its Heideggerian-Marxian and Nietzschean modes, and presents a theory of posthumanism that is faithful to Sartre's philosophy but that also creatively carries the mantle of the established logic further. What she writes is that,

> What we need today is a way to take into account the helpful insights of perspectivalism and the recognition of social construction, without abandoning the possibility of describing a common human condition altogether. We need a new understanding of social identities, as both socially constructed and yet real elements of experience, and this will require a new understanding of the relationship of the individual to the social, and of the experiences of freedom and necessity."[23]

And so she turns to *CDR* in order to develop a "new understanding of the social" that will aid in the construction of social relations thematized around "mutual recognition, cooperative group praxis, and even authentic love."[24]

Toward this end, Kevin Boileau claims that *CDR* does not sufficiently ground a space for the primordial "we" to emerge. In other words, Sartre does not properly pose the question of "Man" in a way that allows for the pre-subjective transcendental field to perpetually create humanisms that would resist the atomization of his early work in *BN*. Following Foucault, Boileau remarks,

> [The] pre-personal, temporal dispersion (at the pre-reflective level) is not a substantial self, i.e., the self of knowledge that can be known. Rather, it is a self-in-process, an unfinished, pre-self. This unfinished "self" is not the atomized, isolated self that Sartre describes in *BN*. Its boundaries are not so distinct and therefore "its" relation to the world is not so dualistic (recall the subject-object ontology of *BN*). This is the ontological domain from which a primordial "we" can emerge. This is the ontological grounding Sartre does not develop in his practical discussion of groups in *CDR*.[25]

Ignoring his obvious ontological and normative hermeneutic, Boileau's claim seems to be that Sartre's thought would be strengthened if it were supplemented by an appeal to the pre-subjective transcendental field from which it emerged, which he finds in the work of Michel Foucault. He claims that Foucault's project brings to light "the relations and interests of power that result in the historically contingent ways that thought itself controls its own range."[26] Through "revolt" it is possible to reconstruct the self. "We can invent new concepts to structure the world and our relationship to it."[27] And by developing "new technologies of the self," we can "enter into dialogue with others about identifiable power relations within which we live. We must try to understand what this dialogue about power entails and whether or not it offers us the possibility of exposing underlying relations of power in a way that promotes genuine reciprocity and group authenticity."[28]

But is this not precisely what *CDR* allows? Thus far, through the development of the imaginative logic of action, a path has been charted within the Sartrean paradigm whereby "the relations and interests of power" of Kaironic Seriality are made intelligible so that "we can invent new concepts to structure the world and our relationships to it" through totalization. Likewise, the dialectical logic of *CDR* exposes the "underlying relations of power in a way that promotes genuine reciprocity and group authenticity."

Further, it is no small point to note that Deleuze was perceptive to the presence of a tendency toward the pre-subjective transcendental in Sartre's earliest of writings. In his final essay, "Immanence: A Life," buried in a footnote, he writes: "Cf. Jean-Paul Sartre, who posits a transcendental field without a subject that refers to a consciousness that is impersonal, absolute, immanent; with respect to it, the subject and the object are 'transcendents' (La transcendance de l'Ego)." This of course does not indicate that *TE*. is sufficient to answer Boileau's criticism. But it does indicate that the very thing he criticizes Sartre for and praises Foucault for might not be as stringent a criticism as he supposes. When we chart this germinal tendency that Deleuze notes in *TE* through *BN* and into *CDR*, his criticism becomes further deflated.

This is not to claim that Sartre's project cannot be strengthened in dialogue with Foucault's. Rather, it is to note that two are not so far apart as is generally supposed, as represented in Boileau's criticism. In fact, in 1984, Foucault remarked that:

> [Relations] of power are not something bad in themselves, from which one must free oneself. [. . . The] problem is not of trying to dissolve them in the utopia of a perfectly transparent communication [as it is for Habermas], but to give one's self the rules of law, the techniques of management, and also the ethics, the *ethos,* the practice of self, which would allow these games of power to be played with a minimum of domination.[29]

The giving of one's self the ethos "which would allow these games of power to be played with a minimum of domination" is precisely what the construction of the imaginative logic of action seeks. And it must be repeated that this logic is explicitly derived from the work of Sartre himself. It is a creative reading, but it is thoroughly rooted in exegesis. As such, the project of Sartre in *CDR* can be seen to have crossing paths of resonance with the post-structuralist project of Foucault.

This is where Butterfield's work also begins. She does not take the presumptive interpretations of Sartre that are stuck within methodological individualism, or the typical normative and ontological readings of *CDR* as her starting point. Rather, she approaches *CDR* as a formal, logical investigation into the conditions of lived experience, and then derives useful concepts that can aid in the construction of socio-political theory.

The primary difference between Sartre and the post-structuralists (Foucault in particular) is that Sartre still retains the notion of subjective constitution in a dialectical relational field with objectivity. That is, the subject and the object (structures, systems, institutions, etc.) are co-constituting. So, there is a sense in which the subject is a constituted site of pre-subjective forces, but this doesn't negate the freedom and effectiveness of praxis, as it seems to in many post-structuralist endeavors, which hesitate to give much credence to the individual forcing of a particular person. Of course, for them, "bodies" or "selves" as collections of forces do have the power to act, but this action isn't given the same positive power as it is in Sartre. Likewise, the objective is also constituted by a swirling network of forces. But rather than speak of the indeterminate production of desiring machines or relations of power,[30]

Sartre wants to locate the causal power in the mediatory relation between praxis and material conditions.

So, while a person is thrown into a situation that is not of her own choosing, that person has the ability to act (through totalization) and transcend the situation toward future possibles. Ultimately the differences don't seem so stark. Perhaps the great difference is that Sartre still held a supreme place for the acting praxis, whereas Foucault et al. were more interested in the pre-subjective flows of desire or practices that constitute a subject and that work through her. But where they agree is in the development and proliferation of the underlying logics that condition life. And both Sartre and Foucault believed that through the transformation of the objective there would be a transformation of subjectivity—and *vice versa*.

8.1.3 The Process of Subjectivization in Context

Although he famously declared the "death of man," Foucault was not a nihilist when it came to thinking the "human." Rather, he was an inventive critic of modernist conceptions of humanism. Like Sartre in *CDR*—who declares that "man does not exist"[31]—Foucault explored the conditions of history that gave rise to subjectivity and the broader structures of power that condition the former. As was mentioned above, the later Foucault wanted to develop an *ethos* that would enable "technologies of the self" to revolt against exploitative powers in the perpetual diminishing of their efficacy.

One way he spoke of this perpetual undertaking was by suggesting that we "create ourselves as a work of art."[32] Called the "aestheticization of self" by subsequent theorists, this undertaking is a perpetual project whereby would-be humans create themselves to refuse "the type of individuality that has been imposed on us for several centuries."[33] While Sartre does not use this terminology, the imaginative logic of action that is being developed here operates by a very similar logic. Nik Farrell Fox claims as much when he states that, "Since Sartre and postmodernists both envisage the subject as something which must be created, they tend as a result to aestheticize the subject and the project of authentic self-determination."[34] It is this project of aesthetic creation that this project suggests can only be driven by an imaginative logic of action.

As was stated above, the deployment of the imaginative logic of action is directed both externally and internally. It is directed externally insofar as it transforms the objective condition in which praxis is embedded. It is directed internally insofar as it undertakes the perpetual process of subjectivization. This dual relation is yet another example of Sartre's dialectical logic, for neither the external nor the internal can be separated in actual fact. They are co-constituting aspects of totalization in the social milieu that is conditioned and enacted by the imaginative logic of action. Only the latter is sensitive to the Real in such a way that it can respond to the opening in Being that will allow for novelty to emerge—i.e., the apocalyptic moment—and transform inhumans into humans, equipping them to confront the dominant monstrosity of Kaironic Seriality. Understanding this gives us greater insight into how subjectivity is constituted *in situ*.

As Robert Bernasconi points out, it is the antagonism of the group that shows "how violence not only creates the group but transforms reality." And through the transformation of reality what this violence achieves is "solidarity."[35] This is the dual nature—the external and internal activity—of the imaginative logic of action in its enactment: it transforms reality and the group in common praxis.

It must be kept in mind that this activity emerges in context, in antagonism to Karionic Seriality. The latter is the condition that makes intelligible the particularities of life lived under its dominance. Characterized by the serial logic of inaction, life lived in Kaironic Seriality is predestined to perpetuate inhumanity. The imaginative logic of action, by contrast, is the emergence of human life in opposition to this dominance. This means that the logic that dictates life in Kaironic Seriality is eschewed when the imaginative logic of action irrupts from within the interstices of the social milieu. The emergence of this counter-logic must be understood dialectically. That is, it is the result of the apocalyptic moment that is both initiated from without and from within. In other words, it is a dialectical emergent that is both attributable to objective material conditions and subjective praxis. What this means is that the imaginative logic of action necessarily operates through the transformation of reality and of subjectivity. It is, in one sense, the result of the spark of this dual transformation, and, in another sense, it is the further expression of this transformation. These two modes must be tethered together in a dialectical tension in order to understand the concrete complexity of this counter-logic.

Now, it must be reiterated that the recreation of subjectivity is not merely the creation of bodies that are *tabulae rasae*. Rather, the depths of Infinite Seriality's impingement upon inhuman bodies is so vast that prior to the emergence of human life, in a particular context, inhumans have been so constituted that their very serial existence must be unraveled. As Sartre was wont to say,

> The worker will be saved from his destiny only if the human multiplicity as a whole is permanently changed into a group praxis. [. . . There must be a] joint negation of two reciprocal aspects of the practical field: a negation of the common object as destiny and a connected negation of multiplicity as seriality . . . seriality itself [is] a link of impotence; this seriality is the being-to-be-transcended toward an action tending to socialise the common object.[36]

Setting aside the appeal to the *permanent* salvation of the worker (a point we will return to below), the crucial point for now is to note that Sartre avowed that only through a dual "negation" of "common object" and of "multiplicity as seriality" would the worker be "saved from his destiny." In fact, Sartre seems to emphasize that seriality, as the impotence of the multiplicity, is the key term to be transcended in praxis toward freedom. It is the "being-to-be-transcended" in praxis's seeking commonality.

The point of emphasizing this now is not to backtrack on the dialectical tension mentioned above. Rather, it is noted how crucial subjective transformation is for the dialectical logic of *CDR*. Most interpreters focus on the grand events noted throughout the text: the storming of the Bastille, Chinese deforestation, or the gold coins of Spain. But they neglect the role of subjectivity within such objective conditions. The present contention is that this oversight drastically diminishes the efficacy of the logic that is presented in *CDR*. In its place, it is of vital importance to understand Sartre's text as providing a logic for the emergence of subjectivity itself, one that is ever-embedded within and mediated by material conditions. For, the aim of the development of his philosophy was the creation of "Another man: a man of higher quality."[37] And the latter would only be done through the perpetual transformation of the objective, through the transformation of subjectivity. In his words:

> [The] *praxis* of the group is constantly to reorganise itself, that is to say, to interiorise its objective totalisation through the things produced and the results attained, to make of it its new differentiations and its new structures, and thereby to transcend this rearrangement toward new objectives—or rather, to make *this internal rearrangement*, as structures which have to be transcended (because *attained*) the transcendence of old objectives and of interiorised instrumentality.[38]

Interestingly enough, though, Sartre would claim that this reorganization "is not fundamentally different according to whether it depends on centralisation from above or on a spontaneous liquidation of seriality within the series itself and on the common organisation which follows." The only thing that matters is that it is understood as a "practical recognition within action."[39] What could this mean? Does this contradict what has been established thus far, that freedom emerges within the interstices of Kaironic Seriality? Not at all. Rather, what Sartre is suggesting is that the perpetual reorganization of reality and subjectivity takes place according to a fundamental logic that is not dependent upon a micro-political outburst of action. Rather, the fundamental logic only has purchase insofar as it is "practical recognition within action." In other words, the fundament of group praxis is the imaginative logic of action.

8.1.4 The Perpetual Withering of Seriality and the Perpetual Creation of Free Praxis

In a thought-provoking essay by Betty Cannon, what we are calling the imaginative logic of action is filtered through the lens of group therapy. Cannon's contention is that group therapy provides "the possibility for radical change in a person's orientation toward the world, which groups tend to provoke and reinforce in a way that is more difficult in other forms of therapy."[40] For her, the goal of the group "is not to develop the efficiency of the machine, but rather to aid its members in deconstructing and reconstructing in a more healthy fashion life choices made in other groups."[41] The therapy group, therefore, is a manifestation of the reorganization driven by the imaginative logic of action that refuses to ossify. Its primary goal is the continual transformation of the members so that they can live healthier lives in the other groups or collectives or institutions to which they belong. In this way, the therapy group is a useful tool, so to speak, in that one of its primary functions is the transformation of the inhuman person into a genuine free subject. This person can then move through various ensembles throughout his or her life, having been transformed by the logic of freedom.

While group therapy is not the typical mode of engroupment that is considered in relation to *CDR*, Cannon argues that it is in fact "a powerful antidote to oppression."[42] Operating according to the imaginative logic of action, the therapy group is one expression of antagonism to Kaironic Seriality—that is, its very form. By exposing the serial constraints and seeking to identify freedom, enacting it, and then, through the transformation of the person(s), releasing such persons into the world again, it operates as a sort of fused-pledged-organized group by confronting the serial logic of inaction through piecemeal transformation. Therefore, what Cannon's investigation provides is an application of the imaginative logic of action that is faithful to the fundamental logic of group praxis in *CDR*, but that also applies it in a creative way. For, what the logic does not suggest is the radical overturning of seriality *tout court*. Rather, it is the perpetual withering away of its dominance in the perpetual creation of free praxis, with the goal eventually being that the human race will be "fully matured [and] will not define itself as the sum of the inhabitants of the globe, but as the infinite unity of their reciprocities."[43]

But this goal will require serious understanding and effort. As Nik Farrell Fox notes, "Transgressive and aesthetic practice is vital for the creation of new forms of subjectivity." But this practice of creating ourselves as works of art must be continually made and unmade by "constant activists for whom it is necessary to prevent enabling limits from congealing into constraining limitation, and to generate new limits and new forms of subjectivity which constitute selves."[44] And this can only happen through a philosophical outlook that is both analytical and creative. But identifying subjects who are properly equipped for such an undertaking requires a bit more investigation. Namely, if it is the case that the transformation of reality and of subjectivity is a dialectical activity that takes place in piecemeal fashion, how are we to understand the mechanism(s) that drive(s) this transformation? While this question is far too large to delve into here in any sufficient sense, the next section provides an example of one way in which this transformation takes place—through micro-psychobiological shifts. Such shifts make intelligible the process of subjectivization as driven by the imaginative logic of action.

8.2 MICRO-PSYCHOBIOLOGICAL SHIFTS

The voices that will guide the following discussion are Herbert Marcuse, Gilles Deleuze and Félix Guattari, Catherine Malabou, and William Connolly.[45] Each of them develops, in his, her, or their own way, a logic of subjective transformation that resonates with the imaginative logic of action, supplementing the investigation thus far by making new connections that bring more color to this discussion of dialectical logic.

Bringing these disparate thinkers into dialogue with Sartre is a large-scale project that can only be cursorily undertaken at present. But this brief creative investigation will yield great benefits in four ways: 1) by creating an historical narrative into which *CDR* fits that has up until now been absent, 2) by demonstrating ways in which the imaginative logic of action can be utilized in philosophical discourse, 3) by providing further explication into the efficacy of this logic, and 4) by demonstrating how a fresh reading of *CDR* brings Sartre up to date with developing trends in Continental Philosophy.

8.2.1 The Prophetic Imagination

In Spinoza's *Theological-Political Treatise*, he sets out to confront the religious presuppositions of his day to expose them as mistaken notions. Of primary import is the traditional dogma of prophecy. For Spinoza, the ancient prophets were not individuals with divine minds, superior knowledge, or unique access to God. Rather, they were persons with "vivid imagination."[46] Thus, they really did "encounter" God. However, this encounter was mediated by their historical, contextual, and personal intellectual frameworks, which in turn influenced the interpretation of said encounter.[47] The result was that the prophets spoke forth and proclaimed highly imaginative messages that both reflected and confronted their particular situations.

For Spinoza, the "prophetic imagination" is not something to be characterized as good or bad. However, he does make it clear that prophetic imagination is not akin to natural knowledge—which he does see as *superior*.[48] Natural knowledge is viewed as superior in that it has no need of a theological or supernatural interpretation of Nature. It provides certainty by its very nature without the need of signs.[49] Prophetic imagination on the other hand is deemed inferior to natural knowledge as a "capricious" exception that only arose during certain historical epochs in order to substantiate and shore the foundation of the preexistent moral law.[50] However, his aim was not solely directed at the prophetic imagination, but toward imagination *tout court*:

> Those who are most powerful in imagination are less good at merely understanding things; those who have trained and powerful intellects have a more modest power of imagination and have it under better control, reining it in, so to speak, and not confusing it with understanding.[51]

The stakes for Spinoza are veritably high: namely, to place theology in its proper, subordinate place to philosophy (i.e., "natural knowledge") is essential if one is to understand the power of God and the effects such power enacts.

> For *everything* is done by the power of God. Indeed, because the power of nature is nothing other than the power of God itself, it is certain that we fail to understand the power of God to the extent that we are ignorant of *natural causes*. Therefore it is *foolish* to have recourse to this same power of God when we are ignorant of the natural cause of some thing, which is, precisely, the power of God. [Emphasis added][52]

Although Spinoza affords a certain measure of philosophical capital to prophets, by denigrating the status of the prophetic imagination to a moral forthtelling, he verges toward a reductive rationalism. This reductive perspective limits the robustness of the prophetic tradition which was concerned with a productive mythologizing that has much in common with the political concerns of this present project.[53] What is more, it does not seem clear that the imagination and knowledge, in Spinoza's sense, are necessarily at odds. As this project has been attempting to argue, in fact, both the imagination and knowledge are moments of praxis that themselves refract through one another in dialectical totalization. This indicates a slight resonance with Spinoza's desire to have a full accounting of the causes of Nature, as the intent of the latter maps well onto the desire to develop the imaginative logic of action that is well-attuned to the material conditions in which it finds itself so that it can create future images to transcend these conditions toward the field of possibles. Deep analysis and a utopic thinking are needed to the neglect of neither.

8.2.2 The Foolish Imagination

However, there is a conservative imaginative logic that would be "foolish" (to borrow Spinoza's term) according to the dictates of the present project. This would be a logic conditioned by the serial logic of inaction. Corey Robin describes this conservative imaginative logic as being conditioned by a sense of nostalgia that is refracted through a counter-revolutionary spirit.[54]

Essentially, conservatism is an ideology of reaction that bears a logic not so dissimilar to the mark from which it seeks to separate itself. Of course, things must be understood in their unique expression, but the point is that conservatism has a malleability to it that enables conservative thinkers to perpetually reinvent themselves (albeit within serialized parameters). As Robin notes, for Edmund Burke, in particular, part of this is because of the power of the sublime. The sublime is that "terrible" beyond that shatters our comfort and rearranges how we comport ourselves with the world. Most notably, God is sublime. God serves as this fearful "lightness" and "darkness" that presents both "fear and pain" in his awesomeness (awfulness?). God is the transcendent beyond that stirs up opposition within the soul and constitutes the self in the process. The result is that the constituted self before the transcendent God-sublime is one that is made through tension, fear, pain, anxiety.

This is a creative process for Burke. The self is forged before the sublime. And Robin rightly notes that this Burkean tendency resides to varying degrees within the conservative logic as such. However, this tendency is precisely *not* creative. It is the literal antithesis to creation. Reproduction? Sure. Repackaging? Undoubtedly. Transformation? Possibly. But creation? No. The God that Burke claims disrupts and makes the self is a transcendent practico-inert externality. It is the transcendent inverted inflation of those qualities of men (literally *men*) that are deemed valuable. Projecting this image before the self, to only have that constructed image deconstruct said self, is to circularly flagellate oneself into submission. This may have similarities with the fear-image of the pledge that we discussed in chapter 5, but the key difference is that the logic of the pledge is not entirely cut through with seriality, but retains genuine elements of praxis within it; whereas the sublime that Burke touts, and that undergirds much of conservatism's imaginative logic, is essentially stale and suppressive. It is the interiorization of a practico-inert image that reproduces and intensifies serial existence. A truly creative Sublime would be apocalyptic (in the sense of *CDR*) in its potency, not merely reproductive.

Thus, if this is accurate, there is a sense in which the conservative imaginative logic—as an expression of the serial logic of inaction—must be understood as having an affective and constitutive capacity, as does the imaginative logic of action. The difference, however, is that, where the serial logic of

8.2.3 Imaginative Critical Theory

Contra Spinoza's pessimistic take on imagination, Herbert Marcuse, in his manifesto and polemic *An Essay on Liberation*, argues that imagination qua liberatory faculty is the mediator between sensation and reason.[56] As such, he sees imagination *not* as something to be immediately denigrated. In fact, for Marcuse, the imagination is not something that is necessarily inferior, capricious, and uncommon, but rather is a ubiquitous productive human capacity insofar as it mediates the rational and the sensual in "the reconstruction of society."[57] A few pages earlier we read that "human sensibility which rebels against the dictates of repressive reason . . . invokes the sensuous power of the imagination." He would continue on to remark that rather than liberatory political action "being shaped and permeated by the rationality of domination, the sensibility would be guided by the imagination."[58]

At this point it is important to interject two notes. The first: a preliminary distinction must be drawn between the myriad of various incarnations of imagination: the artistic imagination, the scientific imagination, the political imagination, the religious imagination, etc. Within these various forms of imagination there seem to be two generalizable similarities.

The *first* is that they all arise in a given context. For the artist, her imagination is conditioned by her given situation (her psychological makeup, her desires, her financial pressures, etc.). Likewise, the seer is one who is immersed in a given situation that presses upon her. Much like producing a diamond out of coal, the pressure of a given situation condenses and particularizes the plurality of imaginative possibilities and produces a style of thought that imagines in accord with a given set of conditions.

The *second* similarity between the sundry imaginative impulses is that they exceed the given situation and aim toward futures not yet realized. For the physicist, this might resemble the development of an as-yet undeveloped field of experimentation on wave-particle duality that will aid her in better comprehending the quality and movement of light. For the seer, this might be where she proclaims a utopic vision of a future possible existence in which radical egalitarian principles will govern the social order.

The second important note to interject is that although imaginative traditions have particular and often times discordant content, they are all equal before the Real. Not one of them—*in se*—has *absolute* primacy over any other. Each arises in a localized context for a specific purpose. Be that as it may, as Marcuse intimates, imagination is not so neatly divided topologically. Art, specifically, is an interpenetrative imaginative impulse that can aid political action. What is more, he would claim that an aesthetic imagination is needed to imagine future possible political and/or social organizations:

> Released from the bondage to exploitation, the imagination, sustained by the achievements of science, could turn its productive power to the radical reconstruction of experience and the universe of experience. In this reconstruction, the historical *topos* of the aesthetic would change: it would find expression in the transformation of the *Lebenswelt*—society as a work of art.[59]

It is apparent that Marcuse places high value on the social efficacy of science—to an extent—at which time an artistic imagination is required to redraw the outlines of societal possibilities. The reason science can only go so far is that by definition science is a discourse that is constructed within limits—limits that abet and perpetuate the knowledge of the *status quo* and of "Law and Order."

It might be said that science, as understood in the present context, is susceptible to capture within the general framework of Kaironic Seriality. That is, it is a *limited* and *limiting* discourse that necessarily progresses within strict parameters. Not denigrating science's historically proven usefulness, such endeavors inevitably fail to achieve the goals toward which critical theorists strive; namely, the "transition to a higher stage of development: 'higher' in the sense of a more rational and equitable use of resources, minimization of destructive conflicts, and enlargement of the realm of freedom."[60] What is more, Marcuse believed that even critical theory was unable and unwilling to think beyond such goals for fear of "losing its scientific character."[61] Thus, there is an element to critical theory that itself has been too wedded to a self-limiting paradigm of knowledge. To break the confines of the compressed discourse of the *status quo,* therefore Marcuse wants to reintroduce the idea of "utopia":

> I believe that this restrictive conception [the "scientific character" of critical theory] must be revised, and that the revision is suggested, and even necessitated, by the actual evolution of contemporary societies. The dynamic of their productivity deprives "utopia" of its traditional unreal content: what is denounced as "utopian" is no longer that which has "no place" and cannot have any place in the historical universe, but rather that which is blocked from coming about by the power of the established societies.[62]

In a word: the Master's tools will never dismantle the Master's house. It is only by envisioning the novel that the "refusal of the Establishment" and human freedom will come to fruition.

8.2.4 Toward the Construction of a New Body-Politic

Addressing the bio-productive impetus of advanced capitalism, Marcuse insists that there is a sense in which capital offers a Utopian vision of the future that constructs human nature and modifies organic behavior.[63] And as Philip Goodchild has shown, capitalism is creative.[64] This descent into the "biological dimension," therefore, is at once both a threat and a possible ally to liberation. The threat seems fairly obvious: society, any given aggregate of human desire and behavior, is determined by the logic and insatiable appetite of the market. Thus, "the gadgets which, produced in accordance with the requirements of profitable exchange, have become part and parcel of the people's own existence, own 'actualization.'"[65] In Sartrean language, the constitutive serial conditions of the market have serialized inhumanity living in Kaironic Seriality to such an extent that the affective forces of the market themselves (which include the gadgets produced) have constructed biological beings made in the image of the market. This is why it must be said that capitalism does not merely *ex-sist*—it *in-sists*. Marcuse notes, "The power of corporate capitalism has stifled the emergence of [utopic] consciousness and imagination; its mass media have adjusted the rational and emotional faculties to its market and its policies and steered them to defense of its dominion."[66] In Foucauldian and Deleuzian parlance respectively, capitalism is a "technology of desire" and the "relative limit of desiring-production."

But this threat to human freedom is precisely the signal of Kaironic Seriality's own dissolution, even at the biological level. Nietzsche's "man of the future" lays the tracks for twentieth and twenty-first century post-humanist ideas on biological production: "[He] awakens on his behalf the interest, excitement, hope, almost the confidence, of his being the harbinger and forerunner of something, of man being no end, but only a stage, an interlude, a bridge, a great promise."[67]

By considering how to turn the tools of the Master against himself, proper conditions can arise that will recreate society at the biological dimension, which will allow truly innovative, imaginative political projects to be fabulated. This happens through a two-pronged approach: 1) the recreation of the bio-social order and 2) by releasing the powers of imagination from the stifling grip of serial reproduction. The latter cannot obtain anterior to the former. In fact, the release of the powers of imagination presupposes a new bio-order. However, biological production alone cannot dismantle the Master's house, for it uses the tools of the Master (the system as it currently exists is its starting point). Therefore, prior to the emergence of a revolutionary "aesthetic ethos" that would create "society as a work of art," the construction of a new body-politic must be effected.

8.2.5 Constructing the Body-Politic and Thinking Without Limit

Although Marcuse does not discuss a "prophetic vision" *per se*, his work on the positive mediatory role of imagination (as that fabulating faculty between sensation and reason) settles well in the prophetic tradition and is useful for present purposes in that it presupposes Spinoza's criticism of supernaturalism but also utilizes the creative impetus of utopic fabulation in the recreation of society. Therefore, the choice to examine his work in relation to Spinoza as we develop ways to deploy the imaginative logic of action is not arbitrary.

The most basic and striking feature about this understanding of Marcuse's utopic imagination is that it is way of *thinking*. However, contra Spinoza, it is best to understand this way of thinking as something common and ubiquitous. It is the very imaginative capacity that impels *homo cultura*. It merely needs to be released from the stifling constraints of serial reproduction. *À la* Deleuze, utopic thinking is the unbounded flow of desiring-production that scrambles the codes of social production, creating new forms of organization as it breaks the frozen confines of molarity. Said otherwise, utopic thinking arises *in situ* to meet a need and then exceeds that situation as it imagines a novel future in which such needs are met.

In order that new futures might be imagined, there must be a shift in the biological dimension of human existence. Such a shift is not necessarily (or exclusively) one in which wholesale biological functions or physiological construction as such change. Rather, it is better understood as a shift in the micro-psychobiological order. As noted above, Marcuse insists that capitalism has such a power. By controlling the marketplace of desire, capitalism is able to reorder basic human functionality according to a particular logic. The resultant effect is that participants in the capitalist logic are constructed to function accordingly. Like the development of the opposable thumb alongside tools in the protohuman species, there is a biological change—a structural coupling—that occurs in the psychosomatic unit's relation and interaction with its environment.

The most basic psychobiological element that is captured and ordered by the capitalist system is *desire*. Defined not as lack but as creation, Gilles Deleuze and Félix Guattari view desire as an unbounded flow of production. It is the pre-individual flow of energy that *in-sists* in pure lines of flight, dispersing not from a singular point but *rhizomatically*.[68] Not pure chaos, but metastable chaos within order (or perhaps more appropriately a constant state of order-*ing*), *desire is indeterminate activity*. As such, it is the pure creative impulse on which capitalism feeds. Like a bloodletting leech, capitalism arises only in relation to desire—and is ultimately dependent on desire.

However, rather than pure suppression of the flow of desiring-production (as in despotism), capitalism is a type of creation. As Goodchild states,

"What this entire debacle known as the history of capitalism may teach us . . . is that there is such a possibility of creation."[69] This is because capitalism is a system of both decoding and recoding desire. This dyadic process occurs wherever desire is detected—"nothing must escape coding."[70] But unlike the despotic system's need to code, capitalism functions as a *type* of immanence—one in which the flow of desire is decoded and recoded endlessly. The problem for Deleuze and Guattari is that this dyadic process is determinate—capitalism is a creation with a *relative limit*.[71] It forms as a sheath around the creative desiring-energy of vital life (we might say subjectivity or the differential) and thereby guides, harnesses, suppresses, and releases minor bursts by which it can create further, toward its own ends of value extraction. The latter of course being pre-determined by previously extracted surplus-value. Which means that the limit established by capital is the very limit of the logic of capital itself.

The only solution, therefore, is to devise a way of thinking without limit—one in which the flows of desiring-production escape capture *in toto*. Deleuze and Guattari use the model of the schizophrenic to signify a figure of unbounded productive desire. While this model does offer theoretical merit, envisioning a society of clinical schizophrenics hardly solves the practical needs of the oppressed. That said, how their concept of schizophrenia is useful is that it carves a path toward alternative models of creation that resist capitalism's reallocation of desire.

One such path is through a regressive analysis of the imaginative logic of action's relation to the virtual.

> Philosophy is the theory of multiplicities, each of which is composed of actual and virtual elements. Purely actual objects do not exist. Every actual surrounds itself with a cloud of virtual images. This cloud is composed of a series of more or less extensive coexisting circuits, along which the virtual images are distributed, and around which they run. These virtuals vary in kind as well as in their degree of proximity from the actual particles by which they are both emitted and absorbed.[72]

Described as mutually inextricable, virtual images and actual objects are veritably inseparable. In fact, according to John Mullarkey, the virtual as such *is* not.

> The "virtual" exists only virtually within a virtual ontology, and by that I mean that it is a performative concept, it is produced from our point of view or frame of reference as an "image." [. . . One] can virtualise without anything existing other than what we call and see as "the virtual." It is a frame or system of reference for "seeing as," for taking up the actual world.[73]

This means that the virtual is a transcendental coordinate (or field) within which human beings think the world.

Akin to Deleuze and Guattari's schizophrenic, the thinker of the virtual is not bound to the actual, is not bound to that which is, but is rather in a constant state of encountering the indeterminate. That is, the virtual is a concept that enables one to think beyond the relative limits of social production. Therefore, the virtual serves as a sort of depository into which actuality steadily flows. In turn, the virtual surrounds the actual (like an electron cloud to a nucleus) and acts as the situation out of which actuality emerges (the "actualization of the virtual"). We might call the virtual the *matériel* with which actual desire creates. Therefore, *schizophrenics* are not needed in order to create, but *seers*.

For the imaginative logic of action, the virtual corresponds to the transcendental conditions revealed by regressive analysis in that the virtual is the condition that gives rise to any present state of affairs. The imaginative logic of action therefore takes up the performative *matériel* of the virtual in its supersession of the material conditions in fabulating future possible worlds. In other words, the virtual is the basic *situation* in which utopic thought thinks, and the imaginative logic of action is a creative *logical disposition* that uses the virtual conditions of material existence for the endless production of future possibles.

This occurrence is not rare but is the ubiquitous capacity of human imagination that issues forth from the virtual field. However, creating a world in which human beings will recognize this capacity is no easy task—for it must arise through a shift in social relations; it must arise through the reconstruction of social life as such.

8.2.6 Marcuse and the Biological Root

Following the heels of the May '68 student protests in France and squarely embedded within the counter-culture movement in the United States, Marcuse sought to make intelligible the revolutionary fervor that seemed to be taking hold. At the same time, he wanted to articulate the reasons that this spirit would either fail or succeed. Of course, "failure" and "success" are loaded terms. But suffice it to say that, for Marcuse, success would come in the form of rebellion against the dominant ideological power structures of the day. And more than anything, he wanted to theorize about the *biological root* of this rebellion that would change human *nature*.[74]

Like Sartre, Marcuse believed that social life was predestined. Unable to be truly free, contemporary society was bound by its entanglements with the established value systems and power structures of the day. This entanglement predestined who people were, how they were to live, and defined what it meant to be "human." The result is that life under such conditions is nothing more than "voluntary" servitude.

But Marcuse did see a way out. Through the reconstruction of humanity at the biological level, this voluntary servitude could be broken "through a political practice which reaches the roots of containment and contentment in the infrastructure of man."[75] This "practice" is precisely what he set out to ground in the essay. He does this by opposing two logics. On the one hand is the dominant ideology of the day. And on the other hand, is a new practice that would "break with the familiar, the routine ways of seeing, hearing, feeling, understanding things so that the organism may become receptive to the potential forms of a nonaggressive, nonexploitative world."[76]

He identifies the dominant ideology of the day with capitalist society. As he states:

> The so-called consumer economy and the politics of corporate capitalism have created a second nature of man which ties him libidinally and aggressively to the commodity form. The need for possessing, consuming, handling, and constantly renewing the gadgets, devices, instruments, engines, offered to and imposed upon the people, for using these wares even at the danger of one's own destruction, has become a "biological" need.[77]

This "second nature of man" is the constituted inhumanity of those living under capitalist dominance. They are constituted by a socio-economic tendency that, in turn, introjects the capitalist logic into their very nature, determining the scope, outlook, and trajectory of their lives.

In line with the current stage of our investigation, it can be claimed that this logic is akin to the serial logic of inaction. And like the latter, this logic is incapable of releasing the flows of humanity in freedom. Perpetually, those dominated by the capitalist logic, appropriate the dictates of the serial system and live lives of predestined inhumanity. More to the point, their very organic structures are reconstituted in line with this alienating logic. This "second nature" sinks down to the "biological dimension and [modifies] organic behavior."[78] Once this occurs, "The organism receives and reacts to certain stimuli and 'ignores' and repels others in accord with the introjected morality. [. . . In] this way, a society constantly re-creates this side of consciousness and ideology, patterns of behavior and aspiration as part of the 'nature' of its people."[79] This affective *a priori* becomes the new *statut* by which such persons take up the world. They become the self-generators of their own dominance by their complicity with the system as they have been literally constructed by the logic, and according to the logic, of this serial system.

In order for there to be a transformation of nature, therefore, there must be a "rupture with the self-propelling conservative continuum."[80] This rupture must take place prior to revolution. However, in dialectical fashion, it can also only be understood in the revolution. Echoing themes from Sartre's group logic that we explored in chapter 5, this revolution must "be driven by the *vital need* to be freed from the administered comforts and the destructive productivity of the exploitative society."[81] It is the threat of the Impossible that stirs vitality in the differential, at the affective level, and which is sparked to life in opposition to the "destructive productivity of the exploitative society." Only in such condition can the new biological organism be constructed. And only the new organism can create a new society.

However, although Marcuse claims that "The imagination of such men and women would fashion their reason and tend to make the process of production a process of creation,"[82] he was ill-equipped to suggest precisely how this socio-biological transformation would take place. He did suggest that drug use among the hippie generation enabled them to "see, hear, feel new things in a new way." But this deregulation of the senses only contained "an artificial and short-lived" reprise from the "ego shaped by the established society."[83] This is because the narcotic "trip" can release one from the confines of the established system, but it can also release one from the exigencies of the liberatory order—the withdrawl creates its artificial paradises within the society from which it withdrew, without transforming the society as such, and it pacifies the revolutionary spirit by providing an escape into a Utopia. Therefore, what is required is a more holistic rebellion, one that will dissolve the established ego but that will not diminish a concrete revolutionary orientation.[84]

8.2.7 Malabou, Plasticity, and Making Our Brains

In *What Should We Do with Our Brain*, Catherine Malabou develops a logic of neuronal plasticity that maps well onto the imaginative logic of action as developed in this project. Although without stating so, Malabou furthers Marcuse's project of grounding the revolutionary transformation of subjectivity in the biological dimension. Her project is the flower to Marcuse's bud. Her stated effort is to take Marx's dictum that, "Humans make their own history, but they do not know that they make it" and modify it to, "Humans make their own brain, but they do not know it."[85] It is of no small consequence that Sartre, too, takes this Marxian dictum as his starting point in *CDR*. For, it demonstrates the shared dialectical logic that inspires both Sartre and Malabou. Although Malabou does not refer to Sartre in *What Should We Do with Our Brain*, the resonances with *CDR* are apparent. In a way, she is providing a cutting-edge perspective of the same process of subjectivization, albeit rooted in contemporary findings in neuroscience that were entirely absent in Sartre's day. Therefore, she becomes the perfect interlocutor to supplement the investigation at the present time.

Malabou employs the term "plasticity," borrowed from neuroscience, because it has a dual sense. She remarks that,

> We should not forget that plastique, from which we get the words *plastiquage* and *plastiquer*, is an explosive substance made of nitroglycerine and nitrocellulose, capable of causing violent explosions. We thus note that plasticity is situated between two extremes: on the one side the sensible image of taking form ... and on the other side that of the annihilation of all form.[86]

These two extremes must be conceived together in dialectical tension. They form the basis of the mechanism that drives the transformation of neuronal ideology. Plastic, like rubber, is malleable. It bends and can be shaped and re-shaped. However, unlike rubber, plastic has a limit. It is not endlessly pliable. There is a point at which it will break, thereby taking on a new form.

But plastic is also explosive. What comes to mind are the plastic explosives of demolitions. C-4 is stacked together, molded by hand, and detonated to great effect. For Malabou, such physical metaphor describes the logic of subjective transformation in the brain. The brain has circuits that are pliable to a limit but that eventually break. This rupture opens a space for new connections. And from the ash of exploded neurons emerge new formations of neuronal circuitry, thereby initiating new biological substrata.

If the brain weren't plastic, then it would not be feasible to suggest that novelty would ever truly emerge. For the biological system would merely be a self-perpetuating site of homeostasis. Quoting Antonio Damasio, homeostasis "refers to the coordinated and largely automated physiological reactions required to maintain steady internal states in a living organism."[87] However, Malabou's effort is to develop a critique that will enable *self-generation* by 1) critiquing the logic of flexibility that she claims fits within the existing global capitalist system, and 2) by developing a new logic based on brain plasticity. She asks the following questions: "Can the description of brain plasticity escape the insidious command of the New World Order? Can it introduce something like a resistance within this very order? *Can plastic brains measure the limits of their flexibility?*"[88] We might reword this as: Can the analog of brain plasticity escape the insidious command of Kaironic Seriality? Can it introduce something like a resistance to the serial logic of inaction? Can plastic subjects measure the limits of their flexibility?

Malabou argues that brain plasticity in the sciences has done nothing more than perpetuate the dominant logic of the New World Order. It has "revolutionized nothing *for us*, if it is true that our new brains serve only to displace ourselves better, work better, feel better, or obey better."[89] By operating according to a serial logic, the sciences have turned brain plasticity into a term that is complicit with the endless flexibility of the capitalist system. By proclaiming a narrative that our brains can adapt to the rate of demand set by market forces, this dominant logic has proved to be nothing more than a handmaiden for the reproduction of capital.

But, she argues, this is partly because of a misunderstanding of the application of plasticity. The serial explanation of plasticity forgets the explosive nature of *plastique*. It views plasticity as malleability and in the process creates a serial neuronal ideology. Against this ideology, Malabou wants to theorize resistance to this logic by developing an "intermediate plasticity" defined as "a plasticity-link that is never thought of or recognized as such, allowing us to elaborate a true dialectic of the auto-constitution of the self. . . . If we do not think through this transformation or this plasticity, we dodge the most important question, which is that of freedom."[90] In other words, she wants to develop a theory of subjective constitution that would transform the biological dimension in the creation of free praxis. And this transformation at the biological level would be "the transformation of one motor regime into another, of one device into another, a transformation necessitating a rupture, the violence of a gap that interrupts all continuity."[91]

A final point of note: Malabou's text functions much like *CDR*. It acts as an image that is meant to rouse the affections. In other words, it is not only theorizing about what can be done with our brains, but the text itself is an instantiation of the thesis of the text, which is to aid political subjects, in the creation of such subjects, in their struggle against the dominating "New World Order"—it is a Paradoxico-Critical project. In the final lines of her book, she invites the reader to "do what they undoubtedly have never done: construct and entertain a relation with their brain as the image of a world to come."[92] This transformation at the neuronal level will lead to a new mentality, which means (in one sense) that the transformation at the neuronal level enables reflective thought to create images that aren't determined by serial logic, but that can be created anew, according to a new logic.

Of course, we are taking some liberties with scientific concepts. But this does not negate the efficacy of such analogies for understanding how micropsychobiological shifts might occur. In fact, Malabou's work is steeped in both the scientific literature and in the philosophical tradition. Thus, her work, and by extension our present application of it, is an experimental synthesis based on inference that refuses to settle in the instrumental reason of scientism.

8.2.8 Connolly and Affect

At this point, a brief appeal to William Connolly will signal the way forward to the final section of this chapter. Bringing together Marcuse, Deleuze-Guattari, and Malabou, a speculative sketch for the transformation of subjectivity has been drawn. Both Marcuse and Malabou develop theories that demonstrate the need for counter logics about our very bodies themselves. And they both suggest ways in which these counter logics are different from the systems in which they emerge and against which they are directed. Malabou goes further than Marcuse in detailing a general theory of how a shift in "nature" could occur within the brain—i.e., through the logic of brain plasticity. But now we need to suggest a way in which this logic might materially affect subjectivity. That is, Malabou's final charge to her readers must be undertaken. And this is precisely what Deleuze-Guattari tends toward and what Connolly presents in *A World of Becoming*, to which we now turn. If Malabou was the flower to Marcuse's bud, Connolly is the floating pollen that is carried by the wind.

A sprawling, frenetic, somewhat scattered text, *A World of Becoming* is a barrage of micro-political thought that presents a view of the world that is at one moment chaotic and another creative. Through the dispersal of affective forces (physical, social, spiritual, political, artistic), Connolly provides a pragmatic set of practices that can be employed in the transformation of subjectivity. Starting with the basic idea of affect, he states that "In its most elementary human mode, [affect] is an electrical-chemical charge that jolts or nudges you towards positive or negative action before it reaches the threshold of feeling or awareness."[93] Affect takes place prior to awareness at the very basic level of causal relations within bodies. Affect is the term to describe the initial shift in subjectivity. In Kaironic Seriality, affect would be the charge that initially introjects the serial logic of inaction into an embodied *hexis*. Similarly, affect is also what makes intelligible the first moment of subjective constitution in the apocalyptic upsurge. Affect is the spark of human life, the differential, the logic of subjectivization.

What concerns us now, however, is how to utilize this spark of affectivity, how to work with its ignition in ways that can proactively confront exploitative logics. This is the final task of this project. Stated directly: how can the imaginative logic of action—as affective, active, and imaginative—transform society through the transformation of subjectivity? The answer is through *micro-psychobiological shifts*.

These are micro shifts (intensive variations) in the network of relations within any given body. They take place at the biological and psychological level and encompass the entirety of embodied life. That is, micro-psychobiological shifts are any shift in the network of functions that takes place within the body. This includes the processes from the lowest of complexity to the highest, from the most immediately material to the most abstract, from pure biological instinct to self-consciousness. They vary in scope. They vary in duration. They vary in intensity. They vary in complexity. And they don't follow a linear causal path from body to mental, or from mental to body. In fact, they disrupt the solidity of this binary altogether. But they necessarily always have an effect.

In fact, by nature, micro-psychobiological shifts are effects. Connolly suggests paths by which humans might engage with these effects:

> You do so in part by pursuing tactics of the self in which individuals draw upon tools and small assemblages to affect themselves; you do so more robustly through strategic action on larger networks of desire, and most importantly through resonances back and forth between these levels. Microtactics of the self might involve priming your dream life before you fall asleep, meditation, prayer, neurotherapy, selecting particular films for viewing with others, reading provocative texts, and allowing each of these experiences to engage the others. . . . To alter the networks in which you participate is eventually to alter the relational mode of desire coursing through you, in a model or notable way: you now participate in a modified assemblage of desire that includes and exceeds you. When the next round of action by you or your assemblage expresses that altered quality either or both may be poised to take a more adventurous political stance or accept a new level of ethical responsibility than before. You may be ready to listen to a new mode of inspiration to which you were previously tone-deaf. This is how, on the positive side, spirals of inter-involvement between desire, action, ethics and politics work.[94]

This is precisely what Sartre suggests when he speaks of the risks of the group logic when he states that "at each new stage of the undertaking, the revolutionary consciousness deepens."[95] The interiorized unity of the group transforms the objective and the group bit-by-bit, deepening the revolutionary logic, strengthening the vitality of the imaginative logic of action within Kaironic Seriality.

As the imaginative logic of action increases in potency, so the serial logic of inaction decreases in intensity. The result is that liberatory consciousness expands and alternative models of social and political life can be properly theorized and enacted. Created by a free logic, new images of historical life can be projected; images that are eminently analytical and yet thoroughly creative. Because the subjects themselves have come to life, the images they proffer will be imbued with vitality. They will not be perfect. They are not images of perfect societies or perfect social solutions. Rather, they are *opportune*: they are fitting for the task to which they correspond. They are proper in their origin and in their capacity to continue the transformation of material conditions and subjectivity, for they are products of the very same transformation, carrying forward the mantle of this process in perpetuity.

But this is precisely why the process must be perpetual. Because the images are imperfect, because of the scope of Kaironic Seriality's influence, there must be a perpetual effort of antagonism. Equipped with the imaginative logic of action, individuals and groups must work in common to realize what Sartre called "the perpetual apocalypse."[96]

8.3 THE PERPETUAL APOCALYPSE

This project is not about creating or theorizing the revolution. Such a goal is both overly ambitious and, remaining faithful to the self-diagnosis of our constrained comprehension, perhaps foolhardy. Rather, it is about *grounding* the perpetual maintenance of the group logic; the purpose of which is not a wholesale takeover of one system in favor of a socialist revolution, but rather, a way of developing the contours of a logical disposition that transforms "human beings" in their individual and social lives so that they can better overcome the exigent sites of scarcity in the present and near future, while simultaneously developing new humanisms that will be better positioned to deal with future social and political struggles. It is about *founding* the logic by which we can create better ensembles, those that can be perpetually oriented toward the maintenance of contestation against the capitalist state, objective spirit, institutional alienation, and all forms of diachronic and synchronic seriality—in short, perpetual resistance in Kaironic Seriality.

Following Sartre, this project is seeking to ground a notion of the perpetual apocalypse, which he found to be a "very attractive" notion.[97] Desiring the perpetual apocalypse is not a clamoring for a perpetual state of chaos. Sartre is not espousing a caricatured anarchist outlook. Rather, the perpetual apocalypse is better akin to an agonistic relationship between theoretical anarchism and practical socialism. And in this sense, any Sartre-inspired political project must be both micro- and macro-political.

8.3.1 Cracks in the Parchment

Referring to the Cultural Revolution in China, Sartre notes there "must have been determinate contradictions at the base of the Chinese socialist economy which produced the movement for a return to something like a perpetual fused group."[98] In other words, it was the exigencies of the "determinate contradictions" that potentially sustained "something like a perpetual fused group." Now, Sartre does later admit that he does not think that this is exactly what took place in China, opting instead to suggest that there must be "infrastructural reasons for the Cultural Revolution," but nevertheless we get insight into what a project of perpetual apocalypse would require. Thus, perhaps by the deepening of such "contradictions" in society, by recognizing situations of exigence, and by the creation of affective images we can perpetually force the hand of antagonistic praxis to unravel and transcend Kaironic Seriality in the creation of new humanisms and other worlds.

This means that contestation must be maintained. Antagonism to Kaironic Seriality must become a bedrock of social and political logic. This happens as the imaginative logic of action actually deepens the "feeling" of the Impossible, which then heightens the immediacy of the need for rebellion. Like the unconscious rage of the colonized from *The Wretched of the Earth*, imaginative political subjects are perpetually enraged by Kaironic Seriality. This is one of the defining features of the imaginative logic of action (as affective). It is essentially a logic at a distance from seriality, and as such, in opposition to alienation. Therefore, the perpetual apocalypse derives its impetus from the perpetual rage at the monstrosity of Kaironic Seriality. This again is why the term Kaironic Seriality is so useful. Not only does it demarcate the time as being thoroughly alienating, but it also heralds that the moment is always opportune—the time for transformation is always now; the site of transformation is always here; and the fuel for this transformation is always at hand.

But this antagonism is not merely a negative notion. Certainly, the imaginative logic of action is initiated partly through the violent oppositional upsurge of the apocalyptic spark. But there is also a profoundly positive notion of liberty contained in this opposition. For, the threat of continuing to live the Impossible becomes itself impossible only through a relational contradiction between that which is (the impossible situation of seriality) and that which must become (freedom). This is another way in which a productive dialectical relation must be maintained. For, the very notion of negative freedom contains within it a positive notion of freedom as well. And the same is true in the other direction.

Although Sartre does valorize negative notions of freedom,[99] Thomas Flynn rightly suggests that the future of objective possibility in Sartre's later oeuvre demonstrates a "major shift in Sartre's concept of freedom (towards so-called positive freedom) and constitutes a prime factor in his tilt toward a Marxist theory of history."[100] Therefore, the imaginative logic of action, as wielded by imaginative political subjects, must perpetually contest seriality while simultaneously seeking to realize alternative futures.

Because our history is the history of scarcity, this ensures that there will be no shortage of situations of contestation.[101] Thomas Flynn explains further:

> Besides being the "lack" which illumines present reality, the possible serves as the limit in that it counterpoises the *im*possible. Thus, Sartre speaks of "the real and permanent future which the collectivity forever maintains and transforms," for example, the need for more doctors that industrialized society creates (SM 94).[102]

Thus, the praxis-project, as it aims toward its possibles, overcomes (i.e., negates/transcends) the present condition (through interiorization and subsequent exteriorization), and then simultaneously introduces new possibles that can subsequently be overcome. In the process, one lack is overcome and new lacks are revealed (in the milieu of scarcity). This means that the more we create, the more *need* we also create. The future is that "yet-to-be-achieved totality toward which praxis transcends the present," *and* it is the limit that counterpoises the Impossible—that is, "the real and permanent future which the collectivity forever maintains and transforms."

So, the future opens the present to endless need, as the possible (i.e., the future possible that is subsequently transcended) also maintains and transforms the real and permanent future by continually recreating needs in the continual overcoming/negating of the present. This complex process is echoed by William Connolly in a different though consonant manner:

> Sensory inter-involvement, disciplinary processes, detailed modes of surveillance, media infiltration, congealed attractors, affective disposition, self-regulation in response to future susceptibility—these elements participate in perpetual circuits of exchange, feedback, and re-entry, with each loop folding another variation and degree into its predecessor. The imbrications are so close that it is near to impossible to sort out each element from the other as they merge into a larger complex. . . . Even as they are ubiquitous, however, there are numerous points of dissonance, variation, hesitation, and disturbance in them. These interruptions provide potential triggers to the pursuit of other spiritual possibilities, where the term spirit means a refined state of the body in individual and existential dispositions embedded in institutional practices. [103]

The first half of this quote elaborates the internal variations, co-constitutive flows, and dialectical entanglements that characterize a Paradoxico-Critical logic. And the latter half (from "Even as . . . ") reveals the poetic productivity that virtually insists through the processes of totalization. The "dissonances" are cracks in the parchment of Kaironic Seriality, crevices where the hegemonic whole isn't in *complete* control. This is where there is a site for potential micro-political action.

8.3.2 Micro-Politics

It is generally argued across ideological lines that there are irreconcilable differences between micro- and macro-political theory. For instance, Todd May argues that:

> Poststructuralist political thought has offered, though not precisely in these terms, an alternative vision of political intervention that articulates the tension between the world as it is and the world as it could be, particularly since the collapse of the Marxist project. That the framework it provides has not been much discussed as such is in part owing to its nature: it avoids global discourse in favor of concrete, limited analyses. In poststructuralism, macropolitics gives way to micropolitics. [104]

What immediately jumps out from this quote is the claim that poststructuralism exclusively favors "concrete, limited analyses." But this is precisely what the imaginative logic of action allows, while *also* providing impetus for "global discourse."

Regressive analysis is not detached from concrete concerns in real material conditions. This is where it begins. By analyzing the sites of exigency in the practico-inert field, the imaginative logic of action is a critical, logical disposition that starts with contextualized mediated experience in order to understand the conditions that make this experience *actual*. Then, by revealing the living logic of the unravelled context, it is able to aim forward toward strategies and tactics that can overcome the particular needs of that situation. Further, the scope of the imaginative political subject is not wedded to localized, micro-political concerns, but necessarily has an eye toward global concerns as well—being motivated by an indomitable spirit for the perpetual transformation of the whole. Of course, this does not mean that the transformation of the whole is pre-determined by a logic of totality (we've covered this extensively, particularly in chapter 1). Instead, through a Paradoxico-Critical orientation, the imaginative logic of action is able to perpetually create within the global conditions in which and by which it operates, even as the global and local refract through and inform one another. The either/or between concrete/limited and global discourse is thus not a bifurcation that we must accept.

May continues his argument by drawing a distinction between what he calls "strategic" and "tactical" political philosophies. Strategic political philosophies involve a "unitary analysis that aims toward a single goal."[105] Tactical thought, however, "performs its analyses within a milieu characterized not only by the tension between what is and what ought to be, but also between irreducible but mutually intersecting practices of power."[106] May's general error seems to be in making a stark distinction between micro- and macro-politics. While it may certainly be the case that the "Marxist project" has historically focused on a transformation of economic modes of production, it is not necessarily the case that all Marx-inspired thought, and therefore all macro-political, strategic thinking is necessarily unable to simultaneously have a micro-political, tactical thrust as well.[107]

Sartre's political philosophy was not concerned with a unitary analysis that aimed toward a single goal. May broad-brushes Sartre when he places *CDR* into the strategic camp. He claims that it merely has the same "common strategic base" as structuralist Marxism. The result is that May does not pay specific attention to the details and uniqueness of Sartre's efforts. Instead he focuses his criticism on Althusser and in the process mischaracterizes *CDR* and ignores a unique contribution to the micro-/macro-political debate.

In *CDR*, the implications are that there is no center of power. This is the genius of seriality as a pluridimensional concept: it is dispersed diachronically and synchronically in such a way that there is no concentricity where power can be *singularly* analyzed (in the state or class struggle, for example). Let us quote the great "micro-political thinker" Michel Foucault to get further insight into the quality of the power mechanism itself:

> [The] mechanisms of power in the Soviet Union—systems of control, of surveillance, punishment—are versions of those used on a smaller scale and with less consistency by the bourgeoisie as it struggled to consolidate its power.... One can say to many socialisms, real or dreamt: Between the analysis of power in the bourgeois state and the idea of its future withering away, there is a missing term—*the analysis, criticism, destruction, and overthrow of the power mechanism itself.* [Emphasis added][108]

It is this last line that is precisely what *CDR* allows for and what the development of the imaginative logic of action equips.

May's hope for the revolution is one where there "is not a change from one fundamental form of society to another; rather, it is a change or set of changes whose effects sweep across the society, causing changes in many other parts of the social domain."[109] Sartre would agree. Clarifying some of his ideas from *CDR*, he once stated that, "The idea of an instant and total liberation is a utopia."[110] This is because Sartre's philosophy is one that tethers the balance between lateral political action at the local and micro level, but that also seeks incremental transformations in the pursuit of large-scale socialist images.

The fear of thinkers like May and those of his ilk are that global discourses and large-scale projects tend toward the centralization of power and authoritarianism. Such projects are also supposed to ignore the increased minoritization of the world. And this fear must be granted. There can surely be a tendency to dismiss the ever-increasing dispersal of needs, desires, demands, etc., if grand visions are established as one-size-fits-all. This is Sartre's criticism of Lukács and the logic of totality. But this is why the investigation of *CDR* is so important to continue to undertake and read with fresh eyes. For, it is both concerned with the radical concrete individual and the aggregate concerns of the social. It is both Kierkegaardian and Marxist. And while certain theorists have seen this ideological marriage as inherently contradictory, once the text is understood as a formal, logical investigation into the conditions of history, all the logical notions developed therein resist orthogonal reciprocity and eschew ontological and normative readings that encrust the text into an either/or historical camp.

In an interview, Sartre once claimed that while socialism "may not be able to eliminate all forms of scarcity, alienation, necessity, and suffering, we definitely can eliminate some, and this could improve conditions of our existence."[111] Sartre's notion of an ideal socialism, therefore, is not optimistic in an (admittedly caricatured) Hegelian sense; he does not believe that our progress toward that ideal is in any way necessary or guaranteed; nor is it in anyway pre-fabricated as a singular image. But, as Elizabeth Butterfield notes, "[Sartre] remains hopeful that we can improve human existence incrementally and in taking concrete steps."[112]

8.3.3 Macro-Politics

Of course, the other side of the micro-/macro-political divide requires that incrementality be supplemented by large-scale discourses. In the pursuit of the perpetual apocalypse, there must not merely be the hope for a permanent revolutionary spirit at the lateral level. There must simultaneously be grand vertical projects that are wielded by imaginative political subjects. Part of the reason for this is that micro-politics is too easily re-incorporated back into the clutches of Kaironic Seriality. If the rot of this monstrosity infects every dimension of social life, then merely planting new gardens on the rocky subsoil will not produce long-term fruits. Rather, there needs to be a holistic transformation of the garden itself at every level of complexity and variation. As Nik Farrell Fox states, "A true dialectical understanding of society, in Sartre's view, would make intelligible the 'micro-contexts' of social life and draw these together to see how they continue to affect and in turn be affected by the wider 'macro-structures' of society."[113] Remember that for Sartre it does not matter ultimately if a group is constituted from bottom up or top down—the point for him is to understand the formation of the group: how? why? under what conditions?

In a practical example, if a corporation comes together to implement a new policy to provide, for example, unlimited vacation time so long as the employees complete their projects in a timely manner, their deliberation and subsequent drafting of new corporate policies resembles the logic of the pledged group. It was an ensemble that emerged out of a larger institutional framework and that united various heterogeneous praxes under the common inertia of a new pledge. This pledge of course will supplant existing corporate regulations and will have far reaching consequences (of which we can't go into here). The point is that this common praxis (and the subsequent implementation of it and totalization of it as it is lived by management and employees alike) emerges and creates a new nexus of capacities, exigencies, duties and rights, etc., which can be understood by the logic of the organization.

So, with respect to this new policy, a new regroupment has been effected insofar as it has been driven, in part, by the imaginative logic of action. It will have a productive effect over the larger institutional ossature and activities, but it will also retain various levels of seriality within it. Even in the very language of the contract itself, which promises to create novel social arrangements, there will be serial forces brought into the new phase of corporate development. As such, freedom or de-alienation will not be manifest *in toto*. But there will be a new taste of de-alienation and commonality in so far as each person in the social grouping practically enacts this new policy with each transaction, with each vacation taken, and with each assignment completed from outside the office. And it is the intelligibility of this new policy—how it emerged, what are its effects, what are the mediations that led to its development and how to understand them—that *CDR* allows us to explore, understand, and think (from the perspective of seeking to make comprehensible the logic of dialectical reason).

This is because Sartre develops a heuristic of the formal conditions of group arrangements, serial conditions, material conditions, group being, class being, etc., that we can further formulate and apply in various micro and macro contexts. Hence why the relatively banal example above is valuable. The sexy models of violent revolution tend to overdetermine analyses by romanticizing radical, chaotic, and otherwise exceptional historical circumstances. But for the imaginative logic of action to be best understood, it is important that we do not fetishize moments of social insurrection. For, it is in the day-to-day that the imaginative logic of action operates: sometimes as an inexistent virtual factor; sometimes to small degree; and of course at times expressed more fully.

In fact, there are times when Sartre claims that the revolutionary spirit "must necessarily reproduce—up to a certain limit—the centralization and coercion of the bourgeois state which it is its mission to overthrow."[114] This is because the ultimate difference between a serial leader and a revolutionary agitator is one of difference in distance and mediation. He states, "In fact, what distinguishes the leader from the agitator—apart from the coercive nature of his power—is, frequently, the number of mediations which separate him from the group."[115] Therefore, it can be said that the "limit" that Sartre differentiates between the bourgeois and revolutionary logic has to do with the mediations and the distance between free praxis and centralization.

If centralization is driven by free praxis—that is, by the imaginative logic of action—then it will not infringe upon freedom. Under such circumstances, a political party, for example, will fit within the logical schema of the group (most akin to the logical iteration of the organization). However, if the centralization is driven by the serial logic of inaction, or, what amounts to the same thing, if the centralization of power is at a greater mediated distance from free praxis, then the party will perpetuate seriality. What all of this means is that both the micro- and the macro-political levels of engagement are in themselves benign. They only begin to bear value in the socio-political arena insofar as they are understood by operating according to either the serial logic of inaction or the imaginative logic of action (to greater or lesser degree). If the former, then any micro- or macro-political endeavor will tend toward alienation and/or oppression. And to the contrary, if the imaginative logic of action is the mode of praxis that drives socio-political engagement, then any and all lateral and vertical engagement will be characterized by de-alienation. At the risk of being overly repetitive, it must be kept in mind that this does not mean wholesale de-alienation. We are speaking at the level of logical abstraction here in order to make the project of the perpetual apocalypse intelligible. In lived experience, of course, matters are always variant.

Thus, large-scale visions of imaginative political subjects will not in themselves tend toward authoritarianism. In fact, they will retain the democratic purity that micro-political theorists so desire. Likewise, the imaginative logic of action will actually infuse vitality into the macro-political levels of engagement as well, as the latter will become moments or incarnations of what Nick Srnicek and Alex Williams call "hyperstitions." Arguing for both a micro- and macro-political outlook within Leftist politics, Srnicek and Williams suggest that, "[Progress] must be understood as hyperstitional: as a kind of fiction, but one that aims to transform itself into a truth. Hyperstitions operate by catalysing dispersed sentiments into a historical force that brings the future into existence."[116]

Like the images of the poetic imagination, hyperstitions must not be merely phantasmic ideals, but must be images driven by the imaginative logic of action. They refract the future through the present, in order to transform the latter in realizing the former. Of course, the contours and coordinates of this refraction is not something that is easily determinable. In fact, we have to agree with Sartre: "One can only know something is impossible once one has tried it and failed."[117] This means that there is a sense of play and experimentation that must govern any hope for the effectiveness of the perpetual apocalypse.

8.3.4 The Value of the Perpetual Apocalypse

The reason that the logic of the group must be understood as co-imbricated by serial conditions is that seriality is Infinite and pluridimensional. As such, seriality is never truly overcome (so long as there is scarcity). Even in the apocalyptic moment, the freedom that is experienced is freedom in relation to a particular threat, not to seriality as such. Culture as practico-inert, language, personal identity, class, vocation, university affiliation, race, sport team fanaticism, cuisine culture, etc., all still remain, and are interiorized, in the group. These practico-inert worlds co-imbricate one another and play a role in the constitution of the group as itself a pluridimensional world within worlds. That is why there is still alienation contained within inter-subjective relations; fraternity can only silence it for a time, to direct attention away from its presence. This is why there must be a full-scale war against Kaironic Seriality, and hence why a notion of perpetual apocalypse has use.

There is a perpetual small-scale and large-scale antagonism required to really combat the monstrosity of Kaironic Seriality. Micro-political uprisings are necessary, but insufficient; global economic policies geared toward equitable resource allocation are likewise necessary, but insufficient—there must be a perpetual deployment of both local and global, micro- and macro-political, social, economic, ecological, spiritual, social, artistic, etc., actions. Imaginative political subjects-in-becoming wield the imaginative logic of action as a productive weapon against Kaironic Seriality. This isn't to simply try lateral tactics or micro-political action, but rather, it is a way that we can utilize the micro-political in the transformation of subjectivities while we simultaneously create counter-hegemonic attacks.

Against the common charges of pessimism leveled against Sartre's circularity, it is crucial to note that while, yes, there are moments of circular description in *CDR* from series to group to series, even these cycles are not a mere repetition of the same. As Sartre likes to speak of the spiral movement where men pass the "same" moment, he also notes that this spiral passing takes place at varying "levels of integration and complexity."[118] Thus, when Chiodi says that de-alienation merely has the "temporal dimension of an instant," what he is failing to assess are the transformative effects of the apocalypse and the spontaneous upsurge of freedom in concrete, material terms. By remaining at the level of simple abstraction, he fails to consider the diachronic, synchronic, and thus kaironic effects of this eventual logic, as there are literal intensive shifts that echo from de-alienated human expressions—in qualitative terms. For, in the lives of concrete, material beings, in their unique positions, as particular contracted nodes within the larger social network, there are micro-psychobiological shifts that radically transform them as they move through the various stage(s) of life. Likewise, the eventual logic also produces concrete, material effects within the broad cultural and political landscape. There is a variegating intensity that can't be ignored: an affective transformative power that creates new unbounded situations of life from which further complex layerings of serial-group-serial-group relations will unfold, which themselves will produce profound breaks or fissures in the politico-historical landscape.

Sartre's *Critique of Dialectical Reason* is a heuristic to establish a living logic. As such, it isn't normative or ontological *per se*. Rather, it is a moment of praxis that itself must be taken up and used in order to determine the conditions under which and by which normative and ontological proceedings can be grounded. That is, it is an emergent tool—i.e., a hypo-logic—that is to be applied to various specific contexts as is fitting. For, the insights contained therein are open and applicable to various contextual attachments. In the course of this project thus far, we have endeavored to signal in theoretical directions where such application might be most valuable. In the creative analysis of the logical constructions of *CDR*, and by exploring the logic of the poetic imagination, we have developed the speculative outlines of a dispositional orientation that can aid imaginative political subjects-in-becoming in the perpetual creation of society.

However, with that said, so long as seriality is the dominant force that defines human relations, it will necessarily characterize the human itself as inhuman. Thus, there must be a sort of mortification of sin, a self-directed war to overcome the power of the monstrous serial logic that dominates the destinies of inhuman bodies under global capitalist domination. However, lest one suppose this is a simple morality tale, it must be emphasized that this transformation of self isn't merely an individual pursuit. Rather, it is a group effort. It is a collective antagonism directed against the dominant age but that is awakened within, as it is always the opportune moment to act. And in this sense the transformation of life and society is most assuredly an *experiment*. But it is also a *science*, a *politics*, an *economics*, a *social theory*—and just as equally, it is an *art*.

NOTES

1. Jean-Paul Sartre, "Interview with Benny Lévy," *Sartre and Lévy* (1996), 67.
2. Frantz Fanon, *The Wretched of the Earth*, trans. Richard Philcox (New York: Grove Press, 2004), 239.
3. Nick Srnicek and Alex Williams, *Inventing the Future: Postcapitalism and a World without Work* (London: Verso, 2015), 51.
4. Sartre, *The Wretched of the Earth*, lv.
5. Power, "From Theoretical Antihumanism to Practical Humanism," 185.
6. Flynn, *Sartre, Foucault, and Historical Reason*, Volume 1, 126.
7. Anderson, 274.
8. Power, "From Theoretical Antihumanism to Practical Humanism," 114.
9. Power, "The Terror of Collectivity," 103.
10. See Badiou, *PP*, 25.
11. Power, "The Terror of Collectivity," 103.
12. Badiou, *PP*, 25.
13. Nina Power, "Towards a New Political Subject? Badiou between Marx and Althusser," in Sean Bowden and Simon Duffy, *Badiou and Philosophy* (Edinburgh: Edinburgh University Press 2012), 158.
14. Ibid., 158.
15. Power, "Towards a New Political Subject?," 160.
16. Antonio Negri, "Is It Possible to Be a Communist without Marx?," *Critical Horizons*, 12, no. 1 (2011): 5 and 11.
17. Sartre, *CDR*, 510.
18. Martin Heidegger, "Letter on Humanism," in *Basic Writings* (London: Routledge, 2004), 233–34 and 237.
19. Power, "From Theoretical Antihumanism to Practical Humanism," 9.
20. Sartre, *CDR*, 19.
21. Ibid., 45.
22. Butterfield, 17.
23. Ibid., 17.
24. Ibid., 81.
25. Kevin Boileau, "How Foucault Can Improve Sartre's Theory of Authentic Political Community," *Sartre Studies International*, 10, no. 2 (2004): 85–86.

26. Ibid., 82.
27. Ibid., 82.
28. Ibid., 83.
29. Michel Foucault, "The Ethic of Care for the Self as a Practice of Freedom," in *The Final Foucault*, ed. James Bernauer and David Rasmussen (Cambridge, MA: MIT Press, 1988), 18.
30. See Gilles Deleuze and Félix Guattari, *Anti-Oedipus: Capitalism and Schizophrenia*, Volume 1, trans. Robert Hurley, Mark Seem, and Hellen R. Lane (London and New York: Continuum, 2004), and the later work of Michel Foucault, particularly his essay "The Subject and Power," *Critical Inquiry*, 8, no. 4 (1982): 777–95.
31. Sartre, *CDR*, 110.
32. Michel Foucault, *The Foucault Reader*, ed. P. Rabinow (New York: Pantheon, 1984), 321.
33. Ibid., 308.
34. Fox, 48.
35. Robert Bernasconi, "Fanon's *The Wretched of the Earth* as the Fulfillment of Sartre's *Critique of Dialectical Reason*," 40.
36. Sartre, *CDR*, 309.
37. Sartre, *The Wretched of the Earth*, lvii.
38. Sartre, *CDR*, 385.
39. Ibid., 520, 522.
40. Betty Cannon, "Group Therapy as Revolutionary Praxis: A Sartrean View," *Sartre Studies International*, 11, nos. 1–2 (2005): 133.
41. Ibid., 143.
42. Ibid., 146.
43. Sartre, *The Wretched of the Earth*, lix.
44. Fox, 31.
45. In 1948, Marcuse wrote a stinging criticism of Sartre's *Being and Nothingness* and "Materialism and Revolution." In "Existentialism: Remarks on Jean-Paul Sartre's *L'Entre Et Le Néant*," *Philosophy and Phenomenological Research*, 8, no. 3 (1948): 309–36, he accused Sartre of insufficiently considering history and the body; and also claimed that Sartre's phenomenological notion of freedom withheld any fruitful understanding of social freedom in material existence. However, when Marcuse's essay was republished in 1972, he wrote a postscript in which he claimed that Sartre had gone through a radical "conversion" by embracing Marxism. He claimed that Sartre's phenomenology "[receded] before the invasion of real history, the dispute with Marxism, and the adoption of the dialectic." *Studies in Critical Philosophy*, trans. Joris De Bres (Boston: Beacon Press, 1972), 189. It is this latter position that bridges any gaps between Sartre and Marcuse in the present investigation.
46. Benedict De Spinoza, *Theological-Political Treatise*, ed. Jonathan Israel, trans. Michael Silberthorne and Jonathan Israel (Cambridge, Cambridge University Press, 2007), 20, 27.
47. Ibid., 30–32.
48. Ibid., 27, 28.
49. Ibid., 28.
50. Ibid., 29.
51. Ibid., 27.
52. Ibid., 25.
53. See chapter 5 for the relevance with this project. And see Walter Brueggemann, *The Prophetic Imagination* (Minneapolis: Fortress Press, 2001), to get a full account of the prophetic imagination's theo-political intent.
54. Corey Robin, *The Reactionary Mind: Conservatism from Edmund Burke to Sarah Palin* (Oxford: Oxford University Press, 2011).
55. Jean-Paul Sartre, *What Is Subjectivity?* (London, Verso, 2016).
56. Marcuse, 37.
57. Ibid., 37–38.
58. Ibid., 30.
59. Ibid., 45.
60. Ibid., 3.

61. Ibid., 3.
62. Ibid., 3–4.
63. Ibid., 10.
64. Philip Goodchild, "Capital and Kingdom: An Eschatological Ontology," in *Theology and the Political*, 148.
65. Ibid., 12.
66. Ibid., 15.
67. Nietzsche, *GM*, 57.
68. Gilles Deleuze and Félix Guattari, *A Thousand Plateaus: Capitalism and Schizophrenia*, trans. Brian Massumi (London, Athlone Press, 1988), 6–12.
69. Philip Goodchild, "Capital and Kingdom: An Eschatological Ontology," in *Theology and the Political*, 148.
70. Gilles Deleuze and Félix Guattari, *Anti-Oedipus: Capitalism and Schizophrenia*, trans. Robert Hurley, Mark Seem, and Helen R. Lane (Minneapolis: University of Minnesota Press, 1983), 142.
71. Ibid., 246.
72. Gilles Deleuze, "The Actual and the Virtual," trans. Eliot Ross Albert, in Gilles Deleuze and Claire Parnet, *Dialogues II*, trans. Hugh Tomlinson and Barbara Habberjam (London: Continuum, 2002), 148.
73. John Mullarkey, *Post-Continental Philosophy: An Outline* (London, Continuum, 2006), 28.
74. Marcuse, 5.
75. Ibid., 6.
76. Ibid., 6.
77. Ibid., 11.
78. Ibid., 10.
79. Ibid., 10.
80. Ibid., 19.
81. Ibid., 19.
82. Ibid., 21.
83. Ibid., 37.
84. To be clear, this does not negate the effectiveness of narcotic trips. In fact, the plethora of substances that are ingested have a great effect on subjective constitution. This takes place at almost every level, from basic dietary intake, to health supplements, to recreational chemicals. These biological practices create habits that, in turn, condition subjectivity and how it takes up the world. Not only is there an ethical responsibility attached to eating food that is factory farmed, for example, but there is also a sense in which the substances that are ingested contribute to or challenge the logic that is driving praxis.
85. Catherine Malabou, *What Should We Do with Our Brain?*, trans. Sebastian Rand (New York: Fordham, 2008), 1.
86. Ibid., 5.
87. Ibid., 74.
88. Ibid., 54.
89. Ibid., 68.
90. Ibid., 69.
91. Ibid., 73.
92. Ibid., 82.
93. Connolly, 150.
94. Ibid., 115–16.
95. Sartre, *The Wretched of the Earth*, lvi.
96. Sartre, "The Itinerary of a Thought," 57.
97. Ibid., 57.
98. Ibid., 57.
99. See for example his essay on the differences between American and French notions of freedom in "Individualism and Conformism in the United States," in *Literary Philosophical Essays*.

100. Flynn, *Sartre, Foucault and Historical Reason*, Volume 1, 130.

101. Although Sartre hinted at the possibility of there being a future economy of abundance, he did not elaborate on what this future would look like or even how it would come about. Theorists such as Michael Hardt and Antonio Negri have contested the idea that present society is characterized by scarcity. They claim that capitalism itself is capable of producing an economy of—immaterial—abundance. Thus, to best combat the powers of Empire, one must theorize and act from a position that recognizes capitalism's great power in producing "abundance," and that this power has great appeal for the furthering of neoliberal global domination and to instead develop theories based on the common. See Michael Hardt and Antonio Negri, *Multitude: War and Democracy in the Age of Empire* (New York: Penguin, 2004), 311, and *Commonwealth* (Cambridge, MA: Harvard University Press, 2009), 131–42. Contrary to this, in the future, I would like to explore the ways in which capitalism is essentially a scarcity-producing machine, thereby ensuring that unless there is complete transformation of the economic modes of production across the globe, seriality will reign. In this way, it is sufficient for now to note that, for Sartre, our history is one that is characterized by scarcity and that there will be no shortage of social or political needs that ought to be overcome.

102. Flynn, *Sartre, Foucault and Historical Reason*, Volume 1, 129.

103. Connolly, 55–56.

104. Todd May, *The Political Philosophy of Poststructuralist Anarchism* (University Park: The Pennsylvania State University Press, 1994), 4.

105. Ibid., 7.

106. Ibid., 7.

107. For an excellent treatment of the ways the micro- and macro-politcal can be brought together, see Jacques Bidet, *Foucault With Marx*, trans. Steven Corcoran (London: Zed Books, 2015).

108. Michel Foucault, "The Politics of Soviet Crime" (1976), trans. Mollie Horwitz, reprinted in *Foucault Live*, ed. Sylvere Lotringer (New York: Semiotext[e], 1989), 130.

109. May, 31.

110. Sartre, "The Itinerary of a Thought," 61.

111. Jean-Paul Sartre, "Interview with Sartre," in *The Philosophy of Sartre*, ed. Paul Arthur Schlipp (La Salle: Open Court, 1981), 32.

112. Butterfield, 39.

113. Fox, 99.

114. Sartre, "The Itinerary of Thought," 60.

115. Sartre, *CDR*, 524.

116. Srnicek and Williams, 50.

117. Sartre, "The Itinerary of a Thought," 59.

118. Sartre, *SM*, 106.

Chapter Nine

Prolegomena to Any Future Critique of Political Economy

> "If there can be a philosophy which is something other than and something more than philosophy, this remains to be proved. If there can be a politics that is something other and something more than politics, this also remains to be seen. If there can be a union of reflection and action, and if this reflection and this action, instead of separating those who practise it from all the other, carries them towards a new society, this union remains to be accomplished. The intention of this union was present at the origin of Marxism. It has remained a mere intuition—but, in a new context, it continues, a century later, to define our task."
>
> —Cornelius Castoriadis [1]

Let's read that quote one more time. While we do not engage substantially with Castoriadis in the present project, it is the concern he articulates here that binds him and other similarly sympathetic and critical thinkers of the Marxist project to our present efforts. This final chapter can only indicate a few areas where such critique can take root. But it will hopefully serve as a linchpin for future work to expand upon.

I am very aware that we have been circling around themes and concepts throughout this book rather than settling into them. I'm sure that there is a sense in which such wandering around and quick dashes through social and political concepts has been unsettling at times. However, there is a sense and purpose in this approach. The tendency to need to attach determinate meanings to concepts that are in the process of becoming is a symptomatic effect of the serial logic of inaction. This is not to excuse portions of the text where I could certainly be clearer. My own limits also contribute to any shortcomings. However, it is to note that there is a meta-philosophical underpinning that is intentionally driving this study. I have referred to it in various guises:

dialectic, totalization, a moment of praxis, the Paradoxico-Critical orientation. I want to introduce one more: the philosophy of internal relations.

The reason for introducing this term now is in an effort to ground ourselves before we move on—before you close this book, before you attend your local branch meeting, before class, a date, catching the game on TV, whatever. My hope is to offer, as much as I am able at this time, a parachute to gently set you down from the clouds of high theory. Of course, to start, more theory. However, this is a self-justifying theoretical notion, one that will hopefully give further cause for the formal investigation of this text. The consequences drawn from our brief engagement with the philosophy of internal relations will illuminate, once again, the stakes of this investigation pertaining to dialectical intelligibility. And then, before typing the final word, I will offer some perspective on ways to think through how the present project can help us assess our present hegemonic cultural monstrosity, the serial logic of neoliberalism.

Section 9.1 will unpack the value of abstraction in the philosophy of internal relations. We defend this supposition by arguing that abstractions are not a source of apolitical praxis or pure idealist theoretical speculation. Rather, vital abstractions are the *matériel* by which the dialectic reasons.

In section 9.2, we explicitly draw the stakes of this investigation through a debate between G. A. Cohen and Brian Leiter. Cohen, like Sartre, believed that Marxism had stopped and was in need of further elaboration in order to avoid the reproduction of false consciousness that stifled proletarian solidarity. Leiter's rejoinder is that Cohen slips bourgeois rationality through the back door in his appeal to normative ethics. For Cohen, Marxism needs to be able to explain the shifting quality of the conditions for praxis. For Leiter, the conditions for praxis have already been established by positivist, accelerationist Marxism. While neither position is completely advocated here, their framing of the debate points the way to the final stage of our investigation into the serial logic of neoliberal reason.

The Cohen-Leiter debate brings us to section 9.3 wherein we address the current conditions of mystification. If Cohen is right about the shifting qualities of the conditions of praxis, and if Leiter is correct to criticize the residual bourgeois rationality in Cohen's alternative, then in what way can the imaginative logic of action that we have been developing here, derived from our fresh reading of *CDR* as a formal and logical investigation, inform a dialectical investigation into the conditions for comprehension? We examine the serial logic of neoliberal reason as the most strident expression of Kaironic Seriality for our times. As a source of mystification, neoliberal reason must be understood in order to craft antagonistic strategies to its self-reproduction through anti-praxis. Perhaps then we can join hands in developing perpetual reciprocal contestations to the illusory mechanisms that constrain dialectical intelligibility.

9.1 VITAL ABSTRACTIONS

The purpose of this section is to align the philosophy of internal relations with our development of the imaginative logic of action as a product of Sartre's formal and logical investigation into the grounds of dialectical reason. By understanding the necessity and value of abstraction, we will see how *CDR* is a text that offers so much more than is typically afforded. However, we must attempt to move beyond authorial intent and expand his project into arenas that are calling for attention. We must allow our theoretical work to be sensitive to the exigencies of our material circumstances. With that, this section will seek to defend the deployment of abstraction as a productive technology of praxis that is a central component to the embodiment of the art that is the imaginative logic of action.

9.1.1 Abstraction and the Philosophy of Internal Relations

In common parlance, "abstraction" is a dirty word. It is often associated with obfuscation. To speak in abstractions in political dialogue is to speak the language of detached theory. To engage in abstract semiotic debates is to ponder over language at a level that is acceptable in its proper navel-gazing context, behind the walls of the ivory tower, or over drinks with friends after hours. But on the clock, abstraction merely diffuses our focus and misdirects our attention from the concerns at hand. In effect, the accusation that abstraction is obfuscation is akin to criticizing it for being mystifying. In the same way Marx criticized groundless theory and religion as ideology, so too is abstraction viewed as a mode of the human experience that induces illusory speculation rather than scientific analysis.

The philosophy of internal relations suggests otherwise. It views abstraction as a vital component of human thought *per se*. Rather than abstraction contributing to illusory cognition, the philosophy of internal relations views abstraction as part of the dialectical process of totalization. This does not mean that abstract concepts *per se* are immune from criticism. Rather, the philosophy of internal relations argues that abstract concepts are simultaneously process and form. As such, in the language of the present project, abstract concepts ought to be viewed as both practico and inert. Thus, it is not abstraction *per se*, but the mode of philosophical orientation that determines whether abstraction will be mystifying or not.

Bertell Ollman has gone the furthest in explicitly elaborating the philosophy of internal relations in relation to dialectical rationality. According to Ollman, abstraction omits becoming. It is the containment of the processes that lead to a given thought. As he states, "[People] are essentially what they appear to be at this moment. How they got that way, and what they become as they get older—the stages each of us goes through over a lifetime—are omitted in determining who and what we are."[2] This tendency appears to be a function of linguistic consciousness. Sartre would refer to it as a tendency of imaginative consciousness. The point is that perceiving (and conceiving) the flow of becoming is something abnormal. This is what leads Sartre to describe the "slimy" in the final pages of BN and the awareness of the absurd in his most famous of novels as being something non-standard and overwhelming in typical, lived experience. Heidegger refers to the ontological mood; Husserl appeals to the division between the lived attitude and the *epoche*. For all, the constant is that there seems to be a slippage between modes of lived experience. At the ontological level, there is flux, flow, the processes of becoming. Yet, consciously, we are able to carve out portions of the *hyle* in order to calculate, name, analyze, place, taxonomize, quantify, etc.

Being aware of this slippage is what Ollman wants to address: how it is that thought either retreats from the confrontation with becoming, or how it might harness process productively. He does this by examining the poetic capacity of paradox-turned-contradiction. For Ollman, "A paradox refers to two or more things that seem to be incompatible but manage to exist at the same time."[3] We might think through the relations between seriality and praxis, or between determinism and freedom, or history and structure. One approach to these relations would become frustrated at their apparent external relation that might not have the capacity to think through their productive participation with one another. At that moment, a paradox has been realized. A tension is sensed.

However, in Marxian fashion, Ollman is not content to let the sensing of paradox rest as an insurmountable mystery. Instead, he wants to push through such paradoxical relations to their productive relations as internally related contradictions. Reason being that Ollman claims there is an "'identity' between elements that are first presented as not only different from but logically independent of one another."[4] Exploring this sensed "identity" is what causes Ollman to consider how it is that paradoxical relations might be more complex than perceived in common sense. And through problematizing the paradoxical relations, we might sense how these apparently disparate objects are in fact related *internally*. Ariel Salleh describes this complex and productive tension by an appeal to post-Einsteinian sensibilities and the lived experience of pregnancy:

> Post Einstein, reality is increasingly spoken of as layered, or more accurately, relative to how it is conceptually framed. For example, using a sociological lens, a woman can be seen as the routine carrier of learned roles in a social system that functions by certain time coordinates; using another lens, she becomes a dissipative flux in an environment whose temporal context is elsewhere. As Julia Kristeva records it, pregnancy is an experience in which a woman comes to know herself in contradictory ways at once: "Cells fuse, split,

and proliferate; volumes grow, tissues stretch, and body fluids change rhythm, speeding up or slowing down. Within the body growing is a graft, indomitable, there is another. And no one is present, within that simultaneously dual and alien space, to signify what is going on. It happens, but I'm not there. I cannot realise it, but it goes on. Motherhood's impossible syllogism." A process without a subject; identity in non-identity? The body of the mother is wave and particle, metaphorically speaking. Only the 1/0 logic of philosophers rules this relational truth out of court.[5]

This "1/0 logic of philosophers" is the determinateness of logocentrism. It operates by carving the world into static objects externally related, with boundaries and borders inscribed, established, and accepted. However, when we confront the paradoxes of "impossible syllogisms" such as motherhood described by Kristeva, we cannot rest content with accepting that things simply must be understood in their paradoxical relations without submitting this tension to a deeper orientation of critical analysis. This is what dialectical reason, according to Ollman, does. It is not a theory of external relations, but of internal relations. That is, dialectical reason seeks to apprehend life and its contradictions without accepting that such relations are either necessary or separate.

It is bourgeois thought that is precisely the opposite. For Ollman, bourgeois thinking assumes the frame of external relations. There might be times when contingency and history are feigned components of bourgeois thought, but a thoroughly dialectical rationality would eschew all tendencies that deny the philosophy of internal relations, for the precise reason that the philosophy of external relations cannot truly examine the historical and structural forces that compose how people construct the world. The stakes of this are veritably high for Ollman:

> [Whether] we organise our thinking on the basis of the philosophy of external relations or the philosophy of internal relations [is] the most important philosophical question of the day ... The school of relation one prefers also weighs heavily on how we interpret, criticise and use any philosophy as well as the various economic, political, social and psychological theories constructed with its help.[6]

In other words, the reason where one comes down on the divide between external and internal relations is paramount for Ollman is that either orientation will impact how it is that one takes up the very world in which one participates. Not merely that one might come to a faulty conclusion now and then because of misapplied theories. Rather, the orientation one assumes affects the entire hermeneutical grid by which the world is encountered. This influences the very theoretical apparatuses that constitute the relations between praxis and material contexts themselves.

What this means regarding abstraction is that although abstract concepts divide the world into perceptible or manageable bits, these units have "elastic meanings."[7] The borders that separate the terms are fluid and porous. There is an osmosis between the borders separating intensive variations of individual concepts. Along Badiouian lines, we can speak of these units as being sets containing contingent relations of transcendental coordinates that index the variations that have been so ordered within the given set. Thus, when we speak of abstract concepts, we need to be aware of them as sets within sets relating overlapping and interpenetrating fields of transcendental variation.

Thus, abstraction is not merely static containment. The processes that constitute abstract concepts do not cease to flow or halt in their efficacy. Rather, what occurs is a perpetual pulsating expansion and contraction between the intensive variations that are contained within the previously constituted concept and the processes that relate to its perpetual constitution. James Williams develops a process philosophy of signs that explains this further. He asks, "How can a set be a process? The nature of sets seems to run opposite to movement and change." His pithy response: "No set is independent of the event of its selection."[8] What he means is that a set is an effect of the eventual relations that constitute its selection as *that* given set. Thus, the particular differentiation between concepts (understood as processual sets) is a product of abstraction. The boundaries enable us to distinguish one set of variations from another. But these boundaries are not the foreclosure of process. They are merely the abstract *pausing* of variation.

The participle "pausing" is important as this activity of abstraction from within the orientation of internal relations is an ongoing activity. Williams suggests there is a "moment of hesitation and openness which provides a gap for things to be otherwise, not only as critical alarm but also as creative difference."[9] By contrast, the philosophy of external relations might allow for processes and becoming, but only as pre-established conditions that allow for the static *pause* of abstraction to determine the quality of these relations. The difference is the same difference between totalization and totality. Whereas the pausing of abstraction in the philosophy of internal relations is the *result of* and *allows for* productive creation, the abstract pause of the philosophy of external relations is an imposition of determinateness. This is why we can now speak of the philosophy of internal relations as relating to the Paradoxico-Critical orientation that we have been advocating throughout the present project; while also identifying the philosophy of external relations with analytical reason and the Constructivist orientation.

Therefore, for Ollman, the philosophy of internal relations demonstrates the productive capacity that derives from sensed paradoxical relations between supposedly disparate units of analysis. However, rather than allowing this perceived paradox to set the terms of the analysis, Ollman gestures beyond the external relations that cause the paradox by investigating the intensive variations that constitute the relations and processes of the contradiction that produce the tension in the first place. Politically, this orientation has validity in that Ollman demonstrates how it is not abstraction that induces illusory thinking, but rather that it is the orientation of external relations and its attendant "limited abstractions" that explain "[most] of the distortions found in bourgeois ideology."[10]

9.1.2 Sartre and Abstraction

Sartre, too, values the productive capacity of abstraction. From his earliest writings on the imagination, through his novels and plays, connecting to his existentialist opera, and moving through his materialist and psycho-biographical musings later in his life, Sartre employed abstraction as a method of revealing the truths of life. Through productive fabulation, Sartre sought to unveil Being in its depths through the creation of concepts that would express Being's own infinite capacity for presentation and expression. We might say that Sartre viewed abstraction as the lie that reveals the truth.

In his early explicitly phenomenological texts, abstraction serves the purpose of presenting the relation between the intending consciousness of the for-itself to the inert being of the in-itself. These abstractions are what breathe life into Being as the emergent, transcendent objects of imaginative consciousness. This imaginative act operates by "at once constituting, isolating, and annihilating." This act is constitutive of its object, and as Thomas Flynn observes, "It isolates its object from the larger field of the real."[11] The imaginative act, therefore, ought to be understood in the same vein as Ollman's description of abstraction as omitting the process of becoming. This indicates why Roquentin in *Nausea* gets drawn into a state of overwhelming disquiet when he taps into the *hyle* that is excessive of the imaginative abstractions that constitute typical conscious experience. When he perceives the chestnut tree sinking into the ground; when he details how "the root, the park gates, the bench, the patches of grass" all vanished; in his experience of the veneer melting away, revealing the *dividuality* of naked becoming—he catches a glimpse of what he believes is life behind the veil of abstraction, which induces a profound encounter with the absurd.

For Sartre, formal abstractions are the window that allow consciousness to take up the shifting landscape of the material world, that if experienced without frames would overtake us with existential dread. Analogously they relate to the matter/form distinction in Aristotle, where matter is the determinable and the form is the determined.[12] In Sartrean terms, the determined is the imaginative act of consciousness that irrealizes the material world to which it relates. Later in his life, he would be more specific about the imaginary's role in abstracting in order to make the reality of the world palatable. In *The Family Idiot*, he writes, "To imagine is at once to produce an imaginary object and to become imaginary (*s'imaginariser*); I did not stress that adequately in *The Imaginary*."[13] It is this process of imagining and becoming an imaginary object that makes the activity of irrealizing the world productive, for Sartre. This is because by irrealizing oneself, one becomes *l'homme imaginaire* and becomes aware of her own constitution as part of the same activity of abstraction as the intending act of imaginative consciousness in relation to the *hyle*. Flynn asserts that, for Sartre, "Flaubert will 'imagine being' itself, viewing everything *sub specie phantasiae* by a sustained adoption of the aesthetic attitude."[14] This "sustained adoption of the aesthetic attitude" is the pure retreat into the irreal that Sartre warned against in PI as preferring an "anti-world." There, he identified it with the desire of the schizophrenic, whereas in *FI* he notes that Flaubert's neurotic tendencies required this flight into the irreal in order for Flaubert to be an artist. That is, in order to speak of the world, Flaubert had to irrealize himself.

However, this activity of irrealizing oneself and the world ought not be viewed as a necessary flight into fancy. In *CDR*, Sartre does not abandon the imagination so much as sublate it. It is ever-present even if rarely mentioned explicitly. The reading that we have been working through in the present project views *CDR* as a conscious work of imaginative abstraction. This is why we have characterized it as a formal investigation. When we speak of the formal abstractions of *CDR*, we are acknowledging Sartre's aim to enfold his earlier inclinations pertaining to imaginative abstraction into the Marxian project of raising class-consciousness through dialectical reason. Nicos Poulantzas notes this when he states that Sartre's goal in *CDR* was to "enrich contemporary Marxist theory with certain categories, concepts, methodological procedures, and examples of concrete analysis."[15]

However, we need to stress that this concrete analysis is not devoid of abstraction as though what Sartre discusses is the "really real." We must dispel of the positivist tendency to separate the real from the ideal. For Sartre, concrete analysis must be understood as lived totalization in mediatory conditions. This does not immune the concrete from the internal relations of the dialectic. The concepts of abstraction that Sartre formulates, therefore, cannot be seen as being exempt from the process of totalization that characterizes the dialectical reason that he is seeking to ground. Which means that the examples of concrete analysis, just as much as the categories, concepts, and methodological procedures, are only intelligible insofar as they are lived abstractions that are *part of* and *moments of* dialectical reason's Paradoxico-Critical journey of grounding and unveiling.

Further, the Paradoxico-Critical orientation of Sartre in *CDR* has to be understood through Sartre's explicit efforts to maintain subjectivity without dissolving it in the historical process. Michael Burns stresses the importance of Kierkegaard for Sartre on this point when he writes that "the place of the subjective is the paradox which resists being taken up into an historical process, and from the position of the subject one can exploit the openness and incompleteness of past historical processes to do something new."[16] This paradox is the locus of the site of productive praxis in *CDR*. Rather than seeing the paradoxical relation between subjectivity and history as externally related categories bumping into one another as pre-constituted and logically independent of one another, Sartre moves to engage with their internal, co-constitutive relations. Poulantzas makes this clear when he states that Sartre "will not attempt to add materiality as mere facticity, as mere datum of the situation that human activity encounters in its unfolding in the world, to some original—pure—existential human activity. He will seek to discover the 'constitutive' dialectical relations between human practice and materiality that establish these two terms as meaningful coordinates of society and history."[17] This is Sartre's contribution to the base-superstructure dilemma. However, rather than framing in terms of a binary, Sartre chooses ternary dialectical relations between concrete subjectivity, history, and structure.

Therefore, Sartre's use of abstraction in *CDR* must be understood as a dialectical synthesis of the transcendental, phenomenological, and materialist. That is, by constructing formal and logical abstractions of practical ensembles in *CDR*, Sartre is engaging in the transcendental-phenomenological task of eidetic reduction, refracted through imaginative consciousness, and infused into a hypo-logical investigation into the conditions of dialectical reason. What this means is that the formal investigation that he employs yields abstractions (i.e., practico-inert objects). And these practico-inert objects are *analogons* of the imagination. But because they are both practico *and* inert, they are ever in the process of becoming. Thus, the project in *CDR* is an exercise in synthetic abstraction. It is transcendental in that it is an investigation into the formal conditions of experience. It is phenomenological in that Sartre never wavers from his commitment to intentionality. And it is materialist in that both the phenomenological and transcendental are refracted through the dialectic—what he calls the "living logic of action." When these three approaches are synthesized, the result is a methodology that uses the tools of formal abstraction, or concept creation, to ground a logic that makes the conditions of lived experience intelligible. This approach is both traceable throughout his past works and also novel.

9.1.3 Abstraction and the Imaginative Logic of Action

In our elaboration of what we have termed the imaginative logic of action, we have been sketching the conditions for the embodiment of an art, an art that would be both thought and practice—praxis. Sartre's central concern in *CDR* is that praxis is unknown to itself. More than this, because of Kaironic Seriality, praxis is unknowable. Thus, what he sketches are the abstract blueprints for making the (in)human predicament knowable. The imaginative logic of action is my extension of his blueprints into a next phase of development. It is an orientation of internal relations like the one elaborated by Ollman. It does not avoid abstraction for fear of obfuscation or mystification in the pursuit of comprehension. Rather, the imaginative logic of action must be understood as Paradoxico-Critical, as a philosophy of internal relations, and thus as wielding the tools of productive abstraction. The imaginative logic of action is a logical disposition in the world that derives its impetus from the exigencies of the material conditions and that also remains fervently committed to the beyond. The beyond is not a pre-figured reality that dictates the means, but a speculative field of indeterminateness that is fabricated through the perpetual creation of future concepts that motivate action in the present to seek the actualization of virtual potencies.

This process is highly speculative and experimental. It must be. For the subjects engaged in this process are themselves in the process of becoming. They are not pre-figured humans, but humans-in-becoming, constituted by the autopoetic activity of the dialectical flow itself. As praxis is unknown and unknowable, the imaginative logic of action is the orientation that remains perpetually open to praxis's coming-to-comprehension. We cannot assume that praxis is immune from the serial powers that emerge because of the logic of the practico-inert field. Praxis is very often inhuman praxis—anti-praxis. As such, any structural analysis is conditioned (in various measures) by a bourgeois logic that entraps it within the same serial cycle from which it seeks to distance itself.

Following Sartre, the claim here is that positivist Marxism and scientific socialism, insofar as they are philosophies of external relations, are actually ensnared by the same mystifying tendencies they seek to denounce. The issue becomes strident when the very clarion call for class consciousness is itself conditioned by the false consciousness that is a result of historico-structural conditioning. Would this not stifle the analysis of the material conditions and thus contaminate the suggestions that issue therefrom? Which ought to make us wonder to what extent socialist analysis is often blinded by its own serial ideological biases; if there is not a hubristic tendency toward purity in its ability to analyze the material conditions; if it is not overly informed by a logic of instrumental reason; and whether and under what circumstances socialist theorists end up playing the neoliberal game by reproducing the very technological reason that the anti-capitalist orientation must contest (this last point will be addressed in the final section). Merely sensing injustice does not guarantee that one's sense or interpretation of these phenomena equates to genuine comprehension.

Thus, the imaginative logic of action seeks the perpetual transformation of subjectivities through the dialectical process of totalization as it also perpetually seeks the transformation of the practico-inert exigencies that mediate social relations. Because of the differential (i.e., the subjective spark) that is virtually present at all times, the value of future abstractions is in their ability to spark the unconscious, affective rage of inhumans who are always positioned in the opportune moment to act. These future abstractions are tools that make this *kairos* known. However, the abstractions themselves are imperfect. They are contaminated by the serial forces that construct them. This is the recognition of the persistent tendency toward false consciousness even in feigning contestation to seriality. However, the logic of the philosophy of internal relations teaches us that we are not trapped within a serial, mimetic circle of bourgeois thought. Because objects of mediation are both process and relation. As Ollman claims, "What was a thing for the philosophy of external relations becomes a relation evolving over time (or a process in constant interaction with other processes)."[18] This means that even while the forces of seriality are potent, there is a constant state of disruption that accompanies their tendency toward territorialization.

The quality of the logics that are revealed when examining the formal abstractions in *CDR* and that define the future images and abstract analysis of the imaginative logic of action are the conditions of the concrete relations that concern Sartre's overall investigation into the historical and structural conditions of history. However, the structure of any abstract object as an object-in-becoming requires that we allow for processes of perpetual intensive variation to manifest effects. Which means the terms and their complex webs of meaning themselves are intended for dialectical sublation. Ollman reminds us that "the whole acquires, over time and with its own growth as the pattern of its constituent patterns, some characteristics that appertain to it and it alone."[19] This is the tendency toward vital or productive abstraction. The separation of the whole from the process in a singular notion is an abstraction away from the process. This is the type of abstraction that is unavoidable. This paradox between the processes of relations and the whole that acquires certain characteristics that "appertain to it and it alone" is precisely that paradox that articulates the process of totalization in *CDR*. For the material system is not pure chaos. Neither is it totality with clean borders where the totality is distinct from the sum of its parts (as in the philosophy of external relations). Rather, the whole is a part of the processual flow, with its boundaries and its characteristics in perpetual flux as it is an effect of the intensive variation that defines its constitutive processes.

Referring to Marx's Eleventh Thesis on Feuerbach, G. A. Cohen wrote: "the Eleventh Thesis reflects a viewpoint according to which true theory, an illusionless conception of the world, will not prevail until practice overturns the structures which continually reproduce false theory. But in order that practice may overturn these structures, theory must first deliver an understanding of the world we are in."[20] This dialectical concern between the structures of the world that reproduce false theory and theory that must deliver an accurate understanding of our world is precisely the project of

CDR and the task of the imaginative logic of action. To resist this project, to resist the philosophy of internal relations as the *arche* of such a project, is to accept a vulgar conceptual rationality, the very tendency that the critique of political economy and that dialectical reason must eschew.

But by embracing the imaginative logic of action, we embody a disposition that attunes us to our participation in the perpetual production of the world. This also means that we are complicit in its creation. This is where the ethical enters. We are complicit in erecting its past limits and demands and in the future ones that we perpetually imbue through totalization. This also connects us with the totality of the past that is embedded within the practico-inert field that allows us to see our participation in both the *transcending of* and *contribution to* previous ethical and political concerns. We feel our implication in the perpetuation of exploitative and oppressive logics. But without guilt, for there is no fixed transcendent standard by which the debt-guilt mechanism is necessarily introduced. We are ever aware of how we can always recreate and re-position ourselves in relation to these processual logics. Not afresh. No *tabulae rasae*. But within conditions that are not of our own choosing.

This means that there is always going to be a measure of false consciousness in our praxis. Which means that socialist strategies cannot ever be seen as being immune from serial contagion. The practico-inert mediates all social relations, which may not necessarily affect every aspect of thought and praxis, but there will always be shadows within dimensions that impact on even the most pure of revolutionary thought and/or action. A genuine revolution can break out but people will still have other conditioning factors inflecting the complex of their relations in that moment. Hypothetically, there could be a pure apocalyptic moment in history, but once that moment is settled and roles start to form and reflective consciousness enters, practico-inert mediation guarantees that some measure of serial logic will become determinate. This is because human thought and feeling is never singular or simple. It too must be understood according to the philosophy of internal relations. Which means that most likely, even the staunchest of revolutionary fervor is going to be peppered with serial specters.

This is not to suggest all is hopeless, nor to denigrate the value and beauty contained in street-level antagonism around the world, but to present a more accurate depiction of concrete material life, one that seems so missing in many romantic revolutionary projects. Of course, this also ought to make us more vigilant. Because again, we are perpetually transforming the exigent mediatory conditions as we are perpetually transformed by them. By being aware of our agency and by not ignoring our complicity in this task, we can be better prepared to confront Kaironic Seriality in all its particular historical guises. This is why the imaginative logic of action is not a static idea; it is not a principle; nor is it a system (in the Hegelian or Badiouian sense). It is a process. And it requires the collective efforts of all manner of humans-in-becoming around the globe, throughout the ages, to maximize its efficacy.

9.2 TERMS AND STAKES OF THE DEBATE

The above leads to the two underlying concerns involving any investigation into dialectical reason: 1) self-awareness/comprehension/class consciousness and related to it 2) the reason why people revolt. We are going to briefly investigate these two concerns through a debate between two Marxist orientations. The first is represented by G. A. Cohen and the second by Brian Leiter. The concern for each pertains to the conditions that justify liberatory praxis. For Cohen, like Sartre, Marxism has stopped and is thus in need of further elaboration of ways by which class consciousness will come to recognize itself and the truth of the world in order to motivate revolt. Leiter's criticism of Cohen is that in his effort to reground dialectical reason, he employs the tools of bourgeois thought and thus ends up perpetuating the logic of capital. While Cohen sees scientific socialism as mystifying, Leiter argues that Cohen's bourgeois normative theory is vulgar and in response argues that scientific socialism is not, in fact, mystifying but the genuine orientation by which class consciousness and motivation for revolt are achieved.

9.2.1 Cohen and the Limits of Obstetric Marxism

Cohen is concerned with the status of dialectical rationality. For a number of reasons, he believes that a certain framework of Marxist thought stifles self-awareness. He cites historical reasons that he believes validate skepticism to the Marxist project of liberatory praxis. But it is his theoretical ideas that concern us, as, perhaps surprisingly, they align quite well with Sartre's concerns in *CDR*.

Cohen identifies what he terms the "obstetric" conception of political practice as establishing the mystifying frame of socialist theory.[21] The obstetric model argues that history is pregnant with socialism. It is the inevitable outcome of the historical development of capitalist production. That is, the problem of capitalism contains within it the necessary solution. The role of the socialist theorist, therefore, is to heighten the contradictions of the problem, to make them more known and felt so that the solution will become apparent which will then organically, causally follow. This model operates under the assumption that self-awareness is a necessary and causal factor of the historical process of capitalism's perpetual expansion in its exploitative pressures over the proletariat. Cohen is unconvinced of this project and suggests that, instead, Marxist theorists must not avoid speculative forcing but must rather "abandon the obstetric conception, and that they must, in some measure, be utopian designers."[22]

The central issue for Cohen that informs his criticism of the obstetric conception is that proletarian praxis is not self-aware. What follows from this is that motivating liberatory action is barred until such a time when the conditions of self-awareness can be realized. Cohen defends his supposition that proletarian praxis lacks self-awareness by an appeal to Marx's engagement with the famous, and according to Cohen, oft-misunderstood "opium" passage. The goal is that by demonstrating the true source of alienation Cohen believes there must also be a transfiguration of the locus of proletarian praxis.

For Cohen, the sigh of the oppressed creature must not be seen as a mere top-down imposition of ideological control. Rather, the sigh is the genuine, free response of the oppressed creature that reveals an unjust world which induces the sigh in the first instance. "So: the people need religion. They need it because they inhabit a vale of woe. And it is they who create religion, to service their need. Religion is their sigh. . . . The oppressed creature is disposed to sigh."[23] The point being that, for Marx, the sigh of the oppressed creature issues from the contradictions of the social landscape that produce such stirring. Thus, freedom, as the sigh of the oppressed creature, is a conditioned response to the Impossible of ideological control from the mystification of false-consciousness induced by religious expression from below. This is how religion produces false consciousness. It provides cover and a sense of resolve to endure the contradictions of capitalist exploitation. Religion is therefore not only a tool of the powerful to quell revolutionary sentiment (although it can be used in this way). But, more than this, religion is the genuine expression of proletarian dissatisfaction with a world that ought to be constructed otherwise. Thus, religion is both a foreclosing and disclosing of injustice.

It is religion's disclosure of injustice that most concerns Cohen. This is because religion is a symptom of the underlying problem that Marx was seeking to unveil, with the goal being that disclosing injustice would issue "the demand to give up a condition which needs illusions."[24] In other words, critique must make it clear *why* there is anxiety, frustration, and discontent. The world is in conflict, but it is unaware of this *why*. To reveal the reasons why would be the raising of class-consciousness. And in so doing, praxis would demand that the world be restructured, in a way that would not produce illusory conceptions of the world and praxis's role within it.

Cohen suggests that, "Emancipation comes not by proving that religion is false but by revealing the source of religion in a spiritless world *that needs to have its spirit returned to it, a world that needs to be humanized* [emphasis added]."[25] Thus, the problem is not that religion is fabricated. It is that it is fabricated as a palliative that covers over and justifies injustice *only because the oppressed creature does not have the proper recourse for a more appropriate response*. However, the value of religion is precisely in revealing that there is a clamoring for a world with a spirit, with a heart; for a world that is truly and perhaps for the first time human.

Therefore, the Marxist theorist's role is to "show the oppressed creature what its sigh means."[26] It is to provide the missing explanation that reveals the truth of the contradictions, rather than letting the system maintain itself under the cover afforded to it by false consciousness. Until then, the oppressed creature will remain stifled by an illusory conception of the world and its place within it. Thus, the goal is to construct an illusionless conception of the world, which would require an accurate analysis of the conditions that produce the false-consciousness in the first instance. As Marx wrote in a letter to Arnold Ruge, "The reform of consciousness consists solely in letting the world perceive its own consciousness by awaking it from dreaming about itself, in explaining to it its own actions. . . . So our election cry must be: reform of consciousness not through dogmas, but through the analysis of mystical consciousness that is not clear to itself."[27]

However, if even the act of showing is contaminated by false-consciousness, then the acts of showing will cloud the presentation and thus perpetuate the crisis without it being properly exposed. This is because, in the act of showing, the world of the proletariat is reflected back to them as the products of their own hands. By revealing their integral role in the process of value production, and then explaining how and why they are excluded from receiving the just return on their contributions, a felt sense of injustice will turn from mystified discontent into genuine self-awareness; unless, of course, the act of showing insufficiently reflects the proletariat back to itself. This latter insufficiency is what Cohen charges the obstetric model of producing. It does this by resting in a linear and teleological causal logic that is rooted in a deficient characterization of the proletariat itself.

For Marx, "philosophy would find its material weapon" in the proletariat.[28] However, the problem as Cohen sees it is that defining the proletariat is not a settled case. He outlines four qualities that characterize the proletariat: that they 1) constitute the majority of society; 2) produce the wealth of the society; 3) are the exploited in society; and 4) are the needy in society. He adds two consequences that follow from these qualities: that they 5) have nothing to lose from revolting and 6) could and would transform society.[29] These six characteristics were easily identifiable in the context of nineteenth-century industrial capitalism. However, in the twenty-first century, Cohen avers that Marxism must not accept the nineteenth-century conception of proletarian identity.

He makes this argument based on the claim that there is a contemporary paradox between the third and fourth qualities: exploitation and need.

> Particularly problematic, from the point of view of a socialist political philosopher, is the coming apart of the exploitation and need features. It forces a choice between the principle of a right to the product of one's labor embedded in the doctrine of exploitation and a principle of equality of benefits and burdens which negates the right to the product of one's labor and which is required to defend support for very needy people who are not producers and who are, *a fortiori*, not exploited. This is the central normative problem which Marxists did not have to face in the past.[30]

The problem, for Cohen, is that nineteenth-century Marxism was unaware of the cleavage that would occur as a result of capitalist evolution. No longer is there a single class of exploited workers who are simultaneously the class of the very needy members of a given society. In fact, Cohen suggests that the very needy in the global capitalist society have been displaced to the periphery nations, while the center contains those most exploited (in terms of surplus-value extraction). Of course, he is generalizing for the sake of drawing tensions. He is not ignorant of the needs in the center or the exploitation that occurs in the periphery (nor ought we focus too much on the issue pertaining to quantifying the rate of exploitation in the center versus peripheral nations). His point is to note the diffusion that has taken place that rents the once-centralized logic of exploitation and need. In late-capitalism, what we are presented with is a much more challenging endeavor of identifying points of solidarity between members of center and periphery nations. In other words, what do we do "once the really needy and the exploited producers no longer coincide?"[31]

Cohen's solution is that there needs to be a turn toward moral grounding which can motivate global solidarity across regional, contextual, demographic, etc., particularities. He explains that "the disintegration of the proletariat induces persons of Marxist formation to turn to normative political philosophy, and how the loss of confidence in a future unlimited abundance reinforces their tendency to take that turn."[32] By rejecting the necessary historical notion of material abundance that motivated Marx's nineteenth-century optimism, Cohen offers moral prescription as the binding agent to ground a reformulated vision for global proletarian solidarity. While the issue pertaining to scarcity versus abundance is not settled in the literature, one thing we can admit is that the notion of scarcity in a dispersed late-capitalist landscape cannot mean the same thing that it once meant for nineteenth-century socialist advocacy. Thus, in order to understand Cohen's turn from the obstetric model toward a normative theoretical Marxism, we must keep in the mind the central tensions driving his concern. For, if the proletariat is ever-mystified by a self-illusory conception of the world and its place and participation in it, then genuine class-consciousness and praxis remain ever beyond our grasp.

9.2.2 Leiter and Positivist Accelerationism

Brian Leiter's contestation is a defense of the obstetric conception that Cohen finds insufficient. His claim is that Marx had normative inclinations, but not a normative theory.[33] Thus, in Cohen's efforts to ground a binding moral orientation for a transfigured conception of the proletariat, Leiter sees the introduction of a bourgeois rationality that "offers no threat to capitalist relations of production."[34] In fact, for Leiter, normative theory itself is an inherently problematic discourse in that "we can not know what morality would be characteristic of a society that did not have capitalist relations of production."[35] In other words, all moral theory in the milieu of capitalism is going to be contaminated by the bourgeois logic that issues therefrom.

Leiter seeks to defend Marx from Cohen's criticism by addressing how Marx simply presumed future equality as the necessary outcome of the culmination of historical development. As we mentioned above, in the obstetric conception, the solution was a guaranteed outcome of the fulfillment of the problem's elaboration. Therefore, the proletariat do not "require a normative theory to help them."[36] What is required is scientific analysis that reveals the truth of the historical moment which reveals the opportune moment to act. If the two guiding concerns that frame the contours of this debate are 1) self-awareness/comprehension/class consciousness and 2) the reason why people revolt, we can now reduce Leiter's concern to one: the reason people revolt is that, "[At] a certain point capitalist relations of production evolve in such a way that those who labor for survival wages realize there is no hope of a better future. Such people, unsurprisingly, will agitate for change."[37] Thus, where Cohen sees this singular obstetric concern in terms of two points in need of elaboration, Leiter suggests they are extensions of the same problematic.

Leiter presumes that people will spontaneously feel their alienation at the right historical moment and will be motivated to revolt. And even though he rightly notes that normative theories under the logic of capital will be contaminated by the conditioning influence of bourgeois rationality, he neglects to turn the mirror upon the socialist theorist's capacity for analysis in the first instance. That is, Leiter's conception is thoroughly rooted in the Constructivist orientation of thought. He advocates a positivist Marxism that operates according to the logic of external relations. What is more, in a footnote he hints at an accelerationist conception of Marxism. After earlier decrying Lenin, Mao, and Castro as "incompetent readers of Marx," he goes on to suggest that the basic mistake of much Marxism after Marx is its "failure to realize that capitalism has yet to run its course: there is both more productive power and more misery in the offing. And the misery must be sufficient to motivate the counterfactual *thought that if things were otherwise*, everything would be better. In the United States, for example, we are probably a century or more away."[38] The issue one ought to take with this position is not his suggestion that the contradiction of capitalist exploitation needs to be felt in order to motivate revolt. The issue is in his settled acceptance of historical evolution as the justification for continued "misery." This is precisely the conception that Cohen wants to contest by turning away from the obstetric model. We might say that the obstetric model has a tendency to justify the injustices of the capitalist mode of production by erecting its own ideological control mechanism of historicism. Thus, Leiter's position ends up reproducing an illusory bourgeois logic precisely in his efforts to re-found Marxism in the obstetric model.

Leiter grounds his positivist accelerationism by claiming that Cohen misunderstands human motivation. Leiter suggests that, in fact, Marx and neoclassical economists are better suited to elaborate human psychology in that they both present views of human desire based on instrumental concerns. "The genius of neoclassical economics was to diagnose the only kind of 'thinking' that could count as rational under capitalism, namely, figuring out what means would satisfy one's ends, the latter immune to rational adjudication. It is precisely that fact on which the most plausible Marxian theory of revolutionary motivation depends."[39] The idea that neoclassical economics diagnosed the only kind of thinking that could count as rational under capitalism is an interesting claim. Not that it is false. But it is interesting in the way it is used in this quote. It is tied to Marx's analysis in that Leiter claims that Marx held the same structure of instrumental rationality of the neoclassical thinkers; but with Marx understanding the instrumental appeal in its diagnostic purposes. This is because, for Leiter, instrumental appeals are all one needs in order to make one's situation known and felt, which will then induce action.[40]

However, the problem with Leiter's claim is that instrumental rationality under capitalism is precisely conditioned by the logic of the commodity as a mediating practico-inert object. Neoclassical rationality is not immune from the conditioning factors that contribute to its own articulations. Thus, where Leiter sees a valorization of a form of positivist instrumental reason as a potential diagnostic technology, Marx's criticism (as well as Cohen's) is precisely that the conditions of rationality in capitalism produce false consciousness rather than a model of rationality that is an accurate depiction of human psychology. Not meaning to split hairs, even if instrumental rationality is the dominant form of rationality as conditioned by the logic of capitalism, dialectical reason must be seen as something qualitatively *other* if it is to be dialectical reason at all. This is what Leiter seems to ignore.

In his lecture series *The Birth of Biopolitics*, Foucault calls the market the "site of veridiction."[41] What he means by this is twofold: 1) true prices are determined by market forces through the exchange mechanisms of the market; something different than when a "just" price was determined under previous economic regimes, and more importantly, I think 2) that truth itself is completely detached from notions of "right" or "just" and is completely determined by the logic of marketability. This is to say that truth, under the logic of capitalism, requires market equivalence in order for there to be social exchange. It is this logic of market equivalence between discrete units as the constituted logic of veridiction that conditions the logic of bourgeois rationality. Thus, in a sense, the neoclassical revolution has sought to colonize rationality through the monopolizing determination of crafting thought according to the philosophy of external relations. There is, therefore, a sense in which dialectical rationality is essentially transgressive precisely because it is not analytical, which is inherently veridical and serial—veridical in that it is only concerned with analytical, relative truths, and serial in that it is conditioned by the logic of the practico-inert field. Thus, at issue must be to ground a thoroughly dialectical reason that eschews the colonizing tendencies of instrumental reason offered by the logic of capital.

While Leiter is right for seeking to criticize remnants of bourgeois thought that he senses in Cohen's normative concerns, in the end, he ends up valorizing bourgeois rationality and retrojecting it into the Marxist project as an essential component of a Marxist orientation. Even if Marx did view human psychology in relatively instrumental terms, this does not mean that Marxism *per se* must, of necessity, follow suit. Dialectical rationality ensures that the orientations of reason will also shift as the mediatory material exigencies change. The issue becomes again how to break out of the reproductive cycle of serial rationality. And at least on this point, Leiter's rejoinder to Cohen falls into the very bourgeois trap that he seeks to criticize.

9.2.3 Recipes for Future Kitchens: The Imaginative Logic of Action

At issue for both Cohen and Leiter are the conditions under which the proletariat will comprehend comprehension. For Cohen, the obstetric model of positivist Marxism stifles class consciousness primarily because the diffusion of proletarian concerns has disarticulated the proletariat as a singular and easily identifiable locus of revolutionary praxis. Therefore, he turns to normative theory to offer a way to bridge the gap between dispersed sites of alienated existence. Leiter's concern is that such an effort to bridge these divides misunderstands the necessary historical evolution of capitalism and therefore rushes for an answer by proffering a bourgeois rationality that does not contest the dominance of the logic of capitalism. For Leiter, "an instrumentally rational proletariat that understands how capitalism works, and what the alternatives are, will be motivated to undertake revolutionary acts."[42] Whereas for Cohen, binding a rational proletariat under the conditions of late-capitalism is a problematic that is yet to be resolved.

If there is a bourgeois tendency in Cohen's thought, it is attributable to his over-reliance on *ratio* to the neglect of concrete lived experience. We might say that it is yet insufficiently dialectical. However, we can also say that Leiter makes an unnecessary bifurcation between the immediate sensed contraction of exploitation at the right historical moment and theoretical abstraction. This is precisely what Sartre seeks to overcome in *CDR* and what the imaginative logic of action elaborates further. It is not that theoretical abstraction misdirects our attention that is otherwise more potent at the immediate affective dimension of concrete experience at the right historical moment, but that both inhere and co-imbricate one another. In a word, Leiter establishes an external relation between normative abstraction and immediate causal sense, and thereby reproduces the paradox of their external relations, whereas the imaginative logic of action works productively through the contradiction in order to think through how they co-constitute one another.

The result is that Leiter ends up reproducing a serial logic in his criticism of Cohen because he does not sufficiently account for the serial impact upon his own analysis. That is, he presumes a Constructivist orientation whereby socialist analysis can be purified through empirical study of the conditions of exploitation and oppression under capitalism. In fact, he responds in a footnote to a prompting by a colleague that he would gladly reduce all philosophy to science (with qualification, of course).[43] What this shows us is that Leiter has embraced the Constructivist orientation and the philosophy of external relations, thereby self-domesticating his own theoretical position as a serial logic of inaction.

However, the problem of comprehension has not been solved. If Leiter's obstetric Marxism reproduces a serial logic, and if there is a residual embourgeoisement in Cohen's orientation, what can we say about philosophy's role in overcoming these tendencies? How can we develop an illusionless conception of the world? That is, what would it look like to shift philosophy so that it would become a practice that would be the "Platonic unity of philosophy and power?"[44]

In *The Poverty of Philosophy*, Marx wrote the following:

> The *philanthropic* school is the humanitarian school carried to perfection. It denies the necessity of antagonism; it wants to turn all men into bourgeois; it wants to realize theory in so far as it is distinguished from practice and contains no antagonism. It goes without saying that, in theory, it is easy to make an abstraction of the contradictions that are met with at every moment in actual reality. This theory would therefore become idealized reality. The philanthropists, then, want to retain the categories which express bourgeois relations, without the antagonism which constitutes them and is inseparable from them. They think they are seriously fighting bourgeois practice, and they are more bourgeois than the others.[45]

We can almost imagine Leiter repeating this very passage to Cohen, were they in the same room.

What is interesting to note is that Marx's concern here is that theory separated from practice has a tendency to avoid *antagonism*. There is a safety of thought that isn't as compulsive in practice. The idea, of course, for Marx being that thought is able to abscond from the contradictions of class struggle that are material, lived, present in the lives of workers in factories. Thought is able to remain tucked away and secure from its own self-exposure to the conditions that cause disruption, that condition the sigh of the oppressed creature. Thus, for Marx, the Eleventh Thesis on Feuerbach becomes less about *thought* being bourgeois than about certain strands of *idealist thought* being bourgeois. In that case, he noticed it in Feuerbach's criticism of religion which he further extended to idealist philosophy *tout court*. Thus, his effort to ground a material and lived praxis was not to diminish the importance of thinking, but to think holistically about the human experience as embodied, embedded, enacted, extended, and affective. While he did not explicitly develop a theory of humanity in line with this litany, it is not a stretch to recognize such traits in his critical engagement. The point pertaining to the Cohen-Leiter debate is that even though Leiter's concern to avoid bourgeois theory is important, his rejoinder is not sufficiently *antagonistic* itself. It lacks a dimension of *self-criticism* that is required to instigate a truly dialectical antagonism to the logic of capital. Such a dialectical antagonism is what we have been trying to intimate in our present study of *CDR*, and through the elaboration of the orientation that we are calling the imaginative logic of action.

It is worth noting that there is a measure of criticism that ought to be directed toward Marx himself. Leiter is not necessarily wrong when he notes the instrumental rationality in Marx's thought. Marx does express a positivist rationality at times. After he makes the above remarks, he continues:

> [The] *Socialists* and *Communists* are the theoreticians of the proletarian class. So long as the proletariat is not yet sufficiently developed to constitute itself as a class, and consequently so long as the struggle itself of the proletariat with the bourgeoisie has not yet assumed a political character, and the productive forces are not yet sufficiently developed in the bosom of the bourgeoisie itself to enable us to catch a glimpse of the material conditions necessary for the emancipation of the proletariat and for the formation of a new society, these theoreticians are merely utopians who, to meet the wants of the oppressed classes, improvise systems and go in search of a regenerating science. But in the measure that history moves forward, and with it the struggle of the proletariat assumes clearer outlines, they no longer need to seek science in their minds; they have only to take note of what is happening before their eyes and to become its mouthpiece. So long as they look for science and merely make systems, so long as they are at the beginning of the struggle, they see in poverty nothing but poverty, without seeing in it the revolutionary, subversive

> side, which will overthrow the old society. From this moment, science, which is a product of the historical movement, has associated itself consciously with it, has ceased to be doctrinaire and has become revolutionary.[46]

Clearly Marx believed that self-awareness as a science (a form of knowledge) would not be something forced but would rather become apparent by simply being attuned to the material exigencies that history unfolds. However, how far we are to read this valorization of "science" as positivist is a separate issue, and one that we cannot develop here. Suffice it to say for now, that, regardless, it is not necessary to maintain the mantle of the Marxist spirit in antagonism to the logic of capital by reproducing positivist rationality. That is, along Sartrean lines, it seems apt to suggest that what Marx is establishing in this passage is the trajectory of the process of totalization that will perpetually move dialectically in the co-constitution of both subjects and historico-structural conditions. What is more, if there is a modicum of instrumental rationality in Marx himself, this does not mean that socialist orientations must necessarily repeat this tendency. In fact, we might say that this tendency is precisely what concerns many post-Marxist thinkers who are ever-seeking to press beyond certain nineteenth-century presuppositions that undergird Marx's thought.[47]

Which brings us finally to the imaginative logic of action as an orientation that seeks to resolve the tensions elaborated in the Cohen-Leiter debate. If either position fails to escape its own tendency toward mystification, how are we to conceive of a practice that would overcome this apparent impasse? That is, in what would a philosophical project consist whereby praxis would be better reflected back to itself in order to raise class-consciousness and motivate antagonism to capitalism?

This is what Sartre's project in *CDR* initiates. The return of stolen praxis and its attendant serial consequences make it clear why comprehension is not comprehended. We are not adequately reflected back to ourselves because of the serial logic of inaction. Only when the dissonances of Kaironic Seriality are felt and heralded can the source of oppression and exploitation be made known. But since the serial logic of inaction is so thorough as the expression of praxis (as anti-praxis), Kaironic Seriality is not immediately, causally felt or known. Therefore, there must be a forcing to induce comprehension of the Impossible. This is what the imaginative logic of action seeks to do: to perpetually engage in an orientation that is more and more aware of itself and its place and role in the world in their co-imbrication, which perpetually transforms both praxis and the world.

By embracing utopic thinking, imaginative political subjects need not be wary of normative abstractions *per se*. Not the *telos* of praxis, nor essential totalities that mediate praxis, normative ideas can be understood as vital abstractions that are part of the process of totalization. They can take the form of future images that motivate the proletariat in the present to overcome the material exigencies of Kaironic Seriality. As abstractions-in-becoming, they are endless recreations of images that themselves transform according to the variegating material conditions that mediate their emergence and thus perpetually transform their constitutive character. Which means that in being reflected back to praxis, they have a shifting quality about them; one that is not statically defined by the logic of capital, but that is perpetually excessive of the limiting and static boundaries by which capital necessarily operates as a logic of enclosure.

However, what this implies is that philosophy too is a "sigh" of the oppressed creature. If we are going to claim that Kaironic Seriality conditions life to the extent that we have advocated in this project, then we must admit that philosophy is contaminated as an orientation. In other words, there is a perpetual tendency toward mystification that is inherent in philosophical practice. This is not merely an indictment of academic philosophy or high theory in the name of "just doing praxis." Rather, this is an indictment of the very materialist philosophical conception that characterizes socialist praxis, as Marxist philosophy, *per se*. Therefore, philosophy too must be transfigured. Its concepts must be transformed. New abstractions developed. And with each new constructed concept, that it become more and more conditioned by the orientation that we have called the imaginative logic of action.

While he may not have been entirely successful toward this end, we can heed the well-intentioned words of G. A. Cohen:

> The history of socialist failure shows that socialists do need to write recipes, and not only, as that history suggests, in order to know what to do with power, but also in order to attract the masses of the people, who are, very reasonably, wedded to the devil they know. Unless we write recipes for future kitchens, there's no reason to think we'll get food we like.[48]

Not just recipes for meals, but for "future kitchens." This mangled metaphor is precisely the type of micro-macro strategy that is required, and that the imaginative logic of action seeks to signal toward.

9.3 THE SERIAL LOGIC OF NEOLIBERALISM

Before handing this project off to future participants in the perpetual contestation of Kaironic Seriality, it would behoove us to briefly investigate the current monstrosity that conditions anti-praxis. We mentioned above that Brian Leiter suggests that the genius of neoclassical economists was in their ability to "diagnose the only kind of 'thinking' that could count as rational under capitalism, namely, figuring out what means would satisfy one's ends." This instrumental reason that results from the logic of the market's own philosophy of external relations finds its zenith in the logic of neoliberalism.

9.3.1 The Specific Task

Defining neoliberalism is a difficult task. Some have suggested the concept is redundant.[49] While others suggest it is a political program that resulted from conspiratorial and instrumental agents and strategies.[50] The present approach resists either resignation or essentialization. Instead, our focus will be on how the logic of neoliberalism operates as a serial logic of inaction. A dialectical approach, as a philosophy of internal relations, allows for analysis from various perspectives without seeming neglectful. Understanding how the various fields of analysis (through vital abstraction) inform one another is part of the larger dialectical project. Referring to this philosophical orientation, Salleh reminds us that "Ollman points out that the canvas of social analysis can be intimate or distancing in its 'level of generality'; wide or narrow, diachronic or synchronic. In conventional positivist jargon one might say that the discursive scoping which gives boundaries to an investigation is called its 'extension.'"[51] Thus, our extension will be an intentional abstract investigation into a particular set of concerns within a larger matrix. However, of course, such an abstraction must be understood in the context of this overall project more broadly and within this chapter specifically.

From the perspective of the imaginative logic of action, the logic of neoliberalism is viewed as a disclosure of the process of totalization of which the abstraction "neoliberalism" is a particular set within a greater unfolding process of totalization. As such, neoliberalism *is* not. Rather, any discourse *on* or analysis *of* neoliberalism must maintain a positional humility, recognizing its perpetual transformation as a material system. However, although there is an elasticity to the collective object that is neoliberalism, this does not mean that we cannot speak accurately about it. It means that we need to be aware of how we are speaking about it when we are speaking about it. We must open ourselves up, in our very analysis, to the process of totalization as co-constituting participants. This means that our articulations are only ever partial and fleeting. The benefit of the imaginative logic of action, therefore, is that such fluidity is not a source of frustration, but a welcomed recognition of the character of the relational process in which we participate and are perpetually seeking to overcome in transcending present material exigencies while we aim toward new futures.

As we discussed in section 9.2, Cohen was concerned with the state of the Marxist project. He was not interested in preserving the dogmas of an orthodoxy. Rather, his concern was in grounding dialectical reason in a context that presents different challenges than the ones addressed by Marx in the nineteenth century and that had been assumed by subsequent socialist theorists. His contestation was that Marxism has been unable to achieve its materialist philosophical goals of class consciousness because it has not been able to demystify itself from its own faulty self-reflection. The character of the agents of revolution had shifted, and therefore, a shifting philosophical practice was required in order for class consciousness to be made possible. In perspicuous Hegelese, Cohen remarks, "You cannot know yourself without objectifying yourself—without, that is, making yourself an object of knowledge."[52] The issue for Cohen thus becomes, what type of object of knowledge must the proletariat be in order for it to become self-aware?

The aporia for Cohen is to account for the tendential inverse relation between the increase in capitalist exploitation and the decrease of revolutionary spirit. The point he is addressing is that although exploitation continues, there is also a profound measure of political docility that accompanies global capitalist development through countervailing forces that foreclose the contradictions that the obstetric model presumes would initiate antagonism. In effect, the sigh of the oppressed has shifted from a religious conception of God to the religion of the commodity logic. Offered new forms of "heart" and "soul," inhumans are ever-engaged in activities that direct their attention away from the fracturing that is endemic to the capitalist system. They take new opiums. Hence why chronological frames based on linear and quantitative conceptions of accumulating exploitation are insufficient articulations of dialectical reason, for Cohen. Kaironic and qualitative approaches are needed. These circumvent the stultifying tendencies of the serial logic embedded within the former.

Writing at the turn of the twenty-first century, Cohen was surveying the socio-economic landscape and attempting to offer a model of praxis that would overcome neoliberal alienation. Thus, if it is the case that "Alienation obtains when something issues forth from men which they do not recognize as their own, and which consequently dominates them,"[53] then the task for a liberatory project must be to devise *how* objectification could be recognized as one's own in an epoch that is characterized by neoliberal reason. That is, how are we to understand the particular conditions of false consciousness under neoliberalism, and how can dialectical reason confront these conditions in producing comprehension?

9.3.2 Neoliberal Reason

We began this book by charting a conceptual narrative concerning the separation of *logos* from *mythos*. While we cannot predict the future, we can say that neoliberalism ought to be understood as the culmination of this separation so far. That is, neoliberalism is characterized by the triumph of *techne*; of instrumental reason; of efficiency; of the Constructivist orientation of thought; of the philosophy of external relations; and in the language of *CDR*, of analytical reason. When Foucault refers to the market as the site of veridiction, what he means is not only that the market is concerned with *true* prices rather than *just* prices, but also that neoliberalism is the culmination of the post-modern will to truth. As the objective spirit of our current times, neoliberalism has become the dominant medium of significations that limit and demand what we say, how we think, and how we feel.

The key difference between liberal and neoliberal reason, for our purposes, is that liberalism operated according to a connection with metaphysical beliefs that grounded liberal thought in transcendental signifieds. The notions of the Nation State and Autonomous Self were regulative principles that conditioned liberal governmentality. Neoliberalism, however, is a socioeconomic buttress that has emerged in the wake of postmodern legitimation crises. Thus, the logic of neoliberalism is not a logic of radical individuality. The very secure concept of the individual that was rooted in natural law (Rousseau) or liberal utility (Bentham) characteristic of classical liberalism has been detached from any mooring. Thus, when Frederic Jameson calls postmodernism "the cultural logic of late capitalism,"[54] it is not a disservice to the notion to replace "late capitalism" with "neoliberalism" (if for no other reason that when Jameson published his tome the term "neoliberalism" was not as in fashion as it is now). In fact, neoliberalism and postmodernism are obverse images. What this means is that if there was a legitimation crisis pertaining to metanarratives that signify the concerns of the early postmodern theorists, then neoliberalism as conceptually and historically consonant with postmodernism ought to be understood within a similar matrix.

Therefore, we must not understand neoliberalism as a hyper-logic of the individual, but a diffused logic of the illegitimate individual (and nation state, etc.). It is not an individualist logic that defines neoliberal anxieties as though they are exogenous to the otherwise autonomous concept of the individual. Rather, it is the constitutive anxieties of illegitimate, disarticulated bodies that defines neoliberal reason. The effort to combat this anxiety takes the form of all manner of countervailing socio-economic technical devices, not limited to financial instruments, increased IP protections, datafication, the attention economy, social media platforms, dating apps—all of which offer some promise of "grounding." The result is an ambivalent sense of self and place in an ambivalent world; hence the burgeoning response to gravitate toward solid forms of serial reason (identity politics, ethnonationalism, left/right populism, etc.).

Further elaborating the anxious ambivalence of neoliberalism, Peck, Brenner, and Theodore argue that "neoliberalization should be understood as an uneven, frustrated, creatively destructive, adaptive, and open-ended process of transformation."[55] What this means is that neoliberal reason names a process and not a determinate system or a set of outcomes. That is, neoliberalism is not concerned with realizing a set of ends through, for example, structural adjustment programs. Rather, neoliberal reason operates as "a prevailing pattern and ethos of market-oriented, market-disciplinary, and market-making regulatory restructuring."[56] This prevailing pattern and ethos that is market-related does have a consistency, however. We can read it as a Paradoxico-Critical abstraction that is not defined by *consistency* but by *completeness*. That is, as a material system in totalization, there is an identifiable pattern and ethos: it is market related. This is where Foucault's elaboration of the market as the site of veridication is relevant. This is also why Martijn Konings declares that "there is something that deserves to be termed 'neoliberal reason' (Peck, 2010)—understood not as formal ideational consistency but as a degree of cohesion at the level of practice and the imaginaries that orient it."[57]

How are we to understand this market-related cohesion without consistency? For Konings, it is through the logic of speculation and risk that binds the imaginative processes. "The modern subject, no longer beholden to the notion that the future is unfolding according to a divine plan, understands the future as open and its own relation to the world as involving a key element of risk."[58] Because the subject is unmoored and lost at sea, there is no longer a trust that the course is charted. Thus, the neoliberal subject exposes itself to the fundamental truth of uncertainty. This is the very anxiety that Nietzsche notes when discussing the effects of the death of God. However, in this context, we might say that a death of godding has occurred through the postmodern legitimation crises post–World War II.

Thus, if Marx's criticism of religion was concerned with exposing God as an illusory concept in the pursuit of unveiling the truths of the conditions that necessitated the sigh of the oppressed creature, postmodern criticism undertakes a similar demystifying attitude toward the illusory concepts of modernity. Neoliberal reason emerges as a phoenix from the ashes of these legitimation crises asking, "If we are unmoored from any shores, in what could consist a form of governmentality?" Neoliberalism's response has to be understood in relation to risk mitigation and management as new forms of governmentality. And it does this through the proliferation of the commodity as practico-inert object.

Neoliberalism is an intensified technological reason that carves out units of measure from within a vast unbounded and indeterminate landscape in order to be able to manage variation. If the latter does not occur, the fear is that uncertainty will reign. In order to protect the notion of social order, neoliberal reason responds to the felt sense of the unmooring and de-legitimation of the postmodern condition and offers the commodity as the apogee of risk management. The commodity provides the surety that is so craved in the absence of any fiduciary security provided by God, State, or Natural Law.

If religion, for Marx, was a response to cover the contradictions between labor and capital, the neoliberal commodity is a form of cover over the multivalent uncertainties of postmodern life. However, simultaneously, the commodity reveals to us the crises that undergird the process of covering itself. That is, the promise of satisfaction in the logic of the commodity reveals to us the impossibility of commodities yielding satisfaction, precisely because they are covers. Thus, in their covering, commodities only defer satisfaction 1) by duplicating themselves and 2) through the intensification of the promise of satisfaction that will never be realized through their consumption. Thus, the commodity logic of neoliberalism is a novel type of mystification that stifles praxis's self-awareness; one that operates through the promise of risk management that it cannot fulfill.

According to Konings, neoliberal reason demands that we "make speculative investments even if only to secure the identity that we currently enjoy.... The distinctive imaginary of capitalism is that we may move through risk beyond risk—that, if we play our cards right, we may provide our lives with neutral, non-speculative foundations."[59] This quote details the way neoliberal reason operates as our current mystifying field of conditionality. In the postmodern wasteland of ambivalent ideas, neoliberalism offers a perverse messianism; one that promises satisfaction (i.e., redemption) precisely in taking it away. In making the promise of satisfaction, the fiduciary relation between fulfilled promise and neoliberal subject is established. However, there is no ground by which the promise is made, precisely because the logic of neoliberalism operates as an immanent and atelic logic. Therefore, by creating conditions of uncertainty, it is only able to establish an anxious fiduciary commitment to itself and its reproduction as processual pattern and ethos.

9.3.2 The Serial Logic of Neoliberalism

It should now be clear that neoliberal reason is a narcissistic, idealist form of rationality. Because of the intensification of the logic of the commodity as practico-inert, the magnitude of returned stolen praxis exponentially increases, which means we are living in a saturated field of idealized antipraxis. The limits and demands imposed upon us by the neoliberal practico-inert field produce sets of impossible expectations. Limits that can't be overcome; demands that can't be met.

However, these limits and demands are not the pure Otherness of Lévinas. Rather, what is reflected back to us is *us*. In Lacanian terms, we might say that the neoliberal practico-inert field is a fantasy of our own creation. Philosopher Byung-Chul Han refers to this as the "erosion of the Other. This erosion is occurring in all spheres of life; its corollary is the mounting narcissification of the Self."[60] As everything is flattened into an object of consumption according to the logic of neoliberal reason, the logic that is infused into the very objects that mediate social life and that condition neoliberal reason are self-reinforcing. This produces a phenomenon that Han calls "the inferno of the same." In this inferno, the logic of neoliberalism reproduces itself faster and to a greater degree of intensity as it is both producer and product. Each product is produced through a greater intensity of neoliberalization, which in turn produces producers who produce products to a greater intensity according to the mediation of the previously produced products which limit and demand production according to the logic of neoliberalism (which we must also understand as a grand practico-inert object full of its own limits and demands as a synchronic totality).

One of the things that neoliberalism is adept at is enclosing previously inscribed practico-inert objects (i.e., commodities) and fields (i.e., markets). This means that its scope and therefore mediatory influence increases exponentially. For example, the introduction of new financial instruments has afforded the serial logic of neoliberalism an almost unlimited array of technical devices by which it can inscribe, enclose, and quantify new domains of value into practico-inert objects (commodities). The derivatives market is a perfect example of neoliberal technical devices that have re-inscribed and that perpetually re-inscribe and thus enclose social value in its reproduction of itself through the expansion of the mediatory practico-inert field. One result issuing from this simple example is that the actions of financial markets are becoming more and more determined by the logic of neoliberalism as it is infused into the very instruments that compose the field of finance, and into the commodities that mediate the relations between finance and consumers. Therefore, the activities of derivatives traders, commercial lenders, underwriters, business development officers, securities managers, and their clients (et al.) are mediated by these neoliberal practico-inert objects that are processual in their formal role as mediatory social objects that constantly determine how the actors mediated by them are to live—and all of this increasingly according to the serial neoliberal logic that is perpetually being infused to greater degrees of intensity into the field of practico-inert objects that mediate the particular social landscape. This is the diachronic serial logic of neoliberalism.

This is not to suppose that the neoliberal practico-inert field contains no Otherness whatsoever, but rather that the *logic* of neoliberal reason as pattern and ethos operates according to a "desire" (to speak metaphorically) to isomorphically subsume all relations into an object of itself. Again, we must not speak in black and white terms. There is *tendency*; there are shifting fields of intensive variation; the desire is *for* mastery; etc. However, as in our investigation into Sartre's dialectical exploration of the co-constitutive relations between the serial logic of inaction and the imaginative logic of action, neoliberal reason is both hegemonic and dissonant.

Thus, neoliberal reason is the contemporary model for the sigh of the oppressed creature. The inferno of the same is the mystificatory rationality that characterizes the illusory logic of neoliberalism. However, because it seeks to eradicate radical Otherness, neoliberal reason expands like mold on bread, seeking to eliminate any showing of Otherness while relying on it for its own vitality. This Otherness is the irreducible subjectivity of the Sartrean differential and that we have been discussing throughout pertaining to the logic of the apocalypse. This is important to note, because neoliberalism does not wish to kill Otherness, as in despotism. Rather, neoliberalism seeks to attach to its source and guide it gently through nudging, coaxing, luring, and ultimately transfiguration through self-acceptance that *its* desires are really *all* desire.

The conclusion to draw from this is that the neoliberal sigh of the oppressed creature is the central site for problematization. Like Marx's criticism of religion, we ought to think of neoliberal desire as being a genuine cry that signals to underlying contradictions. However, it is a genuine cry under the circumstances that 1) induce dissatisfaction in the first place; 2) claim that there is only one way to achieve satisfaction; which 3) creates a system of endless chasing which leads to a rationality that 4) tells us that satisfaction is thus the goal of human life. And all of this through a form of risk mitigation and management that ensures the neoliberal imaginary will always be prepared to answer the call of crisis (whether at the micro- or macro-level).

Of course, the most insidious aspect of the logic of neoliberalism is that neoliberal subjects do come to accept the logic of neoliberal reason. Thus, analyzing the neoliberal sigh as a sigh of the oppressed creature requires careful attention. This is why describing neoliberal reason as a serial logic of inaction has potency in the context of this project. For the very same attunement of imaginative political subjects via the imaginative logic of action to the material exigencies of Kaironic Seriality, illuminates the Impossible of life lived according to neoliberal reason, and heralds that the opportune moment is always now. Rather than waiting for the contractions of history to induce some form of compulsive obstetric birthing process of revolt, as Leiter suggests, the logic of seriality in neoliberal reason reveals to us precisely that we are inhumans being reflected back to us in the form of false promises of satisfaction. In seeking to mitigate uncertainty, neoliberal reason, induces more uncertainty and heightens the contradictions of the neoliberal landscape.

That said, the logic of neoliberal reason is not entirely amorphous, even if it is elastic. As a practico-inert object itself, neoliberalism is perpetually recreated. It is both formal as the totality that contains the field of practico-inert objects conditioned by neoliberal reason and also expressed immanently through the practico-inert objects that condition praxis's tendency toward neoliberal reason. Like a balloon being inflated, the piety/labor/attention of praxis is infused into the pluridimensional practico-inert image with every expenditure conditioned according to the logic's own self-reinforcement. In return, the neoliberal practico-inert object imposes limits and demands, which humans subsume themselves underneath. This then creates demands for more piety to the image, and so the image gains more potency, issues more demands; and this process continues. This is the synchronic serial logic of neoliberalism.

However, this process is not linear or circular. There are always dissonances, elements that escape. The particular ways the demands are realized only partially obey the demands and only partially follow the contours of the limits prescribed. Therefore, the practico-inert object of neoliberalism is actually an anxious entity. The anxiety it induces is precisely the unceasing chase that characterizes its reproduction. Rather than feeling exploitation in the direct sense of conflict or strife, neoliberal anxiety produces an unsettled disposition. It comes not during the act of consumption (which really does produce a measure of pleasure), but before and after. It is found in the motivation to consume and consume more where this anxiety is most potently felt. The issue becomes when neoliberal reason encloses that affective disquiet into its own logic and then valorizes it. It does this through the creation of "entrepreneurs." Han refers to such subjects as "achievement-subjects."[61] Fully motivated by the positive drive to consume, achievement-subjects are not consumers of Other-objects, but entrepreneurs of the self through the reproduction of the serial logic of neoliberal reason that mediates their very entrepreneurial activities.

This is why Han says that there must be an apocalypse: "In the inferno of the same, the arrival of the atopic Other can assume apocalyptic form. In other words: today, only an apocalypse can liberate—indeed, redeem—us from the inferno of the same, and lead us toward the Other."[62] Han's concern here is how the apocalypse leads to the Other in overcoming the agony of eros in the inferno of the same. Our reformulation would suggest that the apocalypse is the Other. It is precisely the event that is other than the inferno of the same that neoliberal reason offers. While Han's understanding of apocalypse is different from Sartre's and the one we elaborate in this project, there is a kernel of similarity in that the apocalypse is the truly radical break of hegemonic control. Han's concern is how love can exist between two in a world of the narcissistic reproduction of sameness. Ours considers the conditions under which what is reflected back to us is the multiplicity of mediated reciprocity.

9.3.3 Neoliberalism and Kaironic Seriality

This leads us full circle to the very beginnings of this investigation toward a fresh reading of Sartre's *CDR* as a heuristic into the conditions under which dialectical reason might come to comprehend itself. Sartre's concern was that praxis was not comprehensible. Marxism as the philosophical practice that was supposed to shine a light on the proletariat and its place in the world had failed to serve its purpose. Rather than accurately providing a toolset by which praxis could comprehend itself as the agents of history, Marxism had engaged in serial rationality which stifled its own project from realizing the ends it established. Thus, Sartre's investigation into the conditions under which dialectical reason might be known led him to develop formal abstractions that regressively investigated the transcendental conditions of anthropological life. The most startling conclusion in Volume One of *CDR* is that the conditions by which dialectical reason can tend toward comprehension are themselves not yet discovered. This is because the analysis by which the investigation itself is taken up is contaminated by the very mediatory conditions that it seeks to analyze. Seriality is Sartre's name for the illusory mystification that stifles praxis's self-awareness.

Now we can understand this stifling in the context of neoliberalism, as the latter is understood as a serial logic of inaction. Cohen felt this too. He thought that the obstetric model of Marxism did not possess the proper tools, not only of material analysis of the world *out there*, but of self-analysis. The result is that Marxism had stopped. Marxism had misunderstood itself as a living logic embodied in the shifting landscapes of proletarian demographics. Thus, in order to overcome this illusory stop-gap, he proposed a way to fabulate our way out of the inferno of the same. By binding a global community through the use of universal normative theory, Cohen believed that he would be able to force the hand of class consciousness.

Leiter is right to point out the residual bourgeois logic embedded in Cohen's project. Insofar as Cohen's normative ideals act as Kantian regulative principles, we are entrapped within a Constructivist orientation, within a frame of external relations where the ideas are separated from their material instantiation. However, if we think dialectically, from the Paradoxico-Critical orientation, then normative abstractions are not necessarily regulative (as in bourgeois thought), but formal processes that motivate action in their very articulation. This is because, as future images, they reflect the *kairos* back to us, heralding that it is always the moment to act. This is how we can find sites of antagonism against neoliberal rationality. For even in the polymorphic diffusion of the commodity logic, when understood dialectically, what is reflected back to praxis is praxis. It is reflected back, most certainly, as anti-praxis. Said in a Marxian tone, neoliberal commodities are mystified projects of false consciousness. Thus, in their mediatory role, they reflect neoliberal false consciousness back to praxis as the return of stolen praxis that sets the limits and demands for future praxis. This conditions praxis's feelings, thoughts, and actions to accord with the serial logic that is imposed. Thus, in a sense, all neoliberal praxis is anti-praxis.

David Harvey refers to this all-encompassing phenomenon as universal alienation. Alienation is universal when it reaches beyond the analytic economic categories of "production, the economy and bounded spaces."[63] Its reach is so vast that it seeps into the very constitutive forces that compose human subjectivity itself, "so that aspects of [human] subjectivity are damaged (concerning human activities, well-being, consciousness, mind/psyche, body, worldviews, social relations). Alienation is neither purely objective nor purely subjective, but a negative relationship between social structures and humans in heteronomous societies."[64] This negative relation between "social structures and humans" is a deprivation. It is the social experience of being separated from the aspirational concepts of the human that are held up by society, that are presumed by bourgeois discourse to define who and what we are, but that really cover the truth of social relations. Thus, Harvey's concept of universal alienation that stretches beyond the scope of productive relations between capital and labor in the factory model suggests that Harvey closely approaches advocating a theory of real subsumption in the vein of our articulation of Kaironic Seriality.

Michael Hardt and Antonio Negri, on the other hand, all but affirm it explicitly. Hardt and Negri discuss the logic of real subsumption in their critical analyses of neoliberalism. For them, real subsumption under neoliberalism inflects "muscles, languages, affects, codes"; "images"; "social intelligence, social relations"; and "the cognitive, social, and cooperative components of living labour."[65] Capital is no longer to be understood in its relation to vulgar economic categories of value production, for the categories of value production themselves are ever-shifting. Rather, real subsumption informs us that the productive processes "have now seeped outside the factory walls to permeate and define all social relations."[66] What this does not mean is that the same relations have merely escaped the walls of the factory and remain unchanged in form while yet dispersed. Rather, real subsumption teaches that the factory walls also conditioned capitalist contradiction based on the productive relations contained therein. Therefore, to speak of the productive process having seeped outside the factory is to also note that the productive processes of social value that have determinations far beyond the limited social relations of the factory must be taken into consideration. When Hardt and Negri refer to society as a "factory-society"[67] the point is that the logic of capital has embedded itself in arenas of life other than those strictly determined by value production according to the industrial capitalist mode of production. As such, the real subsumption of capital in the serial logic of neoliberal reason presents us with the persistent problem of false consciousness.

However, *free praxis* is also reflected back to us in the neoliberal practico-inert field. The processual notions of subjectivity are ever embedded in the field of the practico-inert. This is not a nostalgic glance at a humanity that was lost, but rather a recognition that the serial logic is not homogenous. It is an awareness of cracks, of previous antagonism, of that which is ever excessive of the territorializing logic of enclosure. Remember that what returns in the practico-inert is not singular. It is a multiplicity. I am confronted by the multiplicity of others. I am also confronted by myself. However, this me is a me that is an other-me. It is a me that is both me and not me, and because of the extent of the multiplicity, the intensity of otherness is far greater and more determinant than the me, which means that there is a reflection of alterity alongside the other-me. We might say that this is a haunting state of being-for-others.

Granted, this is a very idealist conception of material mediation, something that Sartre noted about his own efforts in *CDR* when critically reflecting on it a few years later.[68] But this is why the project in *CDR* and our expansion of it here is speculative and only partial. While we do not know the precise reasons Sartre did not complete the second Volume, and more importantly why he never completed his finished work on ethics, it does seem very likely that the self-referential nature of this investigation led him to realize that the voices required to complete a genuine materialist theory of dialectical reason could not be theorized once and for all. Thus, Fanon's *The Wretched of the Earth*, in which Sartre crafts the "Preface," very well ought to be seen as another stage in development of dialectical reason's self-awareness emerging out of the clouds of serial haze—a proverbial Volume Three. Who are the crafters of Volumes Five, Six, Seven, Eight, etc.?

Limitations aside, by reading *CDR* as a hypo-logic, what we are given are less final conclusions than an orientation with which to work. This is beneficial because the formal structures do not necessarily provide a complete synthesis but rather allow us to maintain a notion of irreducible otherness. Not an otherness that is conflictual. But a same-otherness. An endless process of sameing . . . of same-othering . . . of othering . . . of other-saming. . . . But never ultimately eradicating the dialectical process *per se*. Even if Sartre mused about a socialism of abundance where there would be no scarcity and thus no way for us to understand how conflict would arise, that would be another history and would require an entire other form of analysis; something he was not concerned with in *CDR*. Perhaps this is unsatisfying as an answer. But this is where the text leads us. And this is why we must not be afraid to keep working within the space opened by Sartre, to consider how far the orientation he signals can be taken and to take his work to that extreme. And if we end up criticizing him for being too idealist, then so be it. But at least, let's make sure we exhaust the resources he lays at our feet.

To summarize, the issue is not one about confronting or engaging the real world as opposed to the ideal world. What is at stake is how to navigate the dialectical synthesis of the two. How to form strategies that overcome the binary of reality and desire. In a Freudian sense, we might say that the task becomes how to bridge the cleavage between reality and pleasure. Thus, the imaginative logic of action is neither a realist nor idealist political program. It is a transcendental materialist orientation to dialectical reason.

NOTES

1. Castoriadis, *The Imaginary Institution of Society*, 61.
2. Bertell Ollman, "Marxism and the Philosophy of Internal Relations; or, How to Replace the Mysterious 'Paradox' with 'Contradictions' that Can Be Studied and Resolved," *Capital and Class*, 39, no. 1 (2015): 8.
3. Ibid, 8.
4. Ibid, 8.
5. Ariel Salleh, *Ecofeminism as Politics: Nature, Marx, and the Postmodern* (London and New York: Zed Books, 2017), chapter 10.
6. Ollman, "Marxism and the Philosophy of Internal Relations," 9.
7. Ibid., 13.
8. James Williams, *A Process Philosophy of Signs* (Edinburgh: Edinburgh University Press, 2016), Kindle Edition, chapter 1.
9. Ibid., chapter 1.
10. Ollman, 15.
11. Flynn, *Sartre: A Philosophical Biography*, 130.
12. Ibid., 88.
13. Sartre, *Family Idiot*, Vol. 1, 912 n.
14. Flynn, *Sartre*, 399.
15. Nicos Poulantzas, "Sartre's *Critique of Dialectical Reason* and Law," *The Poulantzas Reader*, ed. by James Martin (London: Verso, 2008), 47.
16. Michael Burns, *Kierkegaard and the Matter of Philosophy: A Fractured Dialectic* (London: Rowman & Littlefield International), 144.
17. Poulantzas, 53.
18. Ollman, 10.
19. Ibid., 10–11.
20. Cohen, 97.
21. For his full elaboration and criticism of the obstetric conception, see Cohen, chapters 3 and 4.
22. Cohen, 43.
23. Ibid., 80.
24. Karl Marx, *Introduction to a Contribution to the Critique of Hegel's Philosophy of Right*. Collected Works, Vol. 3, https://www.marxists.org/archive/marx/works/1843/critique-hpr/intro.htm, accessed December 22, 2018.
25. Cohen, 81.
26. Ibid., 80.
27. Karl Marx, "Letter From Marx to Arnold Ruge, May 1843," in *Karl Marx: Selected Writings*, https://www.marxists.org/archive/marx/works/1843/letters/43_09-alt.htm, accessed December 22, 2018.
28. Cohen, 99.
29. Ibid., 107.
30. Ibid., 108.
31. Ibid., 111.
32. Ibid., 117.
33. Brian Leiter, "Why Marxism Still Does Not Need Normative Theory," *Analyse & Kritik*, 1 + 2 (2015), 23.
34. Ibid., 29.
35. Ibid., 23.
36. Ibid., 24.
37. Ibid., 26.

38. Ibid., 27 note 8.
39. Ibid., 27.
40. Ibid., 28.
41. Michel Foucault, *The Birth of Biopolitics: Lectures at the Collége de France, 1978–1979*, ed. Michel Senellart and Michel Foucault (New York: Palgrave Macmillan, 2008), 32, 33, 44, 48 note 6, and 328.
42. Leiter, 42–43.
43. Ibid., 41 note 32.
44. Cohen, 99.
45. Karl Marx, "Chapter Two: The Metaphysics of Political Economy, Part 1," *The Poverty of Philosophy*, https://www.marxists.org/archive/marx/works/1847/poverty-philosophy/ch02.htm, accessed December 22, 2018.
46. Ibid.
47. Voices as disparate as the Autonomists, Situationists, Feminist Marxists, Eco-Feminists/Eco-Socialists, Psychoanalytic Marxists (Freudian, Lacanian, and beyond), etc.
48. Cohen, 77.
49. Rajesh Venugopal, "Neoliberalism as Concept," *Economy and Society*, 44, no. 2 (2015): 165–87.
50. Philip Mirowski, *Never Let a Serious Crisis Go to Waste: How Neoliberalism Survived the Financial Meltdown* (London: Verso, 2013).
51. Salleh, chapter 10.
52. Cohen, 91.
53. Ibid., 95.
54. Fredric Jameson, *Postmodernism, or, The Cultural Logic of Late Capitalism* (Durham, NC: Duke University Press, 1990).
55. Jamie Peck, Neil Brenner, and Nik Theodore, "Actually Existing Neoliberalism," in *The Sage Handbook of Neoliberalism*, ed. Damien Cahill, Melinda Cooper, Martijn Konings, and David Primrose (Los Angeles: Sage, 2018), 7.
56. Ibid., 7.
57. Martijn Konings, "Governing the System: Risk, Finance, and Neoliberal Reason," in *The Sage Handbook of Neoliberalism*, ed. Damien Cahill, Melinda Cooper, Martijn Konings, and David Primrose (Los Angeles: Sage, 2018), 414.
58. Ibid., 415.
59. Ibid., 415.
60. Byung-Chul Han, *The Agony of Eros* (Cambridge, MA: MIT Press, 2017), 1.
61. Han, *The Agony of Eros* and *The Burnout Society* (Stanford, CA: Stanford University Press, 2015).
62. Han, *The Agony of Eros*, 3.
63. Christian Fuchs, "Universal Alienation, Formal and Real Subsumption of Society Under Capital, Ongoing Primitive Accumulation by Dispossession: Reflections on the Marx@200-Contributions by David Harvey and Michael Hardt/Toni Negri," *tripleC* 16, no. 2 (2018): 456.
64. Ibid., 456.
65. Michael Hardt and Antonio Negri, "The Powers of the Exploited and the Social Ontology of Praxis," *tripleC* 16, no. 2 (2018).
66. Michael Hardt and Antonio Negri, *Labor of Dionysus* (Minneapolis: University of Minnesota Press, 1994), 15.
67. Ibid., 15.
68. Sartre, "Itinerary of a Thought."

Conclusion

In a way, this project is about reframing the critique of political economy. It is concerned with creating forms of social life that are not inscribed into the monstrosity that we have termed here Kaironic Seriality—the age of seriality. This is not to suggest that all human suffering or concern or desire or lack or strife will be overcome. Perhaps such is the *de facto* status of mortal beings with reflective consciousness who are thrown into worlds that are not of their choosing as they fly through an expanding universe (multiverse?) on a perishing molten rock. But it is an endeavor to transcend the limiting and limited frames of social life that impinge upon the very options with which we have to create therefrom. It is an effort to shift our orientation to the worlds in which we find ourselves so that we can perhaps eventually eradicate the very conditions to which contemporary resistance responds. This is what Sartre meant when he speaks of overcoming Marxism itself in the pursuit of "real freedom beyond the production of life."[1] Not that Marxism is not useful. But rather, situating Marxism as a technology in the pursuit of responding to even greater stirrings that echo from the human predicament made so potent by Kaironic Seriality.

We might listen to the voice of Russell Means here who spoke of Marxism as being part of the same cultural logic as capitalism.[2] Similarly, Baudrillard, who criticized Marxism for being the obverse of political economy.[3] Or, Ariel Salleh, who provokes thought by proclaiming that "A new mode of abstraction is called for in the process of reconstructing our historically deleted human identity with/in nature" in her investigation into an ecofeminist, ecopolitical analysis.[4] And perhaps we must go even further: toward grounding a new materialism altogether, one beyond dualism and monism in the search for a "belonging together" of ideality and materiality that is not reducible to correlationism, as in the recent work of Elizabeth Grosz.[5] While very different, Means, Baudrillard, Salleh, and Grosz, among many others, know that Marxism cannot be the goal. It cannot be means and end. And for Means, it ought not even be the means.

Regardless of their different utterances, what we can take from these thinkers, including Sartre in the lot, is that the tools at our disposal are often corrupted. In the language of this project we would say that they are serial tools. Our technologies of antagonism become impotent when inscribed into the very logic they seek to escape. This is more than just "The Master's Tools. . . ." This is a recognition about the very process of inscription, enclosure, and imaginative construction that constitutes our social realities, from top to bottom, inside-out, mind to heart, logic to pathos. It is a call for something else. A call for an unraveling of the knots that bind us to the commonsensical. Not to keep pulling the ends, but to stop the trajectory of momentum itself. And when necessary, to cut the rope. To create new connections. To start new projects unconditioned by the over-determined logics that we have inherited.

Now, of course, Sartre's ideas remained within the inherited logics of phenomenology, existentialism, historical materialism, and the entire heritage of Western philosophy. Our effort is not to absolve him from any criticism. Nor is it to force illegitimate value into his work. Rather, it is to work according to a similar disposition. To welcome gaps and breaks as the differential sparks and spreads. To find sites where we can become more attuned to the incessant life of subjectivity, even in the midst of its suppression; to first affirm it and then be sensitive to its lead, framing and reframing the boundaries that guide its effects. In the end, the goal is not Marxism, but "a philosophy of freedom [that] will take its place." But as Sartre warns, "we have no means, no intellectual instrument, no concrete experience which allows us to conceive of this freedom or of this philosophy."[6] This is what Sartre is seeking to point us toward. Like a prophet heralding the *kairos*, like Zarathustra proleptically declaring the nowhere/now-here, the imaginative logic of action seeks to equip theorists and activists with a toolbox for further elaboration in actualizing this freedom.

What we have sketched here is a clarification of confusions that prevent Sartre's work from being as valued as it ought toward this end. By shifting tack and embracing the virtual potency of *CDR* as a formal and logical investigation into the conditions under which dialectical reason might be made intelligible, new resources are provided as *matériel*. By embracing the Paradoxico-Critical orientation, through the ever-perpetual process of micro-psychobiological shifts, harnessing the force of the imagination, and fervently committing to the opportune moment's ever presence, the imaginative logic of action essays an *arche* to the unveiling of Being and to the validity of this unveiling.

NOTES

1. Sartre, *SM*, 34.
2. Russel Means, "For American to Live, Europe Must Die," July 1980, https://endofcapitalism.com/2010/10/17/revolution-and-american-indians-marxism-is-as-alien-to-my-culture-as-capitalism/, accessed December 22, 2018.
3. Jean Baudrillard, *The Mirror of Production*, trans. Mark Poster (St. Louis: Telos Press, 1975).
4. Salleh, *Ecofeminism as Politics*.
5. Elizabeth Grosz, *The Incorporeal: Ontology, Ethics, and the Limits of Materialism* (New York: Columbia University Press, 2018).
6. Sartre, *SM*, 34.

Bibliography

Agamben, Giorgio. "Vocation and Voice." *Qui Parle*, 10, no. 2 (1997): 89–100.
Ally, Matthew. *Ecology and Existence: Bringing Sartre to the Water's Edge*. Lanham, MD: Lexington Books, 2017.
Althusser, Louis et al. *Lire le capital*. 2 vols. Paris: Maspero, 1965.
Anderson, Kenneth L. "Transformations of Subjectivity in Sartre's Critique of Dialectical Reason." *Journal of Philosophical Research*, 27 (2002): 265–78.
Andrew, Douglas. "In a Milieu of Scarcity: Sartre and the Limits of Political Imagination." *Contemporary Political Theory*, 10, no. 3 (2011): 354–71.
Aristotle. *On Rhetoric: A Theory of Civic Discourse*. Translated by George A. Kennedy. New York: Oxford University Press, 2007.
Aron, Raymond. *History and the Dialectic of Violence: An Analysis of Sartre's Critique de la Raison Dialectique*. Translated by Barry Cooper. Oxford: Basil Blackwell, 1975.
Aronson, Ronald. "A New Politics of Hope." Excerpted from *We: Reviving Social Hope*. Chicago: Chicago University Press, 2017.
———. *Jean-Paul Sartre: Philosophy in the World*. London: Verso, 1980.
———. *Sartre's Second Critique*. Chicago: University of Chicago Press, 1987.
Atwill, Janet. *Rhetoric Reclaimed: Aristotle and the Liberal Arts Tradition*. Ithaca, NY: Cornell University Press, 1998.
Badiou, Alain. *Being and Event*. Translated by Oliver Feltham. London: Continuum, 2005.
———. *Briefings on Existence: A Short Treatise on Transitory Ontology*. Translated by Norman Madarasz. Albany, NY: SUNY Press, 1998.
———. *Conditions*. Paris: Seuil, 1992.
———. *Logics of Worlds: Being and Event II*. Translated by Alberto Toscano. London: Continuum, 2009.
———. *Pocket Pantheon: Figures of Postwar Philosophy*. Translated by David Macey. London: Verso, 2009.
———. *Theory of the Subject*. Translated by Bruno Bosteels. London: Continuum, 2009.
Barnes, Hazel. "Introduction." In *The Cambridge Companion to Sartre*. Edited by Christina Howells. Cambridge: Cambridge University Press, 1992.
Barthes, Roland. "The Structuralist Activity." *Partisan Review*, 15, no. 3 (1967): 82–88.
Baudrillard, Jean. *The Mirror of Production*. Translated by Mark Poster. St. Louis, MO: Telos Press, 1975.
Benveniste, Émile. "Subjectivity in Language." In *Problems in General Linguistics*. Miami: University of Miami, 1974.
Bernasconi, Robert. "Fanon's The Wretched of the Earth as the Fulfillment of Sartre's Critique of Dialectical Reason." *Sartre Studies International*, 16, no. 2 (2010): 36–47.

Bidet, Jacques. *Exploring Marx's Capital: Philosophical, Economic and Political Dimensions.* Translated by David Fernbach. Leiden: Brill, 2007.
———. *Foucault with Marx.* Translated by Steven Corcoran. London: Zed Books, 2015.
Boileau, Kevin. "How Foucault Can Improve Sartre's Theory of Authentic Political Community." *Sartre Studies International*, 10, no. 2 (2004): 77–91.
Bonhoeffer, Dietrich. "The Church and the Jewish Question." Quoted in Dietrich Bonhoeffer, *No Rusty Swords: Letters, Lectures and Notes, 1928–1936.* Edited by Edwin H. Robertson. Translated by Edwin H. Robertson and John Bowden. Vol. 1, *Collected Works of Dietrich Bonhoeffer.* New York, Harper, 1965.
Boulé, Jean-Pierre. "Revisiting the Sartre/Lévy Relationship." *Sartre Studies International*, 4, no. 2 (1998): 54–60.
Bourdieu, Pierre. *The Logic of Practice.* Translated by Richard Nice. Stanford, CA: Stanford University Press, 1980.
Brueggemann, Walter. *The Prophetic Imagination.* Minneapolis: Fortress Press, 2001.
Burns, Michael. *Kierkegaard and the Matter of Philosophy: A Fractured Dialectic.* London: Rowman & Littlefield International, 2015.
Butterfield, Elizabeth. *Sartre and Posthumanist Humanism.* Frankfurt: Peter Lang, 2012.
Cannon, Betty. "Group Therapy as Revolutionary Praxis: A Sartrean View." *Sartre Studies International*, 11, nos. 1–2 (2005): 133–52.
Catalano, Joseph. *A Commentary on Jean-Paul Sartre's Critique of Dialectical Reason, Vol. 1, Theory of Practical Ensembles.* Chicago: University of Chicago Press, 1986.
———. "The Meaning and Truth of History: A Note on Sartre's Critique of Dialectical Reason." *Sartre Studies International*, 13, no. 2 (2007): 47–64.
Casey, Edward. "Imagination: Imagining and the Image." *Philosophy and Phenomenological Research*, 31, no. 4 (1971): 475–90.
Castoriadis, Cornelius. *The Imaginary Institution of Society.* Translated by Kathleen Blamey. Cambridge: Polity Press, 2005.
Caws, Peter. "Sartrean Structuralism?" In *Cambridge Companion to Sartre.* Edited by Christina Howells. Cambridge: Cambridge University Press, 1992.
Chiodi, Pietro. *Sartre and Marxism.* Translated by Kate Soper. Sussex: Harvester Press, 1976.
Clayton, Cam. "The Psychical Analogon in Sartre's Theory of the Imagination." *Sartre Studies International*, 17, no. 2 (2011): 16–27.
Cohen, G. A. *If You're an Egalitarian, How Come You're So Rich?* Cambridge, MA: Harvard University Press, 2001.
Colombel, Jeannette. "Deleuze-Sartre: pistes." In *Deleuze épars: approches et portraits.* Edited by André Bernold and Richard Pinhas. Paris: Hermann Éditeurs, 2005.
Connolly, William. *A World of Becoming.* Durham, NC: Duke University Press, 2011.
Crary, Jonathan. *24/7: Late Capitalism and the Ends of Sleep.* London: Verso, 2014.
Cummings, Robert D. "Role-Playing: Sartre's Transformation of Husserl's Phenomenology." In *The Cambridge Companion to Sartre.* Edited by Christina Howells. Cambridge: Cambridge University Press, 1992.
Damasio, Antonio. Interview by Manuela Lenzen. "Feeling our Emotions." *Scientific American.* https://www.scientificamerican.com/article/feeling-our-emotions/, accessed December 22, 2018.
———. *Looking for Spinoza: Joy, Sorrow, and the Feeling Brain.* London: Williams Heinemann, 2003.
de Beauvoir, Simone. *La Cérémonie des adieux, suivi de entretiens avec Jean-Paul Sartre, Août-Septembre 1974.* Paris: Gallimard, 1981.
Deleuze, Gilles, "He Was My Teacher." In *Desert Islands and Other Texts 1953–1974.* Paris: Semiotext(e), 2002.
———. "Immanence: A Life." In *Pure Immanence: Essays on A Life.* Translated by Anne Boyman. New York: Zone Books, 2001.
———. "The Actual and The Virtual." Translated by Eliot Ross Albert. In *Dialogues II.* Edited by Gilles Deleuze and Claire Parnet. Translated by Hugh Tomlinson and Barbara Habberjam. London: Continuum, 2002.

Deleuze, Gilles and Felix Guattari. *Anti-Oedipus: Capitalism and Schizophrenia*. Translated by Robert Hurley, Mark Seem, and Helen R. Lane. Minneapolis: University of Minnesota Press, 1983.

———. *A Thousand Plateaus: Capitalism and Schizophrenia*. Translated by Brian Massumi. London: Athlone Press, 1988.

Deleuze, Gilles and Claire Parnet, *Dialogues*. Translated by Hugh Tomlinson and Barbara Habberjam. New York: Columbia University Press, 1987.

Desan, Wilfrid. *The Marxism of Jean-Paul Sartre*. Garden City, NY: Doubleday and Company, 1965.

Dobson, Andrew. *Jean-Paul Sartre and the Politics of Reason*. Cambridge: Cambridge University Press, 1993.

Doran, Robert. "Sartre's Critique of Dialectical Reason and the Debate with Lévi-Strauss." *Yale French Studies*, no. 123 (2013): 41–62.

Dosse, François. *Gilles Deleuze et Félix Guattari: Biographie croisée*. Paris: Éditions La Découverte, 2007.

Engels, Friedrich. *Socialism: Utopian and Scientific*. London: Allen and Unwin,1892.

Fanon, Frantz. *The Wretched of the Earth*. Translated by Richard Philcox. New York: Grove Press, 2004.

Flynn, Thomas. "L'Imagination Au Pouvoir: The Evolution of Sartre's Political and Social Thought." *Political Theory*, 7, no. 2 (May 1979): 157–80.

———. "The Role of the Image in Sartre's Aesthetic." *The Journal of Aesthetics and Art Criticism*, 33, no. 4 (1975): 431–42.

———. *Sartre: A Philosophical Biography*. Cambridge: Cambridge University Press, 2014.

———. *Sartre, Foucault, and Historical Reason*, Volume One: *Toward an Existentialist Theory of History*. Chicago: The University of Chicago Press, 1997.

———. *Sartre and Marxist Existentialism*. Chicago: University of Chicago Press, 1984.

———. "Sartre and the Poetics of History." In *The Cambridge Companion to Sartre*. Edited by Christina Howells. Cambridge: Cambridge University Press, 1992.

Foucault, Michel. *The Birth of Biopolitics: Lectures at the Collége de France, 1978–1979*. Edited by Michel Senellart and Michel Foucault. New York: Palgrave Macmillan, 2008.

———. *The Final Foucault*. Edited by James Bernauer and David Rasmussen. Cambridge: MIT Press, 1988.

———. *Foucault Live*. Edited by Sylvere Lotringer. New York: Semiotext[e], 1989.

———. *The Foucault Reader*. Edited by P. Rabinow. New York: Pantheon, 1984.

Fox, Nik Farrell. *The New Sartre: Explorations in Postmodernism*. London: Continuum, 2003.

Fuchs, Christian. "Universal Alienation, Formal and Real Subsumption of Society Under Capital, Ongoing Primitive Accumulation by Dispossession: Reflections on the Marx@200-Contributions by David Harvey and Michael Hardt/Toni Negri." *tripleC*, 16, no. 2 (2018): 454–67.

Gadamer, Hans-Georg. "Plato as Portraitist." In *The Gadamer Reader: A Bouquet of the Later Writings*. Edited by Richard E. Palmer. Evanston, IL: Northwestern University Press, 2007.

Galbraith, John Kenneth. *The Affluent Society*. New York: Houghton Mifflin Company, 1998.

Goodchild, Philip. "Capital and Kingdom: An Eschatological Ontology." In *Theology and the Political: The New Debate*. Edited by Creston Dave, John Milbank, and Slavoj Žižek. Durham, NC: Duke University Press, 2005.

———. *Capitalism and Religion: The Price of Piety*. London: Routledge, 2002.

Grosz, Elizabeth. *The Incorporeal: Ontology, Ethics, and the Limits of Materialism*. New York: Columbia University Press, 2018.

Habermas, Jürgen. *The Philosophical Discourse of Modernity: Twelve Lectures*. Translated by Frederick Lawrence. Cambridge, MA: MIT Press, 1987.

Hallward, Peter. *Out of This World: Deleuze and the Philosophy of Creation*. London: Verso, 2006.

Han, Byung-Chul. *The Agony of Eros*. Cambridge, MA: MIT Press, 2017.

———. *The Burnout Society*. Stanford, CA: Stanford University Press, 2015.

Hardt, Michael, and Negri, Antonio. *Commonwealth*. Cambridge, MA: Harvard University Press, 2009.

———. *Multitude: War and Democracy in the Age of Empire.* New York: Penguin, 2004.
———. *Labor of Dionysus.* Minneapolis: University of Minnesota Press, 1994
———. "The Powers of the Exploited and the Social Ontology of Praxis." *tripleC*, 16, no. 2 (2018): 415–23.
Heidegger, Martin. *Basic Writings.* London: Routledge, 2004.
Horkheimer, Max. *Eclipse of Reason.* New York: Oxford University Press, 1947.
Howells, Christina. *Sartre: The Necessity of Freedom.* Cambridge: Cambridge University Press, 1988.
Jameson, Fredric. "Foreword." In Jean-Paul Sartre, *Critique of Dialectical Reason: Volume One.* Edited by Jonathan Ree. Translated by Alan Sheridan-Smith. London: Verso, 2004.
———. *Postmodernism, or, The Cultural Logic of Late Capitalism.* Durham, NC: Duke University Press, 1990.
Jay, Martin. *Marxism and Totality: The Adventures of a Concept from Lukács to Habermas.* Berkeley: University of California Press, 1984.
———. *Reason After Its Eclipse.* Madison: University of Wisconsin Press, 2016.
Kant, Immanuel. *Metaphysical Foundations of Natural Science.* Edited by Michael Friedman. Cambridge: Cambridge University Press, 2004.
Kearney, Richard. *The Wake of Imagination: Toward a Postmodern Culture.* Minneapolis: University of Minnesota Press, 1988.
Kelly, Michael. "Towards a Heuristic Method: Sartre and Lefebvre." *Sartre Studies International*, 5, no. 1 (1999): 1–15.
Keynes, John Maynard. "Economic Possibilities of Our Grandchildren." *Essays in Persuasion.* New York: W. W. Norton & Co., 1963.
Klockars, Kristian. *Sartre's Anthropology as a Hermeneutics of Praxis.* Aldershot, UK: Ashgate, 1998.
Konings, Martijn. *The Emotional Logic of Capitalism.* Stanford, CA: Stanford University Press, 2015.
———. "Governing the System: Risk, Finance, and Neoliberal Reason." In *The Sage Handbook of Neoliberalism.* Edited by Damien Cahill, Melinda Cooper, Martijn Konings, and David Primrose. Los Angeles: Sage, 2018.
Koselleck, Reinhart. "Crisis." Translated by Michaela Richter. *Journal of the History of Ideas*, 67, no. 2 (April, 2006): 357–400.
———. *Futures Past: On the Semantics of Historical Time.* Translated by Keith Tribe. New York: Columbia University Press, 2004.
Kotsko, Adam. "Insan Nedir," in Sabah Ülkesi, October 8, 2018. http://www.sabahulkesi.comlivepage.apple.com/2018/10/08/insan-nedir/, accessed December 22, 2018. Translation provided on author's blog: https://itself.blog/2018/10/10what-is-human/, accessed December 22, 2018.
Leiter, Brian. "Why Marxism Still Does Not Need Normative Theory." *Analyse & Kritik*, 1 + 2 (2015): 23–50.
Lévi-Strauss, Claude. *The Savage Mind.* London: Weidenfeld and Nicolson, 1966.
Lévi-Strauss, Claude, Augé, Marc, and Godelier, Marice. "Anthropologie, Histoire, Idéologie." *L'Homme*, 15, no. 3–4 (1975): 177–88.
Lévy, Benny. "Today's Hope: Conversations with Sartre." *Telos*, 44 (1980).
Livingston, Paul. *The Politics of Logic: Badiou, Wittgenstein, and the Consequences of Formalism.* New York: Routledge, 2012.
Lukács, Georg. "Existentialism." In *Marxism and Human Liberation: Essays on History, Culture and Revolution.* New York: Dell Publishing Co., 1973.
———. *History and Class Consciousness.* Cambridge, MA: MIT Press, 1971.
Malabou, Catherine. *What Should We Do with Our Brain?* Translated by Sebastian Rand. New York: Fordham, 2008.
Malraux, André. *Days of Hope.* London: Penguin, 1970.
Mamet, David, *True and False: Heresy and Common Sense for the Actor.* New York, Vintage Books/Random House, 1997
Marcuse, Herbert. *An Essay on Liberation.* Boston: Beacon Press, 1969.

———. *Reason and Revolution: Hegel and the Rise of Social Theory.* Boston: Beacon Press, 1960.
Martinot, Steve. "The Site of Postmodernity in Sartre." *Sartre Studies International*, 5, no. 2 (1999): 45–60
Marx, Karl. *The Eighteenth Brumaire of Louis Bonaparte.* Translated by D. D. L. [1897]. New York: Mondial, 2005.
———. *The German Ideology.* Moscow: Progress Publishers, 1964.
———. *Introduction to a Contribution to the Critique of Hegel's Philosophy of Right.* Collected Works, Vol. 3, https://www.marxists.org/archive/marx/works/1843/critique-hpr/intro.htm, accessed December 22, 2018.
———. "Letter From Marx to Arnold Ruge, May 1843." In *Karl Marx: Selected Writings*. https://www.marxists.org/archive/marx/works/1843/letters/43_09-alt.htm, accessed December 22, 2018.
———. *The Poverty of Philosophy.* https://www.marxists.org/archive/marx/works/1847/poverty-philosophy/ch02.htm, accessed December 22, 2018.
Mason, J. W. "Socialize Finance." Jacobin. November 28, 2016. https://www.jacobinmag.com/2016/11/finance-banks-capitalism-markets-socialism-planning/, accessed December 22, 2018.
May, Todd. *The Political Philosophy of Poststructuralist Anarchism.* University Park: The Pennsylvania State University Press, 1994.
Means, Russell. "For American to Live, Europe Must Die." July 1980. https://endofcapitalism.com/2010/10/17/revolution-and-american-indians-marxism-is-as-alien-to-my-culture-as-capitalism/, accessed December 22, 2018.
Mehrabian, Albert and Epstein, Normal. "A Measure of Emotional Empathy." *Journal of Personality*, 40, no. 4 (1972): 525–43.
Merleau-Ponty, Maurice. "Sartre et l'ulta bolchevisme." In *Les Aventures de la Dialectique*. Paris: Gillimard, 1955.
Mészáros, István. *The Work of Sartre: Search for Freedom and the Challenge of History.* New York: Monthly Review Press, 2012.
Milbank, John. "Materialism and Transcendence." Quoted in Creston Davis, John Milbank, Slavoj Žižek, *Theology and the Political: The New Debate.* Durham, NC: Duke University Press, 2005.
———. *Theology and Social Theory: Beyond Secular Reason.* Oxford: Blackwell, 2006.
Mirowski, Philip. *Never Let a Serious Crisis Go to Waste: How Neoliberalism Survived the Financial Meltdown.* London: Verso, 2013.
Morot-Sir, Edouard. "Sartre's Critique of Dialectical Reason." *Journal of the History of Ideas*, 22, no. 4 (1961): 573–81.
Mullarkey, John. *Post-Continental Philosophy: An Outline.* London: Continuum, 2006.
Negri, Antonio. "Is It Possible to be a Communist Without Marx?" *Critical Horizons*, 12, no. 1 (2011): 5–14.
Nicolacopoulos, Toula and Vassilacopoulos, George. "Philosophy and Revolution: Badiou's Infidelity to the Event." In *The Praxis of Alain Badiou*. Edited by Paul Ashton, A. J. Bartlett, and Justin Clemens. Melbourne: re.press, 2006.
Nietzsche, Friederich. *Beyond Good and Evil.* Translated by Helen Zimmern. New York: Dover Publications, 1997.
———. *Genealogy of Morals.* Translated by Horace B. Samuel. New York: Dover Publications, 2003.
Ollman, Berell. "Marxism and the Philosophy of Internal Relations; or, How to Replace the Mysterious 'Paradox' with 'Contradictions' that Can Be Studied and Resolved." *Capital and Class*, 39, no. 1 (2015): 7–23.
Patterson, Bradley W. *Redefining Reason: The Story of the Twentieth Century "Primitive" Mentality Debate.* Bradley Williams Patterson, 2011.
Pearson, Keith Ansell. "A Dionysian Drama on the 'Fate of the Soul': An Introduction to Reading On the Genealogy of Morality." Quoted in Christa Davis, *Acampora Nietzsche's On the Genealogy of Morals: Critical Essays.* Lanham, MD: Rowman & Littlefield, 2006.

Peck, Jamie, Brenner, Neil, and Theodore, Nik. "Actually Existing Neoliberalism." In *The Sage Handbook of Neoliberalism*. Edited by Damien Cahill, Melinda Cooper, Martijn Konings, and David Primrose. Los Angeles: Sage, 2018.

Poster, Mark. *Sartre's Marxism*. London: Pluto Press, 1979.

Poulantzas, Nicos. "Sartre's Critique of Dialectical Reason and Law." In *The Poulantzas Reader*. Edited by James Martin. London: Verso, 2008.

Power, Nina. "From Theoretical Antihumanism to Practical Humanism: The Political Subject in Sartre, Althusser and Badiou." PhD thesis, University of Warwick, 2007.

———. "The Terror of Collectivity: Sartre's Theory of Political Groups." *Prelom*, 8 (2006): 93–103.

———. "Towards a New Political Subject? Badiou between Marx and Althusser." In *Badiou and Philosophy*. Edited by Sean Bowden and Simon Duffy. Edinburgh: Edinburgh University Press, 2012.

———. "Towards an Anthropology of Infinitude: Badiou and the Political Subject." In *The Praxis of Alain Badiou*. Edited by Paul Ashton, A. J. Bartlett, and Justin Clemens. Melbourne: re.press, 2006.

Rae, Gavin. "Sartre, Group Formations, and Practical Freedom: The Other in the Critique of Dialectical Reason." *Comparative and Continental Philosophy*, 3, no. 2 (2011): 183–206.

Reisman, David. *Sartre's Phenomenology*. New York: Bloomsbury, 2007.

Robin, Corey. *The Reactionary Mind: Conservatism from Edmund Burke to Sarah Palin*. Oxford: Oxford University Press, 2011.

Rump, Jacob. "Lévi-Strauss, Barthes, and the 'Structuralist Activity' of Sartre's Dialectical Reason." *Sartre Studies International*, 17, no. 2 (2011): 1–15.

Salleh, Ariel. *Ecofeminism as Politics: Nature, Marx, and the Postmodern*. London and New York: Zed Books, 2017.

Sallis, John. *Force of Imagination: The Sense of the Elemental*. Bloomington: Indiana University Press, 2000.

Santoni, Ronald E. "In Defense of Lévy and 'Hope Now': A Minority View." *Sartre Studies International* 4, no. 2 (1998): 61–68.

Sartre, Jean-Paul. "Après Budapest Sartre Parle." *L'Express*, November 9, 1956. http://www.lexpress.fr/informations/apres-budapest-sartre-parle_590852.html.

———. "Art and Subjectivity (Part 2)." Originally published April 8, 2016. Accessed April 10, 2016. http://www.versobooks.com/blogs/2593-art-and-subjectivity-part-2.

———. *Being and Nothingness*. Translated and edited by Hazel Barnes. New York: Washington Square Press, 1993.

———. *Between Existentialism and Marxism*. Translated by John Matthews. London: Verso, 2008.

———. *Critique of Dialectical Reason: Volume One*. Edited by Jonathan Ree. Translated by Alan Sheridan-Smith. London: Verso, 2004.

———. *Critique of Dialectical Reason: Volume Two*. Edited by Arlette Elkaim-Sartre. Translated by Quintin Hoare. London: Verso, 2006.

———. *The Family Idiot*. Translated by C. Cosman. Chicago: University of Chicago Press, 1987.

———. *The Imaginary: A Phenomenological Psychology of the Imagination*. Translated by Jonathan Webber. London: Routledge, 2004.

———. *Literary and Philosophical Essays*. Translated by Annette Michelson. New York: Collier Books, 1962.

———. *Preface to The Wretched of the Earth*, by Frantz Fanon. Translated by Richard Philcox. New York: Grove Press, 2004.

———. *Search for a Method*. Translated by Hazel Barnes. New York: Alfred A. Knopf, 1963.

———. *The Transcendence of the Ego: An Existentialist Theory of Consciousness*. Translated by Forrest Williams and Robert Kirkpatrick. New York: Hill and Wang, 1991.

———. *What Is Subjectivity?* Translated by David Broder and Trista Selous. Kindle Edition. London: Verso, 2016.

———. "Un Entretrien avec J.-P. Sartre." Interview with Michel Contat and Michel Rybalka, published in *Le Monde*, May 14, 1971.

Sartre, Jean-Paul, and Contat, Michel. "Sartre at Seventy: An Interview." Originally published August 7, 1975 Issue. Accessed June 12, 2016. http://www.nybooks.com/articles/1975/08/07/sartre-at-seventy-an-interview/.
Schlipp Paul Arthur. *The Philosophy of Sartre*. La Salle: Open Court, 1981.
Seneca, Lucius Annaeus. *Letters on Ethics: To Lucilius*. Translated by Margaret Graver and A. A. Long. Chicago: University of Chicago Press, 2015.
Sherman, David. *Sartre and Adorno: The Dialectics of Subjectivity*. Albany: State University of New York Press, 2007.
Simont, Juliette. "The Critique of Dialectical Reason: From Need to Need, Circularly." *Yale French Studies*, no. 68 (1985): 108–23.
Smith, Brian. "Badiou and Sartre: Freedom From Imagination to Chance." In *Badiou and Philosophy*. Edited by Sean Bowden and Simon Duffy. Edinburgh: Edinburgh University Press, 2012
———. "The Limits of the Subject in Badiou's Being and Event." In *The Praxis of Alain Badiou*. Edited by Paul Ashton, A. J. Bartlett, and Justin Clemens. Melbourne: re.press, 2006.
Spinoza, Benedict. *Theological-Political Treatise*. Edited by Jonathan Israel. Translated by Michael Silberthorne and Jonathan Israel. Cambridge: Cambridge University Press, 2007.
Srnicek, Nick, and Williams, Alex. *Inventing the Future: Postcapitalism and a World Without Work*. London: Verso, 2015.
Stack, George. "Sartre's Dialectic of Social Relations." *Philosophy and Phenomenological Research*, 31, no. 3 (1971): 394–408.
Stewart, Jon. *The Debate between Sartre and Merleau-Ponty*. Evanston, IL: Northwestern University Press, 1998
Taylor, Charles. *Hegel*. Cambridge: Cambridge University Press, 1975.
———. *Modern Social Imaginaries*. Durham, NC: Duke University Press, 2003.
———. *Sources of the Self: The Making of the Modern Identity*. Cambridge, MA: Harvard University Press, 1992.
Toscano, Alberto. "Sovereignty and Deviation: Notes on Sartre's Critique of Dialectical Reason, Vol. 2." *Crisis and Critique*, 3, no. 1 (2016): 280–99.
Turner, Christopher. "The Return of Stolen Praxis: Counter-Finality in Sartre's Critique of Dialectical Reason." *Sartre Studies International*, 20, no. 1 (2014): 36–44.
Venugopal, Rajesh. "Neoliberalism as Concept." *Economy and Society*, 44, no. 2 (2015): 165–87.
Williams, James. *A Process Philosophy of Signs*. Edinburgh: Edinburgh University Press, 2016. Kindle Edition.
———. "If Not Here, Then Where? On the Location and Individuation of Events in Badiou and Deleuze." *Deleuze Studies*, 3, no. 1 (June 2009): 97–123.
Wood, Philip R. "Derrida Engagé and Poststructuralist Sartre: A Redefinition of Shifts in Recent French Philosophy." *MLN*, 104, no. 4, French Issue (1989): 861–79.
Yoder, John Howard. *The Politics of Jesus*. Grand Rapids, MI: Eerdman's, 1994.

Index

Abschattung, 162
abstraction: conceptual, 3, 29, 151; dialectical, 117; formal. *See* formal; logical, 5, 148; productive, 81, 82; speculative, 185; theoretical, 81, 82, 172, 186; violent, 81, 91; vital, 233–243
abundance. *See* socialism of abundance
actual. *See* virtual
aesthetic ethos, 184–185
aestheticization of self, 198
affect, 5, 41, 133–135, 138, 146, 161, 168, 172, 207, 214–216; affective *a priori*, 211; impotent, 150; organized. *See* organization
Agamben, 77
alienation, 61, 69, 78, 82, 83, 86, 89, 99, 100, 108, 109, 123, 147, 152, 170, 176, 247, 262
Ally, Matthew, 11n17, 182, 185
alterity, 4, 55, 90, 91, 96, 143, 151, 186
analogon, 24, 160, 164, 239
analytical reason, 2, 21, 30, 35–38, 41–42, 64, 65, 77–78, 118. *See also* Marxism, positivist
Anderson, Kenneth, 82, 191
anthropology: historical and structural, 2, 60, 67, 68, 69, 148, 151; Marxist, 4, 63; philosophical anthropology, 21; prolegomena to any future, 68
apocalypse, 3, 5, 28, 56, 59, 62, 68, 85, 90, 100, 108, 117, 121–133, 133, 136, 139, 144, 149, 164, 172, 180, 183, 198, 261; logic of, 132–133, 135; perpetual, 217–226
Aquinas, Thomas, 34
Aristotle, 18, 24, 34, 77, 101, 170, 237
Aron, Raymond, 5, 62–69, 119
Aronson, Ronald, 54, 113
Atwill, Janet, 101

Badiou, Alain, 5, 7, 11n15, 28, 31, 32–33, 39, 48n61, 51, 114, 117, 121, 124–133, 142–143, 143–145, 191–192, 236
Barnes, Hazel, 21
Barthes, Roland, 1, 44
Baudrillard, Jean, 267
Beauvoir, Simone de, 28
becoming, 25, 81, 119, 132, 233, 239
being, 5, 16, 20, 39, 45, 81, 93, 138, 162, 194, 198, 237; for-itself. *See* for-itself; for-others; for-others; in-itself; in-itself
Being and Nothingness, 6, 54, 60, 63, 82, 119, 120, 125, 192, 196, 234
Benveniste, Émile, 107, 124, 130, 132
Bernasconi, Robert, 8, 199
Boileau, Kevin, 196
Bonhoeffer, Dietrich, 111–114
Bourdieu, Pierre, 108, 117
bourgeois thought, 235, 237, 247, 249
Burke, Edmund, 204
Burns, Michael, 238

279

Butterfield, Elizabeth, 6, 80, 83, 98, 110, 195, 197, 221

Cannon, Betty, 201
capitalism, 24, 29, 63, 68, 208–209, 211, 213, 226, 243, 245, 247, 249, 263, 267
Cartesian individualism, 5–6, 11n16, 63–64
Castoriadis, Cornelius, 4, 231
Caws, Peter, 60
Chiodi, Pietro, 23, 55, 143
chronos, 101, 102, 122
class-consciousness, 4, 23, 24, 184, 238, 240, 244
class struggle, 251
Cohen, G. A., 23, 184, 241, 243–246, 249–253
the collective, 55, 93–94, 96, 97, 151, 201
collective object, 93, 94, 97, 106
Communism. *See* Communist. *See also* Marxism
Communist, 192
comprehension, 4–119, 10n14, 20, 23, 27, 41, 45, 51, 64, 78, 90, 123, 135–136, 240, 249–253, 262
concrete universal, 93
Connolly, William, 7, 91, 183, 187, 214–216, 219
Constructivist orientation, 28–41, 61, 67, 77, 120, 136, 236, 247
counter-finality, 55, 79, 80–81, 84, 86, 138
Crary, Jonathan, 178–179, 180
critique of political economy, 29, 242, 267
culture, 97

Damasio, Antonio, 134–135, 213
de Beauvoir, Simone. *See* Beauvoir
Deleuze, Gilles, 34, 107, 117, 124, 127–131, 196, 208, 208–210
derivatives, 259
Desan, Wilfrid, 5, 136
Descartes, René. *See* Cartesian individualism
destiny, 4, 57, 62, 97, 200. *See also* freedom, conditioned
dialectic, 16, 19, 20, 41, 53–54, 55, 110, 119; as formal, 75; idealist, 24; as logical, 75; materialist, 73; moments of the, 81; of nature, 21, 32, 35–38, 54;

totalizing. *See* totalization
dialectical, 73, 74–75; investigation, 15, 61, 82–83, 91, 118
dialectical reason, 2, 4, 7, 9, 20, 27, 30, 39, 40, 41, 42, 45, 51, 64, 82, 106, 182, 242, 243, 248, 262, 265; made intelligible, 68, 232
difference: field of, 130; ontological. *See* ontology
the differential, 110, 119, 121, 123, 124, 138, 168, 193, 240; become common. *See* group-in-fusion; the spark of, 114
Dilthey, Wilhelm, 98
Dobson, Andrew, 62
Dussel, Enrique, 7

Eleventh Thesis on Feuerbach, 241, 251
emotional contagion, 134
empathy, 133–135, 136, 172
Engels, 37
eschaton, 102, 104, 105
ethical, 19, 27, 242; motivation, 83–85; responsibility, 27
ethnocentrism, 28–30
Event, 5, 11n15, 103, 117, 124, 132, 192; apocalyptic, 124–127; Christ-Event, 143; evental logic, 127–131
events, 117, 129–130, 132
exigency, 55, 68, 73, 78–86, 92, 126, 137, 140, 142, 149, 161, 169, 193, 212; free exigencies, 85; mediatory material exigency, 166–173; serial exigencies, 85, 109, 177
existentialism, 5, 6, 8, 20, 24, 63, 117, 177, 194; Existentialism is a Humanism, 24, 63, 82
external relations, 235

fabulation, 64, 165, 237
false consciousness, 5, 23, 240, 242, 244–246, 263
The Family Idiot, 237
Fanon, Frantz, 8, 51, 121, 123, 191, 264
fascism, 111
fidelity. *See* institutional fidelity
the field of possibles, 54, 164–165
Flaubert, Gustave, 8, 97, 159
Flynn, Thomas, 5, 11n16, 51, 67, 76, 84–85, 92, 93, 119–121, 124, 132, 133,

135, 147, 169, 179, 191, 218, 237, 238
force of imagination. *See* John Sallis
for-itself, 6, 52–54, 119, 125, 142, 192, 194, 237
formal: abstraction, 5, 46, 67, 118, 169, 237, 238; cause. *See* Aristotle; conditions, 2, 7, 64, 69; defined, 10n3, 46; investigation, 5, 7, 8, 46, 59, 62, 64, 75, 83, 91, 151, 183, 197, 221; as lived, 46, 191
for-others, 6, 52, 194
Foucault, Michel, 34, 38, 182, 196–197, 198, 220, 248
Fox, Nik Farrell, 6, 64, 93, 198, 201, 222
Frankfurt School, 17, 20, 47n18, 47n20. *See also* Marcuse
fraternity terror. *See* terror
freedom, 3, 5, 29, 52, 55, 67, 90, 118–152, 124, 147, 173, 178, 218; conditioned, 61, 84, 119–120, 244; of the sovereign. *See* the sovereign
French Communist Party. *See* PCF
French Revolution, 16, 28–29
fused group. *See* group-in-fusion
future, 141; aiming toward, 83, 184, 218; imagined, 163–164; living, 163–164; man of the future. *See* Nietzsche; possibles, 85; predestined, 96
future image. *See* image

Gadamer, Hans-Georg, 18
Generic orientation, 28–41, 127
Goodchild, Philip, 103, 207, 208
Grosz, Elizabeth, 267
group, 3; formation, 126–127; group-in-fusion, 5, 11n15, 56, 118, 122, 124, 126, 133–139, 141, 148, 150, 173, 192; logic of, 68, 126, 133, 186; pledged, 30, 57, 118, 139–146, 147, 163–164; surviving, 139, 147; therapy. *See* Betty Cannon
Guattari, Félix. *See* Gilles Deleuze

Habermas, Jürgen, 47n27
Hallward, Peter, 51, 130
Han, Byung-Chul, 258, 261
Hardt, Michael, 7, 263
Harvey, David, 262
Haynes, Stephen R., 111–113

Hegel, 2, 4, 53, 66, 78, 98, 135
Heidegger, Martin, 25, 170, 194–195, 234
historical materialism, 15, 20, 195. *See also* Marxism; Marxist
history, 2, 4, 9, 29, 39, 44, 59, 61–69, 75, 89, 148, 186, 221, 239; pregnant with socialism. *See* obstetric model of political practice
hope, 58–59, 132
Howells, Christina, 6, 86
humanism: human nature, 75, 76–78, 210; inhuman. *See* inhuman; new humanisms, 2, 5, 68, 76, 114, 139, 189, 190–202; subtractive, 125
humanity, 3, 62, 68, 76, 77, 85, 95, 104, 110–111, 193; emergence of, 117; rational animal, 77; the human predicament, 91–92, 100
Husserl, Edmund, 26, 234
hyperstition, 224
hypo-logical, 45, 46, 51, 64, 68, 73, 117, 197, 225, 239, 264

idealism, 66, 79, 141, 264; subjective idealism, 181
identity: as serial, 94, 170
ideology, 233
image, 57, 141, 160–163, 216; fear-image. *See* fraternity-terror; future image, 141, 142, 143
The Imaginary, 160–164, 168
imagination, 2, 8, 24, 26, 64, 140–141, 159–173, 184, 203, 205, 239; force of. *See* John Sallis; the imaginary, 159; imaging consciousness, 159, 160–166, 234; poetic; John Sallis; prophetic, 102, 202–203
imaginative logic of action, 8, 46, 62, 159, 170, 173, 180–187, 189, 196, 198, 201, 216, 220, 223, 233, 240, 242, 249–253, 268
imagined future. *See* future
the Impossible, 52, 59, 89, 90, 108, 110, 114, 123, 139, 142, 180, 211
indirect gatherings, 94–95
inferno of the same, 259
Infinite Seriality. *See* seriality
inhuman, 5, 55, 57, 73, 76–78, 90, 91, 93, 97, 99, 114, 123, 172

in-itself, 6, 52, 125, 142, 161, 192, 194, 237
institution, 4, 57, 146, 150, 201; emergence of, 68; institutional fidelity, 143–145; institutional oppression, 69; logic of, 97, 150–152
instrumental rationality, 19–20, 35–38. *See also* capitalism; Leiter, Brian; Weber, Max
intelligibility, 1, 7, 15, 29, 40, 44, 45, 46, 51, 59, 148, 164, 189, 196, 232
intentionality, 83, 160
interiorization, 75, 76, 81
internal relations, 232, 233–237
invasion of Hungary. *See* U.S.S.R.

Jameson, Frederic, 8, 56, 256
Jay, Martin, 17, 22
Jesus, 19, 102. *See also* logos

Kaironic Seriality. *See* seriality
kairos, 91, 100–108, 112, 117, 122, 124, 132, 180, 241, 268
Kant, Immanuel, 31, 34. *See also* formal cause
Keirkegaard, Søren, 238
Klockars, Kristian, 51, 92, 146, 150, 173, 182, 184
Konings, Martijn, 256
Koselleck, Reinhart, 102
Kotsko, Adam, 77–78
Kristeva, Julia, 234–235

language, 38, 98–100, 107. *See also* Constructivist orientation; linguistic turn
Leiter, Brian, 243, 247–253
Lévi-Strauss, Claude, 5, 16, 28–46, 62–69, 106, 118
Lévy, Benny, 58
Liberation Theology, 112
linguistic turn, 31
lived experience, 2, 46, 97, 99, 159, 168, 185, 197, 250
living future. *See* future
living logic of action, 2, 7, 45, 62, 69, 75, 107, 239
Livingston, Paul, 16, 31–39, 43. *See also* Constructivist orientation; Generic Orientation; Onto-theological orientation; Paradoxico-Critical orientation

logic, 2, 7, 8, 9, 45, 46, 61, 62, 175–187, 197, 217, 221; defined, 10n4; dialectical, 40, 196; imaginative logic. *See* imaginative logic of action; serial logic; serial logic of inaction
logocentrism, 20, 235
logos, 4, 16, 17–21, 31, 35, 43, 45, 64
Lukács, Georg, 16, 20, 21–25, 32
Lyotard, Jean-François, 182

macro-political, 7, 217, 219, 222–226
Malabou, Catherine, 212–214
Malraux, André, 59, 117, 122–123
Marcuse, Herbert, 175, 184, 205–208, 208, 210–212
Marx, Karl, 1, 4, 26, 29, 53, 193, 220, 233, 241, 244–245, 245–249, 250–251, 257
marxian, 53, 97, 195, 238
Marxist, 15, 29, 192–193, 194, 219, 220, 231, 238, 243
Marxism, 2, 4, 6, 15, 20, 21–22, 29, 63, 63–64, 231, 240, 243, 245, 249–253, 262, 267; Positivist Marxism, 32, 35–38
material conditions, 4, 9, 20, 24, 45, 53, 55, 66, 73, 137, 148, 170, 173, 193, 197, 200, 235
materialism, 181, 239, 267
Materialism and Revolution, 180–181, 186
materialist dialectic, 73
material system. *See* system of interiority
matter. *See* worked matter
May, Todd, 7, 219–221
May '68, 210
Means, Russell, 267
mediating third, 67, 143. *See also* Flynn, Thomas
mereology, 25, 26
Merleau-Ponty, Maurice, 23, 24
metaphysics, 75, 103
methexis, 17
micro-political, 7, 215, 217, 219–221
micro-psychobiological shifts, 190, 202–216
Milbank, John, 34, 104, 113
milieu of scarcity. *See* scarcity

mimesis, 18
mimetic rivalry, 143
Morot-Sir, Edouard, 5, 63
Mullarkey, John, 209
mystification, 1, 233, 243, 253
mythos, 4, 16, 17–21, 35, 43, 45

natural knowledge. *See* Spinoza
nature, 74, 170; human nature. *See* humanism; worked nature, 79–80
Nausea, 237
Nazi Germany, 111
need, 4, 82–83, 218
negation: of negation, 54, 82
Negri, Antonio, 193; Hardt and Negri. *See* Michael Hardt
new humanisms. *See* humanism
neoliberalism, 232; neoliberal reason, 232, 256; serial logic of neoliberalism, 253–264
Nietzsche, Friedrich, 103–106, 195, 207
nihilism, 103
nostalgia, 140–143

oath. *See* pledge
Obergefell v. Hodges, 111
objectification, 4, 55, 76, 78, 81, 123; of spirit, 98–99
objective spirit, 90, 97–100, 123, 170, 177
obstetric model of political practice, 24, 27, 243–246
Occupy movements, 113
Ollman, Bertell, 233–241
ontology, 51; Badiou's binary, 128; Deleuze's differential, 130; of peace, 101; participatory, 18, 20, 104–105; phenomenological, 6, 63, 75, 125, 142, 192; social, 5, 75, 119–120
Onto-Theological orientation, 28–41, 104, 113
Origen of Alexandria, 102
the organization, 57, 139, 146–150
orthogonal logic, 59–61, 63, 67, 68
otherness. *See* alterity

Paradoxico-Critical orientation, 10n14, 16, 28–41, 61, 73, 78, 118, 120, 127, 130, 183, 214, 219, 236, 238
Parti communiste français. *See* PCF

participatory ontology. *See* ontology
PCF, 22, 29
Pearson, Keith Ansell, 104
perpetual apocalypse. *See* apocalypse
phenomenology, 45, 53–55, 160–163, 237, 239; phenomenological ontology. *See* ontology; post-phenomenology, 2
philosophical anthropology. *See* anthropology
philosophy of internal relations. *See* internal relations
plasticity, 212
Plato, 17, 20; Platonism, 103
the pledge, 30, 56, 138, 145–146, 146–147, 164, 173
pledged group. *See* group
pluridimensionality, 64, 69, 74, 169, 170, 173, 183, 185, 220, 224
political economy. *See* critique of political economy
Positivist Marxism. *See* Marxism
positivist reason. *See* analytical reason
the possible, 54, 76, 83, 97; the field of possible. *See* the field of possibles
Poster, Mark, 136
posthumanism, 194–198
postmodernism, 6, 35, 182, 198, 256
poststructuralism, 182, 197, 219
Poulantzas, Nicos, 238
Power, Nina, 51, 58, 63, 110, 139, 144, 146, 191–194
practical ensembles, 2, 7, 61
practico-inert, 24, 55, 56, 67, 73, 78–82, 83–86, 90, 91, 93, 95, 96, 97, 98, 109, 117, 123, 136, 138, 143, 162, 171, 177, 179–180, 182, 186, 239, 259
praxis, 2, 3, 8, 20, 24, 46, 53, 73, 76, 78, 80, 81, 82, 83, 84, 92, 93, 99, 117, 118–121, 135–136, 137, 148, 149, 161, 173, 184, 195, 234, 235, 239; imagination as a moment of, 168–169; mediated, 118, 197; praxis-project, 3, 54, 84; relating to imagination, 160; return of stolen praxis, 74, 82–86, 99, 110, 138, 162, 169, 252; thought as praxis, 168, 203; translucid to itself. *See* comprehension
predestined. *See* destiny. *See also* freedom, conditioned

process philosophy of signs, 236–237
progressive: progressive-regressive method. *See* regressive-progressive
proletariat, 4, 21. *See also* class consciousness; comprehension; false consciousness
Protagoras, 101
Psychology of the Imagination. *See* The Imaginary

Rae, Gavin, 51, 135, 147, 149
rationality: instrumental, 19, 35–38; serial, 78
rational animal. *See* humanity
the real, 160–163, 198, 205, 238
real subsumption, 263
regressive: regressive analysis, 41, 45, 64, 68, 69; regressive-progressive method, 68
Reisman, David, 161
religion, 34, 244–245, 257
responsibility, 27, 177
Ricard, Matthieu, 134
Robin, Corey, 204
Ruge, Arnold, 245
Rump, Jacob, 42, 67

Said, Edward, 182
Salleh, Ariel, 234, 254, 267
Sallis, John, 160, 170–172
Sanders, Bernie, 113
savage mind. See Lévi-Strauss
scarcity, 4, 54, 61, 65, 68, 91, 94, 165, 246; a human fact, 73–78, 84; a contingent fact of history, 54, 74, 76, 218; as created, 73, 74, 75–78; men of, 75, 76–78; milieu of, 4, 54, 55, 57, 61, 74, 76, 77, 80, 83, 92, 96, 137, 169; as necessary, 73, 74–75
scientific socialism., 24, 35–38. *See also* analytical reason; Engels; obstetric model of political practice
Search for a Method, 5, 21–23, 40
Seneca, 19
serial: alienation. *See* alienation: conditions, 3, 93, 95, 97, 99, 124; logic; serial logic of inaction; rationality, 41, 78, 92, 135, 176–180

seriality, 3, 4, 57, 67–69, 73–74, 81, 86, 89–114, 122, 125, 139, 140, 143, 145, 165, 173, 234; diachronic, 86, 89, 91, 93–96, 96, 100, 123, 137, 220; Kaironic, 45, 62–69, 86, 89, 91, 100–114, 117, 121, 122–123, 125, 126, 131, 132, 135, 137, 141, 148, 152, 162, 170, 176, 180, 183, 196, 206, 213, 222, 239, 252, 261–264, 267; Infinite, 100, 107, 123, 124, 135, 137, 151, 152, 178, 180, 224; pluridimensional, 90, 224; (re)introduction of, 146–148, 151; synchronic, 86, 89, 91, 96–100, 123, 137, 220
serial logic of inaction, 170, 173, 176–180, 190, 204, 211, 231, 250
series, 93–94
signification, 97–98, 99, 107, 236–237, 256
Smith, Brian, 51, 125, 192
social imginaries. *See* Charles Taylor
socialism, 243; of abundance, 76, 246; global, 152; socialist revolution, 152, 217
social ontology. *See* ontology
Sophists, 101
the sovereign, 151
Spinoza, 202–204, 205, 208
Srnicek, Nick, 191, 224
Stiegler, Bernard, 178–179
stored labor. *See* worked matter
structuralism, 43. *See also* Lévi-Strauss
subjective constitution, 5, 7, 75, 122, 124, 129, 135–136, 138, 144, 149, 168, 172, 190, 190–202
subjectivity, 3, 107, 113–114, 124, 124–152, 133, 238; organic, 82–83; system of interiority, 3, 25–28, 40, 41, 46
sublime. *See* Edmund Burke
surviving group. *See* group
system of interiority. *See* subjectivity

Taylor, Charles, 42, 53, 160, 169–170
techné, 20, 41. *See also* instrumental rationality
telepathy, 133–135
terror, 141–143; fraternity terror, 142–143, 144

totality, 15, 16, 20–28, 33, 85, 98, 104, 164, 182
totalization, 16, 20–28, 55, 60, 64, 73, 76, 77, 78, 79, 81, 84, 85, 89, 90, 92, 98, 109, 117, 118–119, 121, 122, 124, 133, 137, 148, 149, 164, 179, 182, 189, 195, 196
Transcendence of the Ego, 82, 196
transcendental, 32, 63, 120, 128–129, 130, 144, 162, 169–172, 189, 196, 210, 239
translucidity of praxis to itself. *See* comprehension
transubstatiation, between matter and praxis, 80
Trump, Donald, 112
Turner, Christopher, 85–86

us-object, 6
U.S.S.R., invasion of Hungary, 21, 27, 38

Utopia, 10, 141, 173, 206, 212, 221; thinking Utopia, 166–168, 181, 184; utopic thinking. *See* utopic thinking
utopic thinking, 8, 166–168, 173, 208, 244, 252

Verstehen. *See* comprehension
virtual, 90, 105, 107, 130, 131, 180, 186, 209–210, 240

Weber, Max, 19
we-subject, 6
Williams, Alex. *See* Nick Srnicek
Williams, James, 127, 129, 131, 236
The Wretched of the Earth, 8, 123, 191
worked matter, 55, 73, 78–82, 186

Zarathustra, 103, 106, 268

About the Author

Austin Hayden Smidt is a researcher in political economy at the University of Sydney. He is the producer of the cinematic adaptation of the best-selling political manifesto *Inventing the Future: Postcapitalism and a World Without Work*. He also co-hosts the podcasts Owls at Dawn and Show Me the Meaning and researches and produces for the popular YouTube channel Wisecrack.

www.ingramcontent.com/pod-product-compliance
Lightning Source LLC
Chambersburg PA
CBHW031546300426
44111CB00006BA/194